075731

Rap Whoz Who

Rap Whoz Who

The World of Rap Music

Steven Stancell

Schirmer Books
An Imprint of Simon & Schuster Macmillan
New York

Prentice Hall International
London Mexico City New Delhi Singapore Sydney Toronto

Schirmer Books
An Imprint of Simon & Schuster Macmillan
1633 Broadway
New York, NY 10019

Library of Congress Catalog Card Number: 95-43926

Printed in the United States of America

Printing Number
1   2   3   4   5   6   7   8   9   10

Design: Rob Carangelo
Photos courtesy of Al Pereira, Brooklyn, New York

Library of Congress Cataloging-in-Publication Data
Stancell, Steven.
    Rap whoz who : the world of rap music / Steven Stancell.
    p.   cm.
    Includes index.
    ISBN 0-02-864520-0 (alk. paper)
    1. Rap musicians—United States—Biography. 2. Disc jockeys-
-United States—Biography. 3. Rap (Music)—Discography. I. Title.
ML400.S77 1996
782.42164—dc20   95-43926
                                                         CIP
                                                          MN

This paper meets the requirements of ANSI/NISO Z39.48—1992 (Permanence of Paper).

INTRODUCTION

In popular music since the turn of the twentieth century a leading musical instrument (or instruments) has always garnered the attention of fans and musicians. From ragtime to rock, an instrument has helped define a particular music genre, whether it be piano, trumpet, saxophone, or electric guitar.

By the early 1970s, however, a new musician with a new instrument emerged. It was someone who more or less did something all of us did, at least once in our lives, and the instrument was something most people had in their homes. The new musician was the disc jockey, or DJ, and the instrument was the turntable.

A DJ plays recorded music on a phonograph, hi-fi, or stereo system with a turntable to entertain a group of people. There have been radio DJs who have entertained audiences over the airwaves since the 1940s. We have all played records at one time or another, either for ourselves or for other people. How can the DJ be considered a musician in the traditional sense? The turntable cannot be plucked, strummed, blown, or pounded on. How can it be considered an instrument?

The answers to those questions can be found in the age when the DJs began to emerge, for they are unknowingly the product of their age—the information or computer age. The information age, beginning during the 1950s when the computer was being developed, helped give rise to the concept of gathering all types of information, storing it, then pulling it out to use for various functions and interests. Records themselves are not computer chips, but something is stored on them (in this case, music), and this music can be brought up, or played, as it were, whenever one desires to do so. The DJ is, in fact, the first widely accepted musician to use information as a musical instrument: that is, information, being recorded music or records.

The actual emergence of the DJ as musician began in Jamaica during the late 1940s, but came to prominence

fab five freddy

during the early 1960s. During this period there was a market in Jamaica for rhythm and blues (R&B) records from the United States. These records were played by DJs, who constructed mobile units called "sounds," or sound systems, consisting of a small truck or car outfitted with a turntable, an amplifier, a radio, and large speakers. These DJs would play records for people in the streets of Jamaica. Often, they had to travel to the United States to obtain these R&B records, because American records were scarce in Jamaica at that time. Of course, those DJs who had the most interesting or entertaining records would get the most people to gather around their sound systems. Sometimes, the street DJs would entertain their crowds by imitating what they heard radio R&B DJs do in the states between records, including reciting rhymes or nonsensical statements over a microphone for effect. Some of the leading DJs and sound system operators in Jamaica at the time include Coxsone Dodd, Prince Buster, and Duke Reid.

During the early 1970s in the United States, specifically in New York City, disco music brought the DJ to the forefront. Originally coming to prominence in underground gay male clubs, disco soon expanded its popularity to all members of society and became a successful product for record companies.

In the various boroughs of New York City in the early 1970s jam sessions in housing project community centers, and particularly in neighborhood parks during the summer, were a source of entertainment for blacks and Latinos. In parks (especially in Brooklyn at the Farragut Housing Projects) musicians would hook their instruments into street lampposts, and play for a crowd of people, late into the night, until the police came and unplugged the musicians, ending the free concerts. (Sometimes musicians waited a while after the police left and then replugged in their instruments.) During these night jams musicians would get a nice-sized crowd for their performances, and people would either dance to or listen to the music, or do both. However, one summer musicians began to notice that their crowds were diminishing. This was due to the emergence of the DJ, in this case DJs like DJ Flowers, one of the first group of mobile DJs in New York.

For some reason, the girls and guys preferred partying to records rather than to live music. They would flock over to the other side of the Farragut Projects to another park, and watch Flowers—who was also plugged into a street lamppost—play his disco records for the crowd, who would either dance, or just stand and listen to the sounds. The DJ had arrived! Many other mobile DJs, like Maboya, Plummer, Kool DJ D, the Together Brothers, DJ Smokey, and Pete DJ Jones, began to emerge around the same time from other boroughs. They all originally played disco music, until the arrival of a new DJ: Kool DJ Herc.

Kool DJ Herc, or Kool Herc, emigrated with his family from Kingston, Jamaica, in the late 1960s, and settled in the West Bronx in New York. He became a DJ during the early 1970s, and deejayed for the people in his community, throwing parties on weekends. However, Herc did not play too many disco records. He had his own selection of obscure R&B and funk dance records that he played for his crowd, which made him unique.

Other factors in Kool Herc's originality included his sound system itself (which was one of the most powerful ones at the time among DJs in New York), which he nicknamed the Herculords. In addition to that, at certain points during his parties Herc would only play the musical break part of these records (the part between the verses of a song), and he would *repeat* that break part for as long as he wanted, or as long as the crowd wanted to hear it. He would do this by using *two* turntables playing *two* copies of the same record. Thus, he would go from one turntable to the other, then back to the first, and so on. Kool DJ Herc, in essence, became known as the first rap DJ, and his technique would later be known as *break-beat deejaying.*

Kool Herc's parties inspired dancers to take to the floor and perform strange acrobatic, twisting dance routines, comprised of splits and leg sweeps. They would perform these dances whenever Kool Herc began to play the breaks of his records.

Herc nicknamed these dancers his "b-boys," as in break boys, because they danced in this manner during the break part of those records. The dances that they did at the time were called "burning," "b-boying," and later, "breakdancing." Kool Herc had an MC at his parties. The MC, whose name was Coke La Rock, would get on the microphone in between or during the records that Herc played, and say certain phrases, some of which were nonsensical, to motivate the party crowd to dance more and enjoy themselves. What he was doing was called "MC'ing"; this would later be termed "rapping."

DJ Hollywood, originally a disco DJ whose parties were predominantly held in Manhattan clubs during the early 1970s, also contributed to MC'ing or rapping, by reciting complete verses of rhymes on the microphone to his disco crowd, again, to help motivate the party goers to have a good time and dance to the music that he played for them. A line in one of his verses contained the words "hip, hop," which much later were used interchangeably to define the music of rap and the culture of those who participated in Kool Herc's parties.

During this period other DJs emerged who took on Kool Herc's style of deejaying, and/or playing a similar style of records, including Afrika Bambaataa, former member of a Bronx street gang, the Black Spades. As the gang activity began to subside, and many of the Black Spades began to involve themselves in the arts and sociopolitical awareness, they became known as the Zulu Nation. Headed by Bambaataa, they are responsible for spreading the culture of hip hop around the world. Their Zulu Nation parties since the 1970s have featured some of the best historical DJ and MC "battles." Battle is the term used to describe events that took place in parks or community centers, where DJs and MCs (rappers) would compete against each other in areas of deejaying (which centered on who had the best records and the loudest sound system) and MC group performances. Rapping was not the only criterion used to determine the best group, as the type of routines the group performed also was considered. Among other innovations, Afrika Bambaataa was recognized for having a larger selection of unique break-beat records than any other DJ had at the time, which came from various musical genres such as rock, hard rock, R&B, mambo, reggae, German disco, and calypso.

A little later, DJ Grandmaster Flash emerged and perfected Kool Herc's break-beat dee-jaying technique by developing a way to mix the break beats on time; Herc's technique was more or less hit or miss. Sometimes he would play the break beats on time (in rhythm); sometimes he would miss. Grandmaster Flash, however, precued his records, a method he had learned from disco DJ Pete DJ Jones. When Flash deejayed his break beats, they were much more in time and rhythm than Kool Herc's. Flash is also the first of the trick DJs; while he deejayed, he performed tricks, like deejaying behind his back, with his feet, and underneath tables, similar to the way rock guitarist Jimi Hendrix performed tricks while he played.

Another DJ, Grand Wizard Theodore, achieved acclaim not only for his deejaying ability, but for his introduction of the technique of *scratching*, a turntable skill that involves spinning a record clockwise and counterclockwise underneath the needle to create a scratching, percussive sound. Here, the turntable came full circle, truly becoming an instrument, in this case, a percussion instrument, producing a sound similar to a string drum or lion's roar. The hip-hop DJ at times will also play a portion of a break beat as an effect, or an accent, while the same record (or a different record) is playing in full on the other turntable. This is done with the help of a device called a mixer; this hip-hop deejaying technique inspired the creation of digital recording devices for musicians called *sampling machines*, or *samplers*, which enable a musician to record break beats digitally and play them over and over with the push of a button.

Rap really took off in the late seventies, beginning with the Sugar Hill Gang's recording of "Rapper's Delight" in 1978, the first rap hit single, and the first release on Sugar Hill Records, run by black-music industry veteran Sylvia Robinson and her husband, Joe. It was followed a year later by "Funk You Up" by Sequence, the first successful female rap group. In 1980 rapper Kurtis Blow scored the first rap single to go gold, "The Breaks," and popular mainstream white group Blondie introduced rap in their single "Rapture," introducing the sound (in a diluted form) to white audiences.

In the 1980s rap took a harder edge, beginning with the electrofunk of "Planet Rock" by Afrika Bambaataa and his Soul Sonic Force, released in 1982. The backing track of this record relied heavily on synthesizers and drum machines, which became the standard in rap. A year later, Bambaataa was among the pioneers in the use of sampling, electronically copying a short riff from a previously released record, on his single, "Looking for the Perfect Beat." The years 1982—83 also saw the first rap singles introducing a harder-edged lyrical content, reflecting the tough life on inner-city streets, including Grandmaster Flash and the Furious Five's "The Message" and Run-D.M.C.'s "It's Like That." At about the same time, popular groups like The Fat Boys continued to turn out rap music with a humorous, party-like atmosphere, belying the notion that all rappers were politically motivated.

UTFO's recording "Roxanne, Roxanne" inspired one of the first, and most influential, answer records, 1984's "Roxanne's Revenge," by female rapper Roxanne Shanté. She was offended by the antifemale message of UTFO's original recording, and her answer record inspired a barrage of imitators, all dealing with the fictional Roxanne character. Roxanne took "dissing" or insult rapping to new heights. The flip side of dissing, records based on boasting, made one of its first appearances on Run-D.M.C.'s seminal 1983 hit "Sucker MCs."

Run-D.M.C. helped bring rap further into the mainstream by collaborating with arena-rockers Aerosmith on their 1986 release "Walk This Way"; in the same year the Beastie Boys were the first white rap group to be accepted by most of the hip-hop community; their album *Licensed to Ill*, which initially sold four million copies, was the most successful rap album to date. The late 1980s saw the full emergence of the gangsta style, particularly as championed by West Coast groups such as N.W.A, whose 1988 album, *Straight Outta Compton*, embodied the tough voice of inner-city L.A. Meanwhile, more mainstream acts helped popularize a less-threatening, dance-oriented rap style, including Hammer with his big 1990 hit "U Can't Touch This" and white rap star Marky Mark, who capitalized on his good looks, even appearing in a series of underwear advertisements, and adolescent rappers Kris Kross.

Rap reached the heights of controversy in the early nineties, being attacked from both within and outside the black community. The Reverend Calvin Butts, a noted African-American clergyman, attacked the lyrical content of rap as promoting violence and being disrespectful toward black women. Meanwhile, conservative politicians jumped on the antirap bandwagon, calling for record companies to cease profiting off of what they considered to be "obscene" recordings. Warner Bros. Records was particularly attacked, first in 1992 following the release of Ice-T's controversial single "Cop Killer" (which some people believed encouraged violence against the police). The song was later removed from Ice-T's album (supposedly with his approval), although he split with the label soon after. In late 1994 conservative former drug czar William Bennett headed a campaign to encourage Time Warner, the parent company of the label, to discontinue issuing rap recordings.

However, the popularity of rap continues to grow, despite the conservative opposition. And rap as a genre embraces a wide variety of musical voices, from the highly political to the purely entertaining. It is a mistake to lump together all rappers as "gangstas" or purveyors of obscenity; many address issues of deep concern to the African-American community, from racism to politics to violence in the streets. The attacks on rap may be motivated by more than just concern over children being exposed to four-letter words. Many critics have pointed out the hypocrisy that the ultraviolent movies of white megastars such as Sylvester Stallone and Arnold Schwartzenegger are rarely attacked by conservatives who seem so upset by the violent words of rappers.

This book contains the names of artists (producers, DJs, rappers) who have either helped pioneer the music known as rap or brought innovative ideas to the art form (which helped to advance it) and those who have made an impact by making rap records that the hip-hop audience liked and bought, establishing the rap-record industry. Also included are some of the hip-hop DJs who pioneered the making of DJ tapes, which are audiocassettes of DJs playing a set of records as if they were before an audience of partygoers. (In the 1990s the tapes—known as mix tapes—serve as a selection of records mixed by DJs with other records to create different interpretations of a song. The tapes also contain basic hip-hop deejaying techniques such as scratching.) In the early years of hip hop these tapes were recordings of actual parties where a particular DJ played. Audiocassettes were also used to record battles, and predate the concept of rap records. They also helped spread rap music from borough to borough (when they were bought, borrowed, or lent to various people), and eventually left New York via persons who undertook military service, for example, or those who traveled outside the state of New York.

The book also lists some of the first record labels to record rap music, and some of the first promoters of rap who helped widen awareness of the music. For those pioneering hip-hop DJs, there is also a brief listing of important break-beat records that they introduced to hip-hop culture. These records have become staples in rap music (via sampling), and have spread to other genres of popular music like R&B. Some people may be missing from this work, due to the lack of written information on them as artists and lack of information from their peers in the music industry.

All mentions of gold and platinum awards for records are based on information from the Recording Industry Association of America (R.I.A.A.), which certifies such awards. All chart information about recordings refers to those published weekly by *Billboard*, unless mentioned otherwise within the text.

A Note on Alphabetization, Names, and Birth Dates

Because many rap groups go by "assumed" names, the entries in this book are alphabetized by the first letter of the group's or individual's name. Thus, "Afrika Bambaataa" will be found under "A" not "B"; "Big Daddy Kane" under "B" not "D" or "K"; "DJ Chuck Chillout" under "D" not "C."

Besides performing under stage names, many rappers are unwilling to reveal their real identities or the place and date of their birth. Every attempt has been made to verify this information, but some data were impossible to obtain.

Record Listings

For most entries, I have listed select singles and albums/CDs that have been discussed in them. Date and record company information are given, including catalog numbers, whenever possible for albums/CDs. Some may no longer be available or may have been reissued under different catalog numbers by different labels. Because this information is constantly changing, it is wise to check with your local record dealer or the companies themselves before ordering.

Acknowledgments

Special special thanks to: Mr. Entertainment (!) Don Thomas and the New York *Beacon* staff, Mike O'Neal (wherever you are), my agent, Carole Abel (a special person indeed), my wonderful wife, Victoria, Al Pereira, Karen Harris, Starrlite Gentry, Vicki Tobak, Lillian Matulic, Kool DJ Red Alert, Debbie Bennett, Anne Kristoff, Kelly Lynn Jackson, Afrika Bambaataa, Van Silk, Kool Lady Blue, Rhonda Mann, Gwendolyn Quinn, Kurtis Blow, Devin Roberson, Sharan Harper, Debra Hunter, George and Evelyn Rodriquez, Tracey Miller, Steve Marlin, Heidi Robertson, Geoffrey F. X. O'Connell, Bill Adler, Mark the 45 King, Charlie Chase, Chuck Chillout, Vandy C, Lovebug Starski, Steven Hager, Jacqualine Canty, Jackie Paul, Jalina Smith, Tatiana Sampson, Brian Adams, and Harry Allen.

Rap Whoz Who

ABOVE THE LAW
●●●●●●●●●●●●●●●●●●●●●●●●●

**Formed in 1983, South Central Los Angeles
(Go Mack, born Arthur Goodman, California; Total K-OSS,
born Anthony Stewart, California; Cold 187um, born Gregory
Hutchinson, California; KMG, born Kevin Dulley, California)**

One of the many L.A.-based rap groups who came to prominence in the early 1990s performing gangsta-style material.

Originally a crew of mobile DJs, Above the Law began to make demos of their rhymes and beats to get a record deal. After several unsuccessful attempts, Go Mack's brother, Laylaw, who had been working at Eazy-E's Ruthless Records, introduced the group to Eazy and his friend Dr. Dre. Both Dre and Eazy were impressed, and Eazy signed them to the label; Laylaw became the group's manager.

In 1990 the group released their debut work, *Livin' Like Hustlers*. The album was produced by Dr. Dre, Laylaw, and the group themselves. Two singles off the work, "Murder Rap" and "Livin' Like Hustlers," got them noticed by hip-hop audiences.

The following year their EP *Vocally Pimpin'* was released, followed by their *Black Mafia Life* album in 1993, both of which were produced by the group's lead rapper, Cold 187um. The single off the latter work was titled "V.S.O.P." In 1994 the group released *Uncle Sam's Curse*.

 Selected albums/CDs: *Livin' Like Hustlers* (1990, Ruthless/Epic 46041); *Vocally Pimpin'* (1991, Ruthless/Epic 47934); *Black Mafia Life* (1993, Ruthless 24477); *Uncle Sam's Curse* (1994, Ruthless 5524).

AFRIKA BAMBAATAA

a.k.a. Afrika Bambaataa Aasim
(Born c. 1955, Bronx, New York)

Afrika Bambaataa is one of the three main originators of break-beat deejaying, and is respectfully known as the "grandfather" and "godfather" of hip hop. Through his co-opting of the street gang the Black Spades into the music and culture-oriented Zulu Nation, he is responsible for spreading rap and hip-hop culture throughout the world. He has consistently made records nationally and internationally, every one to two years, spanning the 1980s into the 1990s.

Due to his early use of drum machines and computer sounds, Bam (as he is affectionately known) was instrumental in changing the way R&B and other forms of black music were recorded. His creation of electrofunk, beginning with his piece "Planet Rock," helped fuel the development of other musical genres such as freestyle or Latin freestyle, Miami bass, house, hip house, and early techno.

Bam is responsible for initiating many careers in the music industry, and his early association with Tom Silverman of Tommy Boy Records helped propel the label to its success. Bam was instrumental in launching the R&B group New Edition, Maurice Starr and the Jonzun Crew, Tashan, and Bernard Fowler of the Peech Boys, to name a few. Bam is also recognized as a humanitarian and a man of peace, who has applied elements of Afrocentric, spiritual, and health-conscious teachings to his philosophy. He is also a historian on hip-hop roots, who traces the culture back to the times of the African griots.

At a time when DJs—hip hop or otherwise—were recognized for the distinctive records they played, Bam was called the "Master of Records," and was acclaimed for the wide variety of music and break records he presented to the hip-hop crowd, which included go-go, soca, reggae, and African music. He is responsible for premiering the following records and songs to hip hoppers, which are now staples in rap and hip-hop culture: "Jam on the Groove" and "Calypso Breakdown" by Ralph McDonald; "Dance to the Drummer's Beat" by Herman Kelly; "Champ" by the Mohawks; themes from *The Andy Griffith Show* and *The Pink Panther*; and "Trans-Europe Express" by Kraftwerk.

Bam joined the Bronx River Project's division of the Black Spades street gang in the southeast Bronx in 1969, where he soon became warlord. Always a music enthusiast (taking up trumpet and piano for a short time at Adlai E. Stevenson High School), Bam was also a serious record collector, who collected everything from R&B to rock. By 1970 he was already deejaying at house parties. Bam became even more interested in deejaying around 1973, when he heard Bronx DJs Kool DJ D and Kool DJ Herc. Kool DJ D had one of the first coffins (a rectangular case that contains two turntables and a mixer) in the Bronx area circa 1972. West Bronx DJ Kool DJ Herc was playing funk records by James Brown, and later just playing the instrumental breaks of those records. Noticing that he had many of the same records Herc was playing, Bam began to play them, but expanded his repertoire to include other types of music as well.

As the Black Spades gang began to die out toward 1973, Bam began forming a perform-

Afrika Bambaataa

ing group at Stevenson High School, first calling it the Bronx River Organization, then later the Organization. Bam had deejayed with his own sound system at the Bronx River Community Center, with Mr. Biggs, Queen Kenya, and Cowboy, who accompanied him in performances in the community. Because of his prior status in the Black Spades, Bam already had an established party crowd drawn from former members of the gang.

About a year later he reformed a group, calling it the Zulu Nation (inspired by his wide studies on African history at the time). Five b-boys (breakdancers) joined him who he called the Shaka Zulu Kings, a.k.a. Zulu Kings; there were also the Shaka Zulu Queens. As Bam continued deejaying, more DJs, rappers, breakdancers, graffiti writers, and artists followed his parties, and he took them under his wing and made them members of his Zulu Nation.

By 1976, because of the proliferation of DJs, many sound system battles would occur to determine which DJ had the best music and sound. Although the amount of people gathered around a DJ was supposed to be the deciding factor, the best DJ was mostly determined by whose system was the loudest. Held in parks and community centers, DJs would set up their gear on opposite sides, playing their records at the same time at maximum volume. However, Bam decided that all challenges to him would follow an hour-by-hour rule, where he would play for an hour, and the opposing DJ would play for an hour.

Bam's first official battle was against Disco King Mario at Junior High School 123 (a.k.a. the Funky 3). A few other important battles Bam had later on were against Grandmaster Caz (known as Casanova Fly at that time and who later was one of the Cold Crush Brothers) at the P.A.L. (Police Athletic League) circa 1978, and a team battle against Grandmaster Flash and an army of sound systems, with Bam teaming systems with Disco King Mario and DJ Tex. Bam formed additional systems for battling as well, like the Earthquake Systems with DJ Superman and DJ Jazzy Jay. There were also many MC battles, where rappers from Bam's Zulu Nation would go against other outside rappers. Later, Bam also jointly promoted shows with Kool Herc under the name Nubian Productions.

Many cassette tapes were made of Bam's parties and MC battles, which were sometimes sold for $20 to $40 apiece. During long music segments when Bam was deejaying, he would sometimes mix in recorded speeches from Malcolm X, Martin Luther King, Jr., and, later, Louis Farrakhan.

Influenced by George Clinton, and the many separate-but-same groups that he created, Bam formed the Soul Sonic Force, which in its original makeup consisted of approximately twenty Zulu Nation members. The personnel for the Soul Sonic Force were groups within groups that Bam would perform and make records with, including:

Soul Sonic Force (#1)—Mr. Biggs, Queen Kenya, DJ Cowboy

Soul Sonic Force (#2)—Mr. Biggs, Pow Wow, G.L.O.B.E. (creator of the "MC poppin'" rap style), DJ Jazzy Jay

Cosmic Force—Queen Lisa Lee, Prince Ikey C, Ice Ice (#1), Chubby Chub; Jazzy Five—DJ Jazzy Jay, Mr. Freeze, Master D.E.E., Kool DJ Red Alert, Sundance, Ice Ice (#2), Charlie Chew, Master Bee; Busy Bee Starski, Akbar (Lil' Starski), Raheim.

Around 1980, Bam and his groups made their first recordings with Paul Winley Records, who recorded Bam's "Death Mix" piece. Winley also released Cosmic Force's "Zulu Nation Throwdown," after which Bam (disappointed with the results) left the company.

Bam's parties had now spread to places like the Audubon Ballroom and the T-Connection. In the early 1980s, news about Bam and other DJs' parties—and the type of music Bam played—started traveling to the downtown sections of Manhattan. Tom Silverman visited Bam at one of his parties and did an article on him and the Zulu Nation for his own *Dance Music Report* magazine. The two became friends, and Silverman later recorded Bam and his Soul Sonic Force with a group of female singers called Cotton Candy. The first song Silverman recorded around 1981 with both groups (without Bam's name listed) was a work titled "Let's Vote," after which a second song was recorded and released, titled "Having Fun."

Thereafter, Silverman met producer Arthur Baker, and together with then–KISS-FM radio mastermix DJ Shep Pettibone, Silverman recorded Bam and the Jazzy Five's "Jazzy Sensation" on Silverman's own Tommy Boy Records label. The record had three mixes, one with Bam and the Jazzy Five, and the other with a group called the Kryptic Krew. The third mix was an instrumental. The record was a hit with hip hoppers.

Around 1982 hip-hop artist Fab 5 Freddy was putting together music packages in the largely white downtown Manhattan new-wave clubs, and invited Bam to perform at one of them, called the Mudd Club. It was the first time Bam had performed before a predominantly white crowd, making it the first time hip hop fused with white culture. Attendance for Bam's parties downtown became so large that he had to move to larger venues, first to the Ritz, with Malcolm McLaren's group, Bow Wow Wow (and where the Rock Steady Crew b-boys became part of the Zulu Nation), then to the Peppermint Lounge, Negril, Danceteria, and the Roxy.

In 1982 Bam had an idea for a record revolving around Kraftwerk's piece "Trans-Europe Express." Bam brought the idea to Silverman and both tried working on it in Silverman's apartment. Bam soon met John Robie, who brought Bam a techno-pop oriented record titled "Vena Carvey" that he was trying to release. Bam then introduced Robie to Arthur Baker, and the three of them, along with Silverman and the Soul Sonic Force (#2), worked on the "Trans-Europe Express" idea, resulting in the piece "Planet Rock"—one of the most influential records in music. Bam called the sound of the record "electrofunk" or the "electro-sound," and he cited James Brown, Parliament, and Sly and the Family Stone as the building blocks of its composition. By September of that year "Planet Rock" went gold, and it continued to sell internationally throughout the 1980s and into the 1990s.

In the autumn of 1982 Bam and other members of the Zulu Nation (which included Grand-mixer D.ST, Fab 5 Freddy, Phase II, Mr. Freeze, Dondi, Futura 2000, and Crazy Legs, to name a few) made one of their first of many trips to Europe. Visiting Le Batclan theater in Paris, Bam and the other hip hoppers made a considerable impression on the young people there, something that would continue throughout his travels as he began to spread hip-hop culture around the world.

Bam's second release around 1983 was "Looking for the Perfect Beat," then later, "Renegades of Funk," both with the same Soul Sonic Force. Bam began working with producer Bill Laswell at Jean Karakos's Celluloid Records, where he developed and placed two groups on the label Time Zone and Shango. He did "Wildstyle" with Time Zone, and in 1984 he did a duet with punk-rocker John Lydon and Time Zone, titled "World Destruction." Shango's album *Shango Funk Theology* was also released by the label in 1984. That same year Bam and other hip-hop celebrities appeared in the movie *Beat Street*. Bam also made a landmark recording with James Brown, titled "Unity." It was admirably billed in music industry circles as "the Godfather of Soul meets the Godfather of Hip Hop."

Around October 1985 Bam and other music stars worked on the antiapartheid album *Sun City* with Little Steven Van Zandt, Run-D.M.C., and Lou Reed. During 1988 Bam recorded another landmark piece as Afrika Bambaataa and Family. The work featured Nona Hendryx, UB40, Boy George, George Clinton, Bootsy Collins, and Yellowman, and it was titled *The Light*. Bam had recorded a few other works with Family three years earlier, one titled "Funk You" in 1985, and the other titled *Beware (The Funk Is Everywhere)* in 1986.

In 1990 Bam made *Life* magazine's "Most Important Americans of the 20th Century" issue. He was also involved in the antiapartheid work "Hip Hop Artists Against Apartheid" for Warlock Records. He teamed with the Jungle Brothers to record the album *Return to Planet Rock (The Second Coming)*.

Around this same period, Greenstreet Records, John Baker, and Bam organized a concert at Wembley Stadium in London for the A.N.C. (African National Congress), in honor of Nelson Mandela's release from prison. The concert brought together performances by British and American rappers, and also introduced both Nelson and Winnie Mandela and the A.N.C. to hip-hop audiences. In relation to the event, the recording *Ndodemnyama South Africa* helped raise approximately $30,000 for the A.N.C. Bam also helped to raise funds for the organization in Italy.

In 1991 Bam received some notice for his remix work on the group EMF's gold single "Unbelievable." He also did an album for the Italian label DFC (Dance Floor Corporation), titled *1990—2000: The Decade of Darkness*.

By 1992 Bam had his own Planet Rock Records label, releasing Time Zone's *Thy Will "B" Funk* LP. In 1993 Bam's Time Zone recorded the single "what's the name of this nation? . . . zulu!" for Profile Records. Toward 1994 Bam regrouped his Soul Sonic Force for the album *Ominous Isthumus*. In that same year he began deejaying on radio station Hot 97 FM in New York City on Fridays, hosting the show *Old School at Noon*.

 **Selected singles:** "Planet Rock" by Afrika Bambaataa and the Soul Sonic Force (1982, Tommy Boy); "Looking for the Perfect Beat," "Renegades of Funk" (1983, Tommy Boy).

Selected albums/CDs: *World Destruction* by Time Zone (1984; reissued 1992, Metrotone 72661); *The Light* (1985, Capitol 90157); *Planet Rock* (1986, Tommy Boy 1007); *1990—2000: The Decade Of Darkness* by Afrika Bambaataa (1991, DFC/EMI 1062); *Thy Will "B" Funk* by Afrika Bambaataa Presents Time Zone (1992, Planet Rock).

AFRIKA ISLAM
•••••••••••••••••••••••
(Born June 19, c. 1962, New York City)

Afrika Islam, known as one of the pioneers of hip hop, has participated in the culture as one of the Zulu Nation's first b-boys (breakdancers) and hip-hop radio DJs. He was the first DJ to work immediately under Afrika Bambaataa, and was responsible for doing the preliminaries at Zulu Nation parties in the 1970s, which is how he earned the title "Son of Afrika Bambaataa." Islam also co-wrote rhymes for the Soul Sonic Force and had his own group, called the Funk Machine, which included Grandmaster Caz and Donald D as members. For two years he hosted the *Zulu Beats* radio show on New Jersey's WHBI (later changed to WNWK-FM, New York) radio.

Islam is known as a virtuoso DJ, who is able to spin as many as four turntables at one time. He has been hired as a scratcher for pieces like Madame-X's "Marry Me," Mr. T's *I'm Somebody* LP, and Rick Rubin's 12-inch single production of the Queen remix "We Will Rock You" and "We Are the Champions." He worked as a DJ/host for the Rock Steady Crew b-boys from 1981 to 1985, and he later toured around the world with the group. Islam is also recognized for his production work with rapper Ice-T, producing four gold albums for the artist, as well as the movie soundtracks for the films *Colors*, *Dick Tracy*, and *New Jack Hustler*, all with Ice-T, with the latter two going gold and platinum, respectively.

As a producer and remixer, Islam has worked on the Eurythmics's "Why" single, New Order's "Tabu," and Michael Jackson's "Bad" for his 1992 "Dangerous" world tour in 1992. He handled Van Silk and Melle Mel's WNBC-TV New York City antidrug commercial and Silk's "The Basepipe" single, and he's also done commercials for Greyhound Bus.

As a DJ at the Roxy, Islam first presented these break-beat records: "Substitution" and "Indiscreet," ESG's "UFO," "Impeach the President" by the Honey Drippers, and songs by the group Liquid Liquid. He also introduced non—break-beat records like "Holiday" by Madonna, Run-D.M.C.'s "It's Like That," "Rock It" by Herbie Hancock, and "Buffalo Gals" by Malcolm McLaren.

Islam was one of the Zulu King dancers in the early 1970s, with Charlie Rock, Amed, Jazzy Jay, Grandmixer D.ST, and Pow Wow. He soon got into writing rhymes, then later, deejaying. By 1977, Islam was involved in the following DJ and MC battles: Islam, Busy Bee Starski and Raheim against Breakout and Baron and the Funky Four (on November 4, 1977); Islam against Grandmixer D.ST (1978); Islam against Grand Wizard Theodore (1978); and Islam and Jazzy Jay against Grand Wizard Theodore and Grandmaster Flash (1978).

Around 1979 Islam began playing Jamaican clubs and deejaying at the Brooklyn College radio station. Not long after, he met Earl Chin and Gil Bailey at WHBI radio, where he was soon given a slot. Islam met the group the Supreme Team and soon brought them on the air with him, calling the show *Zulu Beats*. Due to creative differences, the union was terminated after six to seven months, with the Supreme Team having their own slot, and Islam taking the *Zulu Beats* show to Tuesdays and Wednesdays. Later, Mr. Magic would come to the station, taking Fridays.

Islam played the "Wheels of Steel" night at the Roxy in the early 1980s, and he is also responsible for spurring the underground hip-hop club scene in Los Angeles at Matt Dike's Powertools Club. Islam has also played every important club around the world, from London's the Wag to Tokyo's Seibu and Hallelujah, to name a few.

After his stint as a DJ for the Roxy and the Rock Steady Crew in the early 1980s, Islam relocated to Los Angeles, following his work on the 1984 movie *Breakin' II*. Islam appeared in that film, as well as *Repossessed*, *Pump Up the Volume*, and *Less Than Zero*. From 1989 to 1991 Islam worked with ABC-TV's Saturday morning lineup, where he provided cartoon voice rap for various characters. In 1992 he transported his *Zulu Beats* radio show to Japan. Islam is also the owner of the Universal Zulu Nation club the United Nations, based in Los Angeles, with another branch in Japan. He is the president of the Universal Zulu Nation.

 Selected produced albums/CDs: *Rhyme Pays* by Ice-T (1987, Sire 25602); *Power* by Ice-T (1988, Sire 25765); *Freedom of Speech* by Ice-T (1989, Sire 26028); *Original Gangster* by Ice-T (1991, Sire 26492).

AFROS
· · · · · · · · · ·
Formed c. 1990, Hollis, Queens, New York
(DJ Hurricane; Kool Tee; DJ Kippy-O: all born in Queens)

The Afros were a novelty group known for their huge Afro wigs, which served as a comedic and political statement for the group. They were the first act to be signed to Run-D.M.C.'s Jam Master Jay's record label, JMJ Records.

The group began doing cameos in various rap videos: Run-D.M.C.'s "Pause," 3rd Bass's "Gas Face," and Public Enemy's "911 Is a Joke." They also appeared at a few rap concerts, where they would promote themselves by comically saying their group name in a whining drawl. The group, which included former Beastie Boys' DJ, Hurricane, released the single "Feel It," and the album *Kickin' Afrolistics* in 1990. After promotional tours and some concert appearances for the album, the group disbanded.

 Selected albums/CDs: *Kickin' Afrolistics* (1990, JMJ/Columbia 4675712).

THE ALEEMS
· · · · · · · · · · · · · · · · · · · ·
a.k.a. the Fantastic Aleems, Aleem, Prana People
(Tunde-Ra Aleem; Taharqa Aleem: both born in New York)

The Aleems are twin brother musicians and producers, whose careers in music go all the way back to Jimi Hendrix, when he lived with the brothers for a short period when they all played in Manhattan and Greenwich Village coffeehouses.

The Aleems have worked and recorded under several different names (including Prana People on Prelude Records in 1977), but their contribution to hip hop was the establishment in the early 1980s of their own Nia Records, the label that recorded Marley Marl and MC Shan's "Marley Marl Scratch." The Aleems had worked with Marl earlier, on their own "Release Yourself" single in 1984, which Marl did remixes for. They also put out their Captain Rock singles "Cosmic Glide" and "The Return of Captain Rock" (co-written by the brothers and Dr. Jeckyll & Mr. Hyde).

Another MC on the Aleems's Nia Records was Sparky D, who recorded her answer record to Roxanne Shanté, called "Sparky's Turn (Roxanne You're Through)" in 1985. After Nia Records, the Aleems continued recording as a duo during the latter part of the 1980s. They later began their own recording studio, operating out of upper midtown Manhattan.

 Selected albums/CDs: *Casually Formal* (1986, Atlantic 81622).

Almighty RSO

ALMIGHTY RSO

Formed in 1982, Boston

(Ray Dogg, born Raymond Scott, Boston; E-Devious, born Marco Ennis, Boston; Rock, born Rodney Pitts, 1973, died 1990; Tony Rhome, born Anthony Johnson, Boston; DJ Deff Jeff, born Jeffrey Neal)

The Almighty RSO were known as the RSO Crew during 1982 when they originally formed. As part of Boston's hip-hop scene during the early 1980s, the members frequented hip-hop clubs like Ben's Lounge and Ripley Road.

In 1987 the group received the Boston Music Award for Best Rap Group. They were later banned from appearing in one of their hometown theaters because of DJ Deff Jeff's trick deejaying with fire, à la Jimi Hendrix's Monterey Pop guitar-burning performance. He would set two small trays on fire (sitting them on top of the center of the records), and do DJ tricks while the turntables would spin ablaze.

In 1988 the group independently recorded the single "We're Notorious" and posed for the cover of the work holding fake guns. Later that year one of the group's bodyguards was killed in a drive-by shooting. He was labeled a "gangland godfather" by the *Boston Globe*.

Around 1990 the group was picked up by Tommy Boy Records. Later, group member Rock Pitts was stabbed to death at a local club. During this same year Tommy Boy released the group's single "One in the Chamba." Afterward, the Boston Police Patrolman's Association publicly announced plans to file a suit against RSO, saying that the song "promotes cop killing." Soon after, Tommy Boy dropped the group. They continued to record songs independently, however, and later they were signed to Queen Latifah's Flavor Unit Records, where they released the single "Badd Boyz."

By 1994 the group was recording for RCA Records, where they made the EP *Revenge Ov Da Badd Boyz*, featuring the single "Hellbound (The RSO Saga, Part 2)."

 Selected albums/CDs: *Revenge Ov Da Badd Boyz* (1994, RCA 66444).

ANDRE HARRELL

See DR. JECKYLL & MR. HYDE

ANTOINETTE

•••••••••••••••••••••••

(Born in Queens, New York)

Antoinette, the Gangstress of Rap, made an impressive entry into the hip-hop scene during 1989 and into 1990 with her good looks and hardcore rhyme style. Her rhymes were delivered in a hypnotic monotone vocal texture, similar to rapper Rakim's, of the duo Eric B & Rakim. She is remembered for her verbal attacks on rapper MC Lyte in her rhymes.

Antoinette made her first appearance on the acclaimed piece "I Got an Attitude." The single was featured on producer Hurby "Luv Bug" Azor's compilation album, titled *Hurby's Machine*, in 1989. Her debut album, *Who's the Boss?*, was released that same year, and the work contained similar braggadocio and battle lyrics. By the following year Antoinette released her second album, titled *Burnin' at 20 Below*. She appeared with a sexier image, and her rhymes varied in subject matter, covering such topics as relationships. She did some coproduction on the work as well. Soon after the release of this material, however, Antoinette slowly faded from the scene.

Selected albums/CDs: *Who's the Boss?* (1989, Next Plateau 1013); *Burnin' at 20 Below* (1990, Next Plateau 1021).

Antoinette

APACHE
(Born in Jersey City, New Jersey)

Rapper Apache had a reputation for his skills in the hip-hop underground long before he recorded his 1993 hit song "Gangsta Bitch." Despite the offense some people took (mostly outside the hip-hop community) because of the "b word" and his humorous lyrics mentioning his dream of going to the movies with his girl, carrying his-and-her nines (as in 9-millimeter automatics), this tongue-in-cheek work got the attention of many in hip-hop circles.

Known for his African and Native American features with long braids, Apache (also the brother of Latee) was a writer of poems before being introduced to DJ Mark the 45 King in his Jersey neighborhood. Mark encouraged Apache to work on his material, and would later use him in many of his recording projects. Apache's debut self-titled album, released in 1993 on Tommy Boy Records, included the "Gangsta Bitch" single, which was produced by Q-Tip of the group A Tribe Called Quest.

 Selected albums/CDs: *Apache* (1993, Tommy Boy 1068).

ARABIAN PRINCE
(Born in Los Angeles)

Arabian Prince was one of the original members of N.W.A, and was also part of the High Powered Productions crew at Ruthless Records, along with Dr. Dre, DJ Yella, and label owner Eazy-E. Arabian Prince's production on Ruthless Records's act J.J. Fad's single "Supersonic" propelled the work to gold status in 1989. Prince is also responsible for the piece "Something 2 Dance 2" off N.W.A's *Straight Outta Compton* album.

In 1989 Prince pursued a solo career, signing with Orpheus Records and releasing the single "She's Got a Big Posse" and his album *Brother Arab*. In 1990 Prince produced J.J. Fad's *Not Just a Fad* album with N.W.A's DJ Yella.

ARRESTED DEVELOPMENT

●●●

Formed c. 1989, Georgia
(Speech, formerly DJ Peech, born Todd Thomas, 1969,
Milwaukee; Headliner, born Tim Barnwell, 1968, Savannah,
Georgia; Aerle Taree; Montsho Eshe; Rasa Don; Baba Oje)

Arrested Development is a group that focuses on Afrocentric themes, and displays their rural Southern roots through attire and stage shows with farm scenery. Group leader Speech is also one of the first group of MCs in the 1990s to rap in a half-singing, half-rapping style.

Writer and producer Speech spent most of his summers in Ripley, Tennessee. He got into hip-hop culture at the age of 13 as a DJ named DJ Peech (for his light complexion). He later decided to take up rapping, putting an "s" in front of his nickname.

During college Speech began to coauthor a column with a friend known as Hoover. The column was titled "20th Century African," and it was published by Speech's parents, who owned a publication called the *Milwaukee Community Journal*. Speech's column focused on Afrocentric issues and topics like youth violence, respect for African-American women, drug use, youth parenting, and other issues relevant to the African-American community.

Around 1989 Speech put together a group with his cousin Aerle Taree (who would do background vocals, as well as design the group's clothing) and others, including the elder Baba Oje, known as their spiritual adviser. The group was eventually signed to Chrysalis Records, where their debut album, *3 Years, 5 Months and 2 Days in the Life of . . .* (a reference to how long it took the group to be signed to a label), was released in March 1992. The work went platinum that same year, and two singles off the album, "Tennessee" and "People Everyday," went gold.

In 1993 they were one of the first rap groups to be featured on the popular "MTV Unplugged" television program; this concert was subsequently released as a CD. A year later they recorded their second album, *Zingalamaduni*.

 Selected singles: "Tennessee" (1992, Chrysalis); "People Everyday" (1992).

 Selected albums/CDs: *3 Years, 5 Months and 2 Days in the Life of . . .* (1992, Chrysalis 21929); *Unplugged* (1993, Chrysalis 21994); *Zingalamaduni* (1994, Chrysallis 29274).

Arrested Development

Audio Two

AUDIO TWO

Formed c. 1987, Brooklyn, New York
(Milk Dee, born Kirk Robinson, c. 1972, Brooklyn;
Gizmo, born Nat Robinson, Jr., c. 1970, Brooklyn)

Milk Dee and Gizmo—the Audio Two—are brothers who became very popular in the hip-hop community after the release of their 1987 hit "Top Billin'," which was co-produced by the duo and Daddy-O, of the group Stetsasonic. They are the brothers of female rapper MC Lyte and have produced material for her, including the hit "I Cram to Understand U (Sam)." The two have also produced and remixed work for Sinead O'Connor, Positive K, and others.

The grandchildren of former vaudeville piano player Leslie Walters, Milk and Gizmo occasionally put on talent shows for their family as kids. They later formed a group around 1984, and recorded a piece called "Christmas Rhymes" on the MCM Records label in Brooklyn. Thereafter, the brothers, along with their father, Nat Robinson, decided to form their own label, calling it First Priority Music. Soon after, the Audio Two began to make their musical presence felt.

In 1988 Audio Two released their album *What More Can I Say*. In 1990 their *I Don't Care—The Album* was released, followed two years later by *First Dead Indian*, featuring their sister, MC Lyte.

By 1992 the brothers had split up professionally due to creative differences. Gizmo decided to pursue harder-edged rap, while Milk developed his own Spoiled Milk Products production company. In 1994 he was signed to Rick Rubin's American Recordings, where he released the six-song EP *Never Dated*. He also remixed singer Janet Jackson's 1994 gold single, "You Want This."

 Selected singles: "Top Billin'" (1987, First Priority Music).

 Selected albums/CDs: *What More Can I Say* (1988, First Priority Music 90907); *I Don't Care—The Album* (1990, First Priority Music 91358); *First Dead Indian* (1992, First Priority Music 92145).

AWESOME 2

Formed in 1982, New Jersey
(Special K, born Kevin Bonner, September 28, New Jersey; DJ Ooh
Child Teddy Tedd, born Ted Whiting, October 4, New Jersey)

The Awesome 2 are two cousins known for having the longest running hip-hop radio show, *The Awesome 2 Radio Show*, which began in 1982. They are also known for starting "Rap Talent Night" at the famed hip-hop club the Latin Quarters, and they are responsible for giving professional consultation to some of the most important talents in rap, such as Big Daddy Kane, Nice & Smooth, Positive K, Double XX Posse, Ed O.G & Da Bulldogs, and EPMD. DJ Teddy

Tedd (also known as the "Ooh Child") is recognized for paying homage to pioneer hip-hop artists by always including a couple of their records or tapes in a music set. The duo has worked in the studio with many artists as well, including Boogie Down Productions, Divine Sounds, Rock Master Scott, Nice & Smooth, and Tony Terry. Teddy Tedd has provided his DJ skills on tour for the artist Real Roxanne.

Special K graduated from William Patterson College in New Jersey with a B.A. in communications. He worked as a DJ at local clubs and parties in the area. In his senior year, he began working at the college radio station as a DJ. Teddy Tedd attended the Center of Media Arts in Manhattan, where he learned about studio functions while continuing to perfect his DJ skills.

In the early 1980s Special K approached then-WHBI hip-hop radio personality Mr. Magic, looking for information on rap recordings. Magic suggested that K should take a shot at doing radio in New York, after which K was given Afrika Islam's former Wednesday afternoon slot at the station through radio personality/producer/manager Jerry Bloodrock in 1982. During this period Special K's partner on the show was Donald B, and the union lasted for approximately two years. Later, Sammy "Mysterio" Lee worked with Special K until around 1986, when Teddy Tedd came in as DJ.

The Awesome 2 were getting so many tapes from aspiring rappers and DJs that they decided to start a talent night at the hip-hop club Latin Quarters, in 1986. Called "The Awesome 2's Rap Talent Night," the segment occurred every Tuesday night and was successful, lasting approximately two years.

Around 1990 the Awesome 2 began to get involved with production, putting together the *History of Rap: Volume One* LP, which featured previously released singles from pioneer rap artists. In 1991 they coproduced Ed O.G (another cousin of theirs) & Da Bulldogs' *Life of a Kid in the Ghetto*, which spawned the hit single "I Got to Have It." By 1995 their *Awesome 2 Radio Show* was entering its thirteenth year on the air.

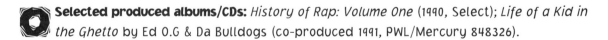 **Selected produced albums/CDs:** *History of Rap: Volume One* (1990, Select); *Life of a Kid in the Ghetto* by Ed O.G & Da Bulldogs (co-produced 1991, PWL/Mercury 848326).

afrocentrism: The study of world culture based on its roots in Africa.

OTHERZ

ALLIANCE
a.k.a. the Brooklyn Alliance
(K-Swift; King of Chill; Style: all born in New York)

This First Priority Music Records group released the singles "Bustin' Loose" and "Ready Set" before releasing their album *We Could Get Used to This* to some critical acclaim around November 1988. The group later disbanded. Group member King of Chill would later be known for his production work for MC Lyte ("Cha Cha Cha," "Stop, Look, Listen") and others.

 Selected albums/CDs: *We Could Get Used to This* (1988, First Priority Music).

ALLMIGHTY MARSKI
(Roggie E. Pettaway, born in Southampton, New York)

Allmighty Marski recorded the single "Leader of the Force."

ANQUETTE
Formed in Miami
(Keta Red; Anquette; Ray Ray: all born in Florida)

This female group made their first record, "Respect," on Luther "Luke Skyywalker" Campbell's label.

A.O.K.
Formed in New York City
(Matt Lewis; Gordon Pettiford: both born in New York)

A.O.K. was an acronym for All Out Kings. This MC and DJ duo recorded the single "Shack It Up" for Profile Records.

AWESOME DRE
(Born in Detroit)

Once signed to Priority Records, Awesome Dre and his group, Hardcore Committee, recorded the single "Frankly Speaking" and the album *You Can't Hold Me Back*.

AFRIKA BAMBAATAA SPEAKS

On Deejaying

To me, a lot of DJs worldwide have gotten real shitty. They're not progressive like they used to be in the 1980s or the late 1970s. When punk rock and hip hop was coming on strong, you had the DJs trying everything, playing from all the hip-hop groups, playing Talking Heads to New Wave and playing oldies but goodies—rare grooves.

But now, everything is separate or apartheid. Where, if you want house, you go here; techno, here. Hip hop might come in when they're not making no money. Reggae, here. We need progressive DJs that's gonna play all the music, to keep the music flowing.

If you're on a radio station and you're playing something on a hip-hop show, and it gets playing on major time, then, it's time to put something else in the spot. Don't play the same thing that they're playing from 9 to 12 midnight on the air now. You already did your job of breaking it.

If that's being played, you go to the next record of an independent, or a major that's not being played. Then you jump that up until people start liking it, and if they pick it up in regular rotation, then you go to the next record that's not doing well, or somebody might not have heard of and start pumping that.

We just gotta tell these DJs, especially in New York—a lot of the DJs here lost the funk. Whereas, when you go down South or to the West Coast, you hear a lot of the funk. You even hear it in a lot of the rap groups that come out there. They try to make you think hip hop is different from funk, which—the birth of it really—comes from funk and reggae.

On History

Our people have to always know our history. It's most important to know our history in everything, in music, culture, anything that deals with blackness from way back to now, we must know, 'cause there are a lot of people who have taken our sound now, which you can't tell anymore.

Back in the 1960s, you could tell if that was a white or black (singer). Now you can't tell who's singing. They're copying the dance steps and everything so perfectly, which is good, 'cause we (Africans) have given everything to the world, but it always ends up with other people making the money and us getting the bad end of the stick.

Impressions

When I was a child, I saw so much that I didn't understand, so much that was happening in the 1960s. TV played a big role. Then, experiencing a little racism here and there with the whites and growing up in street gangs and mixing with the Latino brothers, who are black, too; and hearing the Honorable Elijah Muhammad, Louis Farrakhan, and Martin Luther King, Jr., reading up on Marcus Garvey, going around and hanging around the Black Panthers and the Young Lords parties and then going to demonstrations when I was in school, to fight for bus passes or going up against the Youth Service Agency to get jobs.

Seeing all this, and seeing brothers and sisters die on dope and all the drugs they put out there and then through the hip hop early stages when dust and all that came in. I just started seeing we were wasting our lives. And it was really Minister Farrakhan's words that touched me the most.

On Religion

From the teachings that I learned from the Honorable Elijah Muhammad and Minister Louis Farrakhan, Malcolm X, and everybody else, I just take what I learned and then try to put it in a world perspective. I try to include all nationalities, races, and religions, and I don't get into feuds or arguments over which name you wanna call the Creator, just because you're a Christian, Muslim, Hebrew, or Buddhist. You need to check out everything.

If you're a Buddhist, then you need to check out the Qur'an. If you're Muslim, you need to check out the Bible. You need to get into the messengers that came outside of the books, like Elijah Muhammad or Nostradamus, Confucius, or all those other people that had some insight.

We have to look at this as a real world. There's no more time for falseness. It's time to check everybody out that came and said something and take from all of it. Anything that's gonna uplift you and better yourself as a person and make you a better human being, then we need to take from all the different ideas as long as it helps you and not bring you down.

BEASTIE BOYS

••••••••••••••••••••••

**Formed c. 1979, New York City
(King Adrock, born Adam Horovitz, October 31, [year unknown]; MCA,
born Adam Yauch, August 5, 1965; Mike D, born Michael Diamond,
November 20 [year unknown]: all born in New York City)**

The Beastie Boys were the first white rap group to be authentically received for their skill by most black hip hoppers, which broke ground for other white rap artists entering the field. Their 1986 album, *Licensed to Ill*, was the biggest selling rap album ever up to that date.

At its inception in the late 1970s, the Beastie Boys (a.k.a. the Beasties) was a punk-rock group, consisting of bassist MCA, drummer Mike D, Jill Cunniff, and Kate Schellenbach and John Berry, who played drums and guitar respectively. The group opened for a few other punk bands like Reagan Youth and Bad Brains at venues like Trudy Heller's and Max's Kansas City at the time. In January 1982, they put out a 7-inch EP on Rat Cage Records titled *Pollywog Stew*, which contained eight songs and received some favorable reviews.

Later the group added guitarist Adam Horovitz, who was a member of the group The Young and the Useless, a band who occasionally played with the Beasties. Horovitz (the son of playwright Israel Horovitz) would become Ad-rock, and later, King Adrock. Group members Cunniff, Schellenbach, and Berry eventually dropped out to play with other bands.

In 1983, after experimenting with many types of music, they decided to try their hands at making a rap record. The song, "Cookie Puss" (again on Rat Cage), was a takeoff on a character from the Carvel Ice Cream commercials that aired on TV at the time. British Airways illegally used the record in one of its commercials; the Beastie Boys sued for $40,000 and later won.

The Beasties soon began to do gigs performing that song, with Rick Rubin as their DJ, whom they met through Nick Cooper, an occasional manager of Adrock's former band. Into

1984 the group continued to work with Rubin. MCA also began to work as an assistant engineer for producer Arthur Baker at his Shakedown Studios, with engineer Burzootie.

In 1985 Rubin—who by this time had his Def Jam Recordings label under way with his partner, Russell Simmons—began recording the Beastie Boys, including the songs "Rock Hard," "Party's Gettin' Rough," "Beastie Groove," and "Drum Machine" by the Beasties' MCA and Burzootie. Later the Beastie Boys recorded the song and video "She's on It." In 1986 the Beastie Boys released their first album on Def Jam, *Licensed to Ill.* Its single "Fight for Your Right to Party" catapulted the group to stardom, winning instant success in the hip-hop community. The album went double platinum in a matter of months. It sold four million copies, the largest selling rap album at the time.

Around this time Doctor Dre (from the group Original Concept, and later "Yo! MTV Raps" host) became the group's DJ for a while. Toward the summer of 1986, DJ Hurricane took over. From 1987 to 1988 the Beastie Boys sued Def Jam owners Rick Rubin and Russell Simmons for $2 million in royalties. Later the group changed record labels, signing with Capitol Records, and moved to Los Angeles.

In 1989 they released their second album, *Paul's Boutique,* with the single "Hey Ladies." The album was produced by the Dust Brothers, which consisted of Matt Dike (a former club DJ, owner of L.A.'s Power Tools club and co-owner of Delicious Vinyl Records), John King, and Mike Simpson. *Paul's Boutique* was a masterpiece in its construction of samples from a wide range of recorded music from many genres, and it was critically acclaimed. However, the album only went gold during the year of its release, compared to the platinum sales of their debut work.

In April 1992 the group released their third album on their own label, Grand Royal Records, titled *Check Your Head,* in which the group returned to playing live instruments. It also went gold by the end of 1992.

In 1994 they released the work *Some Old Bullshit,* which is a compilation album of some of their previously released material from the early 1980s. That same year their album *Ill Communication* was released and went platinum.

Selected albums/CDs: *Licensed to Ill* (1986, Def Jam/Columbia 42038); *Paul's Boutique* (1989, Capitol 91743); *Check Your Head* (1992, Grand Royal/Capitol 98938); *Same Old Bullshit* (1994, Grand Royal /Capitol 89843); *Ill Communication* (1994, Grand Royal/Capitol 28599).

Beastie Boys

BEATNUTS

**Formed c. 1988, Flushing, Queens, New York
(Fashion, born Berntony Smalls, 1972, Peekskill, New York;
Psycho Les, born Lester Fernandez, 1972, South Bronx,
New York; Ju-Ju, born Jerry Tineo, 1970, Queens)**

The Beatnuts are a group of Latino artists and producers, originally known for their DJ skills, who are noted for their production work with Pete Nice and Monie Love.

All three members met at the Queens Outreach program for troubled youths. Psycho Les and Ju-Ju were DJs who worked local parties, and soon began making tapes as well. They joined the Native Tongues Posse (which included De La Soul, Jungle Brothers, and others), and later worked with some of its members to produce Monie Love's "Pups Licking Bone." Thereafter, as Ju-Ju and Psycho Les's reputations as producers began to grow, they recruited a third member to handle most of the MC'ing. They chose Fashion, another alumnus from the Outreach program.

They released their *Intoxicated Demons* EP during 1993, and gained considerable notice with three pieces from the work, "No Equal (Competition Is None)," "Story (Pinky in the Twat)," and "Reign of the Tec."

Beatnuts

B-FATS
(Born W. Bowden, El Paso, Texas)

B-Fats is responsible for introducing one of the biggest dance crazes in hip hop, the Wop. His 1986 single on Posse Records, titled "Woppit" (which featured some production work from Teddy Riley), was a major hit in the hip-hop community. The dance itself was still being performed in some states in the late 1980s. Fats was also known for his work with his producer/DJ brother, Donald Dee, at the Renaissance Club in Manhattan.

Raised in New York City, Fats recorded a self-titled work on Rooftop Records in the early 1980s. He was the first rapper signed to Orpheus Records, for which he recorded the single "Music Maestro" and the album of the same name. However, his fame came from 1986's "Woppit." He was unable to duplicate this success later on.

 Selected singles: "Woppit" (1986, Posse).

BECKY DJ JONES
See PETE DJ JONES

BIG DADDY KANE
(Born Antonio Hardy, September 10, 1968, Brooklyn, New York)

Big Daddy Kane is a rapper who was introduced to hip hoppers first as a technician on the microphone—when it came to lyrical skills—and later became an international sex symbol, posing for *Playgirl* magazine and Madonna's coffee-table sex pictorial book. He is noted for his high-top fade haircut and mack image (wearing fine tailored suits and, early on, layers of gold jewelry) while at the same time extolling the teachings of the Five Percent Nation of Islam. Kane has also starred in movies, including Mario Van Peebles's *Posse*, and has donated his time to many charity projects, like KRS-One's H.E.A.L. project. He has made cameo appearances on records, working with Quincy Jones on his *Back on the Block* LP, and Public Enemy's "Burn Hollywood, Burn," to name two. His stage shows are noted for their stylish and sometimes acrobatic choreography, presented by himself and his two dancers, Scoob and Scrap Lover.

Kane (an acronym for "King Asiatic Nobody's Equal") was an early follower of the hip-hop scene, sneaking out of his house late at night in Brooklyn to travel up to the Bronx park jams given by the Cold Crush Brothers and other pioneer groups. Around 1984 Kane met rapper Biz Markie in front of McCrory's department store in downtown Brooklyn. They showed off their rhyme skills to each other and eventually became friends. Markie

Big Daddy Kane

introduced Kane to his friends up in the Queens-bridge Housing Projects in Queens, including producer Marley Marl and Roxanne Shanté.

While attending Sarah J. Hale High School, Kane met and became friends with Mister Cee. They eventually joined a group called Magnum Force, performing shows until the group broke up sometime later. However, Kane and Mister Cee stayed together. Kane soon began working with Roxanne Shanté, traveling on the road with her, and eventually writing rhymes for her, like "Have a Nice Day." Attending studio sessions with Marley Marl, Kane began writing rhymes for Biz Markie as well, and by 1987 Cold Chillin' Records signed him.

During 1988 Kane's *Long Live the Kane* debuted and immediately got him noticed. His nonstop, hardcore lyrical style and cool pimp image caught on with hip hoppers. His single "Raw" (released the previous year) was one of the first pieces that called attention to the artist and DJ Mister Cee, and the album went gold by August 1989. Also in 1989, his second work, *It's a Big Daddy Thing*, was released and went gold. "Smooth Operator" and "I Get the Job Done" were some of the hit singles.

His third album, *A Taste of Chocolate*, was released in 1990. Kane duetted with soul singer Barry White and Gamilla Shabazz (daughter of Malcolm X), as well as film and party-record star Rudy Ray Moore, a.k.a. Dolemite. Around this time staunch hip hoppers were beginning to grow tired of Kane's smooth ladies' man image (which seemed to intensify with every album release), but this album received critical acclaim.

Around 1992 his next work, *Prince of Darkness*, was released. His little brother, Little Daddy Shane, appeared on the work, as well as A Tribe Called Quest's Q-Tip and Leaders of the New School's Busta Rhymes.

In 1993 *Looks Like a Job For* was released. On this work, Kane showed his fans that he still had lyrical skills and proficiency as a rhyme writer, scoring with hip hoppers on the pieces "How U Get a Record Deal" and "Stop Shammin'." In 1994 Kane released the album *Daddy's Home* on a new label, MCA Records. A single, "Show & Prove," was a hit with the hip-hop audience, and included cameos by Wu-Tang Clan's Ol' Dirty Bastard and Shyheim the Rugged Child.

 Selected albums/CDs: *Long Live the Kane* (1988, Cold Chillin' 25731); *It's a Big Daddy Thing* (Cold Chillin' 25941 1989); *A Taste of Chocolate* (1990, Cold Chillin' 26303); *Prince of Darkness* (1991, Cold Chillin' 26715); *Looks Like a Job For* (1993, Cold Chillin' 45128); *Daddy's Home* (1994, MCA 11102).

BILL STEPHNEY
●●●●●●●●●●●●●●●●●●●●●●●●●●●
(Born July 22, 1962, Harlem, New York)

Bill Stephney received wide recognition for his successful marketing of Public Enemy, hip hop's first overtly political rap group. He is also the first cousin of baseball star Bobby Bonilla.

Stephney began his career as a musician. Coming from a musical background (his father played drums), Stephney started out playing the violin, and by the age of two he also took up the drums. Stephney began playing the trumpet when he was 8, and it remained his main instrument until he was 20, although he also played the guitar and bass. He joined his first band in 1973, and by 1978 he started deejaying. Later he worked for a short time at the rock radio station WLIR as a paid intern.

By the early 1980s, Stephney was attending college at Adelphi University, where he met Carlton "Chuck D" Ridenhour, a graphics design major and a member of a party promotion crew called Spectrum City, with brothers Hank and Keith "Shocklee" Boxley. In 1982 Stephney headed his own radio show at the university's WBAU station called the *Mr. Bill Show*. Stephney was bringing the latest rap records to the station's audience—primarily in the Long Island and Queens areas. He also became program director at the station and produced other shows, like *First World News*. Later Chuck D and the Shocklee brothers would also have their own radio shows on this station. Stephney dropped his *Mr. Bill Show* after graduating from

Bill Stephney

college and began working at *College Music Journal*, also known as *CMJ*. (Doctor Dre, later a member of the group Original Concept and "Yo! MTV Raps" host, took over Stephney's radio show). At *CMJ* Stephney set up the journal's first hip-hop column, "Beat Box."

In 1985 he got into video, producing fifteen segments of a show called "W.O.R.D.: The World of Rock and Dance" for Long Island cable. Hank Shocklee and Chuck D also worked with him. During 1986 Stephney was approached by Def Jam Recordings co-owner Rick Rubin and was offered a position at the company. He did not accept the position until months later, but soon became the National Director of Promotion. His first assignment was to help Rubin sign Chuck D to the label, whom Rubin had heard on a tape that Doctor Dre had.

Chuck D was initially reluctant to become a rap artist (believing that he did not want to rap about just anything). To meet these concerns, Stephney decided to create, with Chuck and Shocklee, a rap group with a political edge, similar to punk groups like the Clash. They decided to call the group Public Enemy, based on a demo the Spectrum City crew had done years earlier, titled "Public Enemy Number One," which Chuck had chosen to record. Stephney believed that the name reflected what was happening at the time; many young black males felt that they were public enemies, in large part due to incidents like Howard Beach (where a young black male was killed by an angry group of whites). Other local DJs and musicians, inlcuding Terminator X, Eric "Vietnam" Sadler, Flavor Flav, and Professor Griff, became a part of the group and production crew.

In 1987 Stephney produced Public Enemy's debut album, *Yo! Bum Rush the Show*, in addition to playing guitars and bass on the work. Hank Shocklee and Chuck coproduced the album, while Eric Sadler handled the drum programming. The work created an impressive buzz in underground circles, and was recognized for its emphasis on noise-oriented tracks on top of funk grooves.

In 1988 the group's second album was released, titled *It Takes a Nations of Millions to Hold Us Back*. This time Stephney supervised the production, while Hank Shocklee came more to the forefront, multilayering sampled tracks and increasing the noise factor against rhythms. The album was a success, reaching platinum status the following year.

In 1989 Stephney left Def Jam to start a label with Hank Shocklee called SOUL (the Sound Of Urban Listeners) Records. He had also set up a marketing company called Weasel Marketing to handle the marketing of all SOUL acts. Later disappointed with the SOUL deal, he left to create his own StepSun Music Entertainment in 1992, a joint venture deal with Tommy Boy Records. His first act on the label was comedian Paul Mooney. That same year Stephney was the music supervisor for the soundtrack of the Hudlin Brothers' film *Boomerang*. The soundtrack album was one of the biggest album sellers that year, reaching multiplatinum status. Stephney also did the soundtrack for *BeBe's Kids*.

Selected albums/CDs: *Yo! Bum Rush the Show* by Public Enemy (producer, 1987, Def Jam 40658); *It Takes a Nation of Millions to Hold Us Back* (production supervisor, 1988, Def Jam 44303); *Boomerang* (music supervisor, 1992, La Face 26006).

BIZ MARKIE
. . . .

(Born Marcel Hall, April 8, 1964, Harlem, New York)

Biz Markie is an MC who is known for his humor-seasoned rhymes and beatbox-styled vocal and throat effects. He is also respected as an accomplished DJ and producer. His 1991 court battle over sampling brought the issue into the legal arena.

Biz—who got his name while growing up on Long Island's South Shore because he was always "busy" pulling practical jokes in school—started out professionally as an MC and DJ, working at New York clubs like the Roxy and the Fun House. In 1985 he met producer Marley Marl while beatboxing in Marl's Queensbridge Projects building. Marl liked what he heard, and the two soon began working together, making demo recordings. This led to Biz's signing with Prism Records (which soon became Cold Chillin' Records).

In 1988 Cold Chillin' released Biz's first album, *Goin' Off*, which featured Biz's cousin DJ Cutmaster Cool V. The work was produced by Marley Marl, with some of the lyrics written by Big Daddy Kane. The album, including a number of its songs ("Vapors," "Nobody Beats the Biz," and "Pickin' Boogers"), was a major hit in hip-hop circles and began to establish Biz as an important talent.

Biz Markie

His second album, *The Biz Never Sleeps*, was released in 1989. This time Biz produced and wrote the entire work. Its single "Just a Friend" went platinum in 1990, as did the entire album soon thereafter. At this time Biz and Cool V. began producing other artists (with Biz supplying the records and beats, while Cool V. handled the engineering). DJ Kid Capri, Grand Daddy I.U., and Biz's cousin Diamond Shell were some of the artists they worked with.

I Need a Haircut was his third album, released in 1991. One of the songs on this work, titled "On N On," featured an 8-bar sample of Gilbert O'Sullivan's 1972 hit, "Alone Again (Naturally)." O'Sullivan sued and Biz Markie was later found guilty of copyright infringement, causing a stir in the record industry. The judge in the case ordered Warner Bros. (the distributors) to discontinue the sale of the album containing the song. Biz later remarked that the case nearly ruined him financially.

In 1993 he returned with his fourth album, sarcastically titled *All Samples Cleared*. "Young Girl Bluez" and "Let Me Turn U On" were two hit singles from the work. That same year saw him entering the acting field, working with actor/director Robert Townsend and costarring with him on Townsend's television show, *Townsend Television*.

 Selected singles: "Vapors"; "Nobody Beats the Biz" (both 1988, Cold Chillin).

 Selected albums/CDs: *Goin' Off* (1988, Cold Chillin' 25675); *The Biz Never Sleeps* (1989, Cold Chillin' 26003); *I Need a Haircut* (1991, Cold Chillin' 26648); *All Samples Cleared* (1993, Cold Chillin' 45261).

Black Sheep

BLACK SHEEP

Formed in 1989, New York
(Dres, born Andres Titus, 1969, Queens, New York; Mista Lawnge, born William McLean, December 11, 1970, Brooklyn, New York)

Black Sheep introduced a moderately lighter sound to rap, with less emphasis on traditional funk patterns. Their sample choices were generally light in texture and wide in musical variety, à la producer Prince Paul, and lyrically the duo is known for their playfully sexist rhymes. They later became associated with the Native Tongues Posse.

Dres and Lawnge (a.k.a. 9.5) both hail from New York, but met each other in North Carolina in 1983. They both belonged to the same rap group there for a while.

Some time later Lawnge was performing in a show in North Carolina with female rapper Sparky D, when he met pioneer hip-hop Kool DJ Red Alert, who was deejaying for Sparky. They became friends, with Red telling Lawnge to look him up when he came back to New York. Around 1985, Lawnge moved back to New York and began hanging out with Red Alert and other Native Tongues members. Inspired by all the Native Tongues groups, Lawnge called Dres around 1989 with the idea of forming a group.

By 1991 the duo was signed to Mercury Records and their debut album, *A Wolf in Sheep's Clothing*, was released. It immediately struck a chord with hip hoppers, especially the twentysomething crowd. Theirs was an alternative sound to the more harder-edged material at the time, and by April 1992 the album went gold. "Flavor of the Month," "The Choice Is Yours," and "Strobelite Honey" were some of the hit singles. During the latter part of 1994 the group released the album *Non-Fiction*, with the single "Without a Doubt."

 **Selected albums/CDs:** *A Wolf in Sheep's Clothing* (1991, Mercury 848368); *Non-Fiction* (1994, Mercury 5226852).

BOBBY ROBINSON

See ENJOY RECORDS

BODY & SOUL

Formed in 1987, Los Angeles
(Dzire, a.k.a. Sista Dee, born Denise Barnes, January 1968, Queens, New York; Almight T, a.k.a. Lady T, born in Los Angeles)

The female duo of Lady T and Dzire, known as Body & Soul, received some notice during the late 1980s with the singles "Dance to the Drummer's Beat" and "High Powered" on

Body & Soul

Delicious Vinyl Records. By 1990 the two had split up due to marketing differences with their label, resulting in the company deciding not to release the duo's album.

Formerly a resident of Queens, New York, Dee began her career recording demos with DBC (of Stetsasonic fame). After graduating from high school, she traveled to California and back to New York again several times, before deciding to settle in California. She met another female MC named Lady T there, along with another former New Yorker named Def Jef, and all three were signed to the Delicious Vinyl label.

After Body & Soul split, Dzire pursued solo activities. In 1990, she became the host Sista Dee for the FOX-TV rap video show "Pump It Up." She also hosted the "Sisters in the Name of Rap" pay-per-view television event produced by Van Silk in 1992. Dee is remembered for her $22.7 million civil suit, filed against Dr. Dre, whom she charged with assaulting her in the ladies room of a Los Angeles club in January 1991. The attack came in response to a segment on her "Pump It Up" show, which had shown an offensive videotaped comment about Dre and his group, N.W.A, made by former group member Ice Cube during an N.W.A interview. According to Dee the taped comment was spliced in by her show's producer without her knowledge. Her lawsuit was later dropped.

BONE THUGS N' HARMONY

a.k.a. Bone: Thugs N' Harmony; B.O.N.E. Thugs-N-Harmony
Formed c. late 1980s, Cleveland
(Krazie Bone, Wish Bone, Flesh N' Bone, Lazy
Bone, Bizzy Bone: all born in Cleveland)

Bone Thugs N' Harmony is one of the fastest-charting groups in rap music. Consisting of five MCs, the group's style is a mixture of semispeed rap with a singsong freestyle delivery and occasional harmony, with subject matter focusing on ghetto life in the 1990s. The acronym B.O.N.E. stands for several things, including Brewed Out Niggas Everyday, Brothers on Normal Elimination, and Budded Out Niggas Everyday.

Hailing from Cleveland, Ohio's, St. Claire, East 99th Street area, the group members have been friends since childhood. Just before entering junior high, they were performing as a crew called the Band-Aid Boys, doing talent shows, winning prizes, and gaining fans. They even recorded a work called *Faces of Death* for the Platinum Label Group during the late 1980s to early 1990s.

Around this same period, the friends decided to pursue their dream of meeting Eazy-E. Group member Flesh N' Bone, who worked at a Kentucky Fried Chicken, purchased one-way bus tickets for the group to travel to Los Angeles to meet Eazy during the early 1990s. Upon arriving in Los Angeles, they took turns calling Eazy, staying with some of Flesh N' Bone's college friends. After several attempts (including performing a few freestyle rhymes in rapper Tone Löc's yard), the group finally got a chance to perform rhymes for Eazy's secretary over the phone. Eazy called them back a week later, and soon signed them to his Ruthless Records label.

Thanks to their association with Eazy-E, their 1993 EP, *Creepin' on Ah Come Up*, bypassed *Billboard*'s number 1 spot on their Heatseeker chart and went directly to the Top 200 (pop) Albums chart in seven weeks, without the usual stages of promotion and publicity. By 1994 the work was multiplatinum. The single from the EP was titled "Thuggish Ruggish Bone." The group's second album was released in 1995, after the premature death of Eazy-E due to complications from the AIDS virus. The group dedicated the work to him. The single from the album was "1st of tha Month."

Selected albums/CDs: *Creepin' on Ah Come Up* (1993, Ruthless 5526); *E. 1999 Eternal* (1995, Ruthless 5539).

BOOGIE DOWN PRODUCTIONS

See KRS-ONE

BOO-YAA T.R.I.B.E.

(The Devoux Family: Ted "The Godfather"; Donald "Don L";
David "E.K.A."; Danny "O.M.B."; Paul "The Riddler"; Roscoe:
all born between 1963 and 1969 in Los Angeles)

The six-man family of Samoan brothers known as the Boo-Yaa T.R.I.B.E. made an impressive entry into the hip-hop scene with their debut album of the 4th & B'way label, *New Funky Nation*, in 1990.

Muscular and huge in size, the brothers were Los Angeles-based gang members until the death of one brother due to gang violence forced the others (there were eight in total) to try their hands at another means of making ends meet.

The Boo-Yaa T.R.I.B.E. ("boo-yaa" is the sound a shotgun made when the brothers had their gang wars), noted for their acrobatic performances and funk-rock influences, melted into a hip-hop sound.

After their 1990 debut they were signed in late 1993 to the Hollywood Basic label before that company's demise in early 1995.

 Selected albums/CDs: *New Funky Nation* (1990, 4th & B'way 4017).

BOSS

(Boss, born Lichelle Laws; Dee, born Irene Moore: both born in Detroit)

 Boss

Boss is a female rapper who writes and performs rhymes exclusively in the so-called gangsta genre. By 1992 she was the first female rapper to be signed to Russell Simmons's Def Jam West label.

Boss and her friend Dee hail from Detroit, and originally sought a record deal there, to no avail. She later dropped out of college and, with Dee, traveled to New York City where they were met with what they felt were shady business offers from some record industry heads. The two later decided to travel to Compton, Los Angeles.

After three years of near homelessness, sometimes sleeping on park benches, they came to the attention of DJ Quik and his manager. They were signed to Def Jam West, where their 1993 album, *Born Gangstaz* (formerly titled *They Don't Have the Body Count*), was released. They made appearances at various venues during that year, performing several pieces from the album, including the single "Deeper."

 Selected albums/CDs: *Born Gangstaz* (1993, DJ West/Chaos 52903).

Brand Nubian

BRAND NUBIAN
••••••••••••••••••••••••
Formed c. 1988, New Rochelle, New York
(Lord Jamar, born Lorenzo DeChalus, September 17, 1968, New Rochelle; Sadat X, formerly Derek X, born Derrick Murphy, December 29, 1968, New Rochelle; Sincere, born in New York. Former members: Grand Puba, formerly Grand Puba Maxwell, born Maxwell Dixon, August 24, 1967, New Rochelle; DJ Alamo, born in New York)

Although they were not the first hip-hop group to present rap lyrics dealing with lessons of the Five Percent Nation of Islam, Brand Nubian was the most skillful at it. The quality of the group's work was enhanced by the lyric skill of Grand Puba, an original member who left the group in 1990.

Puba had originally recorded with his cousin Dr. Who as Masters of Ceremony on DJ Jazzy Jay's Strong City Records label, before that group broke up. Puba then began working with a couple of neighborhood friends named Jamar and Derek, later known as Lord Jamar and Derek X. After producing several demos with them, Puba, along with the others, decided to seek a record deal as a group.

Dante Ross, who had just been appointed head of A&R at Elektra Records, knew Puba and his work, and quickly signed the new group. In 1989 the label released Brand Nubian's "Feel So Good" single, which created an underground buzz for the group. By 1990 the group's full-length work *One for All* was released and was well received by hip-hop audiences, mostly on the East Coast. The album became a classic in underground circles. Within a year, however, the group had split due to creative differences between the Brand Nubian members and Grand Puba.

The remaining members, Jamar and Derek (now known as Sadat X), continued with the Elektra label and put out a second album, *In God We Trust*, in 1992. They maintained their creative status with hip-hop audiences with songs like "Love Me or Leave Me Alone" and "Punks Jump Up to Get Beat Down" off their album. In 1994 their third album for the label, *Everything Is Everything*, was released, with its single "Word Is Bond."

 Selected singles: "Feel So Good" (1989, Elektra).

 Selected albums/CDs: *One For All* (1990, Elektra 60946); *In God We Trust* (1992 61381); *Everything Is Everything* (1994, Elektra 61682).

BUSY BEE
a.k.a. Busy Bee Starski, Chief Rocker Busy Bee
(Born David Parker, New York)

Busy Bee's career in hip hop spans about the length of the culture itself. Busy has worked with most of the major artists and developers of hip hop since the 1970s: The L Brothers, Afrika Islam, Kool DJ AJ, Disco King Mario, Jazzy Jay, Mele Mel, Pumpkin, and Afrika Bambaataa, to name just a few.

Busy earned the name "The Chief Rocker" primarily because of his natural ability to move party crowds with his rhyme delivery. Busy has also been known to move crowds without rhymes, by simply shouting exhortations like "Everybody get up! Clap your hands!" and involving everyone in his call-and-response routines.

Busy's rhymes have always been based in comedy for the most part, and he has been involved in many MC battles during rap's early years. He won the New Music Seminar's MC World Supremacy belt in 1986, and he has won similar rap contests in Staten Island, New Jersey, Brooklyn, and other parts of New York's tristate area.

Busy first started being recognized in the hip-hop community around 1977. A long-time admirer of MCs Mele Mel and his brother Creole from Grandmaster Flash's Furious Five, Busy would watch the two trade rhymes with each other. During a battle in that same year, with Afrika Islam and Raheim challenging DJ Breakout with Baron and the Funky Four, Islam gave Busy a shot at MC'ing. Busy actually recycled some of Mele Mel's and Creole's rhymes during the battle, adding his own lines and verses, but his performance was successful, convincing him that he could truly compete with the top MCs around.

Soon afterward Afrika Bambaataa asked him to join his Zulu Nation, where Busy would

MC for many of Bambaataa's Zulu Nation parties. Busy later joined Grand Wizard Theodore and his brothers, known as the L Brothers. After working with this group for some time, he began working with Kool DJ AJ.

In 1982 Busy appeared in the classic hip-hop film *Wild Style*, where he gave a memorable performance as one of the MCs. He is also remembered for being one of the first people in hip hop to introduce the slang term "dope," meaning extremely excellent.

Busy has recorded for many record labels (Brass, Sugar Hill, Independent), but achieved some of his top successes with Jazzy Jay's Strong City Records label, where he recorded the 1987 hit, "Suicide" (with lyrics written by Mele Mel). His album *Runnin' Thangs* was released in 1988. In 1992 Busy had released an album titled *Thank God for Busy Bee*.

 Selected singles: "Suicide" (1987, Strong City).

 Selected albums/CDs: *Runnin' Thangs* (1988, Strong City/UNI Records 2); *Thank God for Busy Bee* (1992, Pandisc 8819).

BIG LADY K

(Born Rosa Lee Chambers, Riverside, California)

Big Lady K received some critical praise in various music publications for her singles "Ffun" and "Don't Get Me Started." Also called "The Poetress," Lady K released her album *Bigger Than Life* in 1990.

 Selected albums/CDs: *Bigger Than Life* (1990, Priority).

BLACK BY DEMAND

Formed in Astoria, Queens, New York
(CJ, born C.J. Moore; Cut Professor, born Dathan
Williams: both born in Astoria, Queens, New York)

Black By Demand was a duo of cousins. They had originally formed a few singing groups, as well as rap groups. CJ usually served as the MC, and Cut Professor handled the music, although they reversed their roles in one of their last incarnations as the group Trio Connection. They played in the community centers and parks, mostly in the Astoria, Queens, area. Toward the early 1990s, the duo recorded the single "Can't Get Enough," backed with "All Rappers Give Up" for Tommy Boy Records.

BLACKMALE

Formed in New Jersey

(Tracey Cobb; Reggie Williams; Robert Adams: all born New Jersey)

The group Blackmale received some notice with the single "Let's Go." Around 1991 they recorded the single "Body Talk," while their album *Let It Swing* was released on Enigma Records.

BLACK ROCK & RON

Formerly the Vicious 4

(David Coutryer, Greg Walsh, Ron Walsh)

As the Vicious 4, Black Rock & Ron recorded on the Next Plateau label. They later recorded the single "Stop the World"; their album of the same name was released on RCA Records in 1989.

BOB AND THE MOB

(MC Speedo, born Robert Crawford; DJ Slayer, born Thomas Morrison)

Bob and the Mob were a Nastymix Records recording act, who released the single "It's a Shame" backed with "I'm Wild." The group was formerly on Holiday Records.

BOBBY JIMMY AND THE CRITTERS

(Born Russ Parr, Los Angeles)

Bobby Jimmy is recognized for his satirical rhymes, which cover everything from relationships to the authenticity of a woman's hair. Some of his notable singles include "Roaches," "Big Butt," "Somebody Farted," and "Hair or Weave."

Bobcat

BOBCAT
. . . .
(Born in Los Angeles)

Pioneer West Coast DJ Bobcat received wide recognition in 1987 for his production work with the L.A. Posse on LL Cool J's *Bigger and Deffer* LP, which sold three million copies. During this same period he deejayed for LL and headed the group Microphone Mafia, which consisted of artists like Threat, Nefertiti, and Yamel.

By 1989 Bobcat had done production on the K-9 Posse's album, and released his own solo effort titled *Cat Got Ya Tongue*, featuring the single "I Need You." Since that time, he has ceased to be active on the rap scene.

Selected produced albums/CDs: *Bigger and Deffer* by LL Cool J (1987, Def Jam/Columbia 40793).

BREEZE
··········

(Born in New York)

Breeze originally resided in New York before he moved to Los Angeles, where he worked with the L.A. Posse on his album, *The Young Son of No. 1*, which was released on Atlantic Records.

BRUCIE B
···········

(Born in Bronx, New York)

Brucie B was one of the first DJs in the early 1980s to create cassette mix tapes (along with DJ Starchild), which are audiotape recordings of a DJ's music repertoire, recorded at home studios or at parties. His style, which was in the party-rocker mode, paved the way for DJs like Kid Capri, who displayed their personalities on the microphone while playing records, in the way that radio DJs did during and between record sets. During this same period, Brucie B also made a name for himself as a house DJ at the Rooftop Club. He has continued to make his mix tapes into the 1990s.

Backspinning: Alternately spinning two records backward under the needle of each turntable to repeat a drum pattern or instrumental phrase.

Battle: An MC who engages an opposing MC in a test of skill, one on one. The same is said for the hip-hop DJs, who originally participated in sound system battles, which consisted of determining who had the most powerful sound system, according to the strength of the dynamic frequency (or volume) on that DJ's system. The DJ who drew the most people in a crowd of onlookers and partygoers to his system would usually be the winner. Hip-hop DJs also battled each other one on one in the turntable skills of cutting, scratching, and back-spinning, as well as with the occasional tricks they would do while performing those skills.

B-boy: A term coined by hip-hop pioneer Kool DJ Herc to describe the people who danced to his break-beat music sets. The term is synonymous with the later-used term *breakdancer*. Hence, to b-boy is to breakdance.

Beatbox: To imitate vocally the sound of a drumbeat or pattern, usually as an MC (or rapper) raps over it. (One who beatboxes is also called a Human Beatbox.) The term beatbox was also sometimes applied to the early drum machines artists used.

Boasting: To exaggerate one's capabilities or skills; in rap, boast records feature exaggerated, sometimes tongue-in-cheek claims made on the part of the rapper.

Break beat: A particular instrumental phrase and/or drum pattern on a record. The break beat is extended by alternately repeating the phrase or pattern on both turntables, using two copies of the same record. This type of deejaying was developed by Kool DJ Herc.

Breakdance: A word first used outside the hip-hop community to describe dance routines done by dancers at Kool DJ Herc's parties. The dances were originally done whenever Herc played *break-beat* music, and the routines themselves consisted of acrobatic dance moves done on the floor. In hip-hop culture *b-boy* became the accepted word for those who breakdanced.

SAMPLING

Rap music created the art of sampling, which is the audio duplication of break-beat music via digital recorders. Originally, DJs like Kool DJ Herc manually repeated a favorite breakoff of a record by cuing up two identical copies of the record on two turntables and alternately playing them back and forth. This took considerable skill, because DJs had to have the speed and precision to play just the short section they wanted and nothing else. An electronic sampler is a digital recording device that allows a musician to record (or "sample") a selection from either a live performance or another source (a record, for example). It can then be electronically played and repeated, allowing for much greater precision.

By the mid- to late-1980s, sampling (led mostly by artists on the Cold Chillin' Records label) completely changed the way rap records were made. Initially, the backing tracks were made using live and electronic instruments like synthesizers and drum machines. Then, samples from other records were assembled into a backing track. This naturally raised questions about copyright and the legality of using material from preexisting recordings.

Sampling is simply applying the latest technology to an age-old musical tradition of musical quotation or borrowing from earlier performers. When a guitarist plays a short phrase or riff learned from an earlier musician, he or she can't be sued for "copyright infringement," even if that riff is a signature phrase. Yet, if that same guitarist recorded the earlier player's performance using a sampler and then played it back as an accompaniment to her or his own recording, copyright problems would come into play.

As various recording artists recognized that their songs were being used as looped breaks in a rap record, they became more vocal about it, requesting financial compensation for the use of their material, not understanding the rap artist's "borrowing" technique as part of the creative process.

No rap artist took the brunt of these opposing artists' anger more than the group De La Soul and rapper Biz Markie. In 1989 De La Soul went through a sampling lawsuit, involving the 1960s rock group the Turtles. Sued by the group for $1.7 million for sampling one of their songs, titled "You Showed Me," De La Soul eventually settled out of court for a smaller amount.

In 1992 Biz Markie was found guilty of copyright infringement by a New York federal judge in a suit filed by singer/songwriter Raymond "Gilbert" O'Sullivan. Markie had used eight bars of O'Sullivan's 1972 song "Alone Again (Naturally)" as a backing track in one of his songs. Warner Bros. (the company that distributed Cold Chillin' Records at the time, which was Biz Markie's label) was ordered to discontinue the sale of Markie's album that contained the song. In an interview one year after the decision, Biz Markie reportedly said the incident nearly ruined him. Markie ironically titled his next album *All Samples Cleared*.

After the Biz Markie incident, however, rap artists began to get more creative with their sampling, recording a musical note or a quarter of a measure of music from a record, instead of an entire bar. However, the legal and ethical issues of sampling are still troubling the rap and hip-hop recording industries.

Kool Herc

CHILL ROB G
• • • • • • • • • • • • • • • • • • •
(Born Robert Frazier, New York)

Chill Rob G is an MC who is remembered for his socially and politically conscious rhymes, which were structured in phonetically funky lines and delivered in an oratorical fashion. Rob was a member of the Flavor Unit and worked extensively with producer/DJ Mark the 45 King. Rob is also remembered for the controversy that arose in 1990 over the sampling of his song "Let the Words Flow" by two German producers (Benito Benites and John "Virgo" Garrett III) for their studio group Snap. The incident showed the confusing and sometimes contradictory side of sampling, as well as its legal entanglements.

"Let the Words Flow" was released as a single by Rob's record label, Wild Pitch. Some time later, producers Benites and Garrett sampled four verses and a horn part from Rob's work, added a sample from disco singer Jocelyn Brown's "Love's Gonna Get You" (where she sings, "I got the power!"), and released the work as a single called "The Power."

Wild Pitch Records' president, Stu Fine, sought compensation for the work from the producers' record company (Logic/BMG). He discovered that Arista Records had picked up the U.S. rights to make a third version of the piece based on the German recording. The Arista version used Turbo B, an American serviceman and aspiring rapper stationed in Germany to replace the Chill Rob G sampled verses, with the exception of one line, which went, "It's gettin' kinda hectic" (Turbo B's cousin, Jackie Harris, added vamped vocal lines). The end result was that all three versions gained much attention, garnering international sales and chart-topping positions.

Chill Rob G grew up in Rockaway, Queens, and Jersey City, and was introduced to Mark the 45 King in New Jersey by his friend, rapper Latee's brother, Apache. Rob rehearsed with Mark and the other Flavor Unit members in Mark's basement, where Mark encouraged and recorded the Flavor Unit artists.

Mark called Rob one day and asked if he was interested in making a record. The two made a demo and gave it to Kool DJ Red Alert, who played it on his radio show. Wild Pitch Records' Stu Fine heard Rob's piece, and soon signed him to the label.

Toward 1989, Rob released singles (with the 45 King's production) that were hits with the hip-hop crowd, including the classic "Dope Rhymes" and "Court Is Now in Session." During this same period Rob's album *Ride the Rhythm* was also released, with Mark the 45 King producing the entire work.

 Selected albums/CDs: *Ride the Rhythm* (1989, Wild Pitch 97545).

CHUBB ROCK

(Born Richard Simpson, West Indies)

Chubb Rock is known for his skillful dexterity in MC styles, and is recognized as one of the major rap technicians. His 6'3" height and huge girth, along with a cool demeanor, also help him stand out in the rap crowd. His rhyme content can range from serious social topics to cartoon-like battle lyrics. Chubb has also written rhymes for other acts, like Finesse and Synquis and the Soul Sisters.

Chubb started rapping at the age of 12, and he soon started rapping with his cousin, future DJ/producer "Hitman" Howie Tee, in the group called Sureshot 4. At the age of 16 Chubb won a National Merit Scholarship to enter college as a premed student. He dropped out after two years to pursue a career in the rap field, working with Howie Tee—who by this time was working with the Real Roxanne. Soon after, Chubb was signed to Select Records.

His first work for the label in 1988, titled *Chubb Rock Featuring Howie Tee*, presented Chubb to hip hoppers with the song "Caught Up," gaining the rapper some attention. In 1989, his second album, *And the Winner Is . . .*, got Chubb even more notice with the singles "Ya Bad Chubbs" and "Stop That Train."

Chubb Rock

In 1990 he released the five-song EP *Treat 'Em Right*, with the title track becoming a hit. *The One* was released in 1991, including the songs "The Chubbster" and "Just the Two of Us."

The album *Gotta Get Mine, Yo* was released in 1992, with the hit singles "Yabba Dabba Doo" and "Lost in the Storm." During this period, Chubb also wrote and produced Real Roxanne's *Go Down (But Don't Bite It)* LP.

 Selected albums/CDs: *Featuring Howie Tee* (1988, Select 21624); *And the Winner Is . . .* (1989, Select 21631); *The One* (1991, Select 21640); *Gotta Get Mine, Yo* (1992, Select 61299; "clean version," Select 61437).

COKE LA ROCK
•••••••••••••••••••••
(Born in Bronx, New York)

Coke La Rock is recognized as the first person to MC, using crowd motivating lines, during the break-beat music sets that were developed by Kool DJ Herc at his parties, which would later become the foundation of most aspects of hip-hop culture. It is for this reason that many original Bronx hip hoppers call him the first MC.

Performing as Kool Herc's MC at his parties in the early 1970s, La Rock did not deliver extensive rhymes, as MC'ing or rapping later came to be identified. However, he presented the standard hip-hop phrases (most of which were used by Kool Herc) in party-rocker fashion, to keep Herc's party crowd dancing.

Speaking on the microphone through an echo chamber (or reverb frequency) on Herc's renowned sound system, Coke La Rock would say:

> Yes yes, y'all. Yo, you're listening to the sounds of "Kool DJ Herc" (and the reverb would echo the "Herc" in Herc's name a few times), "Coke La Rock" (the reverb would echo "Rock"), "Nigger Twins" (again, the reverb on "Twins"), "Clark Kent" (on "Kent," the same), "El Dorado Mike" (the same on "Mike"), etc.

Then, as the party crowd immersed themselves in dancing, Coke La Rock would continue on the microphone, delivering phrases like: "Ya rock, and ya don't stop, to the rock rock rock, the rock rock, the rock. Ya rock, and ya don't stop, to the rock rock rock, the rock rock, the rock," and so on. This was the method of MC'ing La Rock used to help motivate Herc's crowd.

As with Kool Herc, Coke La Rock would also call out the names of dancers or familiar faces in the crowd and tell them to "rock on my mellow, rock on" and the like.

Known for his tall height, sideburns, and glasses, Coke La Rock was a fixture at Herc's parties when the DJ was at the peak of his popularity in the early 1970s. He worked strictly for the love of the music and hip-hop culture, and never worked in any other music capacity.

COLD CHILLIN'/PRISM RECORDS

Formed in September 1986, New York City

Cold Chillin' Records, formerly Prism Records, was an influential rap label during the mid- to late-1980s. With Marley Marl as the official house producer, Cold Chillin's product was distinguished by an extensive use of sampling, helping usher in the use and recording of sampling by other producers and record labels. By 1986 the company's successful product had earned the label an approximate worth of $25 million.

Cold Chillin' Records' main roster consisted of Roxanne Shanté, Biz Markie, Big Daddy Kane, MC Shan, Kool G Rap & DJ Polo, and Marley Marl. These artists were also known as the Juice Crew, named after pioneer radio DJ Mr. Magic (also called Sir Juice). They were noted for their ability to create rhymes off the top of their head on the spot, in freestyle fashion, with impressive results.

The main motivating force behind the label was Tyrone "Fly Ty" Williams, who hailed from Brooklyn, New York, and later attended Howard University. He studied business there, and also played for the Howard Bisons football team as a linebacker. Williams later worked as a tax superviser for Citibank. He was also a radio sports announcer before eventually coproducing Mr. Magic's rap radio show.

By 1983 Williams had met Marley Marl. Magic, Marl, and Williams started calling themselves the Juice Crew when they began doing Magic's *Rap Attack* radio show on WBLS-FM. In 1984 Marley Marl recorded his neighbor Roxanne Shanté performing an answer record to UTFO's "Roxanne, Roxanne," which Magic had played on his radio show. Impressed with the audience response, Williams decided to manage Shanté.

Through Shanté, Williams picked up other acts, managing Biz Markie, MC Shan, and others. Soon Biz Markie was signed to Len Fichtelberg's Prism Records. At Prism Biz Markie recorded an EP that was produced by Marley Marl, featuring the piece "Make the Music with Your Mouth." Its success, along with other Markie songs like "Nobody Beats the Biz" and "Pickin' Boogers" convinced Fichtelberg to combine his venture capital with Williams's acts and create a label especially for the rap material, calling it Cold Chillin' Records.

Around 1987 the label got a distribution deal with Warner Bros., and by 1992 Cold Chillin' launched a second label, Livin' Large. By 1995 the company's product was being released by Sony Music Entertainment's Epic Street label.

COLD CRUSH BROTHERS

Formed in 1979, Bronx, New York
(Grandmaster Caz, formerly Casanova Fly; the Almighty KG;
Tony Tone; Easy AD: JDL, born Jerry D. Lewis; DJ Charlie Chase)

The Cold Crush Brothers are pioneer rappers who were among the first group of MCs to emerge in the late 1970s. They are known for their routines based on popular melodies (developed by group member KG) and their rhymes, particularly those of Grandmaster Caz.

Caz is known as one of the most prolific writers in hip hop, one of the first to introduce the narrative structure in rap, as well as one of the first to deejay and MC simultaneously. The group's DJ, Charlie Chase, is remembered as one of the few Latino hip-hop DJs at the time of the culture's emergence. The group was known for their powerful sound system (including Crown DC 300s, Macintosh 2300s, and Marantz amplifiers, to name a few of the components). They were recognized for being one of the first self-contained groups, operating with their own photographer, promoter, tape manufacturer, and sound system.

Caz was originally known as Casanova Fly during the early 1970s, and was involved with many aspects of hip-hop culture from graffiti to b-boying and deejaying. As a b-boy, Caz danced with the Casanova Crew (not to be confused with Grandmaster Flash's security team, the Casanovas). By 1978 Caz had battled Afrika Bambaataa as a deejay. He worked in many groups, including the Mighty Force with DJ Disco Wiz, JDL, and Afrika Islam's Funk Machine Crew.

Tony Tone had been working as DJ Breakout's sound man and with other groups before becoming part of the Cold Crush Brothers. Around 1977 Charlie Chase was part of the group Tom & Jerry, two Latino DJs who played mostly disco records. Chase would play break-beat music during their shows when the crowd went dead. Later Chase formed a group with Lil' Black, T-Bone, and the Sisco Kid. With Tony Tony accompanying them, they battled Disco King Mario and Busy Bee at Monroe High School in the Bronx.

Around 1978 Chase worked with MCs Mele Mel, Creole, Cowboy, Mr. Ness/Scorpio, and Raheim, who had left Grandmaster Flash due to differences with promoter Ray Chandler. The union with Chase lasted through that summer. Soon after, Chase formed another group with MCs Dot-A-Roc, Prince Whipper Whip, Tony Tone, the Almighty KG, and Easy AD. They were to-gether approximately three weeks. Tone came up with a name for the group, "Cold Crush," based on a phrase he'd seen on a party flier; Chase added "Brothers" to the phrase and it became the group's name. Not too long after, however, Whipper Whip and Dot-A-Roc decided to move up, joining with DJ Grand Wizard Theodore's group and becoming part of his Fantastic 5 MCs. Meanwhile, Caz and JDL were dissolving the Mighty Force; Chase invited them to join the Brothers, and the final lineup was born.

The Cold Crush Brothers practiced their routines as a group nearly seven days a week for approximately a year and a half at Caz's house in the Bronx. They then began doing shows. Some of the group's famous battles were with Grand Wizard Theodore and the Fantastic 5 MCs, particularly a showdown at Harlem World in 1981. The group promoted them-selves by distributing tapes of their performances through two cab companies: Community Cab Service and O.J. Cabs. Both companies had powerful speaker systems in their cars, and would play the tapes; their riders would ask about the tapes, wanting to know who the group was that they were playing.

Eventually, the Brothers began to make records, first signing with promoter and Ecstasy Garage owner Arthur Armstrong, recording the single "The Weekend" on his Elite Records label in 1982. Later that year the group appeared in the landmark hip-hop film *Wild Style*. By 1983, they were among the first rappers to visit Japan, during the Wild Style Tour, which fea-tured twenty-five MCs, DJs, b-boys, and graffiti artists.

Around 1984 the group signed with Aaron Fuch's Tuff City label, which released several of their singles, including "Heartbreakers" and "Fresh, Wild, Fly, Bold." They gradually separated by 1986; Caz began writing rhymes for various artists, notably Biz Markie ("Just a Friend" and "A Thing Called Kim") and Ice-T. Easy AD began working with Afrika Bambaataa, while the Almighty KG released two singles in 1987 and '88 on B Boy Records, "Feel the Horns" and "She's a Dog." Charlie Chase began to work on WBLS-FM in New York City, doing mixes for radio personality Lady B in the early 1990s.

By 1994 the group was performing again, appearing on Terminator X's *Super Bad* album with other pioneer hip-hop artists.

COMPTON'S MOST WANTED
a.k.a. CMW
(MC Eiht, born in Compton, Los Angeles; Chill MC, born in Compton; DJ Mike T, born in Los Angeles; DJ Slip, born in Los Angeles; Ric Roc, born in Los Angeles; Boom Bam, born in Los Angeles; Unknown, a.k.a. the Reanimator, born in Los Angeles)

Compton's Most Wanted (CMW) appeared in the early 1990s as exponents of the so-called gangsta rap genre. Head rapper MC Eiht has received the most attention of all of the group's members; he appeared in the acclaimed 1992 film *Menace II Society* as the character A-Wax, and provided the hit song "Streiht Up Menace." He had previously received notice for "Growing Up in the Hood" off of CMW's 1991 *Straight Checkn 'Em* album, which was used as the theme for film director John Singleton's Academy Award-nominated *Boyz N The Hood*. Eiht and his principal collaborator, DJ Slip (a former member of Uncle Jam's Army), also work as Half-Ounce Productions, and have produced Spice 1's "Murder Show" and D.F.C.'s "Caps Get Peeled."

 Selected albums/CDs: *It's a Compton Thing* (1990, Orpheus 75627; edited version, 75632); *Straight Checkn 'Em* (1991, Epic 47926); *Music to Driveby* (1992, Epic 52984); *We Come Strapped* (1994, Epic TK)

COOKIE CREW
Formerly Warm Milk and Cookie Crew
Formed c. 1985, South London
(Suzie Q, born Susan Banfield, Jamaica, West Indies; MC Remedee, born Debbie Pryce, Barbados; DJ Dazzle, born in South London)

The Cookie Crew is a group of female rappers from South London, England, who perform rhymes dealing with people of African descent and sociopolitical issues.

Rappers Suzie Q and MC Remedee knew each other since nursery school. They also went to college together, and soon their love of hip hop (developed from the rap tapes they heard from the United States) made them decide to form a group. The duo performed as the Warm Milk and Cookie Crew, eventually performing with pioneer female rapper Lisa Lee in 1985. Later Suzie and Remedee took on an additional member named "Mad Maxine" Stirling, changing their group name to the Cookie Crew.

The group eventually signed with an independent label, and released the single "Females," which did well on the dance charts in the United States and on the R&B charts as an import. Another single, "Rock Da House," quickly reached the U.K. Top 5. Thereafter, the group signed a record deal.

In 1989 the Cookie Crew (with their DJ, Dazzle) released their debut album, titled *Born This Way*. Mad Maxine left the group to pursue a solo career, and the group released their second work, *Fade to Black*, in 1991, before fading from the scene.

Selected albums/CDs: *Born This Way* (1989, London/ffrr 828134); *Fade to Black* (1991, London/ffrr 828251).

COSMIC FORCE

Formed c. late 1970s, Bronx, New York
(Prince Ikey C, born in New York; Chubby Chubb, born in New York; Ice Ice, born in New York; Lisa Lee, born in Bronx, New York; DJ Rocky G)

The Cosmic Force was the first of the groups from Afrika Bambaataa's Zulu Nation to make a record.

With DJ Rocky G, this Throgs Neck Projects group recorded their only single, "Zulu Nation Throwdown," on Paul Winley Records in 1980. They have also performed in numerous Zulu Nation events and anniversary parties as a group, and individually, after the group's separation. Prince Ikey C would go on to do solo MC work, performing at classic hip-hop venues like Negril's. In the early 1990s he recorded independent singles, including "Butter."

CRAIG MACK

(Born in 1970, Brentwood, Long Island, New York)

Craig Mack first appeared on the scene in 1988 with the group MC EZ & Troup. They recorded the singles "Get Retarded" and "Just Rhymin'" for Sleeping Bag Records, the first of which was an underground hit. The group then faded from the scene. Thereafter, during the late 1980s and early 1990s Mack drifted into a life of occasional crime, living on the streets, until he approached the group EPMD for a job. EPMD member Parrish Smith hired him to carry the group's bags and perform other menial duties while they were on tour. In an attempt to land a record deal, he recorded a couple of demos during this period, including the songs "You Can't Funk with the Style" and "Like D'at Y'all."

Mack traveled back and forth to Manhattan, visiting major record labels trying to get a record deal, with no luck. In the early part of 1994 he was introduced to manager/producer/label owner Puffy Combs outside a club. Mack performed a few freestyle rhymes for Combs, after which Combs offered to sign him, but only if he performed on a recording with one of the artists he was managing, R&B singer Mary J. Blige. Mack agreed and appeared on Blige's "You Don't Have to Worry" single. Combs soon released Mack's single "Flava in Ya Ear," which went platinum, and then his album *Project: Funk Da World*.

 Selected albums/CDs: *Project: Funk Da World* (1994, Bad Boy 73001).

CRASH CREW

Formed in Harlem, New York
(MC Reggie Reg; MC Bistro; MC G-Man; MC
Shoo-Bee; MC E.K. Mike C ; DJ Darrel C)

The Crash Crew was a six-man group from Lincoln Projects in Harlem, and was popular during the late 1970s to early 1980s. They were known for their MC'ing skills and vocal harmony, which they combined in their songs. They later received wider notice after pressing their own record, called "High Powered Rap," which used R&B group Freedom's "Get Up and Dance" as its basis.

They were later signed to Sugar Hill Records, where they recorded hits like "Breaking Bells (Take Me to the Mardi Gras)," "We Are Known as Emcees (We Turn the Party's Out)," and "On the Radio." One of their main performance venues in the late 1970s was Club 197 in Lincoln Projects.

Cypress Hill

CYPRESS HILL
••••••••••••••••••••

**Formed c. early 1990s, Southgate, Los Angeles
(DJ Mixmaster Muggs, a.k.a. Grandmixer Muggs, born Larry
Muggerud, Queens, New York; Sen Dog, born Senen Reyes,
Havana, Cuba; B-Real, born Louis Freeze, California)**

Cypress Hill burst on the scene with their open advocacy of marijuana smoking expressed in their rhymes. The group was also noted for its use of Spanglish rhymes (street Spanish and English mixed), delivered by their two Latino MCs, B-Real and Sen Dog, the brother of Mellow Man Ace. B-Real is also recognized for his James Cagney/Jerry Lewis-esque MC delivery, reminiscent of graffiti artist Rammelzee.

Group member and producer DJ Mixmaster Muggs produced the group 7A3 in the late 1980s. He already knew Sen Dog and B-Real before working with them, because they were all raised in Cypress Hill, located in Southgate, Los Angeles (not far from Compton). The group released its debut self-titled album (which originally had a title that referred to marijuana intake) in 1991, and by the following year the album went gold, and later, platinum. Hit singles off the work included "Latin Lingo," "How I Could Just Kill a Man," and "Hand on the Pump."

In 1993 they released their second work, *Black Sunday*, which contained the single "Insane in the Brain." The album and single went platinum and gold, respectively. In 1995 they recorded the piece "Roll It Up, Light It Up, Smoke It Up" for the motion picture soundtrack *Friday*.

 Selected albums/CDs: *Cypress Hill* (1991, Ruffhouse/Columbia 47119); *Black Sunday* (1993, Ruffhouse/Columbia 53931; "clean version," 57296).

Chill: Calm down.

Coffin: A rectangular case that contains two turntables and an audio mixer for deejaying.

Cool or cool out: Chill; relax.

Cutting: The spinning of one record backward under the needle of one turntable, to repeat a drum pattern or instrumental phrase, and to cut these patterns and phrases into smaller pieces and play them out in a rhythmic fashion, similar to a drum solo in a song.

RAP AND THE MORAL QUESTION

Throughout the years of its existence, various groups and organizations have blamed rap music for the evils of society. As with much of youth-oriented music historically, particularly rock 'n' roll, forums and protest groups have expressed outrage over the art form. One of the more famous critics of rap is the Reverend Calvin Butts of the Abyssinian Baptist Church in Harlem, New York.

Declaring in 1993 that he was not antirap but against lyrics he deemed offensive to people of African descent, Reverend Butts organized several campaigns protesting the marketing and distribution of those records that contained the type of lyrics that he felt were objectionable. On a drizzly Saturday morning, the Reverend Butts and a small group of protesters dumped a load of rap CDs in front of the Sony Entertainment building (home of Columbia and Epic Records), attempting to smash them with a steamroller. When the steam-roller they brought failed to produce an adequate effect, the protesters had to stomp physically on the CDs.

Butts announced his antirap campaign from the pulpit on Mother's Day. In a statement, quoted in *Rap on Rap* by Adam Sexton, he said,

> I and a broad cross-section of people consider vulgar, offensive to women, and contrary to the progress and goals of African Americans [certain rap lyrics and music videos]. . . . My objection to these lyrics and videos is spurred not only because I am a minister but because I am a black man, husband, and father. I want to supplant these negative music lyrics and videos with positive ones. . . . This protest against offensive lyrics . . . is not an assault on our First Amendment right to free speech and expression. I cherish this very important privilege, but I also believe that African-American women such as Harriet Tubman, Rosa Parks, Ella Baker, Soujourner Truth, and Fannie Lou Harner, among others, did not . . . jeopardize their lives to give young black music artists the temerity to refer to black women as bitches and whores and, with abandon, characterize African-American people as niggers.

Because of Reverend Butts's respected position in the black community, he did not receive a more vehement amount of criticism from black artists, producers, and label owners who were very much involved in the business side of rap music. They viewed this incident as divisive and theatrical, with possible political overtones: they felt that somewhere down the line this would lead to him announcing his candidacy for a political office. However, by July of 1995, the Reverend had not yet made any announcements about his intentions to run for office.

By the middle of 1995, 1996 Republican Presidential candidate Bob Dole began attacking entertainment conglomerate Time Warner, a producer and distributor of many record labels and movies, for what he called "putting profits before decency." Dole singled out the company for its distribution of rap product from Interscope Records, which handles material from major rap artists like Snoop Doggy Dogg, Dr. Dre, and Tupac Shakur.

After Dole's attacks, others followed, particularly those affiliated with the Republican party, such as former Secretary of Education William Bennett, who also had harsh words for Time Warner. C. DeLores Tucker of the National Political Congress of Black Women complained as well about Time Warner's interest in rap music, reportedly stating, "I won't be satisfied until Time Warner stops selling this garbage to kids."

Many rappers have responded to this threat by citing the first amendment protection on free speech. Luther "Luke Skyywalker" Campbell is quoted on *Rap on Rap* saying, "The government has no power to restrict expression because of its message, its ideas, its subject matter, or its content. So what's the problem? I write a few songs that are purely for adult entertainment." He continued, citing another defense of rap, that the lyrics only reflect general societal conditions: "Today's society is based on sex—just look at how many strip bars and how much pornographic literature is available. Why condemn me—a black artist and entrepreneur—for my particular brand of adult entertainment?"

Following the controversy over the single "Cop Killer," also widely condemned by conservative critics, Ice-T had this to say about the song in his book, *The Ice Opinion*:

What's "Cop Killer" about? A black youth takes justice into his own hands after his buddies are unjustly murdered by corrupt cops . . . I don't give a fuck about the police's problems, if I offend them or I cause them to be mad at records. They are not above scrutiny. They're not above ridicule. . . . Believe me, if I could give them one night of inconvenience for the four hundred years they done fucked over my people, I would be happy to do it.

DADDY-O
(Born in Brooklyn, New York)

Daddy-O is the founder of the group Stetsasonic. He is also a top producer, responsible for producing and co-producing rap and R&B hits, including the Black Flames' "Watching You," Audio Two's "Top Billin'," and Levert's "Just Coolin'." He has written songs for artists in various music genres, such as Ipso Facto ("My Only Girl"), Queen Latifah ("We Are the Pro's"), EEK-A-Mouse ("You Are the Only One I Need"), Jeffrey Osborne ("Good Things Come to Those Who Wait"), and the title track for the film *Straight Out of Brooklyn*. Daddy-O has also worked as a jingle writer and producer in both radio and television, for products like Polly-O String Cheese, Alka-Seltzer, Pepsi, and Dark & Lovely. In 1993 Daddy-O released his first solo work, *You Could Be a Daddy, But Never Daddy-O* (Brooktown 518203).

DANA DANE
(Born Dana McCleese, New York)

Dana Dane is known for his playful, narrative rhymes with occasional cartoon-like characters, which he delivers in an English accent, like fellow rapper (and high-school friend) Slick Rick.

Raised in the Walt Whitman houses in Fort Greene, Brooklyn, Dana later attended the High School of Music and Art, where he met Slick Rick. Becoming good friends, Dane and Rick even dressed alike (matching shoes, pants, and their signature Kangol hats). The duo—along with three other friends—began calling themselves the Kangol Crew (because of the hats), and practiced in the school's cafeteria.

Dane eventually began performing solo. His initial appearance at the club Broadway International was so successful he was immediately invited back. Around 1982 he began

Dana Dane

working with Super DJ Clark Kent as his DJ. Three years later Dane landed a record deal with Profile Records, which released his single "Nightmares" (produced by Sam Jacobs, Sr. and Jr.). He also attracted the attention of rap producer/promoter Hurby Luv Bug Azor.

In July 1987 Dane's debut album, *Dana Dane with Fame*, was released. The single off the work "Cinderfella Dana Dane" was a big hit, helping to boost the album to gold status by January 1988. Other hit singles followed, including "Delancy Street" and "This Be the Def Beat." At the same time, Dane became business partners with Play (of Kid 'n Play), opening a boutique that specialized in custom-made clothing, called IV Plai.

Dane's second album, *Dana Dane 4-Ever*, was released in 1990. Although "Tales from the Dark Side" was released as the single, the album track "Lonely Man" drew the most critical attention, because of its story about the death of a girlfriend in an automobile accident.

In 1993 Dane was working with James Smith's Rap-A-Lot Records. By 1995, however, he was recording for singer Madonna's Maverick label, releasing the album *Rollin' Wit Dana Dane*.

 Selected singles: "Nightmares" (1985, Profile); "Cinderfella Dana Dane" (1987, Profile).

 Selected albums/CDs: *Dana Dane with Fame* (1987, Profile 1233); *Dana Dane 4-Ever* (1990, Profile 1298); *Rollin' Wit Dana Dane* (1995, Maverick 45770).

DAS EFX
. . . .

Formed c. 1989
(Krazy Drayz, born Andre Weston, September 9, Jamaica; Books,
a.k.a. Skoob, born Willie Hines, November 27, Brooklyn)

DAS EFX stormed the hip-hop scene with their style of rapping, which consisted of adding occasional prefix-like "iggedy" words to the first initial of certain words in their rhymes, creating an original style of rapping that caught on with hip hoppers. Their appearance and lyrical style always stressed the underground side of hip hop, while remaining accessible to the kids as well as appealing to the staunch hardcore hip hoppers.

Das EFX

The duo got together in college at Virginia State, where Drayz originally planned to study child psychology but soon decided to major in English. Books originally planned to enter broadcast communications but also became an English major. The two got a chance to show off their writing skills when the group EPMD came up to Richmond, Virginia, to judge a rap contest. Drayz and Books didn't win, even though they did have a high score. However, Parrish Smith of EPMD approached them and offered them a record deal, and the two were signed to eastwest Records.

Their debut album, *Dead Serious*, was released in 1992 and went gold that same year, and later, platinum; the single off the work "They Want EFX" also went gold that year. Their second work, *Straight Up Sewaside*, was released in 1993.

 Selected singles: "They Want EFX" (1992, eastwest).

 Selected albums/CDs: *Dead Serious* (1992, eastwest 91827); *Straight Up Sewaside* (1993, eastwest 92265).

DAVY D
Formerly Davy DMX
(Born David Reeves, Queens, New York)

Davy D, a.k.a. Davy DMX (named after the Oberheim DMX drum machine that he used), is known for his DJ work, on and off tour, with MC Kurtis Blow for five years. He is also known for making one of hip hop's classic scratch records, 1984's "One for the Treble." Davy is also one of the first DJs to use samples and sample loops, which he created on the then-popular Fairlight computer during the early 1980s.

Originally a guitarist, Davy joined the group Rhythm & Creation when he was 16 years old. Davy also worked as a guitarist for the band Orange Krush, with Larry Smith and Trevor Gale. Davy began to get into deejaying as well, because he could make more money working alone than with a band. He worked as a mobile DJ, and also started a DJ organization called Solar Sound, before working with Kurtis Blow, and replacing Blow's then DJ, Run (of later, Run-D.M.C. fame).

Davy deejayed for Blow when the rapper opened for the R&B act the Commodores at Madison Square Garden in 1982. Davy also wrote and co-wrote songs for Blow and rapper Jimmy Spicer ("Money: Dollar Bill Y'all"), and contributed guitar work to some of the rapper's pieces. He began doing production work by the 1990s, producing material for various artists, including Doctor Dre & Ed Lover on their 1994 *Back Up Off Me!* album.

 Selected singles: "One for the Treble" (1984, Tuff City).

DA YOUNGSTA'S

a.k.a. Illy Funksta's
Formed in Philadelphia
(Qu'ran Goodman, born in 1977; Taji Goodman, born in 1976;
Tarik Dawson, born in 1975: all born in Philadelphia)

Da Youngsta's is made up of the Goodman brothers, Qu'ran and Taji (sons of Pop Art Records co-owner Lawrence "L.G. The Teacher" Goodman), along with their cousin Tarik. They were "discovered" by their father while working as background vocalists for one of his label's acts, Mentally Gifted, on the song "Something for the Youngsters." Thanks to the favorable responses this record received from listeners, Goodman decided to work with the boys as a group. Mentally Gifted became their principal rhyme writer.

Da Youngsta's released their debut album in 1991. By 1993 their single "Crewz Pop," featuring Treach from the group Naughty By Nature, began to get the boys more serious attention from hip hoppers. Da Youngsta's released their second album, *The Aftermath*, that same year. In 1994 they released the album *No Mercy*, featuring the single "Hip Hop Ride."

Selected album/CDS: *The Aftermath* (1993, eastwest 92245); *No Mercy* (1994, eastwest 92370).

DEF JAM RECORDINGS

Formed in 1984, New York City

Def Jam Recordings is known as the most influential record label in rap music. Launched officially by Rick Rubin and DJ Jazzy Jay, the label developed its position in the market through Rubin's production and A&R capabilities, and later, cofounder Russell Simmons's Rush Artist Management roster. It was Simmons who brought the label into prominence through his distribution deal with CBS Records, and that essentially launched his Rush Communications empire, which by 1992 was worth $34 million.

In 1981 Rick Rubin was attending New York University (NYU) as a film student and working in various bands as a guitarist and a DJ. In 1983 he met DJ Jazzy Jay of Afrika Bambaataa's Soul Sonic Force at a club called Negril. The two became friends, and Jay began to turn Rubin on to many records that were popular with the hip-hop crowd, as well as introducing him to the art of beat programming. Later that year the two decided that they wanted to make a record. Although they hoped to use Special K of the Treacherous Three on their record, they settled on K's brother, T La Rock, to record their song titled "It's Yours." Rubin sought distribution for the record, first approaching Profile Records (whose offer he turned down), then producer Arthur Baker's Partytime label, which Rubin accepted.

The year 1984 saw the release of "It's Yours" to favorable reviews in hip hop's underground, and Rubin's dormitory room at NYU's Weinstein Hall (room #802) officially became Def Jam Recordings. Later that year Rubin met Russell Simmons at a club called Danceteria and

Da Youngsta's

Def Jef

they quickly became friends. Deciding to become fifty—fifty partners in Def Jam Recordings, they each put in $4,000 by November of that year to bring the deal to fruition.

Rubin and Simmons's first act as partners was LL Cool J, a rapper whose demo was first heard by the Beastie Boys's Adam "Ad Rock" Horovitz, and later Rubin. They released LL Cool J's "I Need a Beat" that same year, selling 120,000 copies its first time out.

In 1985, CBS Records approached Def Jam and an agreement was made between the two companies, with CBS handling the promotion and marketing of Def Jam product. The deal was worth $600,000. Later Def Jam released LL Cool J's first album, *Radio*, which eventually went platinum. Some of the company's other releases around this time were MCA and Burzootie's "Drum Machine," Jimmy Spicer's "Beat the Clock," and the Hollis Crew's "It's the Beat" (produced by Run-D.M.C.).

In 1986 Def Jam released the Beastie Boys' *Licensed to Ill*, which sold five million copies, and became the largest selling rap album at that time. In 1987 the company released LL Cool J's *Bigger and Deffer*, which sold two million copies. Later that year Def Jam signed and released Public Enemy's debut album, *Yo! Bum Rush the Show*.

By 1988 the creative relationship between Rick Rubin and Russell Simmons began to dissolve. Rubin took his share of the company and moved to Los Angeles and created his Def American record label (which later became American Recordings), where he worked with acts like comedian Andrew Dice Clay, the Black Crowes, Slayer, Sir Mix-A-Lot, the Geto Boys, and country artist Johnny Cash.

In 1990 Simmons renegotiated the CBS deal (which by then had become part of Sony, Inc.). Def Jam Recordings gave rise to RAL (Rush Associated Labels), which consisted of other labels (along with Def Jam) created by some of Simmons's artists from his Rush Artists Management roster. This joint deal with CBS was the largest subsidiary label deal in the history of the record business at the time, with Def Jam receiving an annual $3 million for operating costs and a splitting of the profits. Simmons's labels and additional companies then became part of his Rush Communications parent company.

DEF JEF
• • • • • • • • • •
(Born Jeffrey Fortson, New York City)

Def Jef is a rapper who is recognized for the Afrocentric and socially conscious rhymes that he writes and performs. He is also noted for the wide variety of musical work he does in various entertainment media. He has done motion picture soundtrack work for the films *Marked for Death*, *The Adventures of Ford Fairlane*, *Downtown*, and *Superfly II*. He has worked in television, composing and producing the theme songs for the Fox Network programs *Pump It Up* and *Studs*. Jef has done commercials, composing and performing on advertisements for Bugle Boy Jeans, the California State Lottery, and Bell Atlantic. Jef has also written rhymes for various artists like Mellow Man Ace, Ed O.G. & Da Bulldogs, Kurtis Blow, Five Star, Ready for the World, and Biscuit, and he was part of the West Coast Rap All-Stars' antigang violence single and video "We're All in the Same Gang." He was involved with the *Souled Out Mandela* project at the L.A. Coliseum, with Tone-Löc and Ice-T, making the record "Freedom Kings" with them. By the early 1990s Jef was also a prominent speaker on the college lecture circuit.

Jef grew up in the Bronx and Harlem and became interested in hip hop in the late 1970s. He soon began to learn about Africa and African-American history, as well as politics in America, later dropping out of school at the age of 14, disenchanted with what he had been learning about those subjects. After moving to Washington, DC, Jef got involved with the go-go music scene there, and continued to be turned on to Afrocentric studies through friends. With the intention of pursuing a career in music, Jef moved to California with a few of his partners in 1985, where they lived in a high school for approximately three months, until they were able to afford an apartment. That same year Jef deejayed and rapped (simultaneously) at several clubs, eventually releasing a 12-inch single entitled "Have You Seen Her," backed with "Dis Dis Dis."

Jef continued doing demos until he was signed by Delicious Vinyl Records. Another 12-inch single was released, titled "On the Real Tip," and by 1989 his debut album, *Just a Poet with Soul*, was released, and received critical notice.

In 1991 Jef's *Soulfood* album was released and was noted for its album cover, a rendition of Leonardo da Vinci's *The Last Supper*, with people like James Brown, Bob Marley, George Clinton, and other well-known pioneer black artists replacing da Vinci's images. Jef has been inactive since then.

 Selected albums/CDs: *Just a Poet with Soul* (1989, Delicious Vinyl 92199); *Soulfood* (1991, Delicious Vinyl 92174).

DE LA SOUL
****
Formed c. 1988, Amityville, Long Island, New York
(Posdnuos, born Kelvin Mercer, August 1969, Bronx, New York;
Trugoy the Dove, born David Jolicoeur, September 21, 1968,
Amityville, Long Island; DJ Pace Master Mase, born Vincent
Mason, March 1970, Brooklyn, New York)

When De La Soul's debut album, *3 Feet High and Rising*, appeared in 1989, it marked a turning point for hip-hop music. This was the first album to liberate sampling from the usual James Brown samples that dominated hip hop during the late 1980s. Former Stetsasonic DJ Prince Paul came into his own as a producer, creating a work that was replete with samples of music from every conceivable genre imaginable. Thus came the idea that anything could be sampled and put into a record to make a work of art. The album is one of the very first full-length rap works to contain comedy skits throughout as well.

The look of De La Soul—Posdnuos, Trugoy the Dove, and DJ Pace Master Mase—was also a turning point. Their attire suggested the flower-power days of the 1960s; the group referred to something called the D.A.I.S.Y. Age, which they translated to "Da Inner Sound, Y'all." The work was also full of inside jokes and terms indigenous to the group themselves, which made deciphering some of the lyrics similar to deciphering works by French symbolist poets of the nineteenth century. Their album cover was adorned with daisies and peace signs, and bright colors like pink and yellow, which was also reminiscent of the 1960s and the posters designed by artist Peter Max.

Prince Paul was looking to do other things outside the Stetsasonic projects when he hooked up with a neighborhood acquaintance, DJ Mase, who gave Paul a demo of a couple of MCs he was working with, named Trugoy and Posdnuos, who worked as floor sweepers at a mall in Massapequa, Long Island. Paul then decided to produce two demo songs for the three (after they pooled their money), and shopped the group to a few record labels. They were signed to Tommy Boy Records.

Their album and the single "Me, Myself & I" both went gold in 1989, putting the group on the map. The album and group is also remembered for the $1.7 million lawsuit filed against them by the rock duo Flo and Eddie, formerly of the Turtles, for the group's use of four bars from their song "You Showed Me." De La Soul used samples from that song for their piece "Transmitting Live from Mars." De La Soul is also remembered for being part of the Native Tongues Posse, which included groups like the Jungle Brothers and A Tribe Called Quest.

Some time after the release of their debut album, De La Soul began to receive some criticism from some hip hoppers who believed that the group was weak materially and timid physically, due to their use of images of daisies and peace signs. In 1991 they immediately set out to destroy their hippie-type image with their second work, titled *De La Soul Is Dead*. Their appearances had changed (they dressed in more casual hip-hop attire), but their sound was still heavily reliant on sampling. The album went gold, and certain cuts off the work like "Millie Pulled a Pistol on Santa" and "A Roller Skating Jam Named 'Saturdays'" got the attention of critics and hip hoppers. By 1993 De La Soul's third album, *Buhlōōne Mindstate*, was released. The work was similar musically to their first work.

Selected albums/CDs: *3 Feet High and Rising* (1989, Tommy Boy 1019); *De La Soul Is Dead* (1991, Tommy Boy 1029); *Buhlōōne Mindstate* (1993, Tommy Boy 1063).

DIGABLE PLANETS
•••••••••••••••••••••••••••••
Formed c. early 1990s, Philadelphia
(Butterfly, born Ishmael Butler, Brooklyn, New York; Ladybug,
born Mary Ann Vierra, Silver Springs, Maryland; Doodlebug,
born Craig Irving, Philadelphia)

Digable Planets received immediate attention when their single "Rebirth of Slick (Cool Like Dat)" appeared toward the latter part of 1992. The work went gold in 1993 and won the group a Grammy.

Principal group architect and Brooklyn, New York, native Butterfly was an engineering student attending college in Massachusetts when he met Ladybug, a Brazilian from Maryland who had danced for a few local rock and hip-hop groups. Through their travels together, they met Doodlebug in his hometown of Philadelphia, where they first shared their love of hip hop as a group. They began to get more serious with their endeavors in Washington, DC, where Doodlebug was attending classes at Howard University. Digable Planets recorded their second album in 1994, titled *Blowout Comb*.

Selected albums/CDs: *Reachin' (A New Refutation of Time and Space)* (1993, Pendulum 61414); *Blowout Comb* (1994, Pendulum 6087).

DIGITAL UNDERGROUND

Formed in mid-1980s, San Francisco

(Shock G, a.k.a. Humpty Hump, MC Blowfish, born Greg Jacobs, New York; DJ Fuse, born David Elliot, October 8, 1970, Syracuse, New York; Schmoovy Schmoove, born Edward Earl Cook, California; Money-B, born Ron Brooks, California; Big Money Odis, a.k.a. Gold Money, born Odis Valentine, California; MC Clever, born in New Jersey; Pee Wee, born Ramone Valentine, Virginia; Chopmaster J, a.k.a. Jimmy Dright, born in California; 2Pac, born Tupac Amaru Shakur, June 16, 1971, Bronx, New York)

Digital Underground is really an organization rather than a group. The group has many groups within the group, à la George Clinton and Afrika Bambaataa: Raw Fusion; Gold Money; Force One Network; and the solo act 2Pac. Their style is humorous and visual, and has elements of George Clinton's P-Funk music.

Group leader and keyboardist Shock G is known for the various characters he portrays within the group (that he had earlier denied were portrayed by him), like Humpty Hump and MC Blowfish. It was his portrayal of the wild, big-nosed character Humpty Hump that brought the group immediate attention, on their piece "The Humpty Dance" in 1989. By the beginning of 1990 the work had gone platinum, as did their album *Sex Packets*, which was released in 1990.

Shock G had lived in New York and Florida before settling in California. He played in small funk bands before meeting electronics equipment salesman Chopmaster J at a music store in San Leandro near Oakland, California. They began working together, with Chopmaster recording Shock's ideas and Shock teaching Chopmaster how to work the electronic equipment that he sold. The two soon put together a group and began looking for a DJ in 1987; they found DJ Fuse, who performed with Money-B (as a duo known as Raw Fusion). The group released several singles during this period, including "Underwater Rimes" and "Your Life's a Cartoon" on their own TNT Records label. The works were distributed by Macola Records, a Hollywood distribution and pressing company.

Digital Underground first began to get noticed with the song "Doowutchyalike." The single and the video began to generate interest in the group, and hip-hop audiences got their first glimpse of Shock G's character Humpty Hump. By 1989 the group released "The Humpty Dance," with the Humpty Hump character in full focus, due to Humpty's comical solo rhymes.

Digital Underground

It was featured in a successful video, which showed Humpty and the group performing the song and the dance as well.

Due to the platinum successes of both the single and the later released *Sex Packets* album (the title of which was supposed to refer to a nonphysical sexual experiment packet, supplied to astronauts by NASA), Shock G's Humpty Hump character became immensely popular. At live shows Shock would have his blood brother (and sometimes friends) play Humpty on stage when he performed his own rhymes and played keyboards.

In 1991 Digital Underground released the EP *This Is an EP Release*, which went gold that year. The single "Kiss You Back" and the album *Sons of the P* were released that same year and both went gold in 1992. During 1993 the group released the single "The Return of the Crazy One" and the album *The Body-Hat Syndrome*.

 Selected albums/CDs: *Sex Packets* (1990, Tommy Boy 1026); *This Is an EP Release* (1991, Tommy Boy 964); *Sons of the P* (1992, Tommy Boy 1045); *The Body-Hat Syndrome* (1993, Tommy Boy 1080).

DISCO KING MARIO
• •
(Born in Bronx, New York; died c. July 1994)

Disco King Mario was one of the first DJs to emerge from the Soundview area of the Bronx (second to Kool DJ D) during the mid-1970s. He was known for his sound system, which consisted of MacIntosh 4300s with six to eight speakers on both left and right sides, which were usually Gauss, Cerwin-Vega, and Altec-Lansing makes. Mario was one of the first DJs to notice the deejaying skills of Jazzy Jay; Jay worked under him until approximately 1978, when he began working under Afrika Bambaataa.

Mario came out of the street-gang era of the Bronx with Bambaataa and others. Although never known for the quantity of his records, he was influenced by Bambaataa and Kool Herc in his preference for playing break music. He also participated in many important sound-system battles during his reign, including against Bambaataa (Bambaataa's first official battle) during the mid-1970s at Junior High School 123 in the Bronx; with Busy Bee in 1977 at Bronx's Monroe High School against later Cold Crush Brothers' DJ Charlie Chase, Lil' Black, Tony tone, T-Bone and Sisco Kid; and during the late 1970s with Afrika Bambaataa and DJ Tex, against Grandmaster Flash.

Mario's parties were usually held at Junior High Schools 123 or 131 in the Bronx, and his tenure lasted up to approximately 1979. He never worked professionally in the established music business, and gradually drifted into the drug scene until his death in 1994.

DJ BREAKOUT & DJ BARON
Formed in Bronx, New York

DJ Breakout emerged during the mid-1970s, around the same time as Afrika Bambaataa, Kool Herc, and Grandmaster Flash. He was considered one of the most influential break-beat DJs during this period, and he was known for his powerful sound system, called the Sasquatch.

Hailing from the Gun Hill Road and Baychester areas of the Bronx, Breakout was also recognized as being one of the more flashier DJs in terms of style and technique who was proficient in cutting. His DJ partner, Baron, who worked under him, was known for his ability to keep a break beat going indefinitely with precise timing. Breakout would also later be known as the DJ for the Funky Four Plus One, and would continue working with the group until the end of their recording career. Soon after, both Breakout and Baron's activities subsided.

DJ CASH MONEY &
MC MARVELOUS
(Both born in Philadelphia)

J Cash Money gained wide attention with hip hoppers in 1987 when he won the New Music Seminar's DJ Battle for World Supremacy. The following year he also won the DMC World DJ Mixing Championship.

Cash Money started out as a dancer while in junior high school during the mid- to late-

1970s, joining a Philadelphia-based dance group called the Franchise Dancers, which was famous for their performances at various block parties in the Philadelphia area. By the late 1970s to early 1980s Money began to get into deejaying after seeing local DJ Grand Wizard Rasheed perform. He purchased a pair of B-101 turntables and met DJ Jazzy Jeff (of later DJ Jazzy Jeff & The Fresh Prince fame); Jeff introduced Money to the local party promoters in the area.

During the mid-1980s he began working with Philadelphia MC, Marvelous, and the two were eventually signed to Sleeping Bag Records in 1986—87. As a duo they released the singles "Play It Kool" and "Find an Ugly Woman." Their debut album for the label (co-produced by Joe "The Butcher" Nicolo) was titled *Where's the Party At?* In 1989 they recorded the singles "A Real Mutha for Ya" b/w "New Sheriff in Town." During that same year they also took on Gene Griffin (producer Teddy Riley's manager) as their manager. By the early 1990s the duo had separated, and around 1994—95 Cash Money started touring with the group PM Dawn, working as their DJ. In 1995 he was working as a producer with Biz Markie and R&B group Nima.

 Selected albums/CDs: *Where's the Party At?* (1988, Sleeping Bag).

DJ CHUCK CHILLOUT
Formerly DJ Steel, DJ Born Supreme Allah
(Born Charles Turner, October 22, 1962, Bronx, New York)

DJ Chuck Chillout is recognized as one of the foremost pioneer radio DJs in hip hop. He is responsible for getting rapper Doug E. Fresh his first record deal and giving DJ Funkmaster Flex his first job.

Chuck started out with his partner Bantley B in the early to mid-1970s, lending speakers to DJ Breakout. He then deejayed at local high-school parties and other events in the Bronx, New York, area. Chuck was approached by Vincent Davis of Vintertainment Records, where the two engaged in making pioneer scratch records.

Their first record was released under the group name the B Boys (which consisted of Chuck on the turntables and rapper Donald D, a former member of Afrika Islam's Funk Machine Crew). The record was titled "Two Three Break," and it was recorded circa 1983. Chuck also did "Cuttin' Herbie" (drawing on Herbie Hancock's "Rockit" single) and "Rock the House" on a 12-inch single that same year.

Later Chuck met then-program director Barry Mayo, of New York City's KISS-FM radio, at the Manhattan club the Roxy. Chuck was soon doing radio at that station, with his own show in 1983. Into 1984, Chuck continued to release records for Vintertainment, including his classic *Hip Hop on Wax—Volume 1.* Later he would also do after-party gigs on the road for both hip-hop tours Fresh Fest One and Two.

From 1985 on, Chuck began to do production and remixes as well, reworking Run-D.M.C.'s "You're Blind," producing the Dismasters's "Small Time Hustler," and Deuces Wild's "Five

Times the Rhymer." Around 1988 Chuck did a remix on Public Enemy's "Night of the Living Baseheads."

In 1989 Chuck recorded an album for Mercury-Polygram, titled *Masters of the Rhythm*, with rapper Kool Chip, featuring the single "Rhythm Is the Master." That same year he left radio station KISS-FM. In 1990 Chuck joined station WBLS-FM, through famed program director Frankie Crocker and radio DJ Fred Buggs. He also began working with VJ Ralph McDaniels on his video show "Video Music Box," where he hosted the show's "Old School Mondays" segment into 1995. Chuck also had his own cable video show circa 1991, titled "American Hot Video." Later he produced another video show called "Video Zone." By 1992 Chuck was instrumental in getting the group Black Moon signed to a record deal, and executive-produced their single "Who Got the Props." In 1994 he co-produced the single "What You Gonna Do" for the artist Brother Arthur, who was signed to Chuck's C-Ya Entertainment label.

 Selected albums/CDs: *Master of the Rhythm* by Chuck Chillout & Kool Chip (1989, Mercury/Polygram 838406).

DJ EDDIE F
(Born Edward Ferrell II, Mount Vernon, New York)

DJ Eddie F is the president and CEO of Untouchables Entertainment, a music production company that specializes in hip hop and R&B. The company, whose main personnel consists of Pete Rock, Dave Hall, and Neville Hodge, has released many gold and platinum records, producing and remixing works for artists such as Intro, Mary J. Blige, Al B. Sure!, Pete Rock & CL Smooth, Changing Faces, Madonna, Jodeci, and Heavy D & The Boyz.

Eddie began his career recording music with his high school friend Heavy D. Later he became one of the "boyz" in their group Heavy D & The Boyz, working as their DJ. He began working as a producer, producing material on Heavy's 1987 debut album *Living Large*. Toward the early 1990s Eddie worked on the theme for FOX-TV's comedy show *In Living Color*, which Heavy D also rapped on. In 1994 he released a compilation album titled *Let's Get It On: The Album* on the Motown label, which featured many of the artists he produced in the past.

 Selected albums/CDs: *Let's Get It On: The Album* (1994, Motown 314530313).

DJ FLOWERS
a.k.a. Grandmaster Flowers
(Born Johnny Flowers, c. 1955; died 1992)

DJ Flowers was one of the most influential DJs to come out of Brooklyn, New York, in the early 1970s. Hailing from the Farragut Projects, Flowers was originally recognized for his early graffiti tag "Flowers & Dice," which embossed buildings, subway walls, and parks all over Brooklyn and other areas, and later he achieved wide recognition as being one of the first mobile DJs.

Flowers was in the forefront of DJs who used a massive sound system and performed in parks and community centers. He played in many of the popular clubs at the time, such as Leviticus, Nell Quinn's, Justine's, Club Saturn, Super Star 33, and Club 371. He played with and against many of the popular DJs of that period, including Lovebug Starski, Maboya, Fantasia, Riff & Cliff, and Plummer. He performed locally in his community as well, in areas like the nicknamed Shady Rest Park in the Farragut Projects, and the C.P.C. Center on Fulton Street in downtown Brooklyn.

Flowers played mostly disco records during his early years, and his popularity steadily declined as more DJs came on the scene through the years. By the 1980s Flowers (never working in the music business after his span as a DJ) succumbed to drug abuse and later died in 1992.

DJ FUNKMASTER FLEX
(Born in New York)

Funkmaster Flex is a popular DJ, who emerged during the late 1980s and early 1990s. He is known for his perfect timing on the turntables, using the techniques of cutting and backspinning.

Flex started deejaying in 1982. He soon hooked up with one of DJ Chuck Chillout's groups, Deuces Wild, and eventually became their stage DJ. Flex also worked as Chillout's DJ on his radio show on WBLS-FM in New York City for a year and a half. Thereafter, he began to play at major club venues like Kilimanjaros, Marrs, Powerhouse, and the Ritz.

In 1991 Flex and his friend, rapper Nine Double M, recorded the singles "F.A.L.L.I.N. (and ya can't get up)" and "Bodies on the Nine," which received some notice from other hip-hop DJs.

Flex later worked as an A&R representative for Profile Records. In early 1993 he began to do radio again, producing a show that aired in Osaka, Japan. Soon after, he became a permanent fixture on radio station WQHT-FM Hot 97 in New York City. Another single, "Dope on Plastic," on reggae DJ Bobby Konder's Massive B Records, was released that year.

In 1995, billed as the Flip Squad Allstars featuring Funkmaster Flex & Big Kap, he recorded the piece "Flip Squad's in Da House," which appeared on the *New Jersey Drive* motion picture soundtrack.

 Selected singles: "F.A.L.L.I.N. (and ya can't get up)" b/w "Bodies on the Nine" by Funkmaster Flex and Nine Double M (1991, Warlock); "Dope on Plastic" by Funkmaster Flex (1993, Massive B).

DJ HOLLYWOOD

(Born December 10, 1954, New York)

DJ Hollywood paved the way for MCs by originating the practice of delivering extensive rhymes over recorded music; in his case, disco records. By 1973 Hollywood became one of the top DJs in New York, primarily working in the Harlem area. It was his influence as an MC that spread into the hardcore hip-hop scenes that emerged. Hollywood's club crowd was usually older, dressed to impress, and a few of them were even considered to be hustler types. He played in clubs like the 371, Charles Gallery, and all the after-hour spots in Harlem. It was at these clubs where Hollywood introduced his stable of entertainers to partygoers.

Hollywood originally began handling a microphone at age 14 when he began to form his own singing groups, like the Innovations and the Liberators. By 1971 Hollywood was deejaying. One of his first club spots was Charles Gallery in Harlem, once owned by Charles Huggins, former husband of singer Melba Moore. Hollywood learned the art of record mixing from Bojangles, a man who ran the club. (Hollywood originally began deejaying on a microphone mixer with no headphones.) During 1973 Hollywood's popularity began to soar, and later his MC'ing style would soon be picked up and used and interpreted in various different ways and styles.

Hollywood had a large group of apprentices and people who worked with him. One of the most famous was DJ Junebug, a dancer in one of his groups called the Corporation, and one of the greatest music mixers of his time. Also working with Hollywood was DJ Smalls—a rapper—who was also billed as Hollywood's "Disco Son." Other apprentices and workers with Hollywood included Lovebug Starski, Reggie Wells, and Kurtis Blow (who participated in Hollywood's response teams at his shows).

Hollywood is also recognized as the person who coined the term "hip hop," which began to be used as part of a motivating line in his rhymes during parties that went, "To the hip, hop, the hippy, the hippy hippy hip, hop hoppin', ya don't stop the rockin' . . ." Hollywood was also the inspiration for the R&B group The Fatback Band's "King Tim III (Personality Jock)," which is technically regarded as the first rap record. The band had earlier caught one of Hollywood's performances at the Apollo Theater, where he began performing toward the late 1970s, and used that as a model for their record.

Hollywood was one of the pioneers in a DJ innovation during the early 1970s, DJ mix tapes. He sold audio 8-track tape cartridges, which were popular before audiocassette tape cartridges came into prominence, for $12 apiece.

DJ Hollywood reigned from 1971 to 1985. Within that period he maintained his DJ and MC style, introduced other talents, and garnered a reputation that is sometimes under-acknowledged by hardcore hip hoppers, primarily because of the type of crowds that attended his parties, the disco records that he initially played, and the Manhattan location of his reign (as opposed to the Bronx areas, which developed and fostered break-beat dee-jaying—the heart of hip hop music).

Trying to venture into other areas of the music business, Hollywood began working with percussionist Ralph MacDonald, who signed him to Epic Records, where the two worked on a project. Hollywood also recorded the single "To Whom It May Concern" for Posse Records during the mid-1980s.

After 1985 Hollywood succumbed to drugs and remained inactive in the music business until the early 1990s. He then returned on the scene free from drugs and began working with Lovebug Starski again, successfully doing shows throughout the New York, New Jersey, and Connecticut areas.

DJ JAZZY JEFF & THE FRESH PRINCE

Formed in 1986, Philadelphia
(DJ Jazzy Jeff, born Jeff Townes, 1965; the Fresh Prince, born Will Smith, September 25, 1969; both born in Philadelphia)

DJ Jazzy Jeff & The Fresh Prince is a very successful commercially oriented rap act, known for the Fresh Prince's humorous rhymes and Jazzy Jeff's turntable skills. The Fresh Prince is also recognized as the first rapper to make the transition to the small screen, starring in his own successful television sitcom, *The Fresh Prince of Bel Air*, in the early 1990s. He later costarred (with critical acclaim) in the motion picture *Six Degrees of Separation*.

As a DJ, Jazzy Jeff is credited with inventing the scratching art of "transforming": taking the sound of an existing record and altering its tempo and phrasing (although the technique is also attributed to DJ Spinbad, a person who later deejayed for the R&B group, Bell Biv Devoe). Jeff successfully presented these and other DJ skills (scratching two records at once, catching double beats) at the 1986 New Music Seminar, winning the event's "Battle of the DJs."

This duo is also remembered for establishing the first 900-number phone line for a pop music act. The number gave fans a chance to hear different daily messages from the two, and eventually, the line logged approximately 60,000 calls a day. By the beginning of 1989, calls to the line had totaled three million. The two are also recognized for making the first rap double-album, titled *He's the DJ, I'm the Rapper*. Jazzy Jeff and the Fresh Prince are also remembered for boycotting the 1989 Grammy Awards show, due to the NARAS (National Association of Recording Arts and Sciences) decision not to air the presentation of the first Grammy for a rap recording during prime time.

Jeff and Prince met each other at a party in their Philadelphia neighborhood and soon began doing songs together. They did a song for Dana Goodman (of Pop Art Records fame) on his Word Up label, titled "Girls Ain't Nothing but Trouble," three weeks before Prince was to graduate from high school. The song caught on with the hip-hop crowd, and though Prince was scheduled to enter MIT's engineering program that fall, he decided to put it on hold.

In 1987 the duo's debut album for Pop Art Records (later picked up by Jive Records) appeared, titled *Rock the House*, which went gold the following year. They joined Def Jam's tour, along with LL Cool J and other acts. By 1988 the two released their second album, *He's*

DJ Jazzy Jeff & The Fresh Prince

the DJ, I'm the Rapper. Two songs on the work, "Parents Just Don't Understand" and "Nightmare on My Street," helped catapult the duo to stardom, with the album selling 2.5 million copies during this period.

In 1989, their third work, *And in This Corner*, was released and went gold the following year. The single off the work was "I Think I Can Beat Mike Tyson." In 1991 their album *Homebase* went platinum and sparked two singles, "Summertime" and "Ring My Bell," which went platinum and gold, respectively.

The year 1993 saw the release of their album *Code Red*. The single off the work, "Boom! Shake the Room," went gold that year.

 Selected albums/CDs: *Rock the House* (1987, Jive/RCA 1026); *He's the DJ, I'm the Rapper* (1988, Jive/RCA 10921); *And in This Corner* (1989 Jive/RCA 1188); *Homebase* (1991, Jive/RCA 1392); *Code Red* (1993, Jive/RCA 1400).

DJ JAZZY JOYCE

(Born in Bronx, New York)

DJ Jazzy Joyce is one of the most prominent female DJs performing in rap music, recognized for her early work with Sweet Tee on the 1986 piece, titled "It's My Beat." Joyce has performed in many areas of the United States, and she is also known for her mix tapes.

Originally a protégé of DJ Whiz Kid, Joyce has deejayed for artists like the Bad Girls and Shelly Thunder, and she has also performed on Russell Simmons's "Def Comedy Jam" on HBO.

By 1994 she began deejaying for the group Digable Planets, and also toured with them following the release of their *Blowout Comb* album that same year.

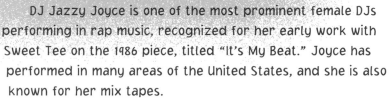

DJ JUNEBUG

a.k.a. Junebug Starski
(Died c. early 1980s, New York)

DJ Junebug was known as one of the greatest mixers of music before his death in the early 1980s.

An apprentice to DJ Hollywood since 1974, Junebug was originally a dancer for Hollywood's Corporation, and worked with him at Club 371 and other venues throughout the boroughs of New York.

As a DJ, Junebug had the ability to surprise partygoers with his choice of disco and R&B records and how he would mix them. They were perfectly connected as far as beat and structure, and the surprise would come from an unexpected record that helped increase the dancing at his parties. Then he would put another record on behind that one, which would have an even greater effect with partygoers. According to many DJs, his mixing style was ingenious. By 1978 Junebug was one of the house DJs at the Disco Fever club in the Bronx.

DJ Junebug was killed in a drug deal, and his life story was the original concept chosen by rap mogul Russell Simmons for the motion picture *Krush Groove*. Simmons's group, Run-D.M.C., dedicated their first album to him.

DJ Kid Capri

DJ KID CAPRI
•••••••••••••••••••••
(Born David Love, Bronx, New York)

DJ Kid Capri is one of the most popular DJs in hip hop. He is noted for his Lovebug Starski-type party rocker exhortations between and during the records that he plays and his flair and timing on the turntables. He became widely known through his cassette mix tapes.

Capri comes from a musical family, with his grandfather once working as an extra trumpeter for Miles Davis and Dizzy Gillespie and his grandmother being a former singer and model. He started deejaying in 1976 after hearing legends like Pete DJ Jones, Grandmaster Flash, Grand Wizard Theodore, and Kool DJ Herc, but couldn't get noticed because of his young age.

In 1986 he began to make mix tapes showcasing his skills with his friend DJ Starchild, as well as deejaying in a few areas of the city. Capri would sell his tapes on the street in Harlem and other select locations for $10 to $20 a pop. From the dubbing and distribution of Capri's mix tapes, he became widely known in hip-hop circles in New York City and across the country. He began to get jobs at larger clubs like the Building and Powerhouse, and eventually wound up performing at Studio 54 on Wednesday nights.

In 1991 he was signed to Cold Chillin' Records and recorded one album for them, titled *The Tape*. For a time in 1992 he worked at New York radio station WBLS, where he did half-hour mix shows five nights a week. After doing some touring with Kid 'n Play, and deejaying in other areas of the country, he was hired as a house DJ also in 1992 for Russell Simmons's HBO "Def Comedy Jam."

 Selected albums/CDs: *The Tape* (1991, Cold Chillin' 26474).

DJ MAGIC MIKE
(Born Mike Hampton, 1967, Orlando, Florida)

DJ Magic Mike pioneered the South Florida bass sound in rap, which is Miami bass's slower-tempo counterpart. Mike is recognized for his turntable skills as a DJ, and he is one of the few DJs in the forefront as a recording artist.

Mike co-owns one of the largest independently distributed record labels in the United States, Cheetah Records. His first album, *Bass Is the Name of the Game*, went gold in 1991, and his *Ain't No Doubt about It* with MC Madness went gold in 1992. In the beginning of 1993 Mike was the first hip-hop artist to release two double-albums simultaneously: *BASS: The Final Frontier* and *This Is How It Should Be Done*.

At the age of 14 Mike hosted a drive-time radio show called *Traffic Jam* on the now defunct R&B station WOKB-AM. He eventually left radio when he reached the age of 17, and began sharpening his DJ skills. A record label soon offered him a deal, but the thickness of the contract compelled him to turn it down.

By 1988 Mike had met independent promoter Tom Reich. Reich was willing to take a chance with Mike's material, and for good measure, they agreed that Mike would own fifty percent of Reich's Cheetah Record label if his material did well.

The first 12-inch singles they released were "Magic Mike Cuts the Record" and "Drop the Bass," and they were both hits. Around 1990 his first album was released, *Bass Is the Name of the Game*. As executive vice president of his label since 1992, Mike has signed and produced T-Isaam, Infinite Jay, and the Almighty Tough Squad.

 Selected albums/CDs: *Bass Is the Name of the Game* (1990, Cheetah); *Ain't No Doubt about It* (1991, Cheetah); *This Is How It Should Be Done* (1993, Cheetah 9411); *BASS: The Final Frontier* (1993, Cheetah 9413); *Bass Bowl* (1994, Cheetah 9427).

DJ MARK THE 45 KING
(Born Mark James, October 16, 1961, New York City)

DJ Mark the 45 King was one of the most prolific producers and beat makers in the late 1980s. Known for obtaining his break beats primarily from 45-rpm records (where he got his moniker), Mark is responsible for many acts being signed to record labels, such as Queen Latifah, Latee, Lakim Shabazz, and Chill Rob G, all of whom were known as the Flavor Unit

Posse, along with several others. Mark is also known for doing occasional house music tracks, and he is responsible for one of the most famous records in hip hop, "The 900 Number."

Mark started out in 1979 as a record boy for DJ Breakout, whom he met through one of Breakout's dancers, Jerry "Basic Breaker" Miller. Initially starting out as trading partners—where Mark and Breakout traded records together—Mark was asked to be a record boy for Breakout, a post he maintained for five parties.

In 1980 Mark moved to Queens and worked with Davy D. He soon began calling himself "the 45 King" during this period, because of his preference for playing 45-rpm records. After working as a DJ for the Fearless Four for a few parties, Mark moved to New Jersey circa 1982 and began deejaying around the Jersey area, where he began to get noticed by the local kids in the neighborhood as one who made good beats.

One of the first people Mark began producing was Markie Fresh. It was Fresh who introduced Mark to radio DJ, Kool DJ Red Alert, circa 1984. It was with Red that Mark began to create ready-made record pressings (actual records) to be played, with hip hop on one side and house-oriented club music on the other. This was done to make it easier for radio DJs to mix in the music, instead of the usual cassette tapes that were used. Mark also began doing remixes, including a version of Eric B & Rakim's "I Know You Got Soul."

Later Mark began working with rapper Latee, who garnered radio exposure and was eventually signed to Wild Pitch Records through his work with Mark, recording "This Cut's Got Flavor." Around 1987 into 1988 Mark began producing tracks for Latee's brother, Apache, Chill Rob G, and Queen Latifah. Mark sold beats outright on occasion as well, supplying the beat for "Microphone Fiend" for Eric B & Rakim. He also did tracks for the group Gang Starr.

Mark soon signed with Aaron Fuchs's Tuff City Records for two six-months periods, where he recorded over autumn releases, including the albums *45 Kingdom* and *Master of the Game,* and the classic single "The 900 Number" (named after the Akai S900 sampling machine). At Tuff City Mark laid down many of his hip-hop break tracks and occasional house-music

DJ Mark

beats. Mark also began collaborating with producer Louie Louie on some projects. He also produced Lakim Shabazz's *Pure Righteousness* album in 1988.

In 1989 Mark produced an album for Chill Rob G, titled *Ride the Rhythm*, which got considerable notice in hip-hop circles. That same year Mark produced eleven songs on Queen Latifah's *All Hail the Queen* LP, which sold over a million copies worldwide.

In 1991 Mark signed a production deal for a compilation album with Warner Bros. The album was to feature Sha Rock, Task Force, Small Wonder, and others. However, the Warner Bros. staff rejected the product. A drug abuser for some time, Mark eventually wound up overindulging in PCP in September 1992, which put him out of action for some time. During 1993 Mark began working again, collaborating with producer Diamond D and others.

 Selected singles: "The 900 Number" (c. 1988, Tuff City).

 Selected produced albums/CDs: *Ride the Rhythm* by Chill Rob G (1989, Wild Pitch 97545); *All Hail the Queen* by Queen Latifah (1989, Tommy Boy 1022).

DJ MIXMASTER MUGGS
a.k.a. DJ Grandmixer Muggs
(Born Larry Muggerud, Queens, New York)

DJ Muggs is the DJ for group Cypress Hill, and has also produced other groups, including House of Pain.

Muggs was working as a DJ in 1985. Around this time he began deejaying for the group 7A3, and produced their album *Coolin' in Cali* in 1988. A year later he produced a successful demo for MC Mellow Man Ace (which was instrumental in getting him signed), and by 1991 he had produced and performed on Cypress Hill's self-titled debut album, which went gold by 1992. That same year Muggs produced House of Pain's self-titled debut album. The album and the single off the work, "Jump Around," both went platinum. He subsequently continued to produce Cypress Hill's works, as well as producing several tracks on House of Pain's second album.

DJ POOH
(Born c. 1966, South Central Los Angeles)

DJ Pooh is a producer who first achieved notice for his DJ work on LL Cool J's piece "Jack the Ripper" with producer Bobcat, and later for his work with Ice Cube on his *Death Certificate* and *The Predator* albums.

Originally a DJ with the Los Angeles DJ crew Uncle Jam's Army (which included the L.A. Posse and Egyptian Lover), Pooh soon branched out into production, working with rapper King Tee, notably on Tee's early work (his *At Your Own Risk* LP and others).

After working with Ice Cube in 1991 and 1992 on his *Death Certificate* and *The Predator* albums, Pooh achieved notice for his production work on commercials for St. Ides Malt Liquor. During 1992 Pooh launched his own record label, called Da' Bomb Records.

By 1995 Pooh expanded his career by becoming a screenwriter. Working with Ice Cube, he co-wrote the script for the movie *Friday*. He also co-produced one of the songs off that movie's soundtrack album, "Lettin' Niggas Know," by the artist Threat.

 Selected albums/CDs: (coproduced): Ice Cube, *Death Certificate* (1991, 4th & Broadway 579); *The Predator* (1992, Fourth & Broadway 542).

DJ QUIK
● ● ● ● ● ● ● ● ● ● ● ●
(Born David Blake, January 18, 1970, Comptom, Los Angeles)

DJ Quik is known for his heavily seasoned funk tracks that are mostly recorded by live musicians, reminiscent of funk artists from the late 1970s and early 1980s. With his creative partner, Rob "Fonksta" Bacon, Quik is known for recording his work with instruments and equipment made during those years.

Quik grew up as the youngest of ten children, and by the age of 3 was entertaining his sister's friends by identifying songs and artists that they listened to. By 1981 Quik's sister bought him a pair of turntables and a mixer. However, it wasn't until 1988 (after working at a real estate company) that Quik began to get seriously into the music scene.

Around 1989 Tracy Kendrick and Courtney Vance of Total Track Productions discovered Quik when he was working with a female keyboardist on a project they were producing. After hearing some of Quik's work with the keyboardist, Kendrick suggested to Quik that he let them do a demo for him. They brought the demo to A&R man Dave Moss at Profile Records's Los Angeles office, and Quik was signed to the label.

In 1991 Profile released Quik's *Quik Is the Name* LP, which nearly went platinum that same year. One song on the album, titled "Sweet Black Pussy" (where he suddenly pretends to forget the words to the piece halfway through the song, and then resumes rhyming without missing a beat), showed Quik's creative streak, and the entire album showed his ability as a producer and a practitioner of traditional funk idioms. "Born and Raised in Compton" and "Tonite" were two of the singles off the album. Soon production offers rolled in, and he provided his production skills to several other artists, including the groups 2nd II None, Penthouse Player's Clique, and rappers AMG and Hi-C.

By 1992 Quik's *Way 2 Fonky* LP was released and went gold that same year. "Jus Lyke Compton" was one of the singles off the work. In 1995 Quick released his third album, *Safe + Sound*, which was also the title of the first single from the work. Another piece off the album, "Dollaz & Sense," appeared on Snoop Doggy Dogg's *Murder Was the Case* soundtrack album. Quik also produced several songs on that album.

 Selected albums/CDs: *Quik Is the Name* (1991, Profile 1402); *Way 2 Fonky* (1992 Profile 1430); *Safe + Sound* (1995, Profile 1462).

DJ Quik

D-Nice

DJ SCOTT LA ROCK

See KRS-ONE

DJ SCRATCH

(Born George Spivey, June 21, 1968, Brooklyn, New York)

DJ Scratch is known as one of the best of the latter-second-to-early-third-generation hip-hop trick DJs, known for his flamboyant style of scratching, and his tricks while performing that skill (e.g., scratching with his buttocks; while juggling a basketball; while stripping; as he dons a *Friday the Thirteenth* Jason mask with a machete; and other tricks). He was the winner of the 1988 New Music Seminar DJ "Battle for World Supremacy," and he achieved even more recognition as the DJ for the group EPMD.

Scratch hails from the Albany Projects in Brooklyn. He started deejaying at age 11, and soon won recognition in his neighborhood during a DJ battle, when no one would challenge him after seeing him do his tricks on the turntables.

He later performed at Manhattan's Milky Way club, which gained him a spot on a sixteen-city European tour with Def Jam acts like Public Enemy and Run-D.M.C. That group's DJ, Jam Master Jay, suggested to EPMD that they should try Scratch for a week. After the group saw him do his tricks at one of their shows in Milwaukee, they were impressed enough to hire him. Scratch has appeared in the 1991 movie *Juice*, and was the house DJ for Fox-TV's *Uptown Comedy Club*. He has not been working more recently.

DJ STARCHILD

(Born in New York)

DJ Starchild is known as one of the first DJs (along with Brucie B) to introduce cassette mix tapes. From 1980 to 1985 Starchild also received wide recognition as one of the house DJs at the hip-hop club Disco Fever.

Around 1986 Starchild began working with DJ Kid Capri, and the two began deejaying together, as well as making tapes. Into the early 1990s Starchild continued making his mix tapes and deejaying at various clubs.

DNA & HANK LOVE

**(DNA, born David Nelson Askew, New York;
Hank Love, born in New York)**

DNA and Hank Love were a noted underground hip-hop radio duo that were on the air during the late 1980s to early 1990s. The duo's *DNA & Hank Love Radio Show* was at the forefront of breaking new acts and records on their "Star for a Night" segment. Some of the groups they discovered include the Ultramagnetic MCs, Super Lover Cee & Cassanova Rud, and Too Poetic.

DNA had originally started out as a record promoter for Russell Simmons and Jive Records, promoting records like "I Need a Beat" by LL Cool J, and artists such as Billy Ocean and Whodini. He started in radio during 1985 with his own *Diamond 2 Radio Show*. Working as host, DNA had two other DJs working for him, and also worked with the Awesome 2 as an occasional producer for approximately five weeks.

By 1987 DNA had teamed with DJ Hank Love, and the two worked the Saturday night/-Sunday morning two-hour slot on radio station WNWK-FM in New York City for approximately seven and one-half years.

Later DNA formed DNA International Records, where he released Too Poetic's "God Made Me Funky" b/w "Poetical Terror," Super Lover Cee & Cassanova Rud's classic "Do the James," and other records for artists, including the Black Mafia and the Nerds of Rap.

Hank Love formed Majestic Control Productions, where he worked with artists like Alemo, MC Lovely, P-King, 1/2 Pint, and MC Tatiana, releasing records with DNA International like "Frontline" b/w "Cold Sweat" in 1990.

By 1993 DNA and Hank Love severed their ties due to creative differences. Hank Love continued the Saturday night/Sunday morning slot teaming with 1/2 Pint as host.

D-NICE

(Born Derrick Jones, June 19, 1970, Harlem, New York)

D-Nice worked under the tutelage of Boogie Down Productions' DJ Scott La Rock, and later became a DJ for that group's MC, KRS-One. (Ironically, it was D-Nice who asked LaRock to help settle a dispute with another rapper, which resulted in LaRock's death.)

In 1989 D-Nice produced the successful gold single "Self-Destruction," which was recorded by the hip-hop all-star Stop the Violence Movement group. By 1990 his debut album, *Call Me D-Nice*, was released and was well received by hip hoppers. Around 1991 his piece "25 Ta Life" garnered interest for its street message, which was enhanced by the work's video. Beginning in 1992 D-Nice was producing material for Queen Latifah's Flavor Unit Records, such as the Flavor Unit MCs' "Roll Wit Tha Flava" and others.

 Selected albums/CDs: *Call Me D-Nice* (1990, Jive/RCA 1202).

THE D.O.C.
● ● ● ● ● ● ● ● ● ● ● ● ● ● ● ●
(Born in Dallas, Texas)

The D.O.C. was originally with a group called the Fila Fresh Crew in Texas when Dr. Dre (from the group N.W.A) got a chance to hear him perform his rhymes and invited him to come to California.

After some differences with his group, D.O.C. came to California and began working with Dr. Dre and his friends Eazy-E, Ice Cube, and others, at Eazy-E's record label, Ruthless Records. He soon began writing material with Dr. Dre and Ice Cube, some of which can be heard on N.W.A's *Straight Outta Compton* album.

In 1989 the D.O.C. came out with his own album on Ruthless Records, titled *No One Can Do It Better*, with Dr. Dre handling the production. Songs like "The Formula" and "Funky Enough" propelled the work to number 1 on the *Billboard* Top Black Albums chart. The album eventually went gold that same year.

Several weeks after this success the D.O.C. was involved in a car accident, which badly damaged his vocal chords. He would later work closely with Dr. Dre and his Death Row Records label until 1992, writing rhymes and advising the label's acts.

 Selected albums/CDs: *No One Can Do It Better* (1989, Ruthless 308).

DOCTOR DRE & ED LOVER
● ●
**(Doctor Dre, born Andre Brown, December 5, 1963, Westbury,
Long Island, New York; Ed Lover, born Ed Roberts,
February 12, 1963, Hollis, Queens, New York)**

Doctor Dre and Ed Lover—DJ and rapper respectively—are a comedy duo, known as the VJ hosts for MTV's daily music video show, "Yo! MTV Raps." They are also known as radio personalities, hosting their own 5:30 A.M. to 9:00 A.M. daily wake-up show on radio station WQHT-FM, Hot 97 in New York City. Dre and Lover have also starred in their own film, titled *Who's the Man?*, which was released in 1993. (Doctor Dre is not to be confused with Dr. Dre, associated with the group N.W.A, from Compton, Los Angeles.)

Doctor Dre was a student at Adelphi University in the mid-1980s when he first got into radio, taking over his friend Bill Stephney's *Mr. Bill Show* at the college station. After abruptly leaving school during the last semester (due to a financial aid discrepancy), Dre soon became part of the group Original Concept. With the group, Dre released the singles "Can You Feel It" around 1986, and "Pump That Bass" in 1987, an underground hit for about two years. Original Concept's album *Straight from the Basement of Kooley High* was released in 1988.

Dre soon left the group and began working as a road DJ for the Beastie Boys. Later he met rapper and musician Ed Lover through Lover's friend Ted Demme, who worked as a producer at MTV. Dre and Lover were paired as a duo for the daily version of "Yo! MTV Raps." During the early 1990s Dre, Lover, and former Original Concept's T-Money also hosted a Satur-

Doctor Dre & Ed Lover

day night hip-hop radio show called *The Operating Room* on WBLS-FM in New York City. In 1994 Dre and Ed Lover released their first album for Relativity Records.

 Selected albums/CDs: *Back Up Off Me* (1994, Relativity 1230).

DONALD D
● ● ● ● ● ● ● ● ● ● ● ● ● ● ● ● ● ●
(Born in Bronx, New York)

Donald D is a Los Angeles-based rapper who got his start in the late 1970s during hip hop's beginnings in New York.

Born in the Bronx, Donald began to get into rapping by 1978. He soon hooked up with Afrika Islam, and eventually became part of his Funk Machine Crew (along with Grandmaster Caz). He was also heard on Islam's *Zulu Beats* radio show. In the early 1980s Donald became part of the B Boys with DJ Chuck Chillout and recorded for Vintertainment Records.

Around 1988 Donald began working with Ice-T, who invited the artist to the West Coast. He took part in Ice-T's *Rhyme Syndicate Comin' Through* compilation album, appearing on the song "Name of the Game" with another native New Yorker, Bronx Style Bob. Soon after, Donald relocated to Los Angeles and became part of Ice-T's Rhyme Syndicate Management. He did rhymes for Ice-T's *Power* LP and worked on the single "Freedom of Speech."

In 1989 Donald's album *Notorious* was released, with the single "F.B.I. (Free Base Institute)" gaining notice. During 1992 his second work, titled *Let the Horns Blow*, appeared.

 Selected singles: "F.B.I. (Free Base Institute)" (1989, Sire).

 Selected albums/CDs: *Notorious* (1989, Rhyme Syndicate/Epic 45298); *Let the Horns Blow* (1992, Sire 45077).

DOUBLE TROUBLE
a.k.a. the Deuce
Formed early 1980s, Bronx, New York
(Lil' Rodney Cee; KK Rockwell: both born c. 1963, New York)

Lil' Rodney Cee originally performed in the group the Magnificent Seven during the years 1977 to 1978. From there he joined the group Funky Four Plus One where his future duo partner, KK Rockwell, had been performing. (Rockwell was one of the first MCs to work with the Funky Four's DJ Breakout.) Rodney Cee and Rockwell performed with the Funky Four through their tenure at Enjoy Records, doing pieces like "Rappin' and Rockin' the House" and "That's the Joint."

Some time after being signed to Sugar Hill Records in 1980, the Funky Four Plus One separated, with Lil' Rodney Cee and KK Rockwell forming their own group, Double Trouble. They performed under that name in the 1982 hip-hop film *Wild Style*. They were later known as the Deuce, and recorded for Capitol Records for a short time until ending their relationship with the company.

Some time later KK Rockwell worked with DJ Scott La Rock at a men's shelter in the Bronx where La Rock and KRS-One spent some time. By early 1993 Rodney Cee was working as a DJ in London on radio station CHOICE-FM.

DOUG E. FRESH
(Born Douglas Davis, September 17, Barbados, West Indies)

Doug E. Fresh is billed as the "World's Greatest Entertainer." His reputation stems from the wide recognition he received on the streets of New York for his rapping skills, and his ability to rhythmically mimic sound effects. For this, he is known as the "Original Human Beat Box."

Fresh grew up in Brooklyn, the Bronx, and Manhattan, and was a young aficionado of the early hip-hop scene, starting to rap seriously at the age of 12. To entertain his friends, Fresh would do his beat boxing for them while walking from school. He continued to develop the skill when he would perform between the changing of records by DJs at outside jams. He later began to incorporate it effectively with his rapping, to distinguish himself from the other MCs who were active at the time.

Doug E Fresh

Based on his music reputation on the street, Fresh was able to do shows with his then-manager, Van Silk, and make enough money from them to begin financing the making of his own 12-inch record circa 1984, which he sold to an independent label.

Fresh was the first rapper to release two different records on two different record labels simultaneously. He got a record deal through DJ Chuck Chillout at Vintertainment Records, which released Fresh's song "The Original Human Beat Box." The other deal was through Bobby Robinson's Enjoy Records label, which released Fresh's "Just Having Fun."

Fresh met rapper Slick Rick at a rap contest in the Bronx. Impressed with Rick's style of rhyming, he later invited Rick to appear on a record with him. Fresh then landed a deal with Jerry Bloodrock and David Luchesi at Reality Records and Fantasy Inc., for which he recorded two songs: "The Show" and "La-Di-Da-Di." Both appeared on a 12-inch single, which became a classic in the hip-hop community in 1985. The songs featured Slick Rick (who went by the name of MC Ricky D) and two DJs named Chill Will and Barry Bee, who Fresh billed as the Get Fresh Crew. By February 1986 the record went gold. Fresh's album *Oh My God!* was also released that year on the same label, minus Slick Rick (with the exception of the piece "The Show"), who quietly left Fresh due to conflicting artistic and financial interests.

In 1988 Fresh's album *The World's Greatest Entertainer* was released. By 1989, however, after the release of his single "Summertime," Fresh's latent business problems with his record label came full circle. He began to look for ways to be released from his contract.

Always active in the black community, Fresh increased his activities that year, working with the Stop the Violence Movement on their song "Self-Destruction." He also helped to organize the "Stop the Racism" rally in Harlem, which was in response to the murder of Yusef Hawkins in Bensonhurst, Brooklyn, and worked on the soundtrack for the film *Ghostbusters II*.

Fresh continued working from 1989 to 1991 by traveling to upstate New York, recording approximately thirty tracks there, then returning to New York City and recording an additional thirty tracks. Various songs were taken to labels by Fresh and the Get Fresh Crew members, in search of another record deal.

In addition to working with rock group Living Colour and Joyce "Fenderella" Irby (on her single "Mr. DJ"), Fresh later visited Jamaica around 1990 and worked with reggae artists there like Cocoa T and Papa San. Fresh came to be represented by Dick Scott Management in this period. He performed at the Reggae Sunsplash in 1991 and also worked with various Washington, DC-based go-go bands, and appeared in director Carl Clay's film *Let's Get Busy*.

In 1992 Fresh's contract with Reality/Fantasy was finally bought out by Hammer's Bust-It Records. Later Bust-It released Fresh's single "Bustin' Out," as well as his first album for the label, titled *Doin' What I Got to Do*.

In 1993 Fresh was recording for 4th & B'way/Gee Street Records, which released the hit single "I-light," based on the Harlem chant originated by Unique and the Mecca Audio Crew. In 1994 he worked with reggae artist Vicious, recording the single "Freaks." In 1995 he appeared again with Slick Rick on his single "Sittin' in My Car."

Selected albums/CDs: *Oh, My God!* (1486, Reality); *World's Greatest Entertainer* (1988, Fantasy 9658); *Doin' What I Got to Do* (1992, Bust-It 98358).

DR. DRE
(Born Andre Young, Los Angeles)

Dr. Dre is known as one of the most successful producers in hip hop. He has garnered countless platinum and gold certifications for his work and for the artists he has introduced, including Snoop Doggy Dogg, the D.O.C., and R&B singer Michel'le, to name a few. Dre was one of the founding members of the group N.W.A, which is known for establishing the influence of the so-called gangsta rap genre that fully emerged during the early 1990s.

Dre was originally a DJ during the early 1980s, who played in various clubs in the Los Angeles area of Compton. Known for mixing electrofunk records with 1960s 45-rpm records, it was at his regular club gig at Alonzo Williams's Eve After Dark that he met another DJ named Yella.

Dre and Yella began to make demo tapes in one of the rooms in Eve After Dark, which had a four-track studio. Dre and the other DJs at the club also would do mix shows on Los Angeles radio station KDAY, and soon (because of good listener response) Alonzo Williams decided to form a group with Dre, Yella, and one of Dre's high school friends, Cli-N-Tel. The group would be known as the World Class Wreckin' Cru'. They recorded several singles, including "Surgery" and "Turn Off the Lights," and the albums *World Class* and *Rapped In Romance*, before dissolving in the mid-1980s.

Around the same time, another one of Dre's friends, Eazy-E, formed a record label. Dre, his friend Yella, and another friend named Ice Cube helped Eazy with the first act he had signed to the label. Teaming with Ice Cube, the two wrote a song for the group called "Boys in the Hood," which was rejected by Eazy's act when they received it. Dre encouraged Eazy-E to cut the song himself, and it became the first song done on Eazy-E's Ruthless Records label.

Dre and the others later formed a group, calling themselves N.W.A, for Niggas with Atti-

Dr Dre

tude. With Dre as the principal producer, along with DJ Yella, they began recording singles for Ruthless like "Dopeman" and "8 Ball," which were popular with record buyers, especially the explicit versions of the songs (they made both clean and explicit versions).

Dre, along with Yella, Eazy, and another producer named Arabian Prince, began producing other acts for the Ruthless label in 1988, calling themselves High Powered Productions. They worked with the female rap group J.J. Fad during this period, producing their *Supersonic, The Album* LP. Dre also worked on Eazy-E's own album, titled *Eazy-Duz-It*. Later Dre worked on the production for N.W.A, handling the group's first two works, *N.W.A & the Posse* and *Straight Outta Compton*. It was with this latter work that Dre began to receive notice as a producer. That album would eventually go multiplatinum.

By 1989 Dre began to work with a solo act, the D.O.C., producing his *No One Can Do It Better* LP, which went gold that same year. Later Dre showed his versatility by producing R&B female vocalist Michel'le's single "No More Lies." That, and her self-titled album, were both gold by 1990. Another act, Above the Law, came to the Ruthless label, and Dre handled the production work on their *Livin' Like Hustlers* album. There was also the second N.W.A work (an EP), titled *100 Miles and Runnin'*, which later went platinum. In 1991 Dre worked on the N.W.A *niggaz4Life* album, which also went platinum. Thereafter, the entire group began to go their separate ways due to creative differences, with Dre and Eazy-E displaying the most bitterness between themselves.

Around 1992 Dre established his own Death Row Records label. He also began to get into film, doing the title song for director Bill Duke's *Deep Cover*. Dre rapped on the piece with the first artist on his label, Snoop Doggy Dogg.

During this same period Dre released his first solo album, called *The Chronic*. This work introduced hip hoppers to Dre's initial Death Row Records acts (along with Snoop Doggy Dogg) and it reached multiplatinum status by 1993. The work also sparked the gold and platinum singles "Dre Day" and "Nuthin' but a 'G' Thang."

In 1994 a compilation album of Dre's early work was released on Triple X Records, titled *Concrete Roots*. That same year, Dre's Death Row label put out the soundtrack album for the movie *Above the Rim*, with Dre listed as supervising producer. The label also released the soundtrack album for the film short *Murder Was the Case*, based on lyrics by Snoop Doggy Dogg. As well as co-writing the screenplay and directing the film, Dre produced several cuts off the album, including the single "Natural Born Killaz," which featured Ice Cube. By May of 1995 the album was double-platinum. Also in 1995, Dre's single "Keep Their Heads Ringin'{|}" from the motion picture soundtrack *Friday* was released.

 Selected albums/CDs: *Straight Outta Compton* by N.W.A (1988, Ruthless 57102); *The Chronic* (1993, Death Row 57128); *Above the Rim* (1994, Death Row 92359); *Murder Was the Case* (1994, Death Row 92484); *Concrete Roots* (1994, Triple X).

DR. JECKYLL & MR. HYDE
• •
Formed late 1970s, Bronx, New York
(Dr. Jeckyll, born Andre Harrell, c. 1961, Bronx, New York;
Mr. Hyde, a.k.a. Lonnie Love, born Alonzo Brown, Bronx, New York;
DJ Scratch on Galaxy, born George Llado, New York)

Dr. Jeckyll & Mr. Hyde arrived on the hip-hop scene in the early 1980s, gaining attention with their 1981 single "Genius Rap." The work helped save their label, Profile Records, from bankruptcy by selling over 150,000 copies. Jeckyll & Hyde were one of the very few rap groups that performed in suits and ties. Jeckyll, or Andre Harrell (his birth name that he later would go by), would go on to become the owner of Uptown Enterprises, responsible for the success of R&B acts Jodeci, Teddy Riley and Guy, and Mary J. Blige, as well as rappers Father, Heavy D, and others.

Harrell hails from the Bronxdale Projects in the Bronx, and started rapping at the age of 16 in 1976 after seeing Disco King Mario perform. He would later begin performing with his friend Alonzo "Mr. Hyde" Brown, who later recorded the song "Young Ladies" for Profile Records under the name Lonnie Love. Harrell attended Lehman College, where he studied business and communications, and was later an account executive at a gospel radio station and at WINS-AM in New York City.

Harrell and Brown recorded several singles as Dr. Jeckyll & Mr. Hyde for Profile Records, including "AM/PM" (produced by Kurtis Blow) and "Gettin' Money." They also worked with the Aleems in the early 1980s on their Captain Rock projects. Jeckyll and Hyde's album *The Champagne of Rap* was released in 1986.

After Dr. Jeckyll & Mr. Hyde broke up, Alonzo Brown worked as an A&R, publicist, and radio promotions man for several labels. Andre Harrell worked as a vice president for the duo's former manager, Russell Simmons's Def Jam Recordings, before starting Uptown Enterprises.

DR. ROCK AND THE FORCE MC'S

See FORCE M.D.'S

DA ORIGINAL

a.k.a. the Original Spinderella
(Born Latoya Hanson, Bronx, New York)

Da Original was among the first crop of female DJs who emerged during the mid-1980s, known for her work with Salt-N-Pepa on their debut album. She was that group's original Spinderella. Her parents were also the owners of one of hip hop's pioneer clubs, the Executive
Playhouse.

Original was introduced to Salt-N-Pepa producer Hurby Luv Bug Azor through one of Salt's friends from Lances Skating Rink, where the ladies occasionally rollerskated. Azor chose her as a DJ for the group, and she appeared on their 1986 *Hot, Cool & Vicious* album. Soon after, she left the group due to creative differences.

In the early 1990s she was managed by pioneer rap promoter Van Silk, and recorded several singles, including "Somebody Else" on Silk's 1994 *Raiders of the Lost Art* compilation album.

DEBBIE DEE

(Born in Bronx, New York)

Debbie Dee was one of the pioneer female MCs during the 1970s, who performed with two early female MC groups, the Mercedes Ladies and the Us Girls.

DIAMOND
a.k.a. Diamond D
(Born in Bronx, New York)

Diamond D became one of the hottest producers in the early 1990s, producing works for Lord Finesse, Showbiz & AG, Apache, and others.

Diamond became a DJ in 1979, and by 1985 he met and began working for DJ Jazzy Jay. Jay asked him to work Master Rob (who was signed to Jazzy's Strong City Records) on the single "I'm Not Playin'." Later Diamond worked with Lord Finesse on his first album (producing four songs). By 1992 Diamond started MC'ing (billing himself as Diamond and the Psychotic Neurotics), and released his first album, *Stunts, Blunts & Hip Hop*, to favorable responses from hip-hop audiences. After releasing his album, Diamond continued producing material for various artists, including the Fu-Schnickens, including their 1994 *Nervous Breakdown* album.

 Selected albums/CDs: *Stunts, Blunts & Hip Hop* (1992, PWL/Mercury 513934).

DISCO BEE
(Born in Bronx, New York)

Disco Bee was a DJ and Grandmaster Flash's right-hand man around 1978. He played with Flash at a number of venues, including the Black Door, Fantasia, and the Audubon Ballroom, and he was later featured as a regular DJ at the hip-hop club the Fever.

DISCO TWINS
(Born in Astoria, Queens)

Twin brothers Rob and Reggie, known as the Disco Twins, were a popular pair of pioneer DJs from the Astoria Projects in Queens, New York, whose reign ran from the late 1970s to early 1980s. The duo was known for their powerful sound system, whose speakers were nicknamed "Berthas," after the famous character from R&B saxophonist Jimmy Castor's "Troglodyte" and "The Bertha Butt Boogie" singles. Their system was one of the most powerful in Queens at the time, and the Twins led the way in being the most recognized DJs in their borough during this period. They primarily played disco music, but occasionally played break-beat records, and displayed some proficiency in the DJ technique of cutting when playing these records. After the early 1980s the Twins' popularity faded, and they soon left the rap scene.

DJ SMOKEY AND THE SMOKETRONS

(Born in Bronx, New York)

DJ Smokey was a popular DJ during the late 1970s, whose main venue was a club called the Dover, located in the Bronx near 174th Street and Southern Boulevard. With his dancers, called the Smoketrons, Smokey also deejayed at a spot called the Burger King Disco during this same period. Located on Prospect Avenue in the Bronx, the Burger King Disco was actually a Burger King restaurant that turned into a disco on the weekends. DJ Smokey and his dancers were one of the main attractions there. Another DJ who worked at this venue was Lovebug Starski.

DJ WHIZ KID

(Born in Bronx, New York)

DJ Whiz Kid was a protégé of Kool DJ Herc, and played under him during the early 1980s at venues like the Roxy and Negril's. He later received wider recognition for his performances at Afrika Bambaataa's Zulu Nation parties.

By the early 1980s Whiz Kid began working with YSL and recording in Seattle for Nastymix Records, where he released the single "Cut It Up Whiz." Toward 1984 Whiz Kid recorded with MC G.L.O.B.E., from Bambaataa's Soul Sonic Force, on the piece "Play That Beat Mr. DJ."

DONALD DEE

(Born in New York; died c. 1993)

Donald Dee served as one of the house DJs at the Manhattan club, the Renaissance (affectionately known as the Reny), working there with his brother, rapper B-Fats.

Hailing from the Drew Hamilton Projects in Harlem, Donald also recorded for Elektra Records, with one of his songs, "Donald's Groove," produced by Grandmaster Flash. Donald worked as a producer as well. Some of his works in that capacity include his brother B-Fats's "Woppit," DJ Hollywood's "To Whom It May Concern," and female MC group Sequence's Cheryl the Pearl, on her song "Don't You Sit Back Down."

Dancehall reggae: The club music genre of traditional reggae music, divided into two categories, which are the *pop/soul* song-oriented style, and the *DJ/toasting* style. The latter is the forerunner of MC'ing or rapping in the United States, and it was pioneered circa the early 1970s by Jamaican artists like U Roy, I Roy, and Big Youth, who combined singing, scatting, and rapping into a unique style of vocal delivery. The musical aspect of dancehall emerged with computerized sound, which was first used circa 1985 by artist Wayne Smith on his "Under Me Sleng Teng," pioneered by producer Prince Jammy. The pop/soul genre of dancehall is made up of re-recordings of current pop and soul songs by dancehall artists, who design their own melodies, or embellish on the existing ones in the songs, with their own distinctive vocal styles and deliveries. Lyrically, both divisions of dancehall focus mostly on sex, love, dancing, ghetto life, and some political consciousness raising.

Dis or Diss: To *dis*respect; to insult verbally.

Disco: A large hall where DJs play music for dancing; in the 1970s a style of dance music characterized by a heavy beat.

Diss wars: An MC battle where the content of the artist's rhymes is meant to disrespect the opposing MC's character.

DJ style: A term used for dancehall reggae MCs who are called in this genre DJs (the inverse of its meaning in rap music, which is one who plays records), with the term DJ style defining what they do, which is rap. The actual dancehall DJ, as the term is known in the United States, is called a *selector*. DJ style is also synonymous with the term *toasting*.

SURVIVORS

Many of the pioneer rap groups of the late 1970s and early 1980s were passed over by the second-generation rap performers. Still, they were important in the development of rap, and many have come back to perform today. The Cold Crush Brothers, originally formed in 1979, paved the way for later MC groups. They were known as the best of the routine groups because, back then, groups came out with routines to accompany their rhymes; in other words, they gave shows. DJ Charlie Chase of the Cold Crush Brothers explained why they broke up: "It's like this. We grew up together. We're each other's best friends. The Cold Crush was a marriage. We lived together, we breathed together and ate together. Everything was Cold Crush. And it's like this: You live with your parents, and you love your parents, but you get to that age where you have to go out on your own and see what's happening. That's what happened with us.

"We matured and we all had ideas and plans and things that we wanted to do, which everybody else didn't see the same—not no disagreements or nothing like that. It's just that everybody had certain things that they wanted to do."

The Brothers reunited in 1993. By that time the group was considered to be "old-timers" by many younger acts. For some reason, a lot of people like to associate most old-school

Salt N Pepa

rappers as being cracked out, or succumbing to some kind of drug situation of some sort, when they've not seen or heard from them for a while. Cold Crush Brother Grandmaster Caz commented, "Most people want you to be doing bad. If people don't see you for a while, they be like 'Yo! what's up? You was locked up?'—first thing they say, you was locked up. So that's just the way people's minds work.

"There are some cases where that happened. But it's not like the whole old school fell off and is drugged out. I mean, some people are married with families now. Or, they saw that they couldn't do nothing (with show biz) and said, oh well, let me try civilian life—or whatever. I saw a guy from the Crash Crew. He's a cop now. But to those people, if you're not who they saw you as, you fell off."

Caz sees an opportunity for older acts to revitalize the music: "Hip hop is coming back around. It's coming back to the stage where we set stuff off at—the music, the raps, the styles. They're like copying the old school styles—the styles of the pioneers. If there was ever a time for us to come back out, it's time now. We left a lot of stuff undone.

"What we're gettin' ready to do is bring back the stuff that inspired all these people to do what they do. But nobody's mastered it. They copy, they take bits and pieces, but no one has been able to capture that style and that sound we got."

Run DMC

EAZY-E
●●●●●●●●●●
**(Born Eric Wright, September 7, 1963, Compton, Los Angeles;
died March 26, 1995)**

Eazy-E was the founder of Ruthless Records, and one of the cofounders of N.W.A—a group that recorded on his label—which was responsible for establishing the so-called gangsta rap genre that began to flourish in the early 1990s. His Ruthless Records was one of the top rap labels in the late 1980s and early 1990s, garnering close to two multiplatinum, four platinum, and four gold albums during that period. Eazy was also a solo artist who had gold and platinum albums to his credit.

Eazy was originally involved with drug dealing during the early 1980s, but was also interested in music. After watching one of his DJ friends, Dr. Dre, make tapes, Eazy started his own record company called Ruthless Records. Eazy signed a group from New York called HBO, and brought them to Los Angeles to record. He asked them to cut a song titled "Boys in the Hood," but the group rejected it. Dr. Dre (who had co-written the song with his friend Ice Cube) suggested that Eazy record the song himself. It was the first record on Eazy's label.

Later, Eazy, Dre, Ice Cube, and another one of Dre's friends, DJ Yella, decided to form a group, calling themselves N.W.A, for Niggas with Attitude. As a group they recorded two songs written by Ice Cube, called "8 Ball" and "Dopeman." Eazy released both clean and explicit versions of the records, but the explicit versions clearly sold more. Eazy eventually hired music industry veteran Jerry Heller as general manager for the N.W.A group.

By 1988 Ruthless Records launched female rap group J.J. Fad. Eazy, Dre, Yella, and another producer called the Arabian Prince began working under the production name of High Powered Productions, producing J.J. Fad's *Supersonic, The Album* for the Ruthless label, which featured the single "Supersonic." The album went gold that year, and the single went gold the following year. Eazy decided to make a solo album in 1988, titled *Eazy-Duz-It*, which was also well received, reaching platinum status in 1989. During this period Eazy and the group N.W.A recorded two albums: *N.W.A & The Posse* and *Straight Outta Compton*, which

Easy-E

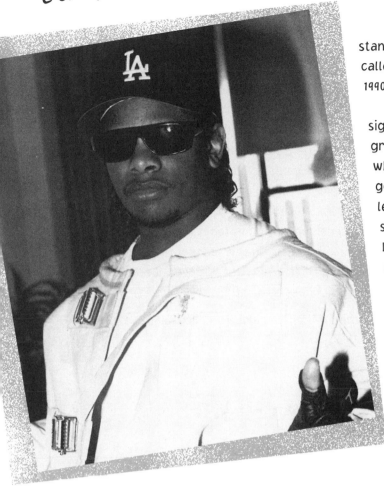

stands as a landmark work for the so-called gangsta genre of rap. By the early 1990s the album was multiplatinum.

From 1989 on into the 1990s Eazy-E signed other acts to the label like the group Above the Law and rapper D.O.C., whose *No One Can Do It Better* LP went gold in '89. Eazy also signed and released female R&B act Michel'le, whose single "No More Lies" (co-written by Laylaw and Dr. Dre) went gold, as did her self-titled album the following year. With N.W.A (minus Ice Cube and Arabian Prince), Eazy released two more albums: the EP *100 Miles and Runnin'* in 1990, and *Niggaz4Life* in 1991. Both albums would go platinum, after which the remaining members of the group went off into other directions. The most animosity was felt between Easy and Dr. Dre, who traded insults both on record and in interviews.

During that same year Eazy made a $2,500 donation to the Republican party and attended a fundraiser for President Bush, both actions shocking those in and outside the hip-hop community. Eazy later said he did this out of curiosity.

Easy continued his solo career, releasing his *5150 Home 4 Tha Sick* EP by the end of 1992, which eventually went gold. He also released a solo EP by former N.W.A member and friend MC Ren, *Kizz My Black Azz*, which went platinum that year. Eazy's next platinum work was his own *It's On (Dr. Dre) 187um Killa* (an EP he developed to counter negative references to him on Dr. Dre's *The Chronic* album), which was released in 1993. That same year he inked a marketing and distribution deal with Relativity and RED (Relativity Entertainment Distribution), which began distributing his Ruthless Records product. The other acts on his label included the Jewish rap group Blood of Abraham, HWA (Hoez with Attitude), and Bone Thugs N Harmony, whose 1994 *Creepin on Ah Come Up* EP was double-platinum by 1995. Eazy also started a Saturday evening party-style radio show in late 1994 on the Los Angeles R&B station KBBT.

People in the hip-hop community were shocked when it was discovered in early 1995 that Eazy had contracted the AIDS virus. Eazy is reported to have said (about his getting the disease) that he guessed his success was too good for him. When he died in March of that year at age 31, he had left behind eight children, borne by six different women.

Selected album/CDs: *Eazy-Duz-It* (1988, Ruthless 57100); *Straight Outta Compton* by N.W.A (1988, Ruthless 57102).

ED O. G & DA BULLDOGS

(Ed O. G, born Edward Anderson, c. 1971, Roxbury, Boston)

Ed O. G gained attention in 1991 when he hit the scene with the single "I Got to Have It."

Ed was originally a b-boy before he got into MC'ing and beat boxing, working with local groups in Roxbury such as Fresh to Impress and the 3 Def Notes. Around 1985 he recorded a single titled "Suzie Q" and subsequently spent a few years learning about how to structure his songs and work in the studio before returning to the music scene, working with Joe Mansfield and reteaming with a member of Fresh to Impress, T-Nyne. Following his 1991 hit single, Ed's album *Life of a Kid in the Ghetto* received attention for his socially conscious rhymes and the quality of the production work, handled by the team of Joe Mansfield and Ed's cousins, the Awesome 2. His 1994 follow-up album, *Roxbury 02119*, continued to deliver rhymes of consciousness, as well as other traditional rhyme styles.

Selected albums/CDs: *Life of a Kid in the Ghetto* (1991, PWL/Mercury 848326); Roxbury 02119 (PWL/Mercury 518161).

EGYPTIAN LOVER

(Born in Los Angeles)

Egyptian Lover is one of the pioneers of hip hop on the West Coast, particularly in Los Angeles. He released one of the first rap recordings from that area, the 1983 single "Egypt, Egypt." By 1989 his Egyptian Empire Records was the second largest black-owned independent record distribution company in the United States, next to Luther Campbell's then-named Luke Skyywalker Records.

A former DJ and member of Uncle Jam's Army, Egypt (as he is affectionately known) started his Egyptian Empire Records in 1984, originally to release his own material. His first album, released around this same period, was titled *On the Nile*. By the late 1980s he began to sign other acts, such as Rodney O & Joe Cooley, whose "Everlastin' Bass" single and debut album, *Me & Joe*, were released during the 1988—89 period. Other acts on the label included the Get Large Posse, and R&B artists Jaime Jupiter and Two O'Clock. Around 1989 Egypt became partners with former World Class Wreckin Cru member Alonzo Williams, and the L.A. Dream Team's Rudy Pardee, forming the West Coast Record Distributors, a coalition of four South Central Los Angeles independent record labels. In 1992 Egypt executive produced Rodney O & Joe Cooley's *F—k New York* album.

ENJOY RECORDS

Formed in 1963, Harlem, New York City

Enjoy Records was second only to Sugar Hill Records in recording major pioneer rap acts.

Label owner Bobby Robinson's (no relation to Sugar Hill's Sylvia Robinson) music career started in 1946 when he opened a record store in Harlem. By 1951 Robinson had become recognized as among the most knowledgeable people in the record business, and soon received calls from A&R men across the country from labels like Chess, Atlantic, Aladdin, and others. Robinson reasoned that he should be able to produce and put out his own acts, so he started his own label.

Robinson first began working with doo-wop groups like the Mellow Moods, the Teenchords, the Channels, and the Charts. He is also credited with spotting early talents like Gladys Knight and the Pips. Robinson also worked in rhythm and blues, recording Wilbert Harrison's "Kansas City," and working with artists like Buster Brown, Lightnin' Hopkins, and Elmore James. Robinson formed many labels, including Red Robin, Whirlin' Disc, Fury, and Fire.

When Robinson established Enjoy Records in 1963, the first artist he recorded on the label was tenor saxophonist King Curtis. After working with several other artists and bypassing the disco genre, Robinson began to seek rap acts in 1979 after watching his friend Sylvia Robinson's success with the Sugarhill Gang.

Grandmaster Flash and the Furious Five and the Funky Four Plus One are among the first rap acts Robinson recorded in 1979, with "Superrappin'" and "Rappin' and Rockin' the House" being the first songs they recorded, respectively, for Enjoy. Robinson was also first in recording the Treacherous Three in 1980, combining them and his nephew Spoonie Gee on the piece "The New Rap Language" and recording Spoonie's "Love Rap." In 1982 Robinson recorded the Fearless Four's first records ("It's Magic" and "Rockin' It"). The Disco Four, Doug E. Fresh, Dr. Ice, and Master Don are some of the other rap acts Robinson has recorded.

 Selected singles: "Superappin'" by Grandmaster Flash and the Furious Five (1979, Enjoy 6001); "Love Rap" b/w "The New Rap Language" by Spoonie Gee and the Treacherous Three (1980, Enjoy 6002); "Rockin' It" by Fearless Four (1982, Enjoy 6028A).

Electrofunk: A style of music pioneered in the early 1980s by one of hip hop's original DJs, Afrika Bambaataa, which consisted of computerized instruments (like synthesizers) playing the music of funk—a form of music that was developed by artists like James Brown, George Clinton, and Sly Stone. Bambaataa's piece "Planet Rock" (which combined computer rock group Kraftwerk's "Trans-Europe Express" melody) introduced this genre of rap. It began to subside in popularity toward the mid- to late-1980s.

EPMD

EPMD
········
a.k.a. EPEE MD
**Formed c. 1987, Brentwood, Long Island, New York
(E-Double E, born Erick S. Sermon, November 25, 1968, Brentwood, Long
Island; PMD, a.k.a. PEE MD, formerly DJ Eazzy P, born Parrish J. Smith,
May 13, 1968, Brentwood, Long Island; DJ K. La Boss, born New York; DJ
Scratch, born George Spivey, June 21, 1968, Brooklyn, New York)**

EPMD (an acronym for Erick and Parrish Making Dollars) were known as a successful hardcore duo, recognized for their strong funky beats and fierce rhyme style and delivery (accented by Erick "E-Double E" Sermon's lisp), which offset their middle-class suburban upbringing. Along with Parrish "PMD" Smith, EPMD had four successive gold albums; all went gold within the year of their release. With their Hit Squad/Shuma Management, the duo was responsible for discovering successful gold and platinum acts like K-Solo, Das EFX, and Redman. All the more reason why much dismay and disbelief were expressed in the hip-hop community when the duo parted ways toward the end of 1992, due to reported financial and creative differences.

Both Erick and Parrish attended the same high school, Brentwood High. Parrish later attended Southern Connecticut State University where he was a wide receiver for the school's football team. An Eagle Scout as well, Parrish began to get into MC'ing during his second year of college. By 1985 Parrish began working as a DJ for the group Rock Squad, where he was known as DJ Eazzy P. They recorded the single "Facts of Life" for Tommy Boy Records and worked with producers the Latin Rascals.

Parrish later hooked up with neighborhood friend Erick and began recording. Using money Parrish had made while working at a bakery, the two recorded the song "It's My Thing" (borrowing one of the break records for the piece from the Awesome 2), which was eventually picked up by Chrysalis Records.

The two were signed to Sleeping Bag/Fresh Records, where they recorded their first two albums, *Strictly Business* and *Unfinished Business*, in 1988 and 1989 respectively. The first album had scratch work by DJ K. La Boss, while the second album had scratching by DJ Scratch, who became the duo's permanent DJ.

In 1991 they recorded the album *Business as Usual* for Def Jam Recordings, and their fourth album, *Business Never Personal*, was recorded in 1992. That same year they also had a single, "Crossover," that went gold.

After the duo parted ways in 1992, Erick began working as a solo artist, as well as doing successful production work for people like basketball star Shaquille O'Neal. Parrish founded his own PMD Records.

 Selected albums/CDs: *Strictly Business* (1988, Sleeping Bag/Fresh 1); *Unfinished Business* (1989, Sleeping Bag/Fresh 8); *Business as Usual* (1991, Def Jam/Columbia 47067); *Business Never Personal* (1992, RAL/Def Jam/Chaos 52848).

ERIC B & RAKIM
●●●●●●●●●●●●●●●●●●●●●●●●●
Formed c. 1986, Long Island, New York
(Eric B, born Eric Barrier, East Elmhurst, Queens, New York; Rakim, born William Griffin, c. 1970, Wyandanch, Long Island)

When Eric B & Rakim emerged on the hip-hop scene in 1986, they introduced a new sound to the genre. Rakim's MC style, showcased on their single "Eric B Is President," featured more complex lyrics than most rappers of the period, delivered with a semideep, hypnotic, monotone tonality. Rakim is also recognized for introducing lessons from the Five Percent Nation of Islam in his rhymes. The duo was one of the first rap groups to extensively sample James Brown's recordings. They were also one of the first groups to introduce atonal textures and obscure sounds in their music, as in their piece "My Melody." Eric B & Rakim was considered one of the most respected groups in hip hop. (Fans would sometimes throw rolled-up dollar bills at Rakim during his performances.) The duo's first three albums went gold within their release years. Both Eric B and Rakim were known for keeping low profiles, rarely giving interviews.

Eric B played trumpet and guitar before taking up deejaying, playing in various local clubs in East Elmhurst, Queens, and at places like the USA Roller Rink. He became a mobile DJ for New York City radio station WBLS-FM around 1985. He met DJ/producer Marley Marl there, who would later do remix work on Eric B & Rakim's debut pieces, "Eric B Is President" and "My Melody."

Eric B & Rakim were initially signed to Robert Hill's Harlem-based Zakia Records label, where their first singles were released in 1986. They were later signed to 4th & Broadway, where their debut album, *Paid in Full*, was released in 1987. By 1988 Uni Records offered the duo a contract that came close to a million dollars. For that label, the duo recorded *Follow the Leader*.

In 1990 they were with MCA Records, recording the album *Let the Rhythm Hit 'Em*. Around this same period, the duo worked with R&B singer Jody Watley (on her single "Friends"). Eric B also established his Lynn Starr Productions and Mega Starr Management companies, working with artists like Kool G Rap & DJ Polo, Freddie Foxxx, and others.

In 1992 Eric B and Rakim cut the Hank Shocklee and the Bomb Squad-produced song "Know the Ledge" (with Rakim playing drums on the looped track), which was part of the soundtrack from the movie *Juice*. During that same year they released the album *Don't Sweat the Technique*, where Rakim expanded his subject matter to include topics like the Gulf War and youth violence.

By 1994—95, the duo agreed creatively to split up, with Eric B starting his own 95th Street Records label and releasing his single "I Can't Let You."

Selected albums/CDs: *Paid in Full* (1987, 4th & B'way 4005); *Follow the Leader* (1988, Uni 3); *Let the Rhythm Hit 'Em* (1990, MCA 6416); *Don't Sweat the Technique* (1992, MCA 10594).

ERIC "VIETNAM" SADLER

(Born c. 1961, Long Island, New York)

Eric Sadler worked as the engineer and electronics man for Hank Shocklee and the Bomb Squad production crew. His thorough knowledge of drum machines—what could be recorded, what would work and not work during recording stages, setting proper sound levels, and the like—propelled the Bomb Squad to the status of major producers during the late 1980s and early 1990s.

Sadler was originally a musician who played in several bands, one of which competed against future colleague Bill Stephney's groups. He met Shocklee, Chuck D, and other Bomb Squad members around 1982 at 510 South Franklin Street in Long Island. Sadler rented the basement of this building with a partner to sell rehearsal time to bands. Shocklee and the others moved in upstairs, using the space to store records and equipment. It was here where Sadler got the nickname "Vietnam," because of his ever-present army fatigue jacket, dark sunglasses, and black cap, which he wore while learning the then-popular Oberheim DMX drum machine that he was keeping for his friend, future actor/comedian Eddie Murphy. Sadler was invited upstairs one day by Chuck D, and with Hank Shocklee's brother Keith, all three began their initial working relationship, collaborating on two songs, "College Collegiate Jam" and "Five Funk."

Besides the Public Enemy projects he co-produced, Sadler also worked on solo production projects with his own Street Element Productions, including rapper/activist author Sister Souljah's 1992 album, *360 Degrees of Power*.

EVERLAST

See HOUSE OF PAIN

OTHERZ

EASY ABADABA

Formed in Harlem, New York
(Steve King; Abdul-Rahman Yoba; Daniel C. Martin: all born New York)
Around 1989 this group recorded an album titled *G.Q. Down.*

EDDIE CHEEBA

(Born c. mid-1950s, New York)

Eddie Cheeba was an MC who performed during the late 1970s, primarily at Charles Gallery in Harlem. He arose with the first generation of MCs, and his MC style was basically that of a party rocker. His style and image was a major influence on rap mogul Russell Simmons.

Cheeba attended Bronx Community College, and hosted a popular radio show on WFUV when he was in school. During his performances in Harlem Cheeba made his mark with the party-rocker routines he did with his DJ Easy G, over records like "Flashlight" by the Parliments. Decked in a plaid sports jacket and baseball cap, Cheeba would expertly motivate his party crowd, along with his three female motivators, called the Cheeba Crew. By 1979 to 1980 Cheeba appeared on the bills of Russell Simmons's parties, performing at venues like the Hotel Diplomat with Kurtis Blow, before leaving the rap scene by the early 1980s.

EINSTEIN

(Born in London)

Einstein was a rapper from England, who was signed to Profile Records. He recorded an album for the label, titled *Friday Night & Saturday Morning.*

FAB 5 FREDDY
••••••••••••••••••••
(Born Fred Brathwaite, c. 1959, Brooklyn, New York)

One of hip hop's premier renaissance men, Fab 5 Freddy's career stretches back to the culture's early days. As one of the first of the many pioneering graffiti writers, Freddy began by tagging walls as a kid ("Fred Fab 5," "Bull 99," and "Showdown 177" were some of his tags), then graduated to full-fledged graffiti art. During this time, he began to study pop art; his last graffiti work depicted subway cars filled with Campbell's soup cans, in homage to one of his heroes, Andy Warhol.

Toward the late 1970s Freddy studied art at Medgar Evers College, where he also had a radio show. Later, he met music columnist Glenn O'Brien, who produced a TV show on Manhattan's public-access channel called *O'Brien's TV Party*. Freddy was a guest on this show, and he ended up doing camera work for O'Brien for two years. He also met some of O'Brien's friends, including Deborah Harry and Chris Stein from the new-wave group Blondie, whose 1981 single "Rapture" mentions Freddy in the lyrics.

For a time, Freddy transferred his art skills to canvas and befriended painters Jean-Michel Basquiat and Keith Haring. But with the opening of the new-wave hangout the Mudd Club, circa 1978, Freddy began MC'ing to try to fuse the two cultures. His success helped bring hip hop downtown. Freddy assembled music packages for popular clubs, like Club 57, that included Afrika Bambaataa among other hip-hop pioneers.

Soon after, Freddy met underground filmmaker Charles Ahearn, portraying Phade—a promoter who tries to get hip hop wider exposure (art imitating life)—in the quintessential hip-hop movie *Wild Style*, done in 1982. With Chris Stein, he also produced the soundtrack for that film. That same year Freddy decided to try his hand at making a rap record, recording "Change the Beat" on Celluloid Records. Fashion illustrator Ann Boyle did the French b-side version of the song.

Into the late 1980s, Freddy began directing music videos, first for KRS-One's "My Philosophy," and then for Shabba Ranks, Queen Latifah, EPMD, and others. Around this time Freddy was approached by executive producer Ted Demme (nephew of film director Jonathan Demme) to host MTV's rap video show "Yo! MTV Raps." Freddy also started doing commercials, directing one for Pepsi, and appearing with actor Billy Dee Williams in Colt 45 ads. He was an associate producer for the 1991 film *New Jack City*, and in 1992, he compiled a dictionary of hip-hop slang, titled *Fresh Fly Flavor*.

FAT BOYS
Formerly the Disco 3
Formed early 1980s, Brooklyn, New York
(Prince Markie Dee, born Mark Morales, 1969, Brooklyn, New York; Kool Rock-ski, born Damon Wimbley, New York; the Human Beat Box, born Darren Robinson, New York)

The Fat Boys were a commercially successful rap group that attained some acceptance in the hip-hop community during their early years. They were known for lighthearted, comic rhymes, with much of their humor based on their large physiques. The Fat Boys made six albums that sold approximately seven million copies. They starred in the movie *Disorderlies* with actor Ralph Bellamy, and they also appeared in the film *Krush Groove*. They had three gold albums, (*Fat Boys*, *The Fat Boys Are Back*, and *Comin' Back Hard Again*), and one platinum album (*Crushin'*) before the group dissolved around 1990. The Fat Boys are remembered for Darren "The Human Beat Box" Robinson's version of Doug E. Fresh's "Human Beat Box." They also were known for their covers of rock classics performed along with the song's originators, including a remake of "The Twist" with Chubby Checker and a single with the Beach Boys.

Prince Markie Dee formed the group in the early 1980s with two of his East New York friends, Darren and Kool Rock-ski. They called themselves the Disco 3. During 1983, Swiss publicist and promoter Charlie Stettler created a citywide talent contest at Radio City Music Hall, which was sponsored by Coca Cola and New York City's WBLS-FM radio. The first prize was a recording contract to anyone who could rap to Stettler's recording of Manhattan street sounds. Markie Dee entered his group and won. Stettler booked a spot for them in Russell Simmons's Fresh Fest Tour, and later suggested that they change their name to the Fat Boys, after their single, also called "Fat Boys," was a hit.

Within their approximate six-year run, the group became more commercial, and continued to have selling power, particularly in albums. At the end of their run the group reportedly filed a $6 million suit against their original record label for back royalties.

In 1991 Darren Robinson was tried for sexual assault of a minor in Pennsylvania. In that same year Markie Dee surprised some people by embarking on a production/writing career, co-producing with his partner, Corey Rooney, successful songs for singers like Mary J. Blige ("Real Love"), Christopher Williams ("Don't You Wanna Make Love Tonight?"), and rapper Father ("Treat Them Like They Want to Be Treated"). In 1992 he released his own solo album with the Soul Convention, titled *Free*.

Selected albums/CDs: *The Fat Boys* (1984, Sutra 100); *The Fat Boys Are Back* (1985, Sutra 101); *Big and Beautiful* (1986, Sutra 077); *Crushin'* (1987, Urban/Polydor 831948); *Comin' Back Hard Again* (1988, Urban/Polydor 835809).

FATHER
. . . .
Formerly Father MC
(Born Timothy Brown, 1970, Brooklyn, New York)

Father is known as a rapper who frequently writes and performs rhymes centering on sex and love. He is noted for his ladies' man image.

Father grew up in Brooklyn and Queens and began to get into rhyme writing while in high school. During 1985, Father entered a rap competition at the USA Roller Rink, which he won. With that, Father began to seriously get into his craft. He went into a studio and made a series of experimental demo recordings to enhance his MC skills, with songs like "I'm Better" and "Father's Going Ill." Some time later former rapper Andre Harrell, the president of Uptown Records, heard one of Father's demos and signed him to his label during the spring of 1989.

Father first gained attention in 1990 with the single "Treat Them Like They Want to Be Treated," which featured vocals by the R&B group Jodeci. His debut album, *Father's Day*, was released during this period, and the second single off the work, "I'll Do for You," went gold in 1991.

Father's second work, *Close to You*, was released in 1992. On this album Father worked with singer Mary J. Blige on the song "One Night Stand," which was a hit on the R&B charts.

In 1993 Father's third album was released, titled *Sex Is Law*. The single off the work was "69."

 Selected singles: "Treat Them Like They Want to Be Treated" (1990, Uptown).

 Selected albums/CDs: *Father's Day* (1990, Uptown 10061); *Close to You* (1992, Uptown); *Sex Is Law* (1993, Uptown 10937).

FEARLESS FOUR
. . . .
Formed circa 1976, New York
(The Great Peso, born Mitchell Grant, December 5, 1959; The Devastating Tito, born Tito Dones, May 27, 1964; Mighty Mike C, born Michael Kevin Clee, March 10, 1963; DLB, the Microphone Wizard, born April 25; DJ Master O.C., born Oscar Rodriguez Jr., September 22, 1962; DJ Krazy Eddie, born Eddie Thompson, July 25, 1960: formerly with Troy B, New York, and Mike Ski, New York)

The Fearless Four was the first rap group signed to a major record label—Elektra Records. They are noted for being one of the first rap groups to have Latinos as members—Devastating Tito and DJ Master O.C.—and they are remembered for having two DJs (DJ Krazy

Eddie and O.C.). They are also one of the first rap groups to use jazz for break beats, such as works from Grover Washington and Herbie Hancock.

During the mid-1970s Master O.C. and Devastating Tito made tapes of their MC'ing and deejaying skills, selling their work for $10 a tape. The tapes established their DJ and MC reputation on the streets.

Later, an MC by the name of Mike Ski joined the duo, and another rapper, Peso, soon followed, who introduced a singing style of MC'ing to the group. Troy B (also known as part of the Disco Four) worked with them for a while, until being replaced by DLB, the Microphone Wizard. They then considered themselves a group, and went by the name the Fearless Five.

When Mike Ski left they became the Fearless Four. They were picked up toward 1982 by Bobby Robinson of Enjoy Records, who released their songs "It's Magic" and "Rockin' It," both of which were handled by multi-instrumentalist Pumpkin. "Rockin' It" hit the mark with hip hoppers, and the piece is regarded as a classic.

By 1983 the group was signed to Elektra Records, where their hit "Problems of the World Today" was released. "Just Rock" was another piece they later released before they parted company with the label. Master O.C. and Krazy Eddie began to work in the field of production, while the Great Peso did solo work on songs such as "Oh Girl" and "She's Wild."

 Selected singles: "Rockin' It" (1982, Enjoy); "Problems of the World Today" (1983, Elektra).

FEVER RECORDS
Formed early 1980s, New York

Fever Records was the label offshoot of the famous hip-hop club Disco Fever owned by Sal Abbatiello, who also owned the Latin freestyle club Devil's Nest. Abbatiello's Fever Records released singles by some DJs and MCs that were popular in his Disco Fever club, like Sweet G's "Games People Play," Lovebug Starski's "You Gotta Believe," and others.

By 1985 the label focused on releasing product in the freestyle genre, with president/producer Andy "Panda" Tripoli releasing works by acts like the Cover Girls and Lisette Melendez.

FORCE M.D.'S
Formerly Dr. Rock and the Force MC's
Formed 1979, Staten Island, New York
(T.C.D., born Antoine Lundy, Staten Island, New York; Stevie D, born Steve Lundy, Staten Island, New York; Mercury, born Charles Nelson; Trisco, born Trisco Pearson)

The Force M.D.'s were a premier hip-hop vocal group who combined rap, vocal harmony, elements of b-boying, a cappella, and impressions in their act, as well as steps à la the Temptations and others before them.

T.C.D. and Stevie D originally performed with their three brothers in 1972 as the LDs, imitating the Jackson Five on the streets of Staten Island. Later two brothers left, and T.C.D. and Stevie D continued to perform on the streets of Manhattan in areas like Broadway and 42nd Street. Soon after, they met Trisco and Mercury, who joined them.

While continuing to perform in as many places as possible, including the Staten Island Ferry, the group added a DJ to the act known as Dr. Rock, who was proficient in DJ tricks. They also had a backup DJ named Dr. Shock, who was an expert in scratching. Billing themselves as Dr. Rock and the Force MC's (and later managed by promoter Van Silk), the group began to gain notice, initially for their rapping. They hit areas of New Jersey and Connecticut with their act, and fans would tape the group, which helped them get even more notice.

New York City radio personality Mr. Magic got a chance to check the group out, after which he brought them to the attention of Tom Silverman of Tommy Boy Records. Silverman signed the group without DJs Dr. Rock and Dr. Shock, after which they went by the name Force M.D.'s (which stands for "musical diversity").

Toward 1984 Tommy Boy released several singles from the group including "Let Me Love You" and "Forgive Me Girl," both co-produced by Mr. Magic. During this same period the group's first album was released, titled *Love Letters*, which featured the single "Tears." Their next album, toward 1985, was titled *Chillin'*, and contained the single "Tender Love," a piece produced by Jimmy Jam and Terry Lewis. The song was alos featured in the film *Krush Grove*.

The album spawned other singles, including "Here I Go Again," and Force M.D.'s was named Best Vocal Group at the 1987 New York Music Awards. During this period they also received the award for Most Promising Group from the R&B Arards. Toward 1987 the group released their second album, *Touch and Go*, after which they did extensive touring. Around 1990 the group's next album was released, titled *Step to Me*.

 Selected albums/CDs: *Love Letters* (1984, Tommy Boy).

freddie Fox

FREDDIE FOXXX
••••••••••••••••••••••••••••••
(Born Fred Campbell, 1969, Westbury, New York)

Freddie Foxxx is a formidable rapper, who occasionally provides rhymes about street life and black pride.

After working various odd jobs Foxxx joined the rap group Royal Nation in 1979. Toward 1982 Foxxx recorded for the Aleems's Nia Records with the group Supreme Force. He eventually went solo, releasing his first album, *Freddie Foxxx Is Here*, for MCA Records in 1989. This work contained the single "Somebody Else Bumped Your Girl," which became a classic with the hip-hop crowd. Thereafter, Foxxx worked with KRS-One in 1992 on his *Sex and Violence* album, and with Naughty By Nature on their *19Naughtyiii* work, appearing on the single "Hot Potato."

He later signed with Queen Latifah's Flavor Unit Records in 1993 and was featured on that label's *Roll Wit Tha Flava* compilation. In 1994 he issued a new solo album, *Crazy Like a Foxxx*.

 Selected albums/CDs: *Freddie Foxxx Is Here* (1989, MCA); *Crazy Like a Foxxx* (1994, Epic/Street 53010).

FUNKY FOUR PLUS ONE

Formed c. 1976—77, Bronx, New York
(DJ Breakout; KK Rockwell; Keith Keith; Sha Rock; Lil' Rodney Cee; Jazzy Jeff: all born c. 1963, Bronx, New York. *Former member*: Raheim, born Guy Todd Williams, New York)

The Funky Four Plus One, from the Edenwald Projects in the Bronx, was one of the premier MC groups of the mid-1970s, who were known for their routines and dance moves modeled on the choreography of the R&B group the Temptations. With their DJ, Breakout, the group had a large following on the streets before they were signed to Enjoy, then Sugar Hill Records. They are remembered for rapping from four to five hours during a show, and for their *Gilligan's Island* routine, where they would change the words to the famous TV theme and replace them with their own. They are recognized for having one of the first female MCs, Sha Rock, and for their battles with Grandmaster Flash and the Furious Five.

DJ Breakout and his partner Baron were among the top DJs to emerge in the Bronx with Afrika Bambaataa, Kool DJ Herc, and Grandmaster Flash during the early- to mid-1970s. One of the first MCs to work with Breakout was KK Rockwell. Keith Keith and Sha Rock later followed, and then Raheim, who stayed briefly with the group until around 1979, when he became part of Grandmaster Flash's Furious Five. Lil' Rodney Cee (formerly with the Magnificent Seven from 1977 to 1978) then joined the group, and later, Jazzy Jeff (not to be confused with Jazzy Jeff and Fresh Prince) became a member.

The Funky Four Plus One was first recorded by music-industry veteran Bobby Robinson on his Enjoy Records label in 1979. Their piece "Rappin' and Rockin' the House" was an immediate hit with hip hoppers. The music was handled by multi-instrumentalist Pumpkin, who was suggested for the session by DJ Breakout. By 1980 the group was signed to Sugar Hill Records, where they recorded the now-classic song "That's the Joint."

The group members then separated and formed other groups: Lil' Rodney Cee and KK Rockwell performed as Double Trouble, and appeared in, and wrote songs for, the 1982 hip-hop film *Wild Style*; Sha Rock got together with other female pioneers Lisa Lee and Debbie Dee, forming the group the Us Girls. They recorded a song for, and appeared in, singer Harry Belafonte's 1984 film *Beat Street*. Lil' Rodney Cee and KK Rockwell also performed for a short time as The Deuce for Capitol Records. Jazzy Jeff, as well, moved on, signing on as a solo act for a while with Jive Records.

FURIOUS FIVE

See GRANDMASTER FLASH AND THE FURIOUS FIVE

FU-SCHNICKENS

Formed c. 1989—91, Flatbush, Brooklyn, New York
(Chip Fu; Moc Fu; Poc Fu: all born in Brooklyn)

Fu-Schnickens is a group influenced by kung fu/martial arts movies in their rhyme styles and deliveries, topped off by the phenomenal rapper Chip Fu, who raps in a super-fast, reggae-tinged MC style, musically equaling thirty-second notes (or demisemiquavers).

The group was discovered at a hip-hop conference that took place at Howard University in February 1991. Dressed in Chinese attire, they threw out fortune cookies and other artifacts associated with Chinese culture, and performed to an impressed audience. Signed to Jive Records, the Fu-Schnickens's debut single was "Ring the Alarm." Their album *F.U.—Don't Take It Personal* was released in 1992. Another single off the work, "La Schmoove," was also a hit with hip-hop audiences.

By 1993, the group (now handled by Queen Latifah's Flavor Unit Management) had a gold single with basketball star Shaquille O'Neal titled "What's Up Doc? (Can We Rock)." In 1994 they released the album *Nervous Breakdown*.

 Selected albums/CDs: *F.U.—Don't Take It Personal* (1992, Jive 41472); *Nervous Breakdown* (1994, Jive 41519).

OTHERZ

FINESSE & SYNQUIS

Formed Queens, New York

The female duo of Finesse & Synquis was based in Lefrak City, Queens, when Uptown Enterprises president Andre Harrell heard about their MC skills. Having finalized a distribution agreement with MCA Records, Harrell signed the duo and around 1988 released their debut album, titled *Soul Sisters*. This was also the title of their single, released during the same period.

FREEZE FACTOR

(Larry Jones; George Green: both born in New York)

Freeze Factor's first album, *Chill*, was released in 1989 by the Epic Records label. It contained two hit singles, "Black All the Way" and "Keep on Groovin'."

FRESH GORDON

(Born in New York)

Fresh Gordon was originally a DJ who made mix tapes during the early- to mid-1980s before expanding to keyboards, working with artists like Master D and the Choice MC's.

Around 1987 Gordon recorded a piece called "Feelin' James," which was released on T.D. Records, and later picked up by the Tommy Boy label. Gordon began working as a producer, notably with artists like Dana Dane and Father, on songs like Dane's "Tales from the Dane Side" and "A Little Bit of Dane Tonight," and Father's "I've Been Watching You."

FULL FORCE

(Paul Anthony George; Bowlegged Lou George; B-Fine George; Curt-t-t; Baby Gerry; Shy Shy: all born in Brooklyn, New York)

Full Force was basically an R&B band and production crew, whose first major success was with a rap record, titled "Roxanne, Roxanne," which they produced for the group UTFO in 1984. The six-man group of cousins and brothers were among the most important producers during the early 1980s, and have also been responsible for the success of Lisa Lisa and Cult Jam, Real Roxanne, Whistle, Cheryl "Pepsii" Riley, Doctor Ice, and others. They have also worked with artists like James Brown, Patti LaBelle, and Samantha Fox, to name a few.

Full Force's work has garnered them seven gold albums and four platinum, with eight gold and platinum singles. Nine of the records they have worked on have reached number 1.

 Selected albums/CDs: Full Force (1985, Columbia 40117).

Five Percent Nation of Islam: A faction of the Honorable Elijah Muhammad's Nation of Islam, created by expelled Nation member Clarence 13X.

Freestyle: MC'ing, or rapping, in its most organic form, which usually involves delivering one's rhymes without music. A person freestyling is sometimes accompanied by a human beatbox, and the term also means delivering rhymes off the top of one's head (rhymes developed as one goes along). Freestyle is also a term used to define a style of music that emerged from rap, which is comprised of Latin rhythms, and created mostly by Latinos.

Fresh: Awesome; excellent.

RAP AND VIOLENCE: SPICE 1

Spice 1's work has always emphasized the reality of life on the streets, leading to the criticism that he is promoting violence. With song titles like "Gas Chamber," "Dumpin' Em in Ditches," and "Trigga Gots No Heart" (which was on the *Menace II Society* soundtrack), folks might think he's a violent man.

The man from Oakland and Richmond, California, whose first, self-titled album nearly went gold with no label support, says some people may feel that way about him indeed.

"People ask me why I'm so violent," Spice reveals. "Why am I talkin' about guns, why am I bringing this upon the black kids, know what I'm sayin'? I'm like, look—I got a son and he's 3 months old, and by the time he's 6 years old, he's gonna know what's up. He's gonna know that when he gets 13 or 14, that anybody can run up on his stuff and take it if they want it.

"I just want my son to know how to protect himself, 'cause there's some dogs out here! There're people—where I'm from?—there are people, who will actually run up in your house, just from knowing what you got in there, run up in there with some AK 47s.

"If they know you got a couple a Gs [$2,000] in your house, they're gonna run up in there and try to take it!

"I hear about that all the time! People can be jealous of you because you got more than they have, or maybe they've been trying longer than you and they felt they should have what you got, ya know what I'm sayin'?

"They just stole my car! I had a $17,000 old school Chevy Impala. They stole it from in front of my house! I'm glad that they knew what type of person I was for them not to run up on me while I was in it.

"Out here you've got to be strapped! [Armed with a gun.] Out here, you would rather be caught by the police with your shit [weapon], than to be caught by some niggas without it!

"This stuff out here is so crazy, people don't believe it! But this shit is really happening out here! That's why, when they hear my lyrics, they be like, 'Aw man, he's just talkin' about killing people.' But half of this stuff on my albums is true! It's so real, people think it's fake!

"You know, you come up and you're able to get what you want, maybe a nice car or somethin' like that. But then you can't drive it, because people wanna car-jack you, and the police wanna pull you over all the time. You might as well not even try to be nobody! 'Cause by the time you get your money, everybody's gonna be on your neck so bad, that you ain't even gonna have anything!

"That's where I'm comin' from [with my music] and I don't wanna be no victim. I'm just talkin' about how I feel on my album. I'm not tellin' anybody to buy it, but everybody who buys it, obviously sees the same point of view. If your record sells 500,000 copies in three weeks, then I got to be sayin' somethin'."

Spice 1

GANG STARR

••••••••••••••••••••

Formed in 1986, New York

(GURU, a.k.a Keithy E, a.k.a. Keith E, born Keith Elam, July 17, 1966, Roxbury, Massachusetts; DJ Premier, born Chris Martin, October 4, 1974, Brooklyn, New York. *Original member*: Michael "Mike Dee" Johnson, born in Boston)

Gang Starr is a duo known for their unique traditional musical approach to rap music, with rapper GURU's monotone, bebop-texture delivery, and DJ Premier's true use of record turntables as solo percussion instruments. Because of this, and their dominant choice of jazz-like breaks and beats, music critics have affectionately labeled their music as "jazz-hip hop," but their overall sound is actually between jazz and funk. Gang Starr is also known for maintaining the traditions of hip hop in their live shows by continuing to perform using turntables instead of DATs (Digital Audio Tapes), as many modern groups do.

GURU—Gifted Unlimited Rhymes Universal—attended Morehouse College in Atlanta in the early 1980s, where he obtained a business-management degree. For a brief period he attended New York's Fashion Institute of Technology, and has worked as a juvenile caseworker for a maximum-detention home. (His father is a Boston municipal court judge.) Premier attended Prairie View A&M University in Texas during the same period, where he majored in computer science. He learned to play several instruments, including bass, guitar, drums, and keyboards. While in college, Premier also ran a record store before returning to his native Brooklyn.

Around 1985 GURU met Michael "Mike Dee" Johnson, a DJ and fellow Bostonite. The two formed the first Gang Starr in 1986, and signed a record contract with a minor label. The group worked with DJ Mark the 45 King on two songs before Johnson left the group due to creative differences. He returned to Boston forming the Gang Starr Posse, which later became Posse NFX.

GURU stayed in Brooklyn and in 1988 met DJ Premier through a demo tape played over the phone. The two soon joined creative forces, forming the second Gang Starr, and were eventually signed to Wild Pitch Records. Their single "Manifest," backed with "Here's the Proof," was released in 1988, followed a year later by their album *No More Mr. Nice Guy*, which initially sold 100,000 copies.

By 1990 Gang Starr was on the Chrysalis label, which released their second album, *Step in the Arena*. The singles "Love Sick," "Who's Gonna Take the Weight," "Just to Get a Rep," and the title track all established their distinctive sound to hip hoppers. That same year the duo cut a song for director Spike Lee's film *Mo' Better Blues*, titled "Jazz Thing." (The song was actually inspired by a piece on their first album titled "Jazz Music.") Co-written and performed with saxophonist Branford Marsalis, "Jazz Thing" officially put Gang Starr on the map. They also collaborated with the duo Nice & Smooth on the single "Dwyck."

In 1993 GURU and Premier took on separate projects, with GURU releasing the album *Jazzmatazz Volume 1*, working with legendary jazz musicians Donald Byrd, Roy Ayers, and Lonnie Liston Smith, to great critical acclaim. Premier also developed his own GURU Productions Inc., and produced songs for female rapper Nefertiti. Premier established his Works of Mart Productions company, producing material for Heavy D, Boogie Down Productions, and Nasty Nas.

GURU and Premier—as Gang Starr Productions—have produced several artists, with Premier working on material by Jeru the Damaja, and both GURU and Premier working with Neneh Cherry.

In 1994 Gang Starr released their fourth album, *Hard to Earn*.

Selected albums/CDs: *No More Mr. Nice Guy* (1989, Wild Pitch 98709); *Step in the Arena* (1991, Chrysalis 21798); *Daily Operation* (1992, Chrysalis 21910); *Hard to Earn* (1994, Chrysalis 28435).

Gang Starr

GETO BOYS
■ ■ ■ ■ ■ ■ ■ ■ ■ ■ ■ ■ ■ ■ ■ ■ ■
Formed in 1986, Houston
(Bushwick Bill, formerly Little Billy, born Richard Shaw,
Jamaica, West Indies; Scarface, formerly Ackshen, born
Bradford Jordan; Willie D; Big Mike, born in Louisiana)

The Geto Boys was one of the first groups to work in the so-called gangsta genre of rap. The group itself has had a revolving door of members, but it was the lineup of Bushwick Bill, Scarface, and Willie D that received wide recognition, under the tutelage of their label owner, Rap-A-Lot Records' James Smith.

The group was founded in 1986 by James Smith. A resident of the fifth Ward in Houston, Smith's decision to put together a group was based on his admiration of Run-D.M.C. Original members of the Geto Boys (then, Ghetto Boys) consisted of Jukebox, Raheim, and James's stepbrother, Sir Rap-A-Lot. They released a single, titled "Car Freaks," which received some notice. Around 1987 the group added a dwarf dancer named Little Billy to their stage act, who later became Bushwick Bill. By 1988 the group members were Jukebox, Johnny C, and Ready Red.

After another break in the group, and also the departure of a business partner, James Smith came to New York, where he sought advice from several record-industry people (Rush Management's Lyor Cohen was among them). Smith then went back to Houston, spending his last dollars putting the group back together. He began working with Willie D (whom he knew from the local barbershop) and multi-instrumentalist Ackshen, a.k.a. Scarface. Ready Red and Bushwick Bill remained from earlier versions of the group, with Bill becoming a rapper toward 1989.

In 1990 the group recorded a self-titled album, which was also known by the title *Grip It! On That Other Level*. Def American Recordings's Rick Rubin heard the material and decided to pick it up, collaborating with the group, adding new songs, and remixing others. A single from that work, "Do It Like a G.O.," was also released. However, when Rubin later submitted the entire album to be distributed by Geffen Records, the label's president, Ed Rosenblatt, balked, calling it "the worse thing I ever heard." In addition, Digital Audio Disc Corporation refused to press the album. These problems brought the group immediate media attention. One of the most talked-about songs on the work was "Mind of a Lunatic" (co-written by former group member Jukebox)—a song that contained elements of necrophilia, murder, and other violent acts. Rubin finally settled on Giant Records as the distributor for the album.

Shortly before the group's second album was to come out, Bushwick Bill, in an intoxicated state, forced his girlfriend to shoot him in the head, resulting in the loss of his eye. When the group's second album, *We Can't Be Stopped*, appeared in 1991, the cover featured Bill on a stretcher being rushed down a hospital corridor by Willie D and Scarface, with Bill's empty eye orbit shown in full view. The album went gold by October of that year, and the single off the work, "Mind Playing Tricks on Me," went gold by December of that year. The album went platinum by February 1992.

The group members began to make solo albums in late 1992. Scarface released three albums, 1992's *Mr. Scarface Is Back*, *The World Is Yours* from 1993, and 1994's *The Diary*, featuring Ice Cube; and Bushwick-Bill released an album titled *Little Big Man* and a single, "Ever So Clear" (a pun on the Everclear liquor he reportedly was drinking when he lost his eye). Willie D quit the group due to creative differences, releasing two solo works, *Going Out Lika Soldier* from 1993 and *Play Witcha Mama* from 1994, which also featured Ice Cube and the group SHO.

By mid-1993 the Geto Boys released a fourth album, titled *Till Death Do Us Part*, this time with new member, Big Mike, and then *Makin' Trouble* in 1994.

 Selected singles: "Mind Playing Tricks on Me," (1991, Rap-A-Lot).

 Selected albums/CDs: *Geto Boys*/a.k.a. *Grip It! On That Other Level* (1990, Rap-A-Lot 40451; re-released Def American 24306); *We Can't Be Stopped* (1991, Rap-A-Lot 40364; edited version, 52171)); *Uncut Dope* (1992, Rap-A-Lot 40368; edited version, 57196); *Till Death Do Us Part* (1993, Rap-A-Lot 40372); *Makin' Trouble* (1994, Rap-A-Lot 40453).

GRANDMASTER FLASH AND THE FURIOUS FIVE
Formed c. 1977, Bronx, New York
**(Grandmaster Flash, born Joseph Saddler, January 1957, Bronx, New York;
Cowboy, a.k.a. Keith Keith Cowboy, born Keith Wiggins, September 1960,
New York, died September 8, 1989; Mele Mel, a.k.a. Melle Mel, born Melvin
Glover, c. 1962, New York; Kidd Creole, born Nathaniel "Danny" Glover,
New York; Raheim, born Guy Todd Williams, New York; Mr. Ness,
a.k.a. Scorpio, born Ed Morris, New York)**

Grandmaster Flash is known as one of the three originators of break-beat deejaying, and is responsible for developing and perfecting time precision on the following DJ techniques: cutting (repeating a beat or musical phrase by moving the record back and forth); backspinning (repeating a beat or phrase on a record, by alternately spinning both records backward to the desired beat or phrase; thus, repeating it); and punch-phasing (playing certain parts of a record on one turntable in quick volume surges, while the same record plays on the other turntable).

Flash was the first to debut trick deejaying skills like mixing records behind his back or beneath tables, kicking mixing faders with his feet, and the like. In the late 1980s, he was also the first DJ to develop and market his own mixer, called the Flashformer. His group the Furious Five was a premier group toward the mid-1970s, known for their choreography, studded leather stage wear, and fierce rapping skills. Group member Cowboy was the first MC for Flash, who pioneered phrases like "Throw your hands in the air, and wave 'em like ya just don't care!," "Clap your hands to the beat!," and "Everybody say, ho!," which have become staples in rap and hip-hop culture. He was also the first MC to hype the skills of his

DJ during their parties, with lines like "the pulsating, inflating, disco shaking, heartbreaking man on the turntables . . . ."

Flash's 1981 single "The Adventures of Grandmaster Flash on the Wheels of Steel" was the first record to exemplify hip-hop deejaying skills, and the group's 1982 hit "The Message" was the first serious rap record. Group member Mele Mel was among the most skillful rap lyricists and technicians of his time. He is also responsible for introducing a more phonetically percussive style to MC'ing.

As one of hip hop's pioneer DJs, Flash is responsible for introducing some of the following break records: "Pussyfooter" by Jackie Robinson, "Heaven and Hell" by 20th Century Steel Band, "Johnny the Fox" by Thin Lizzy, and "Walk This Way" by Aerosmith.

Flash grew up in the South Bronx with a wide appreciation of music. He would sneak and raid his father's record collection, and listen to records by Glenn Miller, Frank Sinatra, James Brown, Aretha Franklin, Thin Lizzy, Led Zeppelin, and other varieties of music. He was also fascinated with electronics, and his mother eventually sent him to Samuel Gompers Vocational High School to pursue this interest.

Flash started to take up deejaying in 1974 after seeing Kool DJ Herc play break music. Flash and his then-partner, Mean Gene (DJ Grand Wizard Theodore's older brother), later played for small house parties and in parks in the neighborhood with a homemade sound system. Flash attended other parties and discos, where he came upon Pete DJ Jones, a popular disco DJ for the older crowd. He noticed that Jones knew more about mixing than Kool Herc did, because Jones precued all his records, as opposed to Herc, whose method of mixing was strictly based on how he dropped the needle.

After asking Jones for an opportunity to play on his system several times, Flash found out why Jones's mixing was perfect. By listening through Jones's headphones, he discovered that a toggle switch allowed him to hear the other turntable before playing it to the crowd. Thereafter, Flash found and devised his own switching system for his sound equipment, and soon began perfecting his timing in break-beat deejaying.

Around 1975 Flash began to apply what he called "the clock theory" to deejaying, where he began to read records by finding a particular spot on the record label (like the label's logo) to enable him to quickly find certain sections on a record. Mean Gene's baby brother, Theodore, began hanging out with Flash around this time and later became Flash's record boy.

Because Flash's deejaying skills at his parties captivated his crowd so much that it hindered them from dancing, he began to assemble a group of MCs to keep the crowd going. Cowboy was his first choice for MC. Mele Mel was the second MC he chose, with Mel's brother, Kidd Creole, being the third. They then were billed as Grandmaster Flash and the 3 MCs. Later Flash would use a Vox drum machine with the group, billing themselves as Grandmaster Flash and the 3 MCs with the Beat Box.

Toward 1976 Flash was approached by ex-policeman and promoter Ray Chandler in St. Ann's Park in the Bronx, who suggested to Flash that he establish a regular spot for his parties. Chandler found a place on Boston Road and 169th Street; the small club had a painted black door, and the two decided to christen the spot in promotions as the Black Door. Later, due to scattered problems by stick-up kids who attended Flash's parties, Chandler decided to hire security for the spot. He hired some former members of the Black Spades street gang, known as the Casanova Crew, led by crew member Tiny.

Within a few months the popularity of Flash's parties forced him to seek larger venues. By September 1976 Flash was playing the Audubon Ballroom to a crowd of nearly 3,000, where he performed many of his familiar tricks, plus added new ones, like dropping the needle on records directly on the beat, on time, without cuing.

Flash, Cowboy, Mele Mel, Kidd Creole, and added member Scorpio (then known as Mr. Ness) appeared in several other venues like the Renaissance and the Savoy Manner as Grandmaster Flash and the Furious Four. By 1977 the Furious Four split with Flash's manager/promoter, Ray Chandler, due to various differences, while Flash continued working minus his MCs. Around this same period DJ and MC battles were frequently occurring in the Bronx. Flash was involved in several notable ones, including challenging DJ Tex and Afrika Bambaataa, where Flash retaliated with an army of sound systems.

Flash began deejaying for Kurtis Blow, and the two would later perform together at various P.A.L. venues in the Bronx. During summer 1978 Cowboy, Mele Mel, Creole, and Scorpio were working with DJ Charlie Chase. By the end of 1978 Flash and his former MCs (with Scorpio) had reunited and resumed doing shows together. Around this same period they took part in a notable battle with Busy Bee Starski, Grand Wizard Theodore, and Afrika Bambaataa. Some time later the group's most famous and intense battles would be with DJ Breakout and the Funky Four.

By 1979 Flash was approached by legendary record producer/store owner Bobby Robinson of Enjoy Records, who wanted to record Flash and the group. During this same period Cowboy, Mele Mel, Kidd Creole, Scorpio, and former Funky Four member Raheim had recorded a record for Brass Records called "We Rap More Mellow" under an assumed name, the Younger Generation.

Soon after, Flash and the Furious Five (with Raheim now a member) began recording for Robinson, with their first 12-inch single for the label being "Superappin'." Disappointed with Robinson's inability to get them on radio, the group soon signed with Sylvia Robinson's Sugar Hill Records, on the strength of her promise to get them to perform on the backing track of a record that was a DJ favorite at the time, titled "Get Up and Dance," by the group Freedom. Flash and the Furious's first record for Sugar Hill was, in fact, titled "Freedom," and was a hit with the hip-hop crowd. During that same year the group recorded the song "Birthday Party."

By 1981 the landmark "Adventures of Grandmaster Flash on the Wheels of Steel" was released. This single gave people the first recorded example of Flash's wizardry on the turntables, and it was the first record of its kind. During this same period Flash and the Furious Five went on a European tour, where they opened some shows for the punk rock group the Clash. They were received poorly by Clash audiences in some venues, while in others they received moderate responses.

In 1982 the group had released another landmark recording called "The Message," a social commentary that was also unique for its "Don't push me, 'cause I'm close to the edge" chorus hook, which expressed urban frustration. Sugar Hill Records' house band percussionist, Ed "Duke Bootee" Fletcher, was one of the main architects behind the work, with Mele Mel's performances making the piece one of hip hop's true classics. That same year Grandmaster Flash made an appearance in the hip-hop movie *Wild Style*.

In 1983 Flash felt there was a conflict of interest with Sugar Hill Records' co-owner Sylvia Robinson managing and producing Flash and the Furious, as well as owning half the label they were recording for. Flash sued Sugar Hill Records for $5 million. Thereafter, the courts ruled that Flash had the right to keep the use of his name, "Grandmaster Flash," but was not entitled to a financial settlement. The lawsuit caused another riff within the group with the Furious splitting down the middle, with Mele Mel, Scorpio, and Cowboy forming one faction, and Mel's brother Creole, Raheim, and Flash forming the other.

Mele Mel, Cowboy, and Scorpio continued to record for Sugar Hill Records. The single "White Lines (Don't Do It)," which was released around 1984, was billed as Grandmaster & Mele Mel. Later Mel and the others did three albums for the label, billed as Grandmaster Mele Mel and the Furious Five, with King Lou, Grandmaster E-Z Mike, Dynamite, Tommy Gunn, and Kami Kaze making up the remainder of the group. Mele Mel also did some cameo work during this same period, appearing on singer Chaka Khan's single "I Feel for You." During 1986, Mele Mel worked with promoter Van Silk on the WNBC-TV antidrug commercial in New York, which won an Emmy.

Flash signed with Elektra Records, working with Raheim and Kidd Creole, along with additional crew members, including Mr. Broadway, Lavon, Shame, and Larry Love. In 1985 this configuration scored big with the piece, "Larry's Dance Theme."

After several albums from both Furious Five factions, the original Furious Five reformed again around 1988, recording the album *On the Strength*. However, by September 1989 Flash's first MC, Cowboy, had died, and the group members had separated again to pursue individual projects. Mele Mel worked with Quincy Jones on his *Back on the Block* album, while Flash began to get into production, working with Roxanne Shanté, Essence (who appeared on the soundtrack of the film *New Jack City*), Color Me Badd, and others.

In 1994 Flash and the four remaining Furious members had united again for a few months, this time on radio, doing the *Mic Check Show* on New York's Hot-97 FM.

 Selected singles: "Freedom" (1980, Sugar Hill); "The Adventures of Grandmaster Flash on the Wheels of Steel" (1981); "The Message" (1982).

 Selected CDs/albums: *The Message* (1982, Sugarhill 1007); *Greatest Messages* (1984, Sugarhill 5552); *They Said It Couldn't Be Done* (1985, Elektra 960389); *The Source* (1986, Elektra 960476); *On the Strength* (1988, Elektra 960769); *The Message from Beat Street: The Best Of* (1994, Rhino 71606).

GRANDMIXER D.ST
(Born Derek Showard, New York City)

Grandmixer D.ST was a dynamic hip-hop DJ who was proficient in the art of scratching and other elements of hip-hop culture, including b-boying. He is known through his work in the late 1970s and early 1980s with Afrika Bambaataa at his Zulu Nation gatherings and parties, and he is also recognized for the work he did with his MCs, called the Infinity Rappers (a.k.a. Infinity Machine).

Along with Infinity Machine's reputation for a powerful sound system, D.ST was also known for the tricks he displayed while deejaying, some of which included leaping on the floor, breakdancing, then jumping back up and mixing records with his foot (kicking the mixer). D.ST's timing on the turntables was also precise. In 1983 he got a chance to display his skills to a wider audience when he worked with jazz artist Herbie Hancock on Bill Laswell's production of the piece "Rockit," which was a major hit. D.ST also appeared in the 1983 hip-hop film *Wild Style*, and worked with Laswell again at Celluloid Records, where he would make approximately five recordings with the Infinity Rappers, including "Grandmixer Cuts It Up."

A drummer and keyboardist, D.ST originally got into deejaying after seeing Kool Herc perform at one of his parties. He soon became one of the Zulu Kings with Jazzy Jay, Afrika Islam, Pow Wow, and others. By 1978 D.ST was also deejaying for Afrika Bambaataa. It was Bambaataa who later brought D.ST and other members of the Zulu Nation downtown to the Manhattan club the Roxy, where D.ST met Herbie Hancock in the V.I.P. section of the club, thus initiating their future collaboration.

Toward the mid-1980s D.ST also got into production, working on Lovebug Starski's 1986—87 *House Rock*. In 1994 he did production work on rapper King Tee's *IV Life* album.

GRANDMIXER MUGGS

See DJ MIXMASTER MUGGS

GRAND PUBA
a.k.a. Grand Puba Maxwell
(Born Maxwell Dixon, New Rochelle, New York)

Grand Puba is an MC and producer who is known for his distinctive husky toned, medium-high vocal delivery, sometimes flavored with reggae tinges, and lyrics drawn from the lessons of the Five Percent Nation of Islam. He is one of the most recognized personalities in hip hop, achieving that fame mostly as a member of two groups: Masters of Ceremony (one of the first groups to combine DJ-style reggae with rap) and Brand Nubian.

Puba's father was a Muslim who raised his son on the principles of the Five Percent. The teaching stayed with him, and by the early 1980s Puba was also getting into hip-hop culture. After hearing Harlem World and T-Connection tapes of the Cold Crush Brothers and DJ Breakout, Puba decided to try his hand at making tapes and writing rhymes in his home.

Later, with his cousin, known as Dr. Who, Puba formed the group Masters of Ceremony. They were signed to Jazzy Jay and Rocky Bucano's label, Strong City Records (formerly Emlo Records); their first single was a song titled "Crime" (with music by Teddy Riley), circa 1986. The group made two other singles, "Cracked Out" and "Sexy," both of which became popular in underground circles.

In 1988 Masters of Ceremony broke up and Puba began producing, hooking up with a couple of friends from his neighborhood known as Lord Jamar and Derek X, who later changed his name to Sadat X. Puba originally had tried to get the duo record deals, but later they decided that they would work together as a threesome, and the group became Brand Nubian. Puba brought his group to the attention of former Tommy Boy Records' A&R and Stimulated Dummies (SD-50's) producer Dante Ross, who had just arrived at an A&R position at Elektra Records. Ross had known Puba and his work before, so when he heard the group he signed them.

The group's *One for All* was released in 1990 and became an underground classic. However, within a year of the release of that album, Brand Nubian broke up, due to creative differences between Puba and group members.

Puba's first solo work, titled *Reel to Reel*, was released in 1992. He continued to do cameo performances on other artists' work, like HEAVY D, the Brand New Heavies, and Mary J. Blige, as well as production and remix work. In 1995 he began doing commercials for Sprite soda.

 Selected albums/CDs: *Reel to Reel* (1992, Elektra 61314).

GRAND WIZARD THEODORE AND THE FANTASTIC 5 MCS

Formerly the Fantastic 4
a.k.a. the Fantastic Freaks, Fantastic Romantics, the Fantastics
Formed c. 1980, Bronx, New York
(Grand Wizard Theodore; Rubie Dee; Water Bed Kevie Kev; Prince Whipper Whip; Dot-A-Roc; Master Rob: all born in Bronx, New York)

Directly from his work with the L Brothers, Grand Wizard Theodore headed the Fantastic 5 MCs during the early 1980s. Along with MCs Water Bed Kevie Kev and Master Rob (who also had previously worked with the L Brothers), Theodore (known for his introduction of the technique, scratching) and his group continued to be a formidable force in hip hop, and were known for their battles with the Cold Crush Brothers.

Theodore and group members Kevie Kev, Master Rob, Rubie Dee, Dot-A-Roc, and Prince Whipper Whip (who had worked with DJ Charlie Chase and the Cold Crush Brothers for a three-week period around 1978) also made an impressive appearance in the 1982 hip-hop movie classic *Wild Style*.

The group later recorded for Tuff City Records, recording works like "Can I Get a Soul Clap, Fresh Out the Pack" for the label. As the group's popularity began to subside during the mid-1980s, Kevie Kev began recording for Sugar Hill Records, recording "All Night Long" for the label. Toward the late 1980s Grand Wizard Theodore was signed to Jazzy Jay's Strong City label.

By 1994 the group came back together to work with Terminator X on his *Terminator X and the Godfathers of Threatt* album.

Gang banger: Member or follower of a gang.

Gangsta: A style of rap that focuses on, and uses images from, the criminal side of life. The term was applied by media experts outside of hip-hop culture. Gangsta-style rap was later associated with the group N.W.A.

Go Go: A style of dance music, practiced in Washington, DC, combining rap, hip hop, and funk popular in the early 1980s.

Griot: West African storyteller who usually accompanies himself with a harp-like instrument known as a kora. Griots specialize in long, rhymed, half-sung, half-spoken narratives, often telling the stories of tribal leaders or myths of early tribal life.

Groove: The rhythm or beat underlying a recording. More specifically, the bass and drum parts that are played together throughout a song.

MC REN: ON ISLAM AND GANGSTA RAP

When you pick up former N.W.A member MC Ren's *Shock of the Hour* the biggest shock will probably be when you open it up and discover that the man has become a Muslim, giving praises to the Honorable Elijah Muhammad and Louis Farrakhan on the cover. Ren is best known for his association with the famed gangsta-rap group, not for his spiritual stance. How'd that come about?

"About a year and a half ago," explains Ren, "a guy by the name of DJ Train used to give me tapes and books, and I just started reading and studying. Everything just clicked. We're [black people] Muslim by nature anyway, but somebody took it away from us and made us something else.

"I drop a little of this on my record. I can't preach to nobody, but I'm speaking the language of my people, 'cause my homies speak like that on the street."

Concerning this whole "gangsta rap" media blitz of late, Ren says, "Today it ain't nothin' really to listen to. The media labeled this, 'gangsta rap.' And after the success we [N.W.A.] had, and Ice-T, Ice Cube, KRS-One, P.E. [Public Enemy] and all that, I see it as hardcore. But the media labeled it, 'gangsta rap.'

N.W.A

"So they got all these brothers coming in record companies sayin', 'We're gangsta rappers,' and all these wack old A&R people, that don't know nothing about rap music, are signing these groups.

"And then they go flood the market with all these so-called gangsta rappers that's talkin' about the same thing—not trying to be creative—and it's killing the music (rap).

"And then they put all the artists that came out before them, and label them with these groups. It gives all of us a bad name. 'Cause I ain't never called myself a gangsta rapper! That's the media! The real gangstas are the Mafia!

"This whole thing is just killing rap. And if rap keeps going like it is with all these wack A&R people signing all these groups, rap is gonna die out. It's gonna deteriorate. 'Cause it makes you not wanna rap anymore.

"Everyday a new rapper comes out. They label him a gangsta rapper. And they be in the videos with a million guns. In the pictures and the magazines everybody's got a gun, everybody's wearing the same clothes. They've commercialized it.

"We need A&R's from the street that know what time it is. We have to start all over again. We have to get people from the street, like Def Jam Recordings was from the street. So many major labels have gotten into this. And they just look at it as a money thing. They look at it like, 'Man, he's from the streets. He's black. Let's make money off him.' It's just an auction block."

HAMMER
•••••••••••••
a.k.a. MC Hammer
(Born Stanley Kirk Burrell, March 30, 1963, East Oakland, California)

Hammer is the first internationally known rap star, with worldwide crossover appeal. He is the first rapper to be known and liked by both young and old audiences outside hip-hop culture, crossing international racial barriers. Lampooned for his limited rapping skills and glitzy appearance by traditional hip hoppers, Hammer's focus originally had been on positive-oriented rhymes and stage shows, with relentless nonstop dance moves, backed by a multitude of performers behind him, equally energetic, and in some cases, acrobatic. His second album, *Please Hammer Don't Hurt 'Em*, dominated *Billboard*'s pop music chart for a total of twenty-one weeks, and its black LP chart for twenty-nine weeks (surpassing Michael Jackson's stay on that chart with his *Thriller* LP), and firmly placed the rapper on the map.

Born one of six children in East Oakland, California, Hammer's other interests besides dancing included baseball. At age 11, he used to take his dancing skills (James Brown splits and the like) to the Oakland Stadium parking lot, performing for complimentary tickets from the Oakland Athletics. Then Athletics owner Charlie Finley finally noticed him, and eventually gave him a job in the front office as a batboy. Two baseball players took an early interest in him: Milwaukee Brewer Pedro Garcia said that Hammer resembled homerun king "Hammerin'" Hank Aaron, and Reggie Jackson began calling him "Hammer" because of that. The nickname stuck. Hammer worked for the Athletics for several years. Later he tried out for the San Francisco Giants but did not make the final cut.

After taking a few college courses Hammer joined the U.S. Navy for three years. When he came home for good he began to concentrate on his musical career. His first move was to become a religious MC, calling himself the Holy Ghost Boy. By the mid-1980s he began to perform at various Oakland clubs, rapping and dancing over music tracks, and locally making a name for himself.

He next received a loan from two Athletics outfielders, Dwayne Murphy and Mike Davis.

With that, Hammer launched Bustin' Records. His first record was titled "Ring 'Em," which was recorded in his basement. Selling 12-inch copies of the single from the trunk of his car, it became number 1 in the San Francisco Bay area. Subsequently, he produced his first album, *Feel My Power*, which sold 50,000 copies. This led to his being signed to Capitol Records in 1988.

His first album for the label, *Let's Get It Started*, went double-platinum, but it was his 1990 *Please Hammer Don't Hurt 'Em* LP that gave him worldwide recognition. It became the third rap album to hit number 1 on the pop charts (behind the Beastie Boys's 1986 *Licensed to Ill* and Tone-Löc's *Loc-ed After Dark*). The album won three Grammys and three "Soul Train" Awards and many other honors. Hammer's performance of the single from the album, "U Can't Touch This," on the "Arsenio Hall Show" helped boost record sales even further. Videos for that song and many others began to receive awards for their state-of-the-art production, and are noted for Hammer's elaborate dance moves that combine the best elements of James Brown and b-boying.

With the success of that album, Hammer began to launch a cottage industry. His own label, Bust It, headed by his brother/manager, Louis K. Burrell, and distributed by Capitol Records, launched the careers of Oaktown's 3.5.7, Angie B., and Special Generation. His management/production company at one time oversaw the careers of Heavy D & The Boyz, Troop, and Ralph Tresvant, among others. He has had a merchandising deal with the Mattel toy company, which introduced two Hammer dolls. He got into the Saturday morning cartoon market also, with the ABC-TV show titled *Hammerman*. He has done numerous TV commercials for Taco Bell, British Knights, and Pepsi.

Hammer

His Bust It label released a soundtrack album for the movie *Rocky V*. His song "This Is What We Do" is featured in the film *Teenage Mutant Ninja Turtles*, as are several of his songs in the motion picture *The Addams Family*. Hammer has garnered acclaim for his home videos, with "Hammer Time" receiving gold status, and both "Here Comes the Hammer" and "Please Hammer Don't Hurt 'Em" going platinum. He also began raising prize-winning racehorses, co-founding the Oaktown Stables, with his brother Louis.

His third album, *Too Legit to Quit*, was released in 1991. It was touted as being a "95% original" album by the artist: Hammer was critiquing hip hop's normal use of sampling, and highlighting his own reliance on live vocalists and musicians instead. The album peaked at number 9 on *Billboard*'s Top 200 Albums chart and went multiplatinum in 1992.

Hammer dismantled Bust It's record and management division in 1993 and turned to boxing management, taking on Evander Holyfield as one of his first clients. In 1994 he was signed to Giant Records, where he released the album *The Funky Headhunter*. "Pumps and a Bump" and "It's All Good" were the singles released off the work. However, it was less commercially successful than his previous albums.

 Selected singles: "Turn This Mutha Out" (1988, Capitol); "U Can't Touch This" (1990).

 Selected albums/CDs: *Let's Get It Started* (1988, Capitol 90924); *Please Hammer Don't Hurt 'Em* (1990, Capitol 92857); *Too Legit to Quit* (1991, Capitol 98151); *The Funky Headhunter* (1994, Giant 24545).

HANK SHOCKLEE
(Born Hank Boxley, Roosevelt, Long Island)

Producer Hank Shocklee is known as the principal musical architect of the group Public Enemy. With his use of noise combined with a multitude of samples, sometimes totaling as many as forty-eight tracks per song, Shocklee brought a new style to rap production based on hip hop, punk, and rock.

Shocklee started his music career as a DJ, heading a party-promotion crew during the early 1980s called Spectrum City, which also included his brother, Keith Shocklee, and Carlton Ridenhour (Chuck D/Carl Ryder), among others. Spectrum City ran a local nightclub, as well as doing mix shows on college radio station WBAU at Adelphi University, through Bill Stephney, a musician and program director at the station. Stephney was acquainted with Chuck D and Shocklee, and offered them a three-hour slot, in which they did live rap mixes, master mixes, and aired demos of local rap groups.

At the radio station Shocklee and the other Spectrum City members discovered multi-track recording and experimented with 4-track tape machines, where they combined tracks of separate deejaying performances and layered them onto single tracks. Soon after, Shocklee and the others began to record demos. "Check Out the Radio" and "Public Enemy Number One" were some of the pieces they did under their Spectrum City moniker. The latter song also featured a regular on their radio show, MC DJ Flavor Flav. In 1985 Shocklee also worked

Hank Shocklee

on a Long Island cable video show with Stephney and Chuck D called "W.O.R.D.: The World of Rock and Dance."

During 1986 Bill Stephney (who by this time was working at Def Jam Recordings) was asked by Def Jam's co-owner Rick Rubin to sign Chuck D to the label based on the "Public Enemy Number One" demo he had heard some time earlier. Because of Chuck D's initial reluctance to make rap records unless he had something significant to say, Shocklee and Stephney worked on the idea of creating a rap group with Chuck D that had a political edge, which became Public Enemy: Chuck performed with Flavor Flav, Shocklee worked with Chuck as co-producer and arranger on the group's first album, while Stephney headed the production. In 1987 the group's debut album was released, titled *Yo! Bum Rush the Show*. Here, the production was noticeable, due to the rhythmic use of noise and unusual sound textures, particularly on "Side F." The album created a positive buzz for the group on the streets.

When Public Enemy's second album was released in 1988, titled *It Takes a Nation of Millions to Hold Us Back*, Hank Shocklee's production skills came more to the forefront, with Chuck, Eric "Vietnam" Sadler, and Hank's brother, Keith Shocklee, working as co-producers. More noise elements over traditional hip-hop break beats were used, as well as a wide array of samples and multitrack layering. The album went gold during that year. Shocklee also produced half of rapper Slick Rick's album *The Great Adventures of Slick Rick* in that same year, with Eric Sadler.

In 1989 Public Enemy performed the title song for film director Spike Lee's movie *Do the Right Thing*. This song showed an increased amount of the production techniques Hank Shocklee used on the last Public Enemy album. Around this time Shocklee and his co-production team began calling themselves the Bomb Squad.

Later that year Shocklee and Bill Stephney (who had left Def Jam Recordings) started their own label, called SOUL: The Sound Of Urban Listeners, to be distributed by MCA. SOUL Records' first act was one of Shocklee's initial brainchilds, a group of white rappers called the Young Black Teenagers. However, they received a lot of criticism from the black community, and in some white circles as well, for what was perceived as the group's opportunism and insincerity.

Shocklee's second act was called Son of Bazerk, a wild four-man, one-woman, suit-and-tie group, which featured Bazerk, a friend of Flavor Flav's, who also made appearances on Spectrum City's radio show. Bazerk is described by Shocklee as Chuck D's ultramaterialistic alter ego with no messages. The third act was Raheim, a singer and rapper, who was billed by Shocklee as an artist who dealt with the problems between black men and women in his songs.

In 1990 Shocklee and the Bomb Squad produced Public Enemy's *Fear of a Black Planet*, which went platinum that same year. During this period, Shocklee was also approached by then-recently resigned N.W.A member Ice Cube. Shocklee and the Bomb Squad produced Cube's *AmeriKKKa's Most Wanted* album with Ice Cube's Lench Mob. The album went gold that year. Around this same period Shocklee and the Bomb Squad began producing other acts, like 3rd Bass, LL Cool J, and Bell Biv DeVoe, and started doing mixes for Sinead O'Connor and Paula Abdul as well.

In 1991 Shocklee's *Son of Bazerk* self-titled album was released and received critical praise. This Bomb Squad production featured even more samples than the Public Enemy projects, coming from a variety of funk, soul, and rock records, with many multilayered tracks, stereo panoramic effects, and occasional short atonal vocal lines from the Son of Bazerk group. The Young Black Teenagers' debut album was also released that year, with Shocklee expanding experimentation by recording car horns and ice-filled glasses of water sound effects to impressive results. Shocklee and the Bomb Squad also began working on the original score for Ernest R. Dickerson's movie *Juice*. That same year Shocklee and the Bomb Squad took a back seat as executive producers for Public Enemy's platinum selling *Apocalypse 91 . . . The Enemy Strikes Black* album.

Around 1992 Bill Stephney left SOUL Records to start his own label. During this period Shocklee and the Bomb Squad executive produced Public Enemy's *Greatest Misses* album, which went gold that same year. Toward the latter half of 1992 into 1993 Shocklee executive-produced the Young Black Teenagers' (billed now as YBT) *Dead Enz Kidz Doin' Lifetime Bidz* album. During 1993 Hank and his brother Keith established the production firm of Shocklee Entertainment, which merged with Hank's own SOUL Records.

Selected produced albums/CDs: *Yo! Bum Rush the Show* by Public Enemy (1987, Def Jam/Columbia 40658); *It Takes a Nation of Millions To Hold Us Back* (1988, Def Jam/Columbia 44303); *Fear of a Black Planet* (1990, Def Jam/Columbia 45413); *Son of Bazerk featuring No Self Control and the Band* (1991).

HEATHER B

* * * * * * * * * * * * * * * *

(Born Heather Gardner, November 13, Jersey City, New Jersey)

Rapper/actress Heather B is best known for appearing in MTV's "The Real World" series in the early 1990s.

Heather began to receive attention in 1992, when she started working with Boogie Down Productions on their *Sex & Violence* album, and appeared on their "Seven DJs" piece. She also released her own "I Get Wreck" single on the Elektra label, and appeared on MTV's "The Real World." Between 1993 and 1995 she opened a hair salon called Nubian Nails & Hair. From 1994 to 1995 she recorded a demo on a DAT cassette called "All Glocks Down" (Glock is the manufacturer of a popular 9-millimeter automatic weapon). DJ/producer Evil Dee from the group Black Moon heard it and played the song on radio station HOT 97 in New York City to favorable responses. Heather then pressed up 300 copies of the work, after which the song was licensed by the Pendulum label. In 1995 she recorded "No Doubt (Get Hardcore)," and appeared in the motion picture *Dead Presidents*.

 Selected singles: "I Get Wreck" (1992, Elektra); "All Glocks Down" (1995, Pendulum).

HEAVY D & THE BOYZ

* *

Formed c. 1986, Mount Vernon, New York
(Heavy D, born Dwight Myers, May 24, 1967, Jamaica, West Indies;
Trouble T-Roy, born Troy Dixon, mid- to late-1960s, died July 1990;
DJ Eddie F, born Edward Ferrell II, New York)

Heavy D gained his name for his 6'4" height and 260-pound girth. Musically, his early work is noted for its use of New Jack Swing music arrangements by producer Teddy Riley, while his complete work is usually filled with R&B vocal textures, complete with an MC style that is phonetic and funk oriented. He also occasionally performs in the dance hall genre of reggae, with artists like Supercat and Frankie Paul.

Heavy was partially raised in the Bronx, New York, before moving with his family to Mount Vernon, New York. It was in the Bronx that he first heard rap and started to perform it at the age of 8. He continued to perfect his rapping by freestyling, and he soon began working with his high-school friend Eddie F, writing rhymes and working on poetry. During a trip to Atlantic City Heavy won $1,500 in a slot machine, enabling him to buy a drum machine, and to work on music more extensively.

Heavy eventually signed with Andre Harrell's Uptown Records, where he first appeared on the label's compilation album *Uptown Is Kickin' It*. Heavy's single "Mr. Big Stuff" put him on the map with hip hoppers. Teddy Riley's drum machine rolls and beat programming, along with producer Marley Marl's mixing in of the Jean Knight record of the same name, went well with Heavy's MC style.

In 1987 Heavy's first album, *Livin' Large*, was released, with Riley contributing some production work. Two years later Heavy's second album followed, titled *Big Tyme*, with the song "We Got Our Own Thang" one of its popular singles. The work went platinum that same year. Around this same period Heavy began doing cameo work, notably on R&B group LeVert's single "Just Coolin'."

In 1990 Heavy's best friend and group member Trouble T-Roy died in a freak accident while the group was on tour. In 1991 Heavy's *Peaceful Journey* album was released in T-Roy's memory. The album and single "Now That We Found Love" went gold that same year, and the album was platinum by March 1992. Heavy also began doing commercials for Sprite soda, and changed his management from Andre Harrell's Uptown Management to Hammer's Bust It Productions. Heavy's next two albums, released in 1993 and 1994, both went gold.

 Selected albums/CDs: *Livin' Large* (1987, MCA/Uptown 5986); *Big Tyme* (1989, MCA/Uptown 42302); *Peaceful Journey* (1991, MCA/Uptown 10289); *Blue Funk* (1993, MCA/Uptown 10734); *Nuttin' but Love* (1994, MCA/Uptown 10998).

Heavy D & The Boyz

HOOUSE OF PAIN

Formed in 1990, Los Angeles
(Everlast, born Erik Schrody; Danny Boy, born Danny
O'Connor; DJ Lethal, born Leor DiMant, Latvia)

House of Pain, which consists of two Irish-American rappers and a Latvian-born DJ, brought Irish pride lyrics to rap, in the same manner that African-American rappers brought African pride lyrics to their songs. Their first single was well received by the hip-hop audience and in pop circles as well.

The group's two Irish members, Everlast and Danny Boy, met while they were attending Los Angeles's Taft High School. Everlast was formerly with Ice-T's Rhyme Syndicate, which released a solo album by the MC. DJ Lethal had worked with Everlast on his first album. Danny Boy had led a punk group with the "House of Pain" name, that Everlast said came from a Bela Lugosi movie titled *Island of Lost Souls*; the trio borrowed the name for their new rap group.

The group signed with Tommy Boy Records, which released their single "Jump Around" in 1992. Their self-titled album (produced by DJ Grandmixer Muggs and Lethal) later followed, and before the year was out, both the single and the album went platinum. In 1994 the group released the album *Same as It Ever Was*.

 Selected singles: "Jump Around" (1992, Tommy Boy).

 Selected albums/CDs: *House of Pain* (1992, Tommy Boy 1056); *Same as It Ever Was* (1994, Tommy Boy).

House of Pain

HOWIE TEE

(Born Richard Thompson, Jamaica, West Indies)

"Hitman" Howie Tee, as he is known, gained wide recognition as a producer from his work with his cousin Chubb Rock, Special Ed, and Real Roxanne. He is also known for producing the demo for the group UTFO's "Roxanne, Roxanne," one of the most imitated and answered songs in rap.

Raised in Birmington, England, and East Flatbush, Brooklyn, Howie originally became infatuated with his father's record collection when he was a child. When he got older, he learned to repair turntables, and later became a DJ. Around 1983 Howie met Peter B. Allen at Manhattan's Rock & Soul Records store. A manager of acts, Allen was trying to get an opinion from Howie concerning one of his act's songs. When Howie told Allen that he wasn't impressed with the material, Allen asked him if he had better material, to which Howie replied that he did, even though he didn't. Howie then quickly put together a group, calling it CD III. They recorded a song called "Get Tough," and presented it to Allen. Impressed with the work, Allen underwrote a professional studio recording of the piece, which was released on Prelude Records, and it became popular on New York radio stations WBLS and KISS-FM.

Howie soon began working with a crew of b-boys by the name of UTFO. With group member Kangol, Howie recorded the drum tracks for the song "Roxanne, Roxanne" in his basement studio at his parent's home, but when it came time to record the piece in another studio, Howie (who was involved with other projects) handed the work over to neighborhood producers Full Force, whose version became a significant hit. When an actual Roxanne was needed to respond to Roxanne Shanté's recorded retort to the record, Full Force developed the "Real Roxanne" using JoAnne Martinez, and made Howie Tee her DJ in the late 1980s. After touring with Real Roxanne, Howie was able to buy more studio equipment and get into full-fledged productions. He worked with Full Force on their "Alice, I Want You Just for Me" single, and also worked with more East Flatbush acts like Whistle (who sang and rapped).

In 1988 Howie produced Chubb Rock's first album, *Chubb Rock Featuring Howie Tee*. By 1989, however, two albums put his production skills on the map: Chubb Rock's *And the Winner Is . . .* and *Youngest in Charge*, by another East Flatbush neighbor named Special Ed. Throughout the early 1990s Howie continued to work with Chubb and Ed. He also expanded to R&B, producing songs for Color Me Bad and other acts.

Selected produced albums/CDs: *And the Winner Is . . .* by Chubb Rock (1989, Select 21631); *Youngest in Charge* by Special Ed (1989, Profile 1280).

HURBY LUV BUG AZOR

(Born Hurby Azor, Queens, New York)

Hurby Luv Bug Azor is a producer with many gold and platinum records to his credit, who is recognized for his groundbreaking work with artists Salt-N-Pepa, Kid 'N Play,

Antoinette, and Sweet Tee. He has also worked with Dana Dane, Kwame, Joeski Love, Super DJ Clark Kent, and producer Steevee-O and his production crew, the Invincibles. Azor's production style gradually developed into a genre of rap that fits between pop/crossover and smooth electrofunk R&B. His initial work with Salt-N-Pepa on the single "The Showstopper" and their following album, *Hot, Cool & Vicious*, helped set the group on the road to success, along with their producer.

Azor attended the Center of Media Arts in Manhattan and worked at a Sears department store along with Salt-N-Pepa. He taped Salt-N-Pepa doing a song called "The Showstopper," which was an answer record to Doug E. Fresh and Slick Rick's piece "The Show" for a school project. Afterward Azor decided to give the song to producer Marley Marl. Marl liked the work enough to let Lawrence and Dana Goodman (owners of Philadelphia's Pop Art Records) hear the piece, and they decided to press it into a record.

After initiating the careers of Salt-N-Pepa and Kid 'N Play (Play was originally in one of Azor's high school groups, the Super Lovers) Azor developed Idol Makers Management and Idol Makers Films, where he placed many of the acts he worked with under his management. He also began working with film and video director Millicent Shelton on video projects for his acts.

Howie Tee

Hurby Azor

Hardcore: A style of rap that contains rhymes with more earthy lyrics that focus on sex and violence, and/or music with more grittier production textures and stronger beats within drum patterns.

Heavy metal: A style of rock 'n' roll characterized by loud volume, basic chord progressions, flamboyant stage shows, and lyrics emphasizing sex, drugs, and violence.

Hip hop: The culture of breakdancing (also known as b-boying), graffiti art and tagging (the practitioners of which were originally called writers), and rap music. Hip hop is frequently used interchangeably with the word "rap" to describe the music.

Homeboy: Person from your neighborhood; friend; compatriot.

Hook: The most memorable part of a melody, which "hooks" the listener.

House: A style of disco music that emerged in the early 1980s, favored by black gay party goers in New York City clubs like the Loft, but made popular in Chicago in clubs like the Warehouse, where the term first emerged. This electronically played music is characterized by its rhythm section, which emphasizes the drum machine's kick and high-hat parts. The songs are accompanied by minimal instrumentation, often produced in bursts of sound.

ICE CUBE

(Born Oshea Jackson, June 15, 1969, Los Angeles)

Ice Cube was a member of and the principal writer for the group N.W.A., recognized for his work on their *Straight Outta Compton* album. He achieved even wider success after leaving the group, embarking on a solo career. Cube's subject matter in his rhymes with N.W.A. centered on street values in the Los Angeles neighborhood of Compton, and it put that area on the map with hip hoppers in and outside the United States. After he left the group, however, Ice Cube's subject matter became more sociopolitical, leaning toward the teachings of the Nation of Islam. Ice Cube also received favorable notices for his acting role of Doughboy in director John Singleton's 1991 film, *Boyz N the Hood*.

Ice Cube is recognized as one of the most skillful rhyme writers of his time. A great deal of his lyrics are visual, and resemble minimovies in structure. His overall technique involves putting many images into his rhymes. Cube started writing rhymes when he was in the ninth grade. Around 1984—85, Cube and his friend Sir Jinx began taping his rhymes, and later, as he got better, he MC'ed at various local parties and skating rinks. He later entered an MC battle that a radio station was holding at the Hollywood Palladium, and wound up being one of the finalists at the event. Sir Jinx's cousin, Dr. Dre (a DJ at a local club at that time), heard one of Cube's tapes and asked him to perform with him at one of his club shows. Dre suggested to Cube that a parody of a song that everyone would know would be a good choice to perform before a crowd. Cube chose to parody UTFO's 1984 "Roxanne, Roxanne" for Dre's audience. The song he did was called "Diane, Diane," and it went over big.

Cube soon met former drug dealer Eazy-E through Dr. Dre. Eazy was interested in making records, and had started a record label called Ruthless Records. For one of the groups he signed to the label, Ice Cube and Dr. Dre wrote a song about street life in Compton titled "Boyz N the Hood," which Eazy wound up doing himself. Later Ice Cube, Dr. Dre, and Eazy-E decided to form a group, along with Dre's friend Yella. They called themselves Niggas with Attitude, or N.W.A. Ice Cube wrote two more songs, this time for N.W.A, "8 Ball" and "Dope-

Ice Cube

man." Both songs focused on the same subject matter as the earlier "Boyz N the Hood" piece. Soon after, Ice Cube attended the Phoenix Institute of Technology, taking a one-year course in architectural drafting, after which he returned to work with N.W.A in 1988. N.W.A made their initial two albums, a compilation called *N.W.A & the Posse* and the classic *Straight Outta Compton*, which initiated the so-called genre of gangsta rap in the 1990s. The album was mostly written by Ice Cube, and it would go multiplatinum by 1992.

Toward 1989 Cube felt that the group's manager, Jerry Heller, was not properly compensating him financially, so he left the group. Almost immediately, Cube began working with Hank Shocklee and the Bomb Squad. With this production crew, and Cube's own group of additional producers called the Lench Mob, headed by Sir Jinx, Cube released his own *AmeriKKKa's Most Wanted* album in 1990. The work received favorable notices, and it lyrically continued the street imagery Cube used in his rhymes for N.W.A, along with narrative rhyme pieces like "Once Upon a Time in the Projects" and "You Can't Fade Me." The work went platinum the following year. The same year he released the EP *Kill at Will*, which he produced with Sir Jinx and Chilly Chill. The work was noted for the song "Dead Homiez." Around this same period he established his own Street Knowledge Productions company with his manager, Pat Charbonnet.

In 1991 Cube released his album *Death Certificate*. Cube divided the album between his usual street-oriented rhymes on the first side, labeling it the "death side," while the second side (labeled the "life side") contained rhymes that showed the influence of the Nation of Islam. Production on the work was handled by Cube, Sir Jinx, and the Boogie Men, which consisted of DJ Pooh, Bobcat, and Rashad. By the end of the year the album was platinum.

Cube's next work in 1992, *The Predator*, debuted at number 1 on both the *Billboard* Top 200 Albums chart and the Top R&B Albums chart. The album went platinum by 1993, and two of his singles, "It Was a Good Day" and "Check Yo Self," went gold and platinum, respectively. Cube continued acting as well, appearing in the 1992 film *Trespass* with rapper Ice-T.

In 1993 his *Lethal Injection* album was released and went gold. In 1994 Cube reteamed with Dr. Dre for the piece "Natural Born Killaz," the single from Snoop Doggy Dogg's *Murder Was the Case* film soundtrack. It was the first pairing of the two on records since their N.W.A days. Cube also co-wrote the lyrics for the song with Dre.

In 1994 Cube released the album *Bootlegs & B-Sides*, which went gold that year, and worked with film director John Singleton again, appearing in his film *Higher Learning*. That same year, he co-produced (with Pat Charbonnet), co-wrote, and starred in the movie *Friday*, as well as appearing in director Charles Burnett's film *The Glass Shield* and directing several music videos.

 Selected albums/CDs: *Straight Outta Compton* by N.W.A. (1988, Ruthless); *AmeriKKKa's Most Wanted* (1990, Priority 551); *Death Certificate* (1991, 4th & Broadway 579); *The Predator* (1992, 4th & Broadway 592); *Bootlegs & B-Sides* (1994, 4th & Broadway 616).

ICE-T
●●●●●●●●
(Born Tracy Marrow, c. 1958, Newark, New Jersey)

Ice-T is one of the first rappers to successfully combine careers as a rapper and film actor. As an MC, Ice-T's rhymes consist of sociopolitical analyses and inner-city street narratives, lyrically delivered in the so-called gangsta style. Ice-T is also recognized for occasionally performing in the heavy metal music genre.

Known for his prerap life as a hustler and thief, Ice-T frequently uses his experiences in his rhymes to subtly educate audiences about the positive and negative aspects of that lifestyle. Taking his name from the ex-pimp novelist Iceberg Slim, Ice-T's film career began to take hold after his appearance as an undercover narcotics cop in Mario Van Peebles's film *New Jack City*.

Ice-T grew up in Newark, New Jersey, until the seventh grade, after which he was sent to Los Angeles to live with his father's sister, a social worker. Both of Ice's parents had died some years earlier. He attended high school in the Crenshaw area of Los Angeles, where he began to hang out with gangs. He left his aunt's house while in the twelfth grade and got his own one-room apartment (using his aunt's Social Security checks to pay his rent), and still managed to finish high school. He entered the Army after learning he would be a father, and stayed for four years. Thereafter, he returned to the States to a life of petty theft and hustling.

Toward the early 1980s Ice became interested in rapping, and he soon began recording for labels like Saturn Records and Electrobeat. One of his first records was a work titled "The Coldest Rap," which also contained performances from future award-winning R&B producers Jimmy Jam and Terry Lewis.

Ice traveled to New York frequently and became involved with writing and performing rhymes for several hip-hop and non—hip-hop-oriented projects. He began working with Afrika Islam, Grandmaster Caz, Mele Mel, and Bronx Style Bob around 1986, appearing on recordings like "The Beach" and "Cars." Back in Los Angeles, Ice was approached to appear in several films during this period, including *Breakin'* and *Breakin' II*.

He met a Bolivian former promotions man named Jorge Hinojosa, who was known for breaking records in Los Angeles like "I'll Take Your Man" by Salt-N-Pepa, and Mantronix's early work. Hinojosa was working for Island Records at this time, when Ice-T and Afrika Islam were turned down for a record deal. Believing in the artist himself, Hinojosa quit Island and began managing Ice-T's career.

Ice was signed to Sire Records, and his first album for the label, *Rhyme Pays*, was released in 1987. Afrika Islam handled the production on the work, as well as Ice's second work, *Power*, which appeared in 1988 and went gold that same year. Ice and Hinojosa formed Rhyme Syndicate Management with Rhyme Syndicate Records, and signed additional artists to the companies. They released the *Rhyme Syndicate* compilation album, which featured many of the companies' artists. Ice performed and wrote the title song for the movie soundtrack *Colors*, which earned him much notice for what some felt were his "frightening" lyrics dealing with the gang lifestyle.

Ice continued to work with Afrika Islam and their albums continued to go gold, including the 1989 work *Freedom of Speech* and *Original Gangster* in 1991. During this same period Ice landed the role of the undercover officer in the movie *New Jack City*, and did the soundtrack song "New Jack Hustler (Nino's Theme)," which was produced by DJ Aladdin. He also appeared in Eddie Murphy's film *Ricochet*.

Ice-T

In 1992 Ice received considerable criticism for his involvement with a black heavy-metal band that he headed called Body Count. Their song "Cop Killer" ignited controversy when police organizations claimed that the piece advocated murdering cops. After releasing a version of Body Count's album without the song (and receiving some flack from hip hoppers for caving in to the pressure that had forced him to take the song off the album), Ice-T split with the Sire/Warner Bros. label and signed with Priority Records. That same year he continued his acting career, appearing in the film *Trespass* with rapper Ice Cube.

Ice's *Home Invasion* album was released in 1993, and went gold by June. Ice-T also continued to act in film and television as well, appearing on the FOX-TV show *New York Undercover* in 1995, and the movie *Tank Girl*.

 Selected albums/CDs: *Rhyme Pays* (1987, Sire 25602); *Freedom of Speech* (1989, Sire 26028); *O. G. Original Gangsta* (1991, Sire 26492); *Body Count* (1992; Sire 45139); *Home Invasion* (1993, Rhyme Syndicate 53858); *The Classic Collection* (1993, Rhino 71170).

ILLEGAL
• • • • • • • • • • •

(Malik, born Malik Edwards, 1980, Holly Hill, South Carolina; Jamal, born Jamal Phillips, 1979, Philadelphia)

The duo of Malik and Jamal, Illegal, gained attention in 1993 for their hardcore lyrics, which were more noticeable because of their young ages (they were 13 and 14 years old, respectively, at the time).

The two were discovered by Lisa "Left Eye" Lopes, of the R&B group TLC. Malik used to hop on tour buses of famous hip-hop acts and perform before the artists. He happened to hop on the group Naughty by Nature's bus once, which resulted in that group taking him along on some dates, where he met Queen Latifah.

Jamal perfected his skills with various rap groups before meeting Lopes, after which he and Malik were signed to Lopes's producer, Dallas Austin's, Rowdy Records.

Illegal's 1993 album *The Untold Truth* had two hits, "Head or Gut" and "We Getz Buzy." Artists Erick Sermon, Diamond D, Lord Finesse, and Biz Markie contributed some production on the work.

Illegal

 Selected albums/CDs: *The Untold Truth* (1993, Rowdy 37002).

INTELLIGENT HOODLUM

a.k.a. Tragedy, MC Jade
(Born Percy Chapman, August 13, 1971, Long Island City, New York)

Tragedy, who records under the name Intelligent Hoodlum, gained immediate attention when he appeared on the scene with his 1990 Marley Marl-produced single "Arrest the President." The politically charged rhymes and his explosive delivery put a spotlight on the artist and his skills.

Growing up in the Queensbridge Housing Projects (where he met Marl), Tragedy was in and out of trouble, dropping out of school, living in group homes, and getting arrested from time to time. However, Tragedy was totally immersed in hip-hop culture, and he eventually started working on material with neighborhood friend Marl. By 1989 Marley Marl recorded a 12-inch single by Tragedy (who was going by the name MC Jade at the time) titled "Coke Is It." The work was released under the name Supa' Kids. He also appeared on Marl's *In Control Volume One* compilation album.

Unfortunately, soon after, Tragedy got into trouble again and was arrested, and this time was sent to prison on a one-to-three-year term. Once there, Tragedy began to turn his life around, studying the sociopolitical system, reading various books, and continuing to sharpen his rhyme-writing and MC skills—all within the confines of his cell.

After his release from jail, Marley Marl worked again with Tragedy, this time producing his first album, titled *Intelligent Hoodlum*. The work was released on A&M Records in 1990, and it called attention to Tragedy as a major artist.

By 1993 Tragedy had another hit with the single "Grand Groove" off his second album, *Tragedy—Saga of a Hoodlum*. Production on the work was again handled by Marley Marl, along with K-Def and others.

 Selected albums/CDs: *Intelligent Hoodlum* (1990, A&M 5311); *Tragedy—Saga of a Hoodlum* (1993, A&M 5389).

 OTHERZ

INFINITY MACHINE

a.k.a. Infinity Rappers
Formed early 1980s, New York
(Godfather KC Roc; Shaheem: both born in New York)

The Infinity Rappers, or Infinity Machine, was Grandmixer D.ST's duo of MCs that performed with his renowned powerful sound system in the early 1980s. Rappers KC and Shaheem recorded with D.ST on the Celluloid label, where they worked on and recorded songs like "Grandmixer Cuts It Up." After recording and working with D.ST, KC later began working as a singer with the R&B group, Entouch.

JAZZY FIVE
● ● ● ● ● ● ● ● ● ● ● ● ● ● ● ● ●
Formerly Jazzy 3 MCs
Formed c. 1979, Bronx, New York
(MC Master Ice; Master Bee; Charlie Chew; AJ Les; Mr. Freeze; Jazzy Jay:
all born in Bronx, New York; Kool DJ Red Alert, born in New York City)

The Jazzy Five was a group of MCs and DJs from Afrika Bambaataa's Zulu Nation, who were responsible for giving Tommy Boy Records its first hit record, titled "Jazzy Sensation."

With the MCs all hailing from the Soundview section of the Bronx, it was Jazzy Jay, along with MC Sundance, Charlie Chew, and Master Bee, who formed the group, originally called the Jazzy 3 MCs. Various members came and went, causing the group's name to change from the Jazzy 3 MCs to the Jazzy 4, and finally the Jazzy Five. The final members of the group were Master Ice, Master Dee, Master Bee, AJ Les, Mr. Freeze, and DJ Jazzy Jay, along with his cousin, Kool DJ Red Alert. The group performed in Bronx area schools and places like the Kips Bay Boys Club and Cardinal Hays school. They also made street tapes of their performances.

Through Afrika Bambaataa's association with Tom Silverman, the Jazzy Five recorded the piece "Jazzy Sensation" in 1981 on Silverman's Tommy Boy label. The record contained three mixes: one with Bambaataa; the second with the group Kryptic Krew; while the third mix was an instrumental. Silverman, Bambaataa, and producer Arthur Baker (along with KISS-FM New York radio DJ Shep Pettibone) were involved with the recording. "Jazzy Sensation" was a big hit with the hip-hop audience.

After the record was released the Jazzy Five did numerous gigs and parties performing it and other material. Soon after, the members dispersed as a group.

 Selected singles: "Jazzy Sensation" (1981, Tommy Boy).

JAZZY JAY
•••••••••••••••••
(Born in Bronx, New York)

Jazzy Jay is a pioneer DJ who was part of Afrika Bambaataa's Soul Sonic Force. He was part of the Zulu King dancers with Afrika Islam and Grandmixer D.ST and also the group the Jazzy Five, whose recording "Jazzy Sensation" was Tommy Boy Records' first hit, and later cofounded Def Jam Recordings with Rick Rubin. Jay is one of the most respected producers and engineers in hip hop, and along with his consultant activities, his Jazzy Jay Studios has turned out important artists like Showbiz & AG, Lord Finesse, Diamond D, Grand Puba, and Brand Nubian.

Jay started deejaying when he was a kid living in the Bronx River Housing Projects. He was noticed by DJ Disco King Mario, and soon worked under him. Because hip hop was very territorial during its early years and competitive, Mario was seen as someone who was treating Jay unfairly by hip hoppers of the Bronx River area, particularly Afrika Bambaataa and his Zulu Nation. Jay was soon taken in by Bambaataa, and became one of his DJs around 1978. Jay participated with Bambaataa in a number of battles, and formed several sound-system crews within the Zulu Nation, including the Earthquake Systems, with Bambaataa and DJ Superman.

Along with his cousin, Kool DJ Red Alert, Jay formed a group called the Jazzy 3 MCs under Afrika Bambaataa. MC Sundance was Jay's first MC, and the group went from three MCs to four (when it became the Jazzy 4), and finally five, becoming the Jazzy Five. After MC Sundance left the group, the final members consisted of Jay and his cousin, Red Alert, as the DJs, along with MCs Master Ice, Master Dee, Master Bee, AJ Les, and Mr. Freeze. The group was originally known for their street tapes and performances before they recorded the piece "Jazzy Sensation" in 1981 for Tom Silverman's Tommy Boy Records.

After the Jazzy Five separated Jay became the DJ for Afrika Bambaataa's Soul Sonic Force, participating in their landmark 1982 recording of "Planet Rock" and other Soul Sonic Force works. He also performed and toured with the group.

Around 1983 Jay met then-DJ, guitarist, and film student Rick Rubin at the club Negril's. Striking up a friendship, Jay began to turn Rubin on to all the popular records with hip hoppers at the time, and showed him how to program beats. They decided to make a record together, and recorded the song "It's Yours" with Treacherous Three member Special K's brother, T La Rock. The song was recorded on what Jay and Rubin called Def Jam Recordings, and it became an underground classic. Jay later performed with La Rock in a number of shows, while Rubin soon began business relations with then-promoter and producer Russell Simmons.

Around 1986 Jay was hired to create the soundtrack for the film *Beat Street*. He utilized his DJ skills to synch turntables to the film for effects, one of the first times that this technique was used in motion pictures. Around this same period Jay began Strong City Records with concert promoter and DJ Rocky Bucano. Some of the artists on the label included Ice Cream Tee, Masters of Ceremony, Busy Bee, and Don Barron.

Toward the late 1980s into the 1990s Jay continued to influence hip hop from his studios, creating and co-creating many record labels, and co-producing various acts in hip hop.

JIVE RECORDS
Formed c. early 1980s, Great Britain

Jive Records was an early British rap label established in the early 1980s and owned by Clive Calder.

The label's first important act was the Brooklyn, New York-based group Whodini. Jive released their Thomas Dolby-produced single "Magic's Wand" (a tribute to hip hop radio personality Mr. Magic) in 1982. They also worked with material from former Funky Four Plus One member Jazzy Jeff.

During the mid-1980s, after the label changed its distribution from Arista Records to RCA, Jive (under the supervision of Barry Weiss and Sean Carasov) began working with Boogie Down Productions, Philadelphia's DJ Jazzy Jeff & the Fresh Prince, and A Tribe Called Quest. With these acts, Jive began to receive increased success. Some of the other successful acts on the label from the 1980s through the early 1990s include Billy Ocean, R. Kelly, the Fu-Schnickens, Too Short, Keith Murray, and Spice 1.

JOESKI LOVE
(Born Joel Roper, Jr., c. 1969, Harlem, New York)

Joeski Love burst on the scene in 1986 with a novelty piece called "Pee Wee's Dance," which was based on the wild dance that TV/film comedian Pee Wee Herman performed. "Pee Wee's Dance" was popular with the hip hop audience, and it sold close to 500,000 copies.

Born in Harlem but raised in the Bronx, Love was originally in a group that had attracted the attention of Vincent Davis—producer, manager, and owner of the Elektra Records-distributed Vintertainment label. However, the group disbanded, and Love decided to stay with Davis as a solo artist. Davis produced and arranged Love's "Pee Wee's Dance." Love later recorded a second single, titled "Say Joe," backed with "My Girl."

Later Love met Bomb Squad producer Hank Shocklee, who brought the artist to Columbia Records. Ron Skoler (then a partner in the management firm Rhythm Method Enterprises, which handled Public Enemy and other acts) brought Love to producer Hurby Luv Bug Azor, who worked on Love's debut album for Columbia in 1991, titled *Joe Cool*, with the single "I Know She Likes Joe."

 Selected singles: "Pee Wee's Dance" (1986, Vintertainment).

JUICE CREW

See MR. MAGIC; MARLEY MARL; COLD CHILLIN' RECORDS;
ROXANNE SHANTÉ; BIZ MARKIE; BIG DADDY KANE; KOOL G RAP & DJ POLO

JUNGLE BROTHERS

Formed c. late 1980s, New York
**(Afrika Baby Bambaataa, formerly Shazam, born Nathaniel Hall, Brooklyn,
New York; Mike G, born Michael Small, Harlem, New York; DJ Sammy B, born
Sammy Burwell, Harlem; Brother J, born Jason Hunter, c. 1971, New York)**

The Jungle Brothers—Mike G, Afrika Baby Bambaataa, and DJ Sammy B—made an impressive debut in 1988 with their attitude and lyrics, which mostly called attention to and celebrated their Afrocentricity. Also of note was their innovative production style, led by Afrika Baby Bambaataa (who named himself in homage to pioneer hip-hop godfather Afrika Bambaataa). The group was managed for a time by Kool DJ Red Alert, and was part of the Native Tongues posse with A Tribe Called Quest and De La Soul.

Group members Mike G and Sammy B (nephew and cousin of Red Alert, respectively) attended the same business high school in Manhattan with Ali Muhammad, Q-Tip—later members of the group A Tribe Called Quest—and Brother J (an early Jungle Brother member, who later joined the group X-Clan). They all were interested in forming a group.

Things took off around 1988 when the Jungle Brothers started recording at label owner Tony D's Idlers Records in Coney Island, Brooklyn, where they did pieces like "Because I Got It Like That." The group began to get more attention with songs like "Jimbrowski" (a humorous song about the male sexual organ). Their *Straight Out the Jungle* album was released on Warlock Records during this same period. One of the surprise hits off the album was house producer Todd Terry's remixed piece "I'll House You"—an experimental work in the hip-hop genre.

In 1989 the group signed with Warner Bros., where their *Done by the Forces of Nature* album was released. Numerous cuts off the album were hits with the hip-hop audience, including "Beads on a String" and "J. Beez Comin' Through."

In 1991 Afrika Baby Bambaataa appeared in the movie *Livin' Single*. The prior year he had begun working on solo production projects with artists like Caron Wheeler, and later, Neneh Cherry. By 1993 the Jungle Brothers released their third work, *J. Beez wit the Remedy*, which was a critically acclaimed work because of its experimental nature.

Selected albums/CDs: *Straight Out the Jungle* (1988, Warlock 2704); *Done by the Forces of Nature* (1989, Warner Bros. 26072); *J. Beez wit the Remedy* (1993, Warner Bros. 26679).

JUST-ICE

(Born Joseph Williams, Jr., Fort Greene, Brooklyn, New York)

Just-Ice was among the first group of rappers to write and perform rhymes in the so-called gangsta style. He is also one of the first group of MCs to add a reggae flavor to his lyrical delivery.

Ice (sometimes called Justice, and also known as Sir Vicious and the Original Gangster) is noted for his pounding delivery that is unrelenting in attack and effect. During 1986 he was falsely accused, in the *Washington Post Magazine*, of murdering a Washington, DC, drug dealer. However, this accusation was thrown out, and the artist was never formally charged.

Just-Ice grew up in the Bronx, and by the age of 9 was already captivated by the hip-hop scene. By age 11 he was able to sneak into clubs like the Black Door and Sparkle, because of his size (making him appear older than his actual age). After seeing all the hip-hop acts of the day, like Grand Wizard Theodore, Kool Herc, and Grandmaster Caz, Ice was finally inspired to pick up a microphone after seeing rapper Mele Mel perform. He started by buying his first rhyme from a friend for $3.

By age 18 he was well into writing his own rhymes. He met producer Kurtis Mantronik at the club Danceteria, along with other people from Sleeping Bag/Fresh Records. Ice and Mantronik began working together and eventually recorded a song called "Latoya." When the piece was heard at Sleeping Bag/Fresh toward 1985, the label immediately signed him. "Latoya" was a favorite with hip hoppers, putting Ice on the map.

Another single, "Put That Record Back On," followed, as well as albums like *Back to the Old School, Kool and Deadly, Masterpiece,* and *The Desolate One*—works that he co-produced with other artists, like KRS-One and the Boogie Down Productions.

After 1989 Sleeping Bag/Fresh closed its business doors, leaving Just-Ice unsigned until 1992, when he was picked up by Savage Records. His *Gun Talk* album was released on this label in 1993, with the 12-inch single from the work, titled "Girls & Guns." Producers on the album are the legendary Kurtis Mantronik and O.C. Rodriguez from the Fearless Four. It offers some of the best MC'ing on record, with a variety of styles all delivered with relentless force.

 Selected albums/CDs: *The Desolate One* (1989, Sleeping Bag/Fresh 005); *Gun Talk* (1993, Savage 50211).

Just-Ice

OTHERZ

JERRY BLOODROCK
....
(Born in New York)

Jerry Bloodrock was originally an early hip-hop radio personality, whose show aired on New York's WHBI-FM (known later as WNWK-FM) from approximately 1980 to 1981. However, his biggest success was as the producer and manager of Rockmaster Scott & the Dynamic 3. The group's song "Request Line," produced by Bloodrock around 1983, was a big hit, and was among the first group of rap records to receive extensive radio airplay. Bloodrock and the group released another single around the same time called "It's Life (You Gotta Think Twice)," which was also a hit. In 1984—86 Bloodrock also worked with the Reality Records/Fantasy label, producing acts like Doug E. Fresh.

Jazz hip hop: A media term used to describe a style of rap, popularized by groups like A Tribe Called Quest, Gang Starr, and others, that uses break beats from jazz records and a smoother textured rhyme delivery.

JUST-ICE: THE ART OF MC'ING

Just-Ice is one of the most skilled of all the MCs in rap. Famous for his 1984 single "Latoya," his 1993 *Gun Talk* album just may be the best work that represents the true art of MC'ing. His verbalist skills here are undeniably relentless. He's got quite a few styles going on in these rhymes, and his delivery is like a sustained explosion, never letting up. At times it seems like he's not even breathing in between.

"You gotta have breath control," he reminds us. "Half of these people out here are smokin' cigarettes, blunts and drinking! Do you think they're actually gonna get on the mic in front of a bunch of people and go freestyle, and take the chance of messing up their careers?

"There's a lot of studio rappers out here," he continues. "Studio gangsters. People who were thinking about doing hip hop when they first started, but they couldn't do that good, so they converted to love song hip hop. Then they couldn't do that good, so they converted back to being a ladies' man. That didn't work, so now the stuff that they were ignoring a few years ago that was hittin' and still hittin' today—but they just slept on it—now, that's what they're trying to do.

"You see, if they knew hip hop, the way it was supposed to be looked at, back then, they would know that the gangsta stuff has been there ever since. Not just now. These people wanted to do everything but that, 'cause they were saying, 'Oh—that's a negative image! You're not being a role model!

"The hell with being a role model! Like Charles Barkley says, I am not a role model! People try to sit there and foresee the future of hip hop in the eyes of these corporate people. You can't do that."

KID CAPRI

See DJ KID CAPRI

KID FROST

(Born Arturo Molina, Jr., May 31, Los Angeles)

Kid Frost is a politically conscious Chicano MC who promotes the recognition of Latino culture and its contribution to hip-hop culture. His music usually contains Latin break-beat records or live percussion instrumentation playing cowbell or clave rhythms. His rhymes are usually composed in Spanglish (English and street Spanish). He was the founder and head of the Latin Alliance—an international organization of Latino hip hoppers similar to Afrika Bambaataa's Universal Zulu Nation.

Frost (a cousin of Cesar Rosas of the rock group Los Lobos) grew up doing a little hustling and gangbanging after dropping out of high school. In the early 1980s Frost started getting into MC'ing and made street tapes, selling them on Hollywood Boulevard

Kid Frost

for $15 to $20. He later performed in clubs and shows like the *Low Rider* magazine car shows, and sometimes worked outside Los Angeles, in places like Houston. By 1981 Frost had met rapper Ice-T, who helped Frost get signed to the Electrobeat label (Frost later drew the label's logo).

By 1988 Frost had a hit with the single "La Raza" on the Virgin label. His album *Hispanic Causing Panic* was released in 1990. Another hit that came off this work was titled "Ya Estuvo."

Frost's second work, *East Side Story*, was released in 1992. A piece off the album, a re-working of R&B singer Bill Withers's hit "Ain't No Sunshine" titled "No Sunshine," was featured in actor Edward James Olmos's film *American Me*.

Selected albums/CDs: *Hispanic Causing Panic* (1990, Virgin 86169); *East Side Story* (1992, Virgin 86275).

KID 'N PLAY
•••••••••••••••••••
Formerly Fresh Force
Formed c. 1987, Queens, New York
(Kid, born Christopher Reid, Bronx, New York;
Play, born Christopher Martin, East Elmhurst, Queens)

Kid 'n Play are a successful rap duo originally known for their dance moves in their videos and Kid's eight-inch high-top fade haircut. Later they also became known as a TV and film comedy duo, in the manner of Bill Cosby and Sidney Poitier or Dean Martin and Jerry Lewis.

Their 1988 debut album, *2 Hype*, went platinum, and they were the first rap group to have their own television cartoon series, which aired on the NBC network during 1990. They were also the first rap group to have their own comic book, which was put out by Marvel Comics in 1991. As movie stars, their *House Party* films were very successful at the box office. The two have done commercials for Sprite and have made appearances on PBS TV's *Sesame Street*. Play is also known as a graphic artist and a designer, who designs a line of clothing called IV Plai.

Kid and Play were in rival groups in high school. Play was in the group Super Lovers, along with the duo's future manager and producer, Hurby Luv Bug Azor. Kid was in the group the Turnout Brothers. After performing in parks and at small parties, the two decided to join forces as a duo. They were soon signed to Select Records, and their first album, *2 Hype*, was released in 1988. Their second work, *Funhouse*, was released in 1990, as was their first soundtrack album for their movie *House Party*.

In 1991 the duo starred in the film *House Party II*, and in 1992 they starred in the movie *Class Act*. By 1993 Kid 'n Play continued the *House Party* series, starring in *House Party 3*.

Selected albums/CDs: *2 Hype* (1988, Select 21628); *Fun House* (1990, Select 21638); *House Party* (soundtrack; 1990, Motown 6296); *Face the Nation* (1991, Select 61206); *House Party 2* (soundtrack; 1991, MCA 10397).

Kid 'n Play

KING SUN
• • • • • • • • • • • • • •
(Born Rahmakhan Todd Turnbow, February 23, 1967, Paterson, New Jersey)

King Sun is known for his 6' 7" height and righteous rhymes, which are seasoned with lessons from the Five Percent Nation of Islam. He is also noted for his smooth-flowing rap style and slightly coarse-textured voice.

Sun (whose father was a former boxer and sparring partner to Muhammad Ali) got turned on to the hip-hop scene when he visited his uncle's house in the Bronx. He began buying all the tapes of groups like the Treacherous Three, Cold Crush Brothers, and Grandmaster Flash. He soon began to freestyle himself, creating rhymes by putting new words into other people's rhymes and ad-libbing. Sun would occasionally get into trouble, and eventually wound up in a juvenile detention center. During his stay another prisoner introduced him to the teachings of the Five Percent Nation of Islam, which intrigued him. He soon joined the group.

When Sun was released from prison at 16, his righteous name had become Universal Sun Born He-Allah. Released in his father's custody (who now lived in Cincinnati), Sun was soon in trouble again by 1983 for attacking his girlfriend's relative who had raped her. Thereafter, he returned to New York and was taken off parole.

Later Sun decided to get back into the rap scene. He met Cutmaster D.C. (of "Brooklyn's in the House" fame) in September 1986 at the New Jersey club Zena's. There Sun battled Kid 'n Play (then known as the Fresh Force) because they wanted to see if he was able to rhyme. Zakia Records' label owner and producer, Robert Hill, showed interest in Sun's skills and told Cutmaster D.C. that he would like to sign Sun and his DJ, D-Moet. Sun's first single for the label appeared in 1987, titled "Hey Love," and it was a hit on radio and in the clubs. The b-side of the record was "Mythological," which was also a hit.

In 1988 Profile Records picked up the artist via a distribution deal with Zakia. In 1989 the label released King Sun's first album, titled *XL*. The work impressed the hip-hop crowd. By 1990 his second album, *Righteous but Ruthless*, was released, which contained production by Tony "Tony D" Depula and King Shameek. In 1994 Sun recorded an EP for Cold Chillin' Records titled *Strictly Ghetto*.

 Selected albums/CDs: *XL* (1989, Profile 1270); *Righteous but Ruthless* (1990, Profile 1299).

KOOL DJ AJ
(Born Aaron O'Bryan, New York)

Kool DJ AJ was a popular DJ during the late 1970s and early 1980s, who was known for having a loyal following of party goers. He was recognized for being able to keep them consistently dancing throughout his music sets. He was also known for deejaying with a drum machine called the Funkbox. AJ is remembered for promoting his own parties, and he was immortalized in the 1984 hit single "AJ Scratch" by rapper Kurtis Blow, for whom he deejayed through the mid-1980s.

AJ first deejayed in the mid-1970s in his neighborhood at the E. Moore Houses in the Bronx. Other areas AJ played include St. Mary's Park, and in the late 1970s, clubs like Harlem World, the Renaissance, and the Celebrity Club. Kenny Gee, Lovebug Starski, and Busy Bee are some of the people who worked with him during this period. Responsible for helping the rap duo Dr. Jeckyll & Mr. Hyde get a record deal in the early 1980s, AJ wrote songs for Kurtis Blow, like the 1985 single "If I Ruled the World," which appeared in the movie *Krush Groove*. He later faded from the music scene as his popularity subsided.

KOOL DJ HERC
a.k.a. Kool Herc
(Born Clive Campbell, c. early 1950s, Kingston, Jamaica)

Kool DJ Herc is the creator of break-beat deejaying, and the originator of parties that inspired the music and dance aspects of hip-hop culture during the early 1970s. Various dancers would perform solo dance routines at Herc's parties that were then known as "burning" or "going off," but would later be termed breakdancing, because of their enthusiastic performances of the wildest dance moves that occurred during the "break" part of a record that Herc played (usually the instrumental part, highlighted by a motivating drum and/or bass pattern). Herc would call these dancers "b-boys," as in break boys, and later, pioneer breakdancers would call their dancing, b-boying.

Attendees at Herc's parties would come dressed in different styles, some sophisticated, sporting alligator shoes and such, others casual, wearing windbreakers and Pro-Keds sneakers. In the beginning young teens as well as 20-year-olds would attend Herc's parties. His spots were known to be dark and packed with people, which gave the parties a feeling that anything could happen.

During the early- to mid-1970s disco was the dominant dance music the DJs played. Herc distinguished himself by playing mostly late 1960s and early 1970s funk records by artists like James Brown, Baby Huey and the Babysitters, the Jimmy Castor Bunch, and Mandrill. These were the records that had the appropriate breaks in them, and Herc would combine those records with some of the disco records he was playing.

Another factor in Herc's popularity was the strength of his sound system, which he named the Herculords. During his tenure at the club Hevalo Herc's sound would overtake one's body, due to the width and intensity of the volume. Partygoers would thus be engulfed by the music emanating from his sound system, which then consisted of two Pioneer PL-15 turntables hooked up to a Sony microphone mixer, which went through a Shure preamp through two Shure column speakers. When Herc moved to his next club spot, the Executive Playhouse, his reputation for having one of the most powerful sound systems increased when he purchased a MacIntosh amplifier, which was the most respected amplifier among DJs at that time.

Kool DJ Herc

Common party phrases such as "rock the house," "rock on my mellow," "to the beat y'all," and "ya don't stop" were pioneered by Kool Herc at his parties. During the music sets Herc would call out the names of friends and party regulars that he knew, telling them on the microphone to "rock on," usually through a reverb frequency or echo chamber. This was embellished upon by his MC, Coke La Rock, recognized as among the first MCs because of his use of crowd-motivating phrases during Herc's deejaying.

Other regulars at Herc's parties included b-boy brothers Kevin and Keith, nicknamed by Herc the Nigger Twins. They performed dance routines dressed in double-knit pants, windbreakers, and crusher hats (with one wearing his hat backward), with drinking straws in their mouths. Wallace Dee did a dance routine called the slingshot, where he would drop to the floor and come up, as if shooting a slingshot. Some of the other regulars at Herc's parties included the Amazing Bobo, El Dorado Mike, Cocaine Smitty, 23rd Street Skip, Trixie (known for his huge Afro that he shook while dancing), and Sha Sha—one of the greatest b-boys of his time. Like other DJs, Kool Herc had DJs that worked under him, including the Original Clark Kent, Little Timmy, Black Jack, and later, Jay Cee, and Whiz Kid.

Herc's repertoire of records and break records at the time was his own, and they later became standards in hip-hop culture via various samples, which have appeared and reappeared in certain songs by different hip-hop artists through the years. A portion of these records that Herc broke to his audience include "Apache" and "Bongo Rock" by the Incredible Bongo Band; "Sex Machine" and "Give It Up or Turnit Loose" by James Brown; "It's Just Begun" by the Jimmy Castor Bunch; "Listen to Me" by Baby Huey and the Babysitters; "Fencewalk" by Mandrill; "The Mexican" by Babe Ruth; "Get into Something, Follow Me" by the Isley Brothers; "Pick Up the Pieces" by the Average White Band; "Soul Makossa" by Manu Dibango; "Hijack" by Herbie Mann; and various Jackson Five records like "It's Great to Be Here."

Herc migrated to America in 1967 from Kingston, Jamaica. He settled in the West Bronx with his mother, and later entered Alfred E. Smith High School. He joined the school's track team, took up weight lifting, and gradually got more into American culture. Kool Herc originally became known for his "Kool Herc" graffiti tag, which he wrote in various spots in his neighborhood. He partied at discos like the Plaza Tunnel on the Grand Concourse in the Bronx, and later got into deejaying around 1973, deejaying at his sister's birthday party. Herc's first party spot was at a place called the Twilight Zone on Jerome Avenue in the Bronx. He later moved to his second venue, known as the Hevalo, and then, over to the Executive Playhouse.

By the mid-1970s Herc was stabbed at one of his parties, which led to a period of less activity. Another factor that contributed to his decline in popularity was the fact that other break-beat DJs had come along by this time, like Grandmaster Flash, who had adapted his style of playing and perfected it, mixing break beats with perfect timing, as opposed to Herc's sight-mixing, which meant dropping the turntable needle on certain areas of a record, hoping that it lands on time.

Some time later Herc resumed deejaying. He joined with Afrika Bambaataa for a while to form Nubian Productions, promoting a few parties. Toward the early 1980s Herc and his DJs

Whiz Kid, Jay Cee, and the Original Clark Kent performed in venues like Negril's, Claremont Center, and others. Herc also appeared in the 1984 movie *Beat Street*.

Afterward, Herc's career subsided as he left the music scene for a number of years. By the early 1990s he had entered the construction field, but gradually began to make appearances at a few music industry gatherings honoring hip-hop pioneers. He also made a cameo appearance on *The Godfathers of Threatt* album by Public Enemy DJ, Terminator X, in 1994, speaking between the selections of songs on the work.

KOOL DJ RED ALERT

a.k.a. Concourse Red, the Propmaster
(Born in Harlem, New York)

Kool DJ Red Alert is one of the most influential DJs in hip hop. He has personally presented more first-time hip-hop acts than any other DJ, and is recognized as the first DJ to air dancehall reggae records on commercial radio.

A former member of the Jazzy Five, and a DJ for Sparky D during the "Roxanne, Roxanne" craze, Red Alert is also noted for being one of the most listened-to hip-hop radio DJs, whose mix shows on KISS-FM (and later HOT-97 FM) radio in New York City have aired since 1983. He has introduced several words and catchphrases to hip-hop culture, such as "props" and his vibrating nasal-pitched exclamation "yeaaaah!," to name a few.

As in the days of the original DJs during the 1970s, Red Alert is known for the records that he plays—a distinct repertoire of songs that identifies him on the turntables. He was an early protégé of Afrika Bambaataa, who taught him the essence of using a variety of music from different genres to create a perfect music set. Thus, he became known for his innovative mixes, which resulted in his show being one of the most taped rap shows on radio. Next to Bambaataa, he is also known for having one of the largest record collections in hip hop, as well as one of the largest collections of hip-hop party tapes covering the earliest MC and DJ battles and mix materials. A small portion of artists Red Alert is responsible for presenting include Boogie Down Productions (whom he participated on stage with as a comic character), Queen Latifah, Mark the 45 King (and the entire Flavor Unit family), and the Native Tongues family, including Black Sheep, A Tribe Called Quest, and the Jungle Brothers.

A few famous records (rap or otherwise) he is responsible for first breaking on radio include "Keep on Moving" by Soul II Soul, "PSK What Does It Mean" by Schoolly D, "Hold On" by En Vogue, "Roxanne, Roxanne" by UTFO, Rob Base's "It Takes Two," Boogie Down Productions' "South Bronx," and the John Wayne impersonated "Rappin' Duke." In the dancehall genre of reggae Red Alert has broken on the commercial airwaves most of Shabba Ranks's early records, including "Roots & Culture" and "Wicked in Bed." He also introduced JC Lodge's "Telephone Love," Shelly Thunder's "Kuff," "Burrp" by Nardo Ranks, "Life (Is What You Make It)" by Frighty & Colonel Mite, "Sorry" by Foxy Brown, "Ram Dancehall" by Tiger, Shinehead's "Who the Cap Fits," and many other classic dancehall pieces.

Born in Harlem and raised in the Colonial Projects, Red Alert began to get interested in deejaying around 1975. A student at DeWitt Clinton High School who later attended the Upward Bound Program at Fordham University, Red Alert watched all the popular DJs at the time, like DJ Flowers, Pete DJ Jones, the Together Brothers, and Plummer. He also frequented party spots like Pippins, Hotel Commodore, Nell Quinn's, and the Riverboat. Red Alert discovered Kool DJ Herc playing at the club Twilight Zone in the Bronx. Herc's method of deejaying greatly affected Red Alert, and soon (along with all the DJs who were operating at the time) he was influenced by Herc's first set of DJ equipment: two direct-drive Technique 1800 turntables with a Clubman mixer.

He started collecting disco and R&B records from his brother's and girlfriend's record collections; then he searched for the records that Kool Herc played and others that nobody had. Later Red Alert (with his roommate) did his first party for the Upward Bound Program, combining their sound systems.

Toward early 1978 Red Alert began to work with Afrika Bambaataa and the Zulu Nation through his cousin, DJ Jazzy Jay, who had been working as one of Bambaataa's DJs. First working as a record boy for Bambaataa, Red Alert gradually worked his way up to being a top DJ in the Zulu Nation, but not before getting his DJ equipment stolen. It took several months after the theft before he was able to begin to regain the skill he had acquired as a DJ, while others who had followed his work at Zulu Nation parties considered him a has-been and laughingstock.

Red Alert was deejaying at various parties, but his status as a DJ with the hip-hop crowd at the time was still at the bottom. By the early 1980s Jazzy Jay began forming part of his group, the Jazzy Five, with Jazzy and Red Alert as the DJs for the group. In 1981 the Jazzy Five recorded the hit "Jazzy Sensation" for Tommy Boy Records. The group per-

Kool DJ Red Alert

formed in various areas of New York before separating. Around the same period Red Alert also made appearances on Afrika Islam's "Zulu Beats" radio show, where he brought the latest party tapes down to the station to play on the airwaves.

After 1982 and Afrika Bambaataa's recording of the "Planet Rock" single, Bambaataa began taking all of the Zulu Nation MCs and DJs downtown to Manhattan clubs like Danceteria, Negril's, and the Roxy, on behalf of promoter Kool Lady Blue. Red Alert was the only Zulu Nation DJ left to deejay the traditional uptown venues. His first spot alone (on his comeback trail) was the T-Connection, which he successfully handled to the audience's delight. Red Alert began doing more parties alone while other Zulu Nation DJs and MCs continued to perform in the downtown clubs.

Around 1983 programmers from radio station KISS-FM met Bambaataa at the Roxy and asked him to do a show for the station. Bambaataa instead offered them his DJs. The first choice was Afrika Islam, who had a scheduling problem and was unable to make the appointment. Bambaataa next offered them Jazzy Jay, who took the 11:00P.M. to 2:00 A.M. spot at the station every other weekend for two months, until he left. Bambaataa next offered them Red Alert, who took the position and remained at the station, where his popularity began to climb. During 1984 Red Alert recorded "Hip Hop on Wax—Volume 2," which was a series of scratch records by various DJs released by Vincent Davis on his Vintertainment Records label.

By 1986 Red Alert also became known as the host at the hip-hop club Union Square for six months, and toward 1987 he was the host at the Latin Quarters club for one year. Red Alert also continued to deejay at other clubs like the Area. Red Alert also became known as the head of the Native Tongues, which was a group of hip-hop artists (Jungle Brothers, A Tribe Called Quest, De La Soul, and others), who took that name after recording a piece called "Buddy" on De La Soul's *3 Feet High and Rising* album. They also referred to themselves as "the vibe tribe," because of their ability to relate to each other's feelings, or vibe.

Along with the other aspects of his career Red Alert has also recorded compilation albums for Next Plateau Records, consisting of records he either broke and/or played heavily on his radio show. By 1994 he did a dancehall compilation album (again, with records affiliated with his radio show) for Epic Records, titled *DJ Red Alert's Propmaster Dancehall Show*. Red Alert was also known as a manager for a short time, handling acts like Queen Latifah, Mark the 45 King, Chill Rob G, Jungle Brothers, A Tribe Called Quest, Monie Love, and acts outside the United States, like Japan's Major Force and Solid Productions from Copenhagen. He has also executive-produced albums like A Tribe Called Quest's *People's Instinctive Travels* and *The Paths of Rhythm* and the Jungle Brothers' *Done by the Forces of Nature*.

 Selected albums/CDs: *DJ Red Alert's Propmaster Dancehall Show* (1994, Epic/Street 57135).

Kool G Rap & DJ Polo

KOOL G RAP & DJ POLO

•••••••••••••••••••••••••••••••••••••

**Formed in 1986, Corona, Queens, New York
(Kool G Rap, born Nathaniel Wilson, July 20, 1969, Jamaica, New York;
DJ Polo, born Thomas Pough, April 5, New York City)**

Known as a rapper with a rapid-fire, lisp-generated style of rhyme delivery, Kool G Rap is recognized as a technician and a storyteller of hardcore street life with gangsta-type scenarios. He is one of hip hop's unsung craftsmen, who early on achieved great recognition for his technique in the hip-hop underground. During the late 1980s G Rap was one of the top rappers in his field, and is one of the few rappers who are known for the stunning cameos they achieve on other artists' works.

G Rap (with the "G" standing for "Genius") and Polo were introduced to each other in 1986 by Eric B. Polo then introduced G Rap to his friend producer Marley Marl and the three then started working together on songs. By 1988 G Rap, Polo, and Marl had recorded "It's a Demo," which was a hit with the hip-hop crowd and eventually became a classic. In that same year G Rap appeared on Marl's single titled "The Symphony," with other artists from the Cold Chillin' Records label. A few other singles were released that year with G Rap and Polo, including "Poison" and "Rikers Island," which gained the duo more notice.

In 1989 their debut album, *Road to the Riches*, was released by Cold Chillin', with the title song firmly putting the duo on the map. By 1990 their even more successful second album, *Wanted: Dead or Alive*, was released, which included the hits "Streets of New York" and "Talk Like Sex."

G Rap began to make appearances on other artists' works, like the Brand New Heavies, MC Shan, Roxanne Shanté, the Poetess, and Heavy D's "Don't Curse" single. He also began producing radio commercials for St. Ides Malt Liquor. DJ Polo was soon working with other artists, and hosting and producing his own rap video show in Philadelphia, called "Strictly Underground."

G Rap & Polo ran into major problems while working on their third album. At this time Warner Bros. Records, which distributed Cold Chillin's product, had refused to handle Ice-T's album, because of the controversy surrounding the song "Cop Killer," which appeared on the work. Many of G Rap & Polo's songs were equally controversial. There was also concern expressed by Warner over sample clearances, which had been raised earlier by the legal problems of another Cold Chillin' act, Biz Markie.

These problems were cleared up by 1992, when their album *Live and Let Die* was finally released. Its production was handled mostly by the Lench Mob production crew's Sir Jinx and the TrakMasterz. The singles "Ill Street Blues" and "On the Run" were popular with hip hoppers. Two years later they released a new album, *Killer Kuts*.

 Selected singles: "It's a Demo" (1988, Cold Chillin'); "Road to the Riches" (1988); "Streets of New York" (1990).

 Selected albums/CDs: *Road to the Riches* (1989, Cold Chillin' 25820); *Wanted: Dead or Alive* (1990, Cold Chillin' 26165); *Live and Let Die* (1992, Cold Chillin' 5001); *Killer Kuts* (1994, Cold Chillin' 5004).

KOOL HERC
See KOOL DJ HERC

KOOL LADY BLUE
a.k.a. Ruza Blue, Lady Blue
(Born in London)

Kool Lady Blue was known as the promoter for the famed roller-skating rink turned club the Roxy in downtown Manhattan during the early 1980s. It was at her parties (thrown with independent film and video director Michael Holman) where Afrika Bambaataa brought his Zulu Nation MCs, DJs, and b-boys to perform, opening up hip-hop culture to a larger, mostly white, new-wave audience.

In 1979 Lady Blue began doing club promotion in London at disco venues. She traveled to New York City in 1981 to run fashion entrepreneur/punk manager Malcolm McLaren's World's End clothing store for one year. Soon after, she ran into a few b-boys who were performing their breakdance routines on the street and decided to get into hip hop.

By 1982 she began promoting shows at the club Negril's, presenting bills like Kool Herc, Whiz Kid, Jazzy Jay, the Treacherous Three, and the Rock Steady Crew b-boys, whom she also managed. At Negril's, Thursday nights were held for these hip-hop events, but they were later moved to the larger Roxy, due to the huge audience at the original venue. Many celebrities frequented Lady Blue's hip-hop shows, such as David Byrne, Herbie Hancock,

Madonna, Rick James, and painter Francesco Clemente. Thus, the genre became exposed to people outside of hip-hop culture.

As the Roxy's heyday began ending after 1983, Blue focused more on managing, handling acts like Afrika Islam, and, by 1995, R&B soul group Two Be F.REE and Man Made, an industrial group. She also began doing music production on commercials for Pepsi.

Kool Moe Dee

KOOL MOE DEE

(Born Mohandas Dewese, 1963, New York City)

Kool Moe Dee is among the first MCs to make records, initially as part of the group the Treacherous Three. He went on to become a successful solo artist. Kool Moe Dee is recognized for his funky rhyme delivery, and for initiating the speed-rapping style of rhyme, which consists of fitting as many as sixteen syllables into a bar of music. Moe Dee is also remembered for his ongoing battle with Busy Bee, and for being involved in heated diss wars with rapper LL Cool J beginning in 1987; Moe Dee's *How Ya Like Me Now* album cover shows a crushed Kangol hat (LL's trademark at the time) underneath a jeep tire, which gave a visual example of the intensity of the wars. Kool Moe Dee was the first rap artist to perform at the Grammy Awards.

Moe Dee was a student at Manhattan's Townes High School with L.A. Sunshine and Spoonie Gee—MCs like himself— along with another rapper named Special K. All four students would eventually battle each other and soon become friends. Spoonie Gee made a record in 1979 called "Spoonin Rap" and was scheduled to make another under the guidance of his uncle, music-industry veteran Bobby Robinson. Moe Dee asked Spoonie if he, Special K, and L.A. Sunshine could record with him, and Spoonie said yes. That summer Moe Dee had been working on a rhyme style that he called speed rapping, and was ready to put it to use.

During 1980 Moe Dee and the others, calling themselves the Treacherous Three, recorded for Bobby Robinson's Enjoy Records label. With their DJ Easy Lee, the Treacherous Three recorded the piece "The New Rap Language," on a 12-inch recording, while on the other side Spoonie recorded his own song, called "Love Rap." The record was successful with hip hoppers. Spoonie Gee eventually left the group to go solo, while Kool Moe Dee and the others continued to record for Robinson, cutting songs such as "Put the Boogie in Your Body" and "The Body Rock." Toward 1982 Robinson sold the group to Sugar Hill Records.

At Sugar Hill Moe Dee and the group made notable singles like "Feel the Heartbeat," "Action," and "Yes We Can Can." However, business relationships began to sour between the group and Sugar Hill Records, and creative ties with the label were soon severed. The Treacherous Three separated by the mid-1980s as well. Moe Dee then focused on college studies, and soon graduated from the State University of New York in old Westbury. Around 1986, Moe Dee began working with producer Teddy Riley, recording a single titled "Go See the Doctor," which became a classic in hip-hop circles. From there he was picked up by Jive Records, where his self-titled debut album was released. The work contained the previous single and another hit, "Do You Know What Time It Is." He soon began touring with Treacherous Three DJ, Easy Lee. During 1987 Moe Dee's second album, *How Ya Like Me Now*, was released and went platinum the following year.

In 1989 his album *Knowledge Is King* was released and made gold that year. During this same period Moe Dee worked with the Stop the Violence Movement on their piece "Self-Destruction." He also worked with Quincy Jones on his all-star *Back on the Block* LP.

By 1990 Moe Dee had released an EP titled *African Heritage*, which contained the song "God Made Me Funke." Moe Dee's next work, *Funke, Funke Wisdom*, was released in 1991. One of the songs on the work, "Rise 'N' Shine," had cameos from rappers KRS-One and Chuck D.

In 1993 Kool Moe Dee and the other members of the Treacherous Three had reassembled, recording "Feel the New Heartbeat" on DJ Easy Lee's own label. A solo album by Moe Dee followed a year later.

 Selected albums/CDs: *Kool Moe Dee* (1986, Jive/RCA); *How Ya Like Me Now* (1987, Jive/RCA 1079); *Knowledge Is King* (1989, Jive/RCA 1182) *Funke Funke Wisdom* (1991, Jive/RCA 1388); *Greatest Hits* (1993, Jive/RCA 41493); *Interlude* (1994, Easylee 8144).

KRIS KROSS
●●●●●●●●●●●●●●●●●●
Formed c. 1991, Atlanta
(Daddy Mack, born Chris Smith; Mack Daddy, born Chris Kelly)

Kris Kross is the first rap duo made up of kids (ages 12 and 13 years old at the time) that became successful in the underground rap market as well as the pop market. Their music is known for its hardcore production, while their lyrics (both by former dancer-turned-producer Jermaine Dupri) are delivered in the same manner as older rappers, thus giving them wide appeal to children and adults. They are also noted for their "krossed-out look": wearing their pants and shirts backward.

Both Chrisses (Chris Smith and Chris Kelly) had known each other since the first grade by the time they met Jermaine Dupri at a shopping mall. After spotting the two, Dupri was reported as saying that they had the look, whereupon he asked them if they could rap. Both said that they could, and from there, Dupri took them in, sculpted the best of their qualities, and presented them to the public.

The duo's debut single, "Jump," was released in February 1992 and was a major crossover hit. Their debut album, *Totally Krossed Out*, sold five million copies. That same year they made *Billboard*'s Top New Pop Artists chart. The duo would later do a popular commercial for Sprite soda, as well as tour Europe with singer Michael Jackson.

In 1993 their second album was released, titled *Da Bomb*. This time Kris Kross contributed some of their own lyrics and ideas to the work. The album and the single "Alright" (featuring dancehall reggae artist Supercat) went gold that same year. Jermaine Dupri also deejays for the duo when on tour.

 Selected singles: "Jump" (1992, Ruffhouse/Columbia).

 Selected albums/CDs: *Totally Krossed Out* (1992, Ruffhouse/Columbia 48710); *Da Bomb* (1993, Columbia 57278).

Kris Kross

KRS-ONE

a.k.a. BOOGIE DOWN PRODUCTIONS
Formed in 1984, Bronx, New York
(KRS-One, born Lawrence Krisna Parker, August 20, 1965, Brooklyn, New York; Scott La Rock, born Scott Sterling, c. 1962, New York; died August 26, 1987).

KRS-One is a rapper who expresses sociopolitical consciousness and Afrocentric awareness in his rhymes, as well as street knowledge and historical analysis of the United States, Europe, and the ancient world. His wide media exposure, both electronic and otherwise, has provided him with the arena to expose historical and social ills through his music, and to display his erudition in areas usually taken up by statesmen.

KRS ("the Blastmaster," "the Teacher," or "Kris" as he is affectionately known—the pronunciation for the acronym "KRS," meaning "Knowledge Reigns Supreme, over almost every One") is also known for his versatile lyrical skills and a variety of rapping styles on the microphone, making him one of the top rap technicians of his generation. His association with influential DJ Scott La Rock, and their formation of Boogie Down Productions early on, was the pinnacle of so-called gangsta rap or gangsta hip hop at the time, epitomized by their *Crimi-*

nal Minded LP. With this album he also helped introduce reggae dancehall style rapping (toasting, chattin', or DJ style) to the rap genre. In the mid-1980s Kris and La Rock were involved in some of the most heated diss wars in hip hop, with pioneer hip-hop radio personality Mr. Magic and his Juice Crew (Marley Marl and the Cold Chillin' Records crew), making records with rhymes airing their disputes. These records from both groups were extremely popular, and became rap classics and staples in hip-hop culture.

Kris regularly writes articles for various publications in which he expresses his views, and he is a constant feature on the lecture circuit, having lectured at Harvard, New York, Yale, Stanford, and Columbia universities. Kris is also recognized for putting together the HEAL (Human Education Against Lies) project, an album that featured diverse acts performing educational rhymes.

In the 1970s and early 1980s Kris was a homeless youth living in the Franklin Men's Shelter in the Bronx, and met his partner there, Scott La Rock, who was working as a counselor/social worker. Around 1984 the two formed a group called Scott La Rock and the Celebrity Three, which consisted of both Kris and Scott, along with Levi 167 and MC Quality. They recorded one record as a group, titled "Advance," after which La Rock and Kris were released from the label's contract and the other members split up. Kris and La Rock continued to perform as a group, renaming themselves the Boogie Down Crew.

In 1985 Kris and La Rock were involved with a group called 12:41, who recorded the single "Success Is the Word" for Sleeping Bag Records. After being cheated out of their rights and payment for the project, the two soon renamed themselves Boogie Down Productions—to emphasize the importance of being producers and artists of their own music. They immediately started recording their own material, and began to shop their demos to no avail. They met Mr. Magic (whose hip-hop radio show now aired on New York's WBLS-FM) at a studio they were recording out of called Power Play. Producer Marley Marl also used this studio, and it was during this particular period that both groups became rivals, with Marl, Magic, Kris, and La Rock charging and countercharging each other with everything from inadequate music skills to tape-reel theft.

Marley produced a record during this period titled "Queensbridge," a.k.a. "The Bridge" (which talked about that area's alleged superiority in rap), for rapper MC Shan. The piece received extensive airplay on Magic's radio show. In 1986 Kris and La Rock were signed to Bill Kamara's B. Boy Records, where they recorded an answer single to Shan's piece, titled "South Bronx." Kiss-FM radio DJ Kool DJ Red Alert began playing both "The Bridge" and Kris and La Rock's "South Bronx," intercutting and interchanging both records together. That same year Shan answered with the piece "Kill That Noise," while Kris and La Rock followed with "The Bridge Is Over." Hip hoppers were again pleased with both works.

By 1987 Kris and La Rock released their first album as Boogie Down Productions, titled *Criminal Minded*, a milestone in hip hop. Not only known for its gangsta type lyrics, the work is also recognized for its co-production by the Ultramagnetics's Ced Gee, and the entire work put the group on the map nationally. However, toward the end of that same year La Rock was fatally shot in the Bronx while trying to break up a dispute between DJ D-Nice and another performer.

KRS-One

In 1988 Kris signed with Jive Records and released the album *By All Means Necessary*, adding his DJ brother Kenny Parker and D-Nice to Boogie Down Productions, calling them the BDP Posse. His first video during this period was for the single "My Philosophy," directed by Fab 5 Freddy.

Kris's *Ghetto Music: The Blueprint of Hip Hop* was released in 1989. The year 1990 saw the release of his *Edutainment* album, after which Kris began to work the college lecture circuit, continuing to combine street lyrics with book knowledge. In 1991 he was featured on R.E.M.'s single "Radio Song." That same year he also released one of the first live hip-hop albums, *BDP Live Hardcore*.

In 1992 Kris released *Sex and Violence*, which contained the singles "Duck Down" and "We in There," which became hits with the hip-hop audience. His next album, *Return of the Boom Bap*, released in 1993, contained many hit songs, including "Sound of Da Police," "Outta Here," "Mortal Thought (I Must Rock the Mic)," and "Black Cop." He also released the single "Hip-Hop VS Rap," which was not on the *Boom Bap* album. In 1994 he collaborated with cartoonist/artist Kyle Baker, Marshall Chess (son of Leonard Chess, of the Chess Records family), and the Marvel Comics group to create the thirty-two-page comic *Break the Chain*, which focused on illiteracy and cultural ignorance. Developed by Marvel's Marvel Music division, called Psychosonic, the comic contained a cassette soundtrack with three untitled songs by Kris.

 Selected albums/CDs: *Criminal Minded* (1987, B. Boy 4787); *By All Means Necessary* (1988, Jive/RCA 1097); *Ghetto Music: The Blueprint of Hip Hop* (1989, Jive/RCA 1187); *Edutainment* (1990, Jive/RCA 1358; clean version: Jive/RCA 1394); *Live Hardcore Worldwide* (1991, Jive/RCA 1425); *Sex and Violence* (1992, Jive/RCA 41470); *Return of the Boom Bap* (1993, Jive/RCA 41517).

K-SOLO
●●●●●●●●●●●
(Born Kevin Madison, Central Islip, New York)

K-Solo hit the hip-hop scene with his distinctive rhyme style, consisting of spelling out words with an in-your-face style. He is also noted for his inventive narratives that are sometimes surreal in imagery, and that occasionally give lessons in life and also explain problems of inner-city youth.

Solo originally started out as a boxer at 12 years of age and started rapping at the same time. After he graduated from high school he was the Empire State Games Champion in the 147-pound division. Solo's rap status was established when he successfully threw out rhymes in battle fashion to New York City's WBLS radio DJ Ken Webb at the Calabash nightclub. Later he met then-Rock Squad member Parrish Smith and joined that group.

In 1985 Solo was harassed by two motorcyclists. A physical brawl ensued, and although Solo was only defending himself, he was sentenced to prison for his acts. After he was released, Parrish Smith (who by now had formed EPMD) decided to feature him on EPMD's platinum-plus *Unfinished Business* LP, on the song "Knick Knack Patty Wack." Solo's work on this

K-Solo

piece was immediately noticed by hip hoppers. After nationally touring with EPMD and
other acts, Smith brought him to Atlantic
Records where he was eventually signed.

In 1990 his debut work, *Tell the World
My Name*, was released. Two hit singles
came off the work: "Spellbound" and
"Your Mom's in My Business," which was
on the national rap charts for over
eight weeks, remaining in the top-five
category. In 1992 his second album,
Time's Up, was released, with "Letter-
man" being the single off the work.

Toward the end of that year
Solo left Atlantic Records and Parrish Smith's Hit Squad management
due to creative differences and established his own
management and production company.

 Selected singles: "Your Mom's in My Business" (1990, Atlantic)

 Selected albums/CDS: *Tell the World My Name* (1990, Atlantic 82108); *Time's Up* (1992, Atlantic 82388).

KURTIS BLOW
....
(Born Kurtis Walker, August 9, 1959, Harlem, New York)

Kurtis Blow was the first rapper to sign with a major record company (Mercury
Records). His first two singles, "Christmas Rapping" and "The Breaks," sold over 400,000 and
approximately 600,000 copies, respectively, with the latter reaching gold status in 1980. Blow
was one of the first big-name producers in hip hop, working with Sweet G ("Games People
Play"), Fearless Four ("Problems of the World Today"), Dr. Jeckyll & Mr. Hyde ("AM-PM"),
Lovebug Starski ("You Gotta Believe," "At the Fever"), and singer Angela Wimbush ("Save
Your Love"), and he won producer of the year in New York for 1983, 1984, and 1985. He
produced entire albums for the Fat Boys, and he did production work with Run-D.M.C. and
singer Allyson Williams as well. Blow is also responsible for the production on the all-star
"King Holiday," a piece dedicated to the Rev. Martin Luther King, Jr.

Blow is one of the first people to use samples and sample loops, which his DJ, Davy D
(known at that time as Davy DMX), created on the Fairlight computer. They used a beat from
the go-go band Trouble Funk's "Pump Me Up" for Blow's single "If I Ruled the World" (written
by Blow's later DJ, Kool DJ AJ), and they used the Fairlight again on Blow's homage single to
that DJ, "AJ Scratch." Blow was also an early user of drum machines on his records since

1982. Blow was the first major rapper to tour Europe (with the R&B act, the Commodores) and the first rapper to work on the soap operas, writing and producing rap segments for *One Life to Live* in 1991 and 1992. Blow was also one of the very first rappers to do commercials (for Sprite soda in 1986).

Blow started out in 1972 in Harlem as a DJ and a b-boy going by the name of Kool DJ Kurl, who did battles with dancers like Dancin' Doug from the Polo Grounds Projects in the Bronx. As a DJ, he did house parties with his then-partner, Tony Rome. Later he would have an MC named Billy Bill (who wrote the songs "Basketball" and "8 Million Stories" for Blow in the mid-1980s).

Around 1973 Blow began to follow the parties of Pete DJ Jones, Kool DJ Herc, and DJ Hollywood (becoming part of his response team at his shows). He frequented all the clubs that were popular at the time for hardcore hip hoppers and adult audiences, like Sparkle, Club 371 in the Bronx, the Renaissance, Chuck Thinner's, and the P.A.L. spots.

In 1976 Blow entered the City College of New York and majored in communications and speech broadcasting. There he met future rap mogul Russell Simmons and the two became friends. Blow would also become the program director at the college's radio station. Blow continued deejaying, playing at Charles Gallery in Harlem for a while, then moving to Small's Paradise, becoming the house DJ there every Friday and Saturday night. He also did the club's "Tantalizing Tuesdays" on Tuesday nights.

Around 1977 Blow met Grandmaster Flash (who had just broken up with the Furious Five) at the 371 club, and began working with him as an MC. They soon began doing all the P.A.L. parties in the Bronx. During this same period Blow also teamed with Russell Simmons and worked at the Night Fever Disco in Queens. Blow was the first to bring Flash out to Queens to perform, and soon after, Furious Five member Mele Mel joined them, and they would occasionally do rhymes together. Sometime later, the other Furious Five members got back together with Flash.

Russell Simmons continued working with (and managing) Kurtis Blow, with Blow using Simmons's younger brother Joey (a.k.a. Run) as his DJ, billing him as "Kurtis Blow's Disco Son." Thereafter, Blow was approached by *Billboard* black music columnist Robert

Kurtis Blow

"Rocky" Ford and his friend J. B. Moore. Through Russell Simmons Blow was told of Ford and Moore's desire to make a rap record about Santa Claus coming to Harlem. Blow recorded the song called "Christmas Rapping," which was written by Ford, Moore, and Simmons. It was later picked up by Mercury Records and nearly went gold, putting the rapper on the map. During 1980 Blow released "The Breaks," which was an immediate success for the artist. He then began touring with his DJ, Davy D.

During 1983 Blow began his first production work with Sweet G on the piece "Games People Play," which was one of the most frequently played records on New York radio for approximately three months.

During 1985 Blow starred as himself in the movie *Krush Groove*. He continued to record for Mercury Records during the late 1980s, making the album *Back by Popular Demand* in 1988. By the early 1990s he had entered the world of film production, working with rapper and actor Ice-T. In 1994 he recorded the piece "G-Party" for the *Raiders of the Lost Art* rap pioneers reunion album, which was put together by promoter/producer Van Silk.

 Selected albums/CDs: *Kurtis Blow* (1980, Mercury 6337137); *Deuce* (1981, Mercury 4020); *Tough* (1982, Mercury 1505); *Ego Trip* (1984, Mercury 822420); *Back by Popular Demand* (1984 {AU: Change o.k.?}, Mercury; *Best Rapper in Town* (1984, Mercury 822283); *America* (1985, Mercury 826141); *Kingdom Blow* (1986, Mercury 830215); *Best Of* (1994, Mercury 522456).

KURTIS MANTRONIK
• •
See MANTRONIX

KWAME & A NEW BEGINNING
• •
Formed c. 1988, Queens, New York
(Kwame, born c. 1971, East Elmhurst, Queens; Tasha, born Natasha Lambert,
New York; DJ Tat S, born in New York; A-Sharp, born in New York;
Nina Love, born in New York)

Multi-instrumentalist Kwame made an impressive appearance with the younger hip-hop audience when he appeared in 1988 at the age of 17 with his group, A New Beginning, dressed in polka-dotted outfits, performing "The Rhythm." Kwame is known for his experimental albums and stage shows, which are similar to musician/performer Prince in terms of theatrical structure. He was formerly one of the Invincibles, a production crew who worked with producer Hurby Luv Bug Azor.

Kwame (named after Ghanian president Kwame Nkrumah) began learning the piano at the age of 7. He later learned guitar, xylophone, drums, and horns. He also got into rap, partaking in MC battles at the USA Roller Rink. In 1986 Kwame took part in a rap contest, coming in second place, which won him a spot on an East Coast rap tour.

Returning home, Kwame began working on a demo tape to present his rap skills, and formed the group A New Beginning. He attended three high schools, including the High School of Art and Design, by the time he played one of his demos for producer Hurby Luv Bug Azor. Azor brought the demo to Atlantic Records, and Kwame was soon signed to the label.

The single "The Rhythm" was one of the first songs Kwame worked on, and it wound up being one of the top-five rap songs by the time his first album, *The Boy Genius, Featuring a New Beginning*, was released in 1989. In 1990 Kwame released his second album, *A Day in the Life—A Pokadelick Adventure*, which contained the single "Ownlee Eue." *Nastee*, his third album, was released in 1992, along with its single "Dontmatta."

 Selected albums/CDs: *Boy Genius* (1989, Atlantic 81941); *A Day in the Life—A Pokadelick Adventure* (1990, Atlantic 82100); *Nastee* (1992, Atlantic 82536).

KENNY GEE
(Born in New York)

Kenny Gee was a DJ who worked with Kool DJ AJ and Lovebug Starski during the years 1978 to '79. They played together mostly in areas located in the Moore Houses in the Bronx, and in some of promoter Ray Chandler's Black Door Production parties with Grandmaster Flash. Gee, AJ, and Starski usually worked as a team during their shows.

KOOL DJ D
(Born in Bronx, New York)

Kool DJ D was one of the first DJs to perform with a sound system in the Soundview area of the Bronx during the early 1970s, before Disco King Mario and Kool Herc. He was one of the first DJs in the Bronx to use a coffin (a one-piece case that houses two turntables and a mixer for deejaying), and he is recognized for his influence on DJ Afrika Bambaataa. Like most DJs during the early 1970's before Kool Herc's emergence, Kool DJ D played disco music and switched to break music after Herc's appearance. He continued for a few years before his popularity subsided.

Kicking the mixer: Trick used by DJs in which they manipulate the mixer by using their feet to adjust the fader (volume control), rather than using their hands.

RAP'S CHARTS

Around 1985—86 a writer and promoter from Jenkintown in Philadelphia, Pennsylvania, noticed that, out of all the music charts contained in the music industry publication *Billboard*, there was one that was missing: a chart for rap music.

"When I first started, I approached Impact Publications, and I had this idea for a rap chart," says Jackie Paul, veteran music industry writer and promotions person for over twelve years. Her Rap Report first appeared in Impact Publications three years before *Billboard* decided to publish its own version of her chart.

"Rap," explains Paul, "was like an infant, with so much life ahead of it and growth and potential. Because the labels were still denying it. Nobody was really supporting it—it was like the stepchild of music.

"So program director Lynn Tolliver at radio station WDAK attacked *Billboard*, saying 'Hey! Wake up! Why is it taking this girl to realize that a rap chart is needed, when you're supposed to be the trend setters?'

"So Terri Rossi (then part of *Billboard*'s chart and research department, and writer for their "Rhythm Section" column) wrote a letter back, and they were both published in the magazine, and *Billboard* came in three years behind me [circa 1988{*}89] with their rap chart.

"Then later I met Darryl Lindsay at *Hits* magazine and worked with him, and Darryl started a rap chart there. Then Darryl and I helped Brian Sampson at Gavin Publications with their rap chart."

Billboard continues to print a rap singles chart, although it has yet to institute an album listing. Rap artists regularly appear on *Billboard*'s pop chart as well.

LADY B
•••••••••••
(Born in Philadelphia)

Lady B is recognized as Philadelphia's pioneer hip-hop radio personality. She also recorded (as DJ Lady B) the single "To the Beat Y'all" on Tec Records. During the early 1980s she gave exposure to many of that city's rising hip-hop acts, including DJ Jazzy Jeff & the Fresh Prince, Steady B, Three Times Dope, DJ Cash Money & MC Marvelous, and Schoolly D. Her show, which began in June 1983 on radio station WHAT, was the most popular of the subsequent rap shows that followed in that area. Called *Streetbeat*, the show moved to radio station WUSL-FM, Power 99, around 1987. She stayed there until July 1989, after which she was fired due to the station's controversial format change.

She became financially involved with Hiriam Hicks (manager of R&B group Bell Biv DeVoe) and his *Seriously Hip Hop* (later known as *Serious Hip Hop*) rap publication during the early 1990s. During this period she relocated to New York City and worked at radio station WBLS-FM for a short time. She left the station and began working in radio in Atlantic City, New Jersey, in late 1994.

L.A. POSSE
•••••••••••••••••••
Formed c. early 1980s, South Los Angeles
(Muffla, born Dwayne Simon; Big Dad, born Darryl Pierce; Byrd, born Clarence Boyce; Bobcat: all born in Los Angeles)

The L.A. Posse gained wide recognition as producers for their work on LL Cool J's 1987 album *Bigger and Deffer* and his 1989 *Walking with a Panther* work.

Principal group members Dwayne "Muffla" Simon and Darryl "Big Dad" Pierce hail from South Los Angeles, and met at Antelope Valley College in 1982. Both joined the DJ group Uncle Jam's Army for a while; however, they grew impatient waiting to make a record with that group. They eventually left to make their own demos in an effort to get a record deal.

Their demos reached rap producer/mogul Russell Simmons, who asked the two to do some demo work with one of his artists, LL Cool J. Impressed with their work, he hired them to work on the artist's album. With pioneer West Coast DJ Bobcat, the L.A. Posse produced LL's *Bigger and Deffer* album, which eventually went triple platinum. They also produced the artist's *Walking with a Panther*, which attained platinum sales in the year of its release, 1989.

The L.A. Posse later produced works for MC Breeze, Real Roxanne, Tashan, the Wise Guyz, and others. They introduced artists like female MC The Lady of Rage and singer Joi Cardwell on their debut album, *They Come in All Colors*, in 1991.

Selected produced albums/CDs: *Bigger and Deffer* by LL Cool J (1987, Def Jam/Columbia t40793).

LARGE PROFESSOR
(Born Paul Mitchell, 1973, Harlem, New York)

The Large Professor is known for his work as a producer and MC with the group Main Source, and for his production work with other acts.

Professor auditioned for brothers K-Cut and Sir Scratch, who made up the Main Source around 1989, and became a member of the group. All three had apprenticed with legendary engineer and producer Paul C at Studio 1212 in Jamaica, New York. The group released their first album, *Breaking Atoms*, in 1991, which was an underground classic, noted for its production and MC rhymes.

The Large Professor left the group over creative differences, and soon got into full-fledged production work. He worked on Kool G Rap & DJ Polo's *Wanted Dead or Alive* album, and he was involved with Eric B & Rakim's *Let the Rhythm Hit 'Em* as well. Large Professor has also produced Akinyele's 1993 *Vagina Dinner* LP, and produced several cuts on Nas's *Illmatic* album in 1994. In 1995 he worked with rapper Common Sense on that artist's "Resurrection" single.

LARRY SMITH
(Born c. 1954, St. Albans, Queens)

Producer Larry Smith was responsible for some of the early hits on the Def Jam Recordings label. His collaborations with Russell Simmons, and his album productions for Run-D.M.C. (*Run-D.M.C.*, *King of Rock*) and Whodini (*Escape*, *Back in Black*) helped establish those two groups and the Def Jam label. Initially a bass player, Smith is also known for his bass work on Kurtis Blow's first singles, "Christmas Rappin'" and "The Breaks."

Smith taught himself to play bass by listening to records by James Brown. He got his first paying job as a musician while still in high school, playing at a club in the Bedford-Stuyvesant neighborhood in Brooklyn, New York. He later toured with a Brooklyn blues singer, and played for the R&B group Brighter Side of Darkness. He also worked as a session musician, playing jazz, punk, rock, and even bar mitzvahs and weddings. Smith was also involved in the theater, working in Albany, New York, leading the orchestra for the play *Your Arm's Too Short to Box with God*, then later in Toronto, Canada, where he led the house band for the musical *Indigo*.

In 1979 Smith was hired to work with Kurtis Blow by his friend Robert "Rocky" Ford. Smith later formed a band with DJ/guitarist Davy D, R&B singer Alyson Williams, and drummer Trevor Gale, called Orange Krush. Around 1981 to 1982 he produced with Russell Simmons their single "Action," which had vocals by Williams. They also worked on Jimmy Spicer's "The Bubble Bunch" and "Money (Dollar Bill Y'All)." Smith and Simmons began working with Simmons's brother Run and his friend Darryl (a.k.a. D.M.C.) in Smith's attic recording studio. They worked on songs like "It's Like That" and "Sucker MCs," subtitled "Krush Groove 1" after the drum programming they used, which was patterned after Orange Krush drummer Trevor Gale's drum pattern on "Action."

Smith worked with Simmons on Run-D.M.C.'s self-titled album in 1984. During that year he produced Whodini's album *Escape*. In 1985 Smith worked on Run-D.M.C.'s *King of Rock*, and in 1986 he produced Whodini's *Back in Black*. On that group's 1987 album *Open Sesame* Smith worked on two songs, before terminating his relationship with Def Jam for a period, due to creative differences.

Smith disappeared from the music scene for a while but returned in 1994, working with Whodini again on their piece "It All Comes Down to the Money," which he co-produced with Public Enemy's Terminator X.

 Selected produced albums/CDs: *Run-D.M.C.* by Run-D.M.C. (1984, Profile 1202); *Escape* by Whodini (1984, Jive/RCA 1226).

L BROTHERS
* * * * * * * * * * * * * * * * * *
Formed c. 1977—78, Bronx, New York
(Gordeo, a.k.a. Gordon Livingston; Mean Gene, a.k.a. Gene Livingston;
DJ Grand Wizard Theodore, a.k.a. Theodore Livingston; Water Bed Kevie Kev;
Master Rob; Rubie Dee; Dot-A-Roc: all born in Bronx, New York;
Busy Bee Starski, born David Parker, New York)

The L Brothers (as in Livingston Brothers) were a premier DJ and MC group during the late 1970s, led by DJ Mean Gene Livingston and his DJ brothers, Gordon and Theodore, the youngest, known as Grand Wizard Theodore. Theodore is recognized for introducing and perfecting the DJ technique known as scratching (which is the quick, back-and-forth spin of a record under the turntable needle, creating a scratching, percussive sound). Because of his short size at the time, Theodore was known to deejay while standing on top of milk crates, and he was also noted for his ability to catch certain parts of a record with the turntable needle without backspinning (alternately spinning two records back to repeat a phrase or beat).

From the Boston Road, 163rd Street-area of the Bronx, the L Brothers were not known for having a powerful sound system. However, they were known for their routines, highlighted by their MCs, Kevie Kev and Master Rob, with their "This is the way we harmonize" number, and later Busy Bee, Rubie Dee, and Dot-A-Roc, who had also worked as one of the Cold Crush Brothers for a short period with DJ Charlie Chase. Kevie Kev and the other MCs also made the then-famous term "fresh" popular, using it in one of their rhyme routines: "We're fresh out the pack so you gotta stay back, we got one Puerto Rican and the rest are black." One of the main venues they performed in at the time was the Fox Street Boys Club in the Bronx.

Around the mid-1970s Mean Gene was working with Grandmaster Flash, and the two deejayed together for a period. Sometime later Gene's brother Theodore also worked with Flash as his record boy. Soon after, Mean Gene soon formed his first DJ group with his brothers, Gordon and Theodore. Gordon occasionally deejayed, but it was Theodore who was the most recognized of the three. It was during a performance at the Third Avenue Ballroom in 1978 where Theodore introduced scratching, using two copies of James Brown's "Sex Machine."

Theodore and the others were also involved in a series of impressive battles during 1978, including teaming with Afrika Bambaataa, Busy Bee, and others against Grandmaster Flash and his Furious MCs; Afrika Islam and Jazzy Jay against Theodore and Flash (a battle that was full of astonishing tricks from each DJ); Theodore also battled Islam during the same period; and toward 1980, the L Brothers battled Kool DJ Herc and the Herculords on University Avenue in the Bronx, which ended with some turbulence and accusations of theft from some members.

One of the last places the L Brothers played as a group was the Executive Playhouse, also around 1980. It was around this period when Mean Gene, Gordon, and Busy Bee dropped out of the group, with Theodore remaining, deejaying for the four MCs, calling themselves the Fantastic Four.

LEADERS OF THE NEW SCHOOL

Formed in 1986, Long Island, New York
(Charlie Brown; Dinco D; Busta Rhymes: all born Uniondale, Long Island; Cut Monitor Milo, New York)

Leaders of the New School (a.k.a. LONS) ushered in the third generation of rappers, whose rap styles are presented with louder deliveries and intermittent ensemble shouts. LONS also revived the concept of three or more MCs in a group, reminiscent of the Cold Crush Brothers and Grandmaster Flash and the Furious Five before them. The group's most heralded rapper, Busta Rhymes, is recognized for his boisterous, off-beat, reggae-flavored rhyme style and semideep voice. His style liberated the art of MC'ing, and enabled later rappers (such as the Wu-Tang Clan and their followers) to find different technical approaches to delivering rhymes.

Charlie Brown and Busta Rhymes began rapping in 1984, and would battle other rappers in front of their junior high school. The two soon met Dinco D, and by 1986 they began to perform as a unit. By 1989 they added DJ Cut Monitor Milo to the group, and later began working with Chuck D and Hank Shocklee of Public Enemy/Bomb Squad fame. Shocklee and Chuck showed the group how to write songs effectively, how to use a music studio and its equipment, and other music industry ins and outs.

The group was signed to Elektra Records, and their debut work, *Future Without a Past*, was released in 1991. With production by another Bomb Squad member, Eric "Vietnam" Sadler, and others, the album was a work that focused on situations and topics related to high school. Musically, samples on the work ranged from everything to Fats Waller-type jazz piano riffs to rock 'n' roll. Its single "Case of the P.T.A." was a hit with hip hoppers, especially those who came from their age group.

In 1993 the group released the single "What's Next?" b/w "Connections." Their second album, *The Inner Mind's Eye (T.I.M.E.)*, featured production work by Sam Sever, Rampage, and Backspin.

Selected albums/CDs: *Future Without a Past* (1991, Elektra 60976); *The Inner Mind's Eye (T.I.M.E.)* (1993, Elektra 61382).

Leaders of the New School

LISA LEE
(Born in Bronx, New York)

Lisa Lee is recognized as one of the most popular of the first female MCs, and one of the first females to join Afrika Bambaataa's Zulu Nation. She is also known for her duets with various MCs.

Hailing from the Lafayette Projects in the Soundview section of the Bronx, Lisa emerged as a rapper around 1978, and in 1979 became a member of one of Afrika Bambaataa's groups, Cosmic Force. With Cosmic Force, Lisa was part of one of the Zulu Nation's first recordings, "Zulu Nation Throwdown." She was also part of the female rap group the Us Girls, and appeared in the films *Wild Style* and *Beat Street*.

LL COOL J
(Born James Todd Smith, January 14, 1968, St. Albans, Queens)

LL Cool J (which stands for Ladies Love Cool James) is one of the first sex symbols in rap, and an artist known for his sharp lyrical technique, delivery of complex lines, and imaginative subject matter, along with his muscular physique. He has also written rhymes for other people (notably MC Lyte's verse for the Stop the Violence Movement's 1989 work, "Self-Destruction") and is one of several rappers who have wide unintentional crossover appeal, reaching all the way to the White House.

LL began rapping at the age of 9. At the age of 16 he sent a demo recording he produced in his basement to Def Jam Recordings's cofounder Rick Rubin—one of many copies LL had sent to other record companies. Ad Rock, of the Beastie Boys, first heard LL's demo and turned Rubin on to it. Rubin was the only record company owner to show interest.

The first single he recorded in 1984 was "I Need A Beat," which initially sold 120,000 copies and launched the career of the artist as well as the record label. LL's original image was changed before he began giving performances, from the slick style of dress that he and most rap groups had in the early 1980s to his then-trademark red Kangol (a round hat with a downward brim) and Adidas sneakers—suggested by Def Jam's other founder, Russell Simmons. When his debut album, *Radio* (with DJ Cut Creator), was released in 1985, it eventually went platinum. His appearance that same year in the movie *Krush Groove*, in a ninety-second cameo, also helped the sales of that album.

In 1987 his second album, *Bigger and Deffer* (produced by Bobcat and the L.A. Posse, with DJ Pooh), was released. This work contained the single "I Need Love," a rap ballad that reached number 1 on the *Billboard* Hot Black Singles chart (which made LL the first rap artist to achieve that feat), propelling the album to triple-platinum status. The same year also saw the beginning of some of the most heated diss wars on record, starting with LL and Kool Moe Dee, and later—to a lesser extent—Ice-T. LL released two songs, "Goin' Back to Cali" and "Jack the Ripper," as a retort to Moe Dee's *How Ya Like Me Now*, which attacked LL visually on

LL Cool J

the album cover (by portraying the crushing of his Kangol cap under a jeep tire). Later that year, after a show LL gave in Columbus, Georgia, he was arrested for "public lewdness." But by 1988 he was placed on *Playgirl* magazine's Ten Sexiest Men in Rock 'n' Roll list.

The album *Walking with a Panther* was his third release in 1989. The single "I'm That Type of Guy" went gold and the album made platinum that same year, even though his status in hip-hop circles was declining. When he made an appearance at a Harlem rally for Yusef Hawkins, a youth slain in a racially motivated attack, during the month of September, he was greeted with tumultuous boos from the crowd, for what they felt was his lack of Afrocentricity, and his less-than-hard loverboy image. But toward the end of the year LL did a remix of one of his songs, "Jingling Baby," with producer Marley Marl, and his street credibility began to rise again.

His 1990 appearance in the pay-per-view concert "Rapmania" also helped restore his image, and he was received favorably by the crowd in the Apollo Theater. When his next album, *Mama Said Knock You Out* (with production by Marley Marl, and some coproduction by LL), was released in September of that year, his credibility in the hip-hop world was totally restored, with the album reaching gold status by November and eventually going multiplatinum. In 1991 two singles from the album, "Around the Way Girl" and "Mama Said Knock You Out," went gold, with the latter song being nominated for a Grammy. LL also began to take on more acting roles at this time, appearing in the film *The Hard Way*, with Michael J. Fox. In 1992 he appeared with actor Robin Williams in the movie *Toys*.

14 Shots to the Dome was his next album in 1993. "How I'm Comin'," "Pink Cookies in a Plastic Bag," and "Stand by Your Man" were some of the singles released from the work. That same year, his song "Strictly Business" received a Grammy nomination. He was also asked to perform at President Bill Clinton's inauguration that year. This was the second time he was asked to perform by someone from the White House. (First Lady Nancy Reagan had asked him to perform at Radio City Music Hall, for her "Just Say No" campaign, c. 1987—88.) He received a positive response from the audience at the inauguration. Later that year LL opened up a camp for children, called Camp Cool J. In 1995 he landed his own network TV show, a situation comedy called *In the House*.

 Selected singles: "I Need a Beat," (1984, Def Jam); "I Need Love," (1987); "I'm That Type of Guy," (1989); "Around the Way Girl," (1991); "How I'm Comin'" (1993).

 Selected albums/CDs: *Radio* (1985, Def Jam/Columbia 40239); *Bigger and Deffer* (1987, Def Jam/ Columbia 40793); *Walking with a Panther* (1989, Def Jam/Columbia 45172; edited version: Def Jam/Columbia 45274); *Mama Said Knock You Out* (1990, Def Jam/Columbia 46888); *14 Shots to the Dome* (1993, Columbia 53325).

LORD FINESSE

(Born Robert Hall, c. 1970, Bronx, New York)

Lord Finesse is recognized for his hardcore rhymes, which usually contain humorous similes and metaphors, and the use of compound words. It is because of his love of fancy language that he is sometimes called the "word technician." His delivery is similar to the style of the original MCs of the 1970s, minus the inflections that MCs used during that period. Finesse achieved an underground following before making records.

Finesse (who hails from Forest Projects in the Bronx) got into MC'ing at an early age, but also performed as a DJ, participating in a few DJ battles and deejaying for several parties. He later performed his rhymes at local block parties, building a reputation for his skills. Soon, with financing from his grandmother, Finesse sought out a record deal, choosing Wild Pitch Records, and recorded the album *The Funky Technician* for the label in 1990.

After some differences with Wild Pitch, Finesse left the company. Ice-T's Rhyme Syndicate Management decided to represent him, and by 1991 Finesse was recording for Giant Records, which released his *The Return of the Funkyman* album.

Finesse has worked extensively with Showbiz & AG, Diamond D, Steve D, the X-Men, and DJ Mike Smooth. By 1994 he began working more as a producer for artists like Biggie Smalls (The Notorious B.I.G.) and others.

Selected albums/CDs: *Funky Technician* (1990, reissued 1992, Wild Pitch 98710); *The Return of the Funkyman* (1991, Giant 24437).

LORDS OF THE UNDERGROUND

Formed in Raleigh, North Carolina
(Doitall; Mr. Funke: both born in Newark, New Jersey; DJ Lord Jazz, born in Cleveland)

The Lords of the Underground met in college at Shaw University in North Carolina. Doitall hails from New Jersey, and was originally a solo performer working with future solo act Redman as his DJ. The two worked together in the New Jersey area for three years, and occasionally appeared in rap contests with Jerseyites Naughty by Nature. Mr. Funke also worked as a solo artist when he and Doitall decided to form a group together and hunt for a DJ. They selected Lord Jazz, a popular DJ at Shaw University, who had his own radio show at the college's station.

The group began giving performances in the North Carolina area. Another schoolmate of theirs told them that he knew legendary producer Marley Marl, and invited him to come see the group. Marl attended a show, and offered the group a chance to record with him. Lords of the Underground worked with Marl and one of his producers, K-Def. They co-produced the singles "Funky Child" and "Chief Rocka," while Marl produced one single alone, "Psycho." All three were number 1 singles on the chart in 1993. Their album *Here Come the Lords* was also released that year. In 1994 the group released the album *Keepers of the Funk*, with the single "Tic Toc."

 Selected albums/CDs: *Here Come the Lords* (1993, Pendulum 61415); *Keepers of the Funk* (1994, Pendulum 30710).

LOVEBUG STARSKI

(Born May 16, Bronx, New York)

Along with Afrika Bambaataa, Grandmaster Flash, DJ Hollywood, and Kool DJ Herc, Lovebug Starski ranks as one of the most important pioneer figures in hip hop, because of the scope of his career, spanning over twenty years (from 1971 on into the mid-1990s), performing as a DJ when the genre itself was developing. His style of deejaying while MC'ing has influenced many performers, like DJs Kid Capri and Ron G, and he has worked with almost every major pioneer DJ in the early days of hip hop, including those who originally played disco and R&B-oriented material, before Kool Herc's break-beat deejaying style emerged. He has also been the house DJ for, or performed in, almost every major early hip hop and pre—hip-hop club throughout Manhattan, Bronx, and Brooklyn.

Hailing from the South Bronx, Starski began his career as a record boy for Pete DJ Jones in 1971. Introduced to Jones by Grandmaster Flash, Starski first worked for Jones at the Stardust Ballroom on Boston Post Road in the Bronx. He soon began deejaying with Jones at other clubs, including Super Star 33, Justine's, Leviticus, Nell Quinn's, and Club Saturn.

Thereafter, Starski began working with DJ Flowers, then with other DJs like Riff & Cliff, Maboya, Fantasia, and Kool DJ AJ, sometimes as a traditional MC, other times as a DJ. He worked at Club 371 in the Bronx, along with DJs Reggie Wells, Eddie Cheeba, Easy G, Hollywood, Junebug, and Richard Hot, and they all occasionally played against each other as well. For a period, he became the house DJ at 371.

In 1978 Starski was the house DJ at the Disco Fever, the famed hip-hop club. He also deejayed at the Audubon Ballroom, and, around 1979, became the house DJ at Club Harlem World and the Renaissance (known as The Reny). Starski also deejayed in what was called the Burger King Disco during this same period, along with DJ Smokey.

By 1981 Starski began recording, cutting his first single for the Club Harlem World's Tayster Records, titled "Positive Life." Kurtis Blow produced his "Do the Right Thing" single in 1984 on the Disco Fever's The Fever label, and in 1985 he recorded the title soundtrack for the movie *Rappin'* on the Atlantic label.

In 1986 Starski recorded his first album for Epic Records, titled *House Rock*. Around this same period he fell into trouble with the law, and was incarcerated for approximately five years. By 1993 Starski was working again, teaming with DJ Hollywood and working in venues in the New York City tristate area. During 1994 the two DJs recorded a single called "Let's Take It to the Old School" for record company executive Sylvia Robinson.

TAG TEAM: RAP BUSINESSMEN

Tag Team is a group that really seems to be on a roll.

For one, their famous platinum-plus single "Whoomp! (There It Is)" was licensed by the ABC television network to introduce the station's 1994 primetime lineup; it was nominated for a 1994 American Music Award under the category of Best Pop Single; received a *Billboard* Music Award nomination; a Spanish version of the single was quickly released; the group was nominated for an NAACP Image Award in the Outstanding New Artist category—all without the record being broken by a single hip-hop DJ in New York.

Group member Steve Roll'n will let you know that they have always run their group in a business-like manner, forming their own publishing company, Tag Team Music Inc., among other ventures.

"We're in control with the whole situation that's happening with Tag Team," Roll'n reveals. "And this record company we're with is the best thing we could've went with. If we had a went with a major [label], a major would've sat us down on the curb a long time ago.

Tag Team

"The name of the company we're with is called Bellmark. A guy by the name of Al Bell is head of it. He used to own Stax Records back in the day. He goes way back to the Black Panthers, and the segregation of the schools in Arkansas. He sat us down many times and had conversations about the industry and his experiences."

Steve Roll'n says he wants anybody who has any misconceptions about the group to squash them.

"They gotta know we come from the streets," he says. "I had to hustle for what I got. I made enough to get me a studio, I got a fleet of cars, gold, whatever I need.

"They gotta realize that we're straight-up hustlers. Straight-up businessmen. Just because other people adapted the song, don't think that we're wack because we had the success we had with it. And don't be jealous either, 'cause we're gonna pick up people. We're gonna help our people out, and that's what it's about. So get it in your minds now. Learn to accept it."

LUTHER "LUKE SKYYWALKER" CAMPBELL

See 2 LIVE CREW

OTHERZ

LAKIM SHABAZZ

(Born in Newark, New Jersey)

Lakim Shabazz was one of the original members of the Flavor Unit, which included Queen Latifah and Chill Rob G. He has worked extensively with DJ Mark the 45 King, and he attained recognition for his rhymes that contained lessons from the Five Percent Nation of Islam. His debut album on the Tuff City label, *Pure Righteousness*, was released in 1988, with the single "Black Is Back," a hit with hip-hop audiences in the United States and London. In 1990 he released the single "No Justice, No Peace." His second album, *The Lost Tribe of Shabazz*, was released in 1991.

Selected albums/CDs: *Pure Righteousness* (1988, Tuff City); *Lost Tribe of Shabazz* (1991, Tuff City 571).

LOVE KID HUTCH

(Born in Bronx, New York)

Love Kid Hutch was one of the many MCs who were part of Afrika Bambaataa's Zulu Nation during the late 1970s and early 1980s. He was known for the rhymes he performed during Jazzy Jay's deejaying sets. He also did rhymes while Afrika Bambaataa played records during his Zulu Nation parties and at other events. He continued to perform at Zulu Nation parties into the early 1990s.

MAIN SOURCE
••••••••••••••••••••
**Formed c. 1989, Queens, New York
(Sir Scratch, born in 1970, Toronto; K-Cut, born in 1972, Toronto; Mickey D, born
in Queens, New York; Original member: Large Professor, born Paul Mitchell,
1973, Harlem, New York)**

The group Main Source began with brothers Sir Scratch and K-Cut, two DJs who were looking for an MC while attending high school. They auditioned rapper Large Professor, who was going by the name of Paul Juice at the time. Impressed with Professor's MC skills, the brothers chose him to become part of the group. The three began working out of Studio 1212 in Jamaica, New York, around 1990. Here, they were shown the ropes of how to record and use a studio by the engineer/producer there, Paul C, who also created break beats for the group.

After completing a few demos, the group shopped around for a record deal to no avail. They then decided to press their own record. On their label, Actual Management (which had a logo designed by Scratch), the group put out two 12-inch singles. The first was titled "Think," with the b-side being "Breaking Atoms." The group then tried to market the work, going as far as Philadelphia, and to Scratch and K-Cut's place of birth, Toronto. They successfully got airtime on Marley Marl's radio show at the time, from DJ Pete Rock.

Their second 12-inch single was called "Watch Roger Do His Thing," backed with Large Professor's self-titled piece. This time they made a video to promote the work and the group. They signed with Wild Pitch Records in 1991. Their first album, *Breaking Atoms*, was a classic underground work, recognized for its production as well as lyrical skill. The album is noted for several cuts, including the singles "Looking at the Front Door" and "Live at the BBQ"—a piece that contained cameos from rappers Nasty Nas (later known as Nas), Akinyele, and Joe Fatal, whose second rhyme verse was written by Pudgee the Phat Bastard. Around 1992 the group also did a song for the *White Men Can't Rap* EP, titled "Fakin' the Funk." Soon after, creative differences between the Large Professor and the other members resulted in the Large Professor leaving the group to concentrate on his career as a producer (which he had started earlier with his production work for Eric B & Rakim and Kool G Rap).

Thereafter, Scratch and K-Cut sought out another MC. They chose someone who had been working with engineer Paul C years earlier, whose name was Mickey D. Mickey D won the 1987 MC Battle for World Supremacy at the New Music Seminar, beating pioneer MC veteran Mele Mel of Grandmaster Flash's Furious Five. The event was noted for Mele Mel's walking off with Mickey's championship belt in disgust. Mickey had previously put out a single, "I Get Rough," under the name Mickey D and the L.A. Posse. With their new MC, Main Source recorded their second album, titled *F**k What You Think*, during 1994.

Selected albums/CDs: *Breaking Atoms* (1991, Wild Pitch 97543); *F**k What You Think* (1994, Wild Pitch 98469).

MANTRONIX
a.k.a. Kurtis Mantronik
(Born Kurtis Khaleel, Canada)

Kurtis Mantronik was a prolific producer of rap and hip hop-oriented dance music during the mid-1980s. Recording for Sleeping Bag/Fresh Records, Mantronik helped establish that company by producing and mixing much of its rap and dance product, such as "This Beat Kicks" by T La Rock, "Cold Gettin' Dumb" by Just-Ice, "All and All" by Joyce Sims, and Nocera's "Summertime Summertime." He is recognized as one of the kings of the then-popular electrofunk genre of hip hop, noted for his innovative sound textures in production.

Mantronik, with his group, or duo, known as Mantronix, consisted of the artist with MC Tee, then later, with Bryce Luvah and DJ D. Mantronik's official appearance began in 1985 with Tricky Tee on the single "Johnny the Fox." As Mantronix, the single "Bassline" was released around the same period, as well as other hit singles like "Fresh Is the Word," and the album titled *Mantronix, The Album*.

By 1990 Mantronik was recording for Capitol Records, where his *This Should Move Ya* album was released. The single off the work was called "Got to Have Your Love." Mantronik continued to produce records in the early 1990s, for artists like Just-Ice and other acts, including Nu-Shooz, Duran Duran, and Chandra Simmons.

Selected albums/CDs: *Mantronix, The Album* (1985, Sleeping Bag/Fresh 6); *This Should Move Ya* (1990, Capitol 91119).

MARKY MARK
AND THE FUNKY BUNCH
●●●●●●●●●●●●●●●●●●●●●●●●●●●●●●●●●●●●
(Marky Mark, born Mark Wahlberg, June 5, 1971, Boston)

Marky Mark received a lot of attention outside hip-hop circles for his 1991 platinum album, *Music for the People*, which included two gold singles, "Wild Side" and "Good Vibrations." Mark's style of rap has always been unacceptable among traditional and hardcore hip hoppers (despite his records' sales), because of its pop/commercial approach. He has, however, garnered many award nominations for his work, including those for his music videos from MTV. Mark is closely associated with his older brother, Donnie Wahlberg, of the singing group New Kids on the Block. Donnie has produced some of Mark's works.

Hailing from Boston, Mark was reportedly a high-school dropout who hung out on the streets before embarking on his recording career. He had great success right out of the box on his first album. This was followed by *You Gotta Believe* in 1992. Mark became recognized as a sex symbol after modeling for Calvin Klein's men's underwear in a series of provocative photos. In 1994 he made his movie debut in the motion picture *Renaissance Man*.

 Selected albums/CDs: *Music for the People* (1991, Interscope 91737); *You Gotta Believe* (1992, Interscope 92203).

MARLEY MARL
●●●●●●●●●●●●●●●●●●●●●●●
(Born Marlon Williams, September 30, 1964, Queens, New York)

Marley Marl is one of the most influential producers, DJs, and remixers in hip hop. He is widely recognized as being one of the first producers to usher in drum sampling, and his music tracks are responsible for the success of early Cold Chillin' Records acts, including Roxanne Shanté, Big Daddy Kane, MC Shan, Biz Markie, and Kool G Rap & DJ Polo. He also recorded Roxanne Shanté's answer record to UTFO's "Roxanne, Roxanne" hit, titled "Roxanne's Revenge." Not only known as an early expert at the turntables, Marl is also one of the top remixers. He was also the partner of pioneer hip-hop radio personality Mr. Magic, and part of his Juice Crew family. He tailored all the music for them in the famous diss wars that took place between the Juice Crew and KRS-One and the Boogie Down Productions. Marl revived the career of LL Cool J by producing his *Mama Said Knock You Out* LP.

Marl got into deejaying at the age of 15, influenced by his brother, known as Larry Larr (from the Up Hi-Fidelity Crew). By 1977 Marl had formed his own group, called the Sureshot Crew, and was known as Doc Magic Hands. Around 1978–'79 he began playing in the parks in his Queensbridge Projects neighborhood. He would also deejay on radio station WBLS-FM's promotion truck. Marl soon began working with musicians, and eventually got into 4-track recording, using his mother's living room as a studio. He cut "Sucker DJs" with his then-girlfriend, Dimples D, and keyboard player Andre Booth. Marl also interned at Unique Recording

Studios, where he met producer Arthur Baker, Afrika Bambaataa, the Force MDs, and the Aleems.

In the early 1980s Marl got into remixing, working with the Aleems on their Nia Records label, handling acts like Captain Rock. By 1983 Marl became Mr. Magic's partner on his *Rap Attack* radio show on WBLS-FM as a DJ. Marl also became part of Magic's Juice Crew (named after Magic's other nickname, Sir Juice).

In 1984 Marl's remix work for the Aleems paid off with the success of their single "Release Yourself," gaining Marl extra notice. That same year, Marl met Roxanne Shanté in front of his building in the projects, where she expressed interest in making an answer record to the group UTFO's hit "Roxanne, Roxanne." Marl made a demo recording of Shanté performing "Roxanne's Revenge," and brought it to Mr. Magic. Magic played the tape on his radio show, introducing it as the "real Roxanne's" response to UTFO's record. Soon after, while in Philadelphia, Marl, Magic, and Tyrone Williams (later Chairman of Cold Chillin' Records) played the work for Pop Arts Records Dana and Lawrence Goodman, after which they released the record to great success.

Marley Marl

By 1985 Marl began working with MC Shan, who also came from Marl's neighborhood. Together they made the single "Marley Marl Scratch," one of the first records to use a sampled drum track throughout an entire song (an idea that was spawned by Marl's accidental sampling of a snare drum). This technique would later be copied extensively by most producers. Soon after, Marl also did "Queensbridge," a.k.a. "The Bridge" (using the same technique), with Shan. This record initiated the diss wars with Blastmaster KRS-One and DJ Scott La Rock's Boogie Down Productions (who answered it with their piece, "South Bronx"). During this period Marl met Biz Markie, who was beatboxing in the hallway of Marl's building.

In 1986 Marl and Shan answered Boogie Down Productions' "South Bronx" with "Kill That Noise." All Marley Marl material for Cold Chillin', as well as the label's roster, got extensive airplay on Mr. Magic's show because of their affiliation as Juice Crew members, while KRS-One and Scott La Rock's work got exposure through Kool DJ Red Alert's radio show. Around this same period Marl also began working with Eric B & Rakim on their singles "Eric B Is President" and "My Melody."

Around 1988 Marl worked with Biz Markie on his album, *Goin' Off*. This record had the song "Pickin' Boogers," which contained a drum track Marl had sampled from a piece done in the 1970s by Larry Graham of Graham Central Station and Sly and the Family Stone fame. Marl's sampled track on Biz Markie's record would later be widely sampled by many producers, including Jazzy B, on Soul II Soul's "Keep on Movin'{|}" single. During this same period Marl worked with Big Daddy Kane and Kool G Rap and DJ Polo, producing their single "It's a Demo." Marl also put together a compilation album titled *In Control Vol. One*, which featured Craig G, Master Ace, MC Shan, Biz Markie, Kool G Rap, and Big Daddy Kane. The work contained the single "The Symphony," which displayed the skills of all these rappers. He also worked on the soundtrack for the motion picture *Colors*.

In 1989 Mr. Magic left WBLS-FM, after which Marl took over his spot, naming it *Marley Marl's In Control Show*. The show was noted for Marl's use of alternating DJs each week, like Pete Rock and others, and it lasted for a few years.

By 1990 Marl had worked on LL Cool J's entire *Mama Said Knock You Out* LP, which went gold by November of that year, then later went multiplatinum. He also worked with the Intelligent Hoodlum (a.k.a. Tragedy), producing his debut album and single "Arrest the President." In 1991 he released the second volume of *In Control*, which featured another single showcasing various rap artists, called "The Symphony, Part II."

In the early 1990s Marl began to branch out into R&B, doing work for Bell Biv DeVoe and continuing his work as a remixer for various artists. He also established his own companies, Marley Marl Productions and the House of Hits, where Marl worked with other producers and artists including K-Def and Lords of the Underground.

In 1994 he did production work on Doctor Dre & Ed Lover's *Back Up Off Me!* album, and worked on Da Youngsta's *No Mercy*.

Selected albums/CDs: *In Control, Volume One* (1988, Cold Chillin' 25783); *Mama Said Knock You Out* (1990, Def Jam/Columbia 46888) by L.L. Cool J; *In Control, Vol. II: For Your Steering Pleasure* (1991, Cold Chillin' 26257).

MASTER ACE
. . . .
a.k.a. Masta Ase Incorporated
(Born Duval Clear, December 4, 1966, Brooklyn, New York)

Hip-hop audiences first got a chance to hear the MC skills of Master Ace on producer Marley Marl's 1988 work "The Symphony, Part 1" on Marl's *In Control, Vol. 1* LP. Ace appeared on two more tracks on that album as well, titled "Simon Says" and "Keep Your Eyes on the Prize." But it was with his 1990 innovative single "Me and the Biz"—a tribute to rap artist Biz Markie—that he garnered attention.

Hailing from the Brownsville section of Brooklyn, Ace took part in many MC and b-boy contests, winning several in both art forms at his high school, Sheepshead Bay. Around 1986{*}87 Ace won a rap contest that took place in Queens. The first prize was six hours of recording time in Marley Marl's studio. After recording several pieces on Marl's *In Control, Vol. 1* album, Ace was signed to Cold Chillin' Records, where he released his *Take a Look Around* album, which contained the "Me and the Biz" single. After the release of the album Ace left Cold Chillin' because of business differences.

He traveled to England in 1991 and recorded with the group Young Disciples on their *Road to Freedom* album. Ace also worked with Marley Marl again on his "The Symphony, Part II," which appeared on Marl's *In Control: Vol. II* album. Ace then appeared on the group Brand New Heavies' *The Heavy Rhyme Experience, Vol. 1*, an album that contained ten of the group's favorite MCs. Thereafter, Ace was signed to that band's label, Delicious Vinyl, where he released his *Slaughta House* album in 1993, billed as Masta Ase Incorporated. One of the big hits off the work was the single "Jeep Ass Niguh." At the time Ace was trying to expand the subject matter of rap beyond the standard gangsta topics, introducing richer social satire into his work. In 1995 his album *Sittin' on Chrome* was released.

Selected albums/CDs: *Take a Look Around* (1990, Cold Chillin' 26179); *Slaughta House* (1993, Delicious Vinyl/Atlantic 92249).

MASTERS OF CEREMONY

See GRAND PUBA

MC CRAIG G

(Born Craig Curry, 1972, Queens, New York)

Craig G's desire to rap started when he was 7; watching his older brothers inspired him to try his hand at it. He managed to use their equipment when no one was around, practicing his MC skills on their microphone. In the early 1980s Craig taped all the hip-hop shows that were on the radio, absorbing the craft of MC'ing and deejaying that poured out over the airwaves.

By 1985 producer Marley Marl (who knew Craig from babysitting for him once) got Craig to help him with a rap version of the rock group Tears for Fears's single "Shout." Their version was released on Pop Art Records, and got the rapper some attention. In 1987 Craig did a song called "Dropping Science," which was featured on Marley Marl's *In Control Vol. 1* album. Craig was also featured on Marley's "The Symphony," a piece that showcased a variety of rappers including Big Daddy Kane and Master Ace.

In 1989 Craig was signed to Atlantic Records, and his debut album, *The Kingpin* (which was mostly in the hip house style), was released, with production by Marley Marl. Craig also began writing rhymes for T. J. Swan and Roxanne Shanté. In 1990 he did some production work on the Force MD's *Step to Me* album.

By 1991 Craig's second work was released, titled *Now That's More Like It*, which contained more hip hop-oriented cuts, including the single "U-R-Not the 1." On into 1995 Craig began to focus on making mix tapes, creating music mixes for that market.

Selected albums/CDs: *The Kingpin* (1989, Atlantic); *Now That's More Like It* (1991, Atlantic 82196.)

MC Lyte

MC LYTE
••••••••••••

(Born Lana Moorer, October 11, 1970, Queens, New York)

MC Lyte burst on the scene as a fresh female voice known for her original rhymes. Her work expresses intelligence and self-awareness, and exemplifies a woman in control of herself and her actions. She is noted for her strong delivery on the microphone and her ability to choose distinctive music tracks for her work. She is also remembered for being the first rap artist to appear at Carnegie Hall.

Lyte started rapping at the age of 12 after hearing artists like Run-D.M.C., the Sugar Hill Gang, and Spoonie Gee. Working with her brothers Milk and Gizmo of the Audio Two, Lyte continued to develop her skills. By 1988 she was already recording for her dad's record label, First Priority Music, debuting there with the Audio Two-produced piece "I Cram to Understand U (Sam)." The song—about a guy named Sam whom she at first likes, then leaves when she finds out he's a philanderer and addicted to crack—earned critical acclaim and acceptance both within and outside the hip-hop community, immediately putting her on the map. Her album *Lyte as a Rock* included three other singles that became hits: "Paper Thin," "10%

Dis," and the title track. Soon after, Lyte worked with rock performer Sinead O'Connor on her "I Want Your Hands on Me" remix.

Her second album, *Eyes on This*, appeared in 1989, with the single "Cha Cha Cha" topping the rap charts, along with "Cappucino" and "Stop, Look, Listen." During this period Lyte also took part in the Stop the Violence Movement's "Self Destruction" song and video, and KRS-One's H.E.A.L. project.

Around 1990, on the release of her album *Act Like You Know*, Lyte expanded her music by working with R&B group Bell Biv DeVoe's producers, Wolf and Epic. The LP yielded the hits "When in Love," "Eyes Are the Soul," and "Poor Georgie."

In 1993 she released the work *Ain't No Other*, with the singles "Ruffneck" and "I Go On" appearing off the work. "Ruffneck" went gold that same year. Around this period she formed a management company with her partners, Kink EZ and rapper Lin Que (formerly known as Blackwatch Movement's Isis), called Duke Da Moon Management.

 Selected albums/CDs: *Lyte as a Rock* (1988, First Priority Music 90905); *Eyes on This* (1989, First Priority Music 91304); *Act Like You Know* (1991; First Priority Music 91731; clean version: 91812); *Ain't No Other* (1993, First Priority Music, 92230; clean version: 92275).

MC SHAN
●●●●●●●●●●●●
(Born Shawn Moltke, September 9, 1965, Elmhurst, New York)

MC Shan was responsible for performing on some of the most famous diss records in hip-hop history. His pieces such as "The Bridge" and "Kill That Noise" were noted for sparking and maintaining the battles between Shan with his Juice Crew (Mr. Magic, Marley Marl, and others) and Boogie Down Productions (Blastmaster KRS-One, DJ Scott La Rock). After retiring from the music business due to a drug problem, he returned successfully in 1993 as a producer for white reggae artist Snow.

Around 1985 Shan hooked up with his cousin, producer Marley Marl, and Tyrone "Fly Ty" Williams. (Williams reportedly met Shan when he caught him "doin' mischief" with Williams's car.) Shan began working with Marley Marl in the Queensbridge Housing Projects in Queens, New York. Their collaboration produced the single "Marley Marl Scratch" on the Aleems' Nia Records. The piece was a hit, and it featured Shan's uniquely high vocal timbre.

Soon after, Shan recorded "Queensbridge," a.k.a. "The Bridge," with Marl. The piece became a classic in hip hop, not only for its artistry, but because of the answer record it spawned from KRS-One and his Boogie Down Productions, called "South Bronx." Both records received wide attention in the hip-hop community.

In 1988 Shan's *Down by Law* album was released on Cold Chillin' Records. The work contained singles like "Jane Stop This Crazy Thing!," "The Bridge," and "Kill That Noise," and it put Shan on the map as a major MC. After two more albums, one in 1989 titled *Born to Be Wild*, and the other, *Play It Again, Shan*, in 1990, Shan disappeared from the music scene, succumbing to a drug problem.

In 1993 Shan returned as a producer, working with reggae artist Snow on his "Informer" single, and working on his *12 Inches of Snow* album, both of which went platinum in the year of their release. Shan also recorded as a solo artist again, releasing his single "Penile Reunion" in that same year. In 1995 Shan worked with Snow again, producing three cuts on that artist's *Murder Love* album.

Selected albums/CDs: *Down by Law* (1988, Cold Chillin' 25676); *Born to Be Wild* (1989, Cold Chillin' 25797); *Play It Again, Shan* (1990, Cold Chillin' 26155).

MC TATIANA
a.k.a. Lady T
(Born Tatiana Sampson, Bronx, New York)

MC Tatiana's 1988 12-inch single "Back Up Jack," b/w "Mission to Rock," called attention to the artist as a major MC of note. She is also recognized for her multifaceted position in the music industry where she works as a record label owner and manager (Clockin' ZZZZ's Music Inc.), and the head of Mouth Almighty Publicity. She has worked as a columnist for the music industry's *Jack the Rapper* magazine and other publications such as *NY Trend, One Nut Network,* and *Fly!*. Tatiana was also the co-host and co-producer of the radio-syndicated *Rap It Up* show.

Tatiana began MC'ing in 1981 as Lady T with the group Missy Dee and the Mellow Dees. They recorded a single titled "Ain't She Sweet" for the Universal Records label. She appeared in many of the known hip-hop venues at the time, including Harlem World, the Renaissance, and the Audubon Ballroom, where she once battled the Funky Four Plus One's Sha Rock. Her problems with being a female recording artist inspired her to embark on six years of research of the music industry before returning to work in it, establishing her own companies and other business projects.

In 1986 she formed Clockin' ZZZZ's Music Inc. with her partner and manager, Doc Morris. By 1987 she was hosting two cable shows, broadcasting out of City College in New York City, *B-Boy TV* and *On Broadway,* which she co-hosted with Darlene Lewis.

By 1994 Tatiana became Executive Vice President of Majestic Control Productions, and began doing guest interviews on that company's *Hank Love & 1/2 Pint Radio Show.* Tatiana is also known as a public speaker who appears in various public schools and colleges.

MONIE LOVE
(Born Simone Johnson, July 2, 1970, London)

Monie Love is known for her rapid-fire rhythmic delivery, clear, Brooklyn, New York, diction, and conscious rhymes. She had a huge amount of word-of-mouth publicity before she ever made an album. Her stunning cameo performances on Queen Latifah's "Ladies First," De

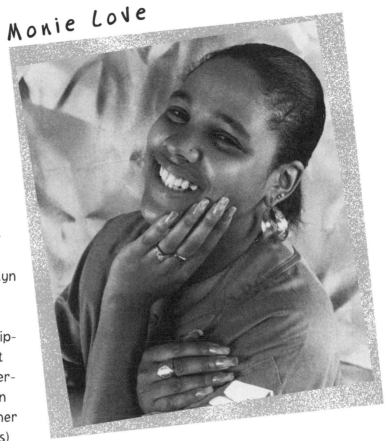

Monie Love

La Soul's "Buddy," and the Jungle Brothers' "Doin' Our Own Dang" created a buzz for Love, and hip hoppers were ready to hear what the London-born rapper had to offer on her own. She would soon join the aforementioned groups' Native Tongues posse, which gave her even more status, and garnered great expectations from hip-hop audiences.

Raised in London and in Brooklyn for a while, it was in Brooklyn that she attended school with MC Lyte, who told her about the weekend hip-hop jams that were taking place at the club Union Square. Love had performed in basement parties back in London, so that by 1990 (based on her work with Queen Latifah and others) she was signed to Warner Bros. Records. Her debut album, *Down to Earth*, included two singles, "Monie in the Middle" and "It's a Shame." The first single was produced by the Fine Young Cannibals's Andy Cox and David Steele.

In 1993 her second album, *In a Word or 2*, was released. The single off the album, "Born to Breed," was produced by Prince, with the remainder of the album being produced primarily by Marley Marl. In 1994{*}95 she ventured into radio, hosting a show in New York City on Hot 97 (WQHT-FM) on Saturday mornings.

 Selected singles: "Monie in the Middle" (1990, Warner Bros.).

 Selected albums/CDs: Down to Earth (1991, Warner Bros./Cool Tempo 1720); *In a Word or 2* (1993, Warner Bros./Cool Tempo 32).

MR. MAGIC
● ● ● ● ● ● ● ● ● ● ● ● ● ● ● ● ● ●
a.k.a. DJ Lucky, Sir Juice, Super Rockin' Mr. Magic
(Born John Rivas, March 15, Bronx, New York)

Mr. Magic is considered to be the pioneer of hip-hop radio. His show, *The Rap Attack Show*, was the first exclusive rap radio show to be aired by a major Arbitron radio station, WBLS-FM in New York City. His ten-year reign on radio (five years on WHBI-FM, six years on WBLS) was instrumental in turning countless young people on to the sounds of hip-hop music.

Magic was originally a DJ living in Brooklyn, known as DJ Lucky in the 1970s, when he started to do mobile DJ work. He played in clubs like Nell Quinn's and Super Star 33, and he also worked for Winston Collection (Group W) for a period. In 1979 Magic had a chance to launch his own show, called *Mr. Magic's Disco Showcase* on Fridays at WHBI-FM (later changed to WNWK-FM), where you paid for your own air time. By 1983 he was invited to work for WBLS, where he met Marley Marl, who at the time was mostly deejaying. Originally not liking him, Marl soon felt comfortable enough to work with Magic on the station's promotion truck called the "Juice Mobile." Here, Marl mixed records for Magic on the truck when they traveled to location sights.

Mr. Magic's *Rap Attack* radio show aired in 1983, with Marley Marl as the show's DJ and Tyrone "Fly Ty" Williams as the show's co-producer. (Williams would later head the Cold Chillin' Records label.) The three began calling themselves "The Juice Crew" after Magic's other nickname, Sir Juice. Airing on the weekends, Magic provided hip hoppers with the latest sounds, giving wider exposure to a music genre that was originally based in community centers, small clubs, parks, and on audiocassettes. Later on, Magic's Juice Crew added more members, like Roxanne Shanté, Biz Markie, and MC Shan. These artists actually became part of Tyrone Williams's management roster.

With his position in radio, Mr. Magic broke countless rap records. Steve Salem brought his group UTFO's piece "Roxanne, Roxanne" to Magic. Magic was one of the first to air the work. Roxanne Shanté would later respond to it, recording "Roxanne's Revenge" with Marley Marl, which also got one of its first airings on Magic's show.

In 1986 Magic and his crew were noted for their battles and feud with rapper KRS-One and his Boogie Down Productions crew. Magic would air MC Shan's and other Juice Crew members' material, while Kool DJ Red Alert (who had his own radio show by this time on KISS-FM, New York) would air and occasionally intercut the Juice Crew's and Boogie Down Productions' material. These back-and-forth radio battles were also good for both stations, with KISS-FM and WBLS raking in listeners by the numbers on the weekends.

Mr. Magic also worked as a producer, doing co-production on the Force MCs "Let Me Love You" and "Forgive Me Girl," as well as working with Whodini (whose first record was actually a tribute to him, titled "Magic's Wand"). He also put out a series of rap compilation albums for Profile Records, titled *Mr. Magic's Rap Attack*, and he has held contests that gave exposure to groups like Stetsasonic. He recorded his own single in 1984, called "Magic's Message" (written by Spyder D). Magic gave cameo performances in films as well, appearing in the movies *Wild Style* and *Krush Groove*.

By 1989 Magic had left WBLS (giving Marley Marl his slot) and headed for Baltimore, where he worked at radio station WABB for about one year. After a two-year hiatus from radio, Magic returned to the New York airwaves in 1993, this time with DJ Mister Cee (previously the DJ for Big Daddy Kane) as his DJ.

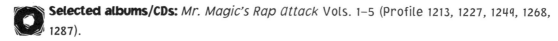 **Selected albums/CDs:** *Mr. Magic's Rap Attack* Vols. 1–5 (Profile 1213, 1227, 1249, 1268, 1287).

OTHERZ

MC EZ & TROUP
••••••••••••••••••••••••
Formed in New York

In 1988 MC EZ & Troup were signed to the Sleeping Bag/Fresh label. They recorded the singles "Get Retarded" (which received some airplay on New York City-area stations) and "Just Rhymin'," which also received some notice. Later one of the group members, Craig Mack, began recording in 1994 for the Bad Boy Records label, doing the single "Flava in Ya Ear" and album *Project: Funk Da World*. The single went platinum during this same period.

MC MARS
•••••••••••
(Born Marchal Silver, San Francisco)

Hailing from the San Francisco Bay area, MC Mars appeared on the scene in 1988. He was signed to Cutting Edge Records, where he released a self-titled EP.

MC RELL
••••••••••
(Born Terrell Davis, Philadelphia)

MC Rell had a hit in 1989 with the single "Life of an Entertainer," which came off his debut album, *Into the Future*. A second release, "Sound Wave Sermon," also attracted some notice.

MC SHY-D
•••••••••••••
(Born Peter Jones c. 1966, Atlanta)

MC Shy-D made his appearance in 1985 with the single "Rap Will Never Die." By 1987 he was recording on Luke Skyywalker Campbell's Skyywalker label, releasing the albums *Gotta Be Tough* and *Comin' Correct in '88*. Around 1989 his single "Shake It" was released, but by 1991 he started his own label, Benz Records, and had a distribution deal with On the Top Records. He later began working with the Wrap/Ichiban label around 1993, releasing the album *MC Shy-D, The Comeback*. In 1994 he won a lawsuit filed against his old label boss, Luke Campbell, for $669,165 in back royalties for the *Gotta Be Tough* and *Comin' Correct in '88* albums. During 1995 Shy-D produced DJ Smurf and P.M.H.I.'s "Ooh Lawd (Party People)" single.

 Selected albums/CDs: *The Comeback* (1993, Wrap 8124).

MC TWIST

(Born Michael Thomas, San Jose, California)

Appearing on the scene in 1988, MC Twist released the album *Comin' through Like Warriors* on Luke Skyywalker Campbell's then-named Skyywalker Records. Toward 1990 Twist released his second album, titled *Bad Influence*, on the Lethal Beat Records label, with its single "Step Off" b/w "S-M-O-K-I-N-G C-O-K-E." In 1991 he released the single "1-900-KKK." The work was noted for its recording of outgoing answering machine messages from racist groups, such as WAR (White Aryan Resistance), which gave out actual telephone numbers that Twist recorded over a back beat.

MC TROUBLE

(Born Latasha Rogers, 1970, Los Angeles; died June 4, 1990, Los Angeles)

MC Trouble was a promising MC whose album *Gotta Get a Grip* was released on the Motown label in 1990. The work had received some critical acclaim, and her performance a year earlier at Harlem, New York's, Rally Against Racism also made an impression. Born with epilepsy, the artist tragically died of the disease in 1990.

 Selected albums/CDs: *Gotta Get a Grip* (1990, Motown 6303).

MELLOW MAN ACE

(Born Ulpiano Sergio Reyes, April 12, 1967, Havana, Cuba)

Mellow Man Ace is a Latino rapper whose rhymes are occasionally written in Spanglish (a mixture of English and Americanized Spanish). He became noticed outside the hip-hop community thanks to his 1990 gold single "Mentirosa." He is also the brother of Sen Dog, from the group Cypress Hill.

Ace was born in Cuba. His family won a lottery that gave them exit visas to the United States, and they soon immigrated. The family first lived in Miami and New Jersey, but eventually settled in South Gate, California, where Ace got into the hip-hop scene by the time he was 15 years old. In 1987 Ace was signed to Delicious Vinyl Records, where his 12-inch single "Mas Pingon" was released.

In 1989 Ace was at a new label, Capitol Records, which released his album *Escape from Havana*, which established him as a premier talent. During 1992 his second album was released, titled *The Brother with Two Tongues*.

Selected albums/CDs: *Escape from Havana* (1989, Capitol 91295); *The Brother with Two Tongues* (1992, Capitol 94608).

Mellow Man Ace

MERCEDES LADIES
•••••••••••••••••••••••••••
Formed c. late 1970s, Bronx, New York
(Debbie Dee; Zena Z; Eva Deff; Sherry Sheryl; DJ RC; DJ Baby D:
all born in Bronx, New York)

The Mercedes Ladies were the first female rap group to truly stand out with performance skills equal to the men in hip hop.

They formed during the late 1970s, and performed in various areas in the Bronx and Manhattan, appearing with many of the acts that were popular during this period. They slowly began to get a reputation for their skills with the early hip-hop audience, but suddenly decided not to continue with their career.

Later, DJ Baby D became a recording artist for West End Records under the name D'bora. Debbie Dee would later join Lisa Lee and the Funky Four Plus One's Sha Rock to form the Us Girls.

Michie Mee

MICHIE MEE & L.A. LUV

Formed c. 1987, Canada
(Michie Mee, born Michelle McCullock; L.A. Luv, born Phillip Gayle:
both born in Canada)

Michie Mee & L.A. Luv were a First Priority Records act based in Canada, who made their appearance around 1988 on shows with Boogie Down Productions and Public Enemy. The two later released the singles "Elements of Style" and "Run for Cover."

MIKE & DAVE

(Born in Harlem, New York)

Mike & Dave were known as one of the original groups of hip-hop promoters who operated extensively in the late 1970s before the advent and rise of rap records.

Hailing from Lincoln Projects in Harlem, Mike & Dave held shows in many areas in New York, but worked mostly out of the IS-201 school in Manhattan. In the early 1980s the two established their own Mike & Dave Records label, where they worked with acts like the Boogie Boys ("Rappin' Ain't No Thing"), and released their compilation albums like *Fast Money*, featuring Positive K. Thereafter, their activities in the music business gradually decreased.

MISTER CEE

(Born Calvin Lebrun, August 17, 1966, Brooklyn, New York)

Mister Cee made his mark as a DJ while working with rapper Big Daddy Kane. He met Kane in 1985 while attending Sarah J. Hale High School. They were both part of a group called Magnum Force until the group disbanded. Cee and Kane continued to work together after the disbandment. Mister Cee remained Big Daddy Kane's DJ throughout the 1980s and into the 1990s. In 1993 Cee began doing radio, deejaying for Mr. Magic on his returned *Rap Attack* radio show.

MOVEMENT-EX

(Mustafa Hasan Ma'd; King, born Khaaliq: both born in New York)

This duo (originally from New York, later residing in Los Angeles) performed rhymes containing lessons from the Five Percent Nation of Islam and focusing on sociopolitical situations in the black community. In the early 1990s the two released a self-titled album that contained a hit single, "Freedom Got a Shotgun."

Movement Ex

MS. MELODIE

(Born Ramona Parker, Brooklyn, New York)

Ms. Melodie was recognized for her work on the Stop the Violence movement's 1989 piece "Self-Destruction." During this same period Melodie released her album *Diva*, which had production work by the Awesome 2, Sam Sever, and KRS-One. Melodie was known as the wife of KRS-One, and was also involved in that artist's H.E.A.L. project.

 Selected albums/CDs: *Diva* (1989, Jive).

MASTER ACE: BEYOND GANGSTA RAP

Innovative MC Master Ace's 1993 album, *Slaughtahouse*, reveals a different side of rap, one that seeks to go beyond gangsta cliches. The man who first made noise on Marley Marl's *The Symphony, Part I* in 1988, then with his own "Me and the Biz" in 1990, doesn't like repeating himself. So what new road has he broken with this work?

"I just wanted to show," Ace begins, "that you can make a real hard rough, rugged, rowdy, rap album, without using the same 40 ounce, blunts, 9-millimeter, bitch, ho, murder murder murder, kill kill kill theme.

"I just really felt that it was important to show that that could be done, so that we wouldn't have every other group comin' out on that tip for the next ten years, 'cause it would really end up killing hip hop, as well as killing urban America."

The work has a lot of social and satirical flavor, without sounding preachy. "Slaughterhouse," the title cut, is definitely a snap with its new group, MC Negro & the Ignorant MCs, billed as the future hardcore group in the song.

"Instead of talking about guns," Ace explains, "they're bragging about chopping people's heads off and eating them, 'cause that's where people have to go next if they want to become harder than hard."

Ace reveals that he's always been one to go against the grain, ever since he was a kid. So it's no surprise that his musical approach would be like this.

"I knew," he says, "that there was definitely a large number of people who wasn't into that (smokin' blunts, drinkin' 40 ounces, etc.), that they were tired of hearing about it, and that they wouldn't mind hearing somebody say, Hey, I don't smoke blunts.

"The problem," Ace continues, "is that nobody in hip hop wants to take any kind of chances. Everybody wants to stay safe and wear the same type of jackets, the same type of hats, and talk the same type of junk."

Mack image: A mack, from the French masculine noun *maquerean*, is a pimp; the mack image refers to the 1973 film *The Mack* starring Max Julien, in which Julien portrays the macks of that day as tough, streetwise businessmen and ladies' men, who wear highly ostentatious, expensive clothing, and drive expensive, flashy cars. The film was particularly influential on hip-hop audiences on the West Coast.

Miami bass: A style of rap music played by synthesizers and drum machines, practiced in Miami, which consists of faster tempos (usually 150 bpms [beats per minute]) and high decibels of bass. The style originated with Afrika Bambaataa's 1982 single "Planet Rock."

MC: Original term for rapper.

Mix tapes: Audiocassette tape recordings by DJs of their music sets, recorded live during a party, or privately in their homes and studios.

Mixer: An electronic device used to "mix" or balance different inputs; for example, two turntables might be run through a mixer into an amplifier, so the volume of each recording could be controlled before it comes out through the speakers.

NAS

a.k.a. Nasty Nas, MC Nas

(Born Nasir Ben Olu Dara Jones, 1973, Queensbridge, Long Island City, New York)

Nas first received attention in 1991 on the group Main Source's piece "Live at the BBQ." He is known for the ear-catching statements and metaphors in his rhymes, as well as the breath control he uses when delivering a multitude of lyrics in his verses.

The son of jazz musician Olu Dara, Nas partook in some of the other aspects of hip-hop culture as a youth, such as graffiti and some breakdancing (with a group called Breakin' In Action), before concentrating on MC'ing. Around 1988 to 1989 he began working with the Large Professor and Eric B in the studio, but believed he was not at the top of his craft, so withdrew from the scene for several months. He began working with the Large Professor again around 1989{*}90, and they cut a few demos, which Nas began to shop around for a record deal. In 1991, when the Large Professor's group, Main Source, was ready to make an album, he invited Nas to perform on "Live at the BBQ." A year later, MC Serch, from the group 3rd Bass, took an interest in Nas. He appeared on Serch's "Back to the Grill Again" single, and around the same time Serch was able to get him signed to Columbia Records.

Nas's first single, "Halftime" (which appeared on the motion picture soundtrack *Zebrahead*), was released around 1993. The following year his album *Illmatic* was released.

 Selected album/CDs: *Illmatic* (1994, Columbia 57684).

NATIVE TONGUES POSSE

See KOOL DJ RED ALERT; A TRIBE CALLED QUEST;
JUNGLE BROTHERS; DE LA SOUL; MONIE LOVE; BLACK SHEEP

NAUGHTY BY NATURE

Formerly the New Style
Formed in 1986, East Orange, New Jersey
(Treach, born Anthony Criss, December 2, 1970, Newark, New Jersey; Vinnie, born Vincent Brown, September 17, 1970, East Orange, New Jersey; DJ Kay Gee, born Kier Gist, September 15, 1970, East Orange, New Jersey)

Naughty by Nature brought a new style into rap when they entered the market with keyboardist Dave Bellochio's live piano loops and group member Treach's unique tommy-gun-style rhyme delivery.

Treach moved to East Orange, New Jersey (with his mother and younger brother), when he was 2 years old. As he got older he got more into the life of the streets. With the exception of a packing job at the Grand Union warehouse, he was unable to find work. His mother eventually asked him to leave the house, because he was too difficult for her to handle. He slept at friends' homes, occasionally went to East Orange High School, and sold drugs on the side, which landed him in jail for a short time.

Treach made friends with Vinnie in school, who was a student in his eleventh-grade health class. They joined with DJ Kay Gee—who lived on Vinnie's block—and practiced beat-boxing and turntables skills, while making demo recordings. Kay Gee decided to take part in his high school's talent show and asked Vinnie and Treach to join him. They called themselves the New Style (after a song by the Beastie Boys). They did a show, and were well received. After that they did shows throughout the New Jersey area.

Naughty by Nature

In 1988, after Vinnie and Treach graduated from high school, the group signed a production deal with Sugar Hill Records' Sylvia Robinson, on her Bon Ami label. They recorded one album for her, titled *Independent Leaders* (a.k.a. *Scuffing Those Knees*). Later the deal went sour and the group subsequently settled with Bon Ami for an undisclosed sum.

In 1989 Kay Gee called DJ Mark the 45 King—a friend and producer of Queen Latifah (both of whom Kay Gee knew from the neighboring community of Irvington). The group would occasionally perform in front of Mark's camcorder as he recorded them. Mark showed the tapes to the rest of his Flavor Unit Posse friends. Treach and his friends threw a fund-raiser at Upsala College in East Orange, and invited Flavor Unit members to attend. Latifah, Shakim Compere, and Apache were there and were impressed.

Latifah and Shakim signed New Style to their Flavor Unit Management company. A demo was taken to the senior vice president of A&R at Warner Bros. Records, Benny Medina. Medina asked Tommy Boy Records (then a subsidiary of Warners) to distribute their work. Tommy Boy president Monica Lynch had first turned them down. After changing their style, the group became Naughty by Nature (a title they took from a song off their first album). Tommy Boy decided to market the group's first single in 1991, titled "O.P.P." It sold over a million copies. Their self-titled debut album was released and went platinum. The group later involved themselves with fashion and introduced their own "Naughty Gear."

In 1993 they released the single "Hip Hop Hooray." It went double platinum. Their second album for Tommy Boy was titled *19 Naughty III* and was released that same year. In 1995 they released the album *Poverty's Paradise*, with the single from the work, "Feel My Flow" b/w "Craziest." Their piece "Connections" appeared in the motion picture soundtrack *New Jersey Drive Vol. 2*, as well as on their *Poverty's Paradise* album.

 Selected singles: "O.P.P." (1991, Tommy Boy); "Hip Hop Hooray" (1993).

 Selected albums/CDs: *Naughty by Nature* (1991, Tommy Boy 1051); *19 Naughty III* (1993, Tommy Boy 1069; clean version: 1072); *Poverty's Paradise* (1995, Tommy Boy 1111).

NEMESIS
● ● ● ● ● ● ● ● ● ● ● ●
Formed c. 1980, Dallas, Texas
(MC Azim, born L. Azim Rashid, Jr.; DJ Snake, born Don A. Brown;
Big Al, born Albert Leon English; Joe Macc, born Joe Wagoner;
Ron C, born Ron Carey: all born in Dallas)

Nemesis is a Dallas-based group known for their funk-structured compositions with loud bass lines. They appeared on the hip-hop scene in 1987, when they released the single "Oak Cliff." They were signed to Profile Records, and in 1990 they released the album *To Hell and Back*, followed a year later by *Munchies for Your Bass*.

By the time the group released the album *Temple of Boom* in 1993, MC Azim had left and Ron C had entered as a member—an artist who had previously released three albums: *"C" ya, Back on the Street,* and *The "C" Theory.* In 1995 DJ Snake left the group, and they released the album *Tha People Want Bass* without him.

 Selected albums/CDs: *To Hell and Back* (1990, Profile 1283); *Munchies for Your Bass* (1991, Profile 1411); *Temple of Boom* (1993, Profile 1441); *Tha People Want Bass* (1995, Profile 1461).

NEXT PLATEAU RECORDS
Formed c. mid-1980s, New York City

Next Plateau Records achieved its first major success with the group Salt-N-Pepa on their debut album *Hot, Cool & Vicious* in 1986. The label also released works by artists like Antoinette, Sparky D, and Ultramagnetic MC's.

Label owner Eddie O'Loughlin initially turned down rap artists who came to him to be signed, including Doug E. Fresh and LL Cool J. Eventually, he got a chance to hear hip-hop radio personality Mr. Magic's show, and was soon convinced to sign rap acts. O'Loughlin's first hit was with former Fearless Four members Master O.C. and Crazy Eddie, with their 1984 "Masters of the Scratch." Their first major hit was Salt-N-Pepa's first album, which eventually garnered sales of 1.5 million copies. The label continued into the 1990s, with Salt-N-Pepa being one of their main acts.

NICE & SMOOTH
Formed c. 1987, New York City
(Greg Nice, born Greg Mays; Smooth B, born Daryl Barnes; both born Bronx, New York)

Nice & Smooth is a duo with a sound that recalls 1970s rap, because of their freestyle-flavored performances, which in large part are due to Nice's nonwritten composing techniques and Smooth B's pen-driven writing style, which add spontaneity to all the rhymes they perform.

Childhood friends, Nice & Smooth originally performed with John "June Love" Butterfield, and the trio wrote a song together, "Skill Trade," in early 1987. However, Butterfield was murdered that spring (for reasons publicly unknown) before the song could be recorded; Nice & Smooth proceeded on their own, raising $1,500 to press copies of the song. Released on their own Strange Family Records label, the duo took crates of their records to all the stores, selling them on consignment and sometimes piece by piece. They eventually sold all the records that they pressed, and were able to get airplay on radio station KISS-FM in New York. The record was a hit in underground circles.

Later, singer Bobby Brown heard the record and hired Smooth B to write rhymes for him. Songs like "My Prerogative" and others on Brown's hit album *Don't Be Cruel*, contained some of Smooth's work, although his contribution went uncredited. Smooth B threatened to

Nice & Smooth

sue the superstar, and later was compensated in an out-of-court settlement. He also worked with Cameo's Larry Blackmon, selling rhymes to him for $500 each.

Nice & Smooth befriended DJ Scott La Rock from the Boogie Down Productions. La Rock brought the duo to Sleeping Bag/Fresh Records, which signed them and released their self-titled debut album in 1989. Its single "Funky for You," featuring DJ Oooh Child Teddy Tedd of the Awesome 2, made number 23 on the R&B charts. However, their label soon filed for bankruptcy, and the duo was never paid for their recording. Russell Simmons and Lyor Cohen of Def Jam/RAL bought the duo's contract from the defunct Fresh label.

In 1991 their new label released the album *Ain't a Damn Thing Changed*, which spawned singles like "Hip Hop Junkies" and "Sometimes I Rhyme Slow." In 1992 they worked with the group Gang Starr on the single "Dwyck." In 1993 Nice & Smooth's "Cash in My Hand" was used in the motion picture soundtrack for director John Singleton's film *Poetic Justice*.

In 1994 they released their third album, *Jewel of the Nile*. It featured cameos from singer Bobby Brown (on the single "Return of the Hip Hop Freaks"), Ki-C from the R&B group, Jodeci, and rappers Slick Rick and Everlast (from the group House of Pain). Another successful single off the work was "Old to the New."

Selected albums/CDs: *Nice & Smooth* (1989, Fresh); *Ain't a Damn Thing Changed* (1991, RAL/Columbia 47373); *Jewel of the Nile* (1994, RAL/Columbia 523336).

NIKKI D
● ● ● ● ● ● ● ● ● ● ●
(Born Nichele Strong, Los Angeles)

Nikki D was the first female rap artist signed to the Def Jam Recordings label. Raised in Los Angeles, Nikki originally worked with Ice-T and performed with him in the Los Angeles area with Run-D.M.C. and Whodini (when they toured there). Various labels offered her contracts, but she turned them down to fulfill her dream of being signed to Def Jam, which had no female acts at the time.

During the winter of 1986 Nikki came to New York with a friend with the hopes of fulfilling her dream. They bounced from place to place with no money, and even wound up sleeping in one of the World Trade Center buildings. Eventually meeting a friend who helped her find a job, Nikki then hooked up with the L.A. Posse, who were in New York producing LL Cool J's album. She talked the group into producing a demo for her. A copy of the demo reached Def Jam's Russell Simmons, and after hearing it he immediately signed her.

In 1989 she did a cameo rhyme on R&B singer Alyson Williams's "My Love Is So Raw." In 1990 Nikki got even more recognition with her own single "Lettin' Off Steam," which was produced by Sam Sever. Her next single was titled "Daddy's Little Girl," and her album of the same name was released in 1991.

She switched record companies, signing with Queen Latifah's Flavor Unit Records in 1993, while continuing to remain with Russell Simmons's Rush Artist Management. She recorded the single "Freak Out" for the label during this period. That same year she appeared on her boyfriend Apache's self-titled album, on the cut "Who Freaked Who."

 Selected singles: "Lettin' Off Steam" (1990, Def Jam).

Nikki D

NOTORIOUS B.I.G.

a.k.a. Biggie Smalls, B.I.G. Poppa, Big
(Born Christopher Wallace, 1973, Brooklyn, New York)

The 6'3", 315-pound rapper who goes by the name of Biggie Smalls in the hip-hop community reportedly started out as a hustler and drug dealer in the Bedford-Stuyvesant section of Brooklyn before getting into MC'ing.

Smalls got his start working with a group of neighborhood friends known as the OGB (Old Gold Brothers) Crew, one of whom had a pair of turntables with whom Smalls began to make rap tapes. The tapes circulated in the community during the early 1990s, and one of them wound up in the hands of DJ Mister Cee, rapper Big Daddy Kane's DJ. Impressed with Smalls's work, Cee played the tape for Matty C, a writer at the rap magazine *The Source*, who featured Smalls in his "Unsigned Hype" column, a section that highlighted the talents of various unknown rappers. Smalls was soon signed to Uptown Records by national A&R director Puffy Combs.

Smalls first appeared on Uptown's soundtrack for the motion picture *Who's the Man?* in 1993, on the song "Party and Bullshit." By the following year he was dropped from Uptown Records after Puffy Combs left the label. Combs then signed him to his own Bad Boy Entertainment label. His first single for Bad Boy, "Juicy" b/w "Unbelievable," was released in 1994 and went gold that year, along with his album *Ready to Die*, which went platinum by 1995. His next single, "One More Chance/Stay with Me," also went platinum.

Smalls also collaborates with his proteges, the Junior M.A.F.I.A.; he co-wrote their 1995 single "Player's Anthem," which went gold during that same year. He has also rapped on R&B singers Total's "Can't You See" single (from the *New Jersey Drive* film soundtrack) and Mary J. Blige's "Real Love" and "What's the 411" singles. Smalls is also the husband of R&B singer Faith.

 Selected albums/CDs: *Ready to Die* (1994, Bad Boy 73000).

N.W.A

Formed c. 1988, Compton, Los Angeles
(Dr. Dre, born Andre Young, 1965; Eazy-E, born Eric Wright, September 7; died March 26, 1995; DJ Yella; MC Ren, born Lorenzo Paterson; Former members: Ice Cube, born Oshea Jackson, June 15, 1969; Arabian Prince: all born in Los Angeles)

The group N.W.A took the so-called gangsta genre of rap and raised it to the leading music genre in hip hop during the early 1990s. Even though the genre had existed earlier with rap artists like Schoolly D and others, N.W.A's impact with this style inspired other similar gangsta-oriented groups to follow, and their exaltation of their South Central Los Angeles hometown, Compton, gave credence to that area as being a major contributor to hip-hop music. Their explicit lyrics and violent subject matter had surprising crossover appeal, and all their albums (*Straight Outta Compton*, *100 Miles and Runnin'*, and *Niggaz4Life*) have gone platinum and multiplatinum. They are also one of the very first hip-hop groups to (with the exception of DJ Yella) release solo albums that have gone platinum and multiplatinum.

Group member Dr. Dre was originally a DJ, who made tapes in his bedroom for his friends, until he was hired to do professional deejaying at a local club in the Compton area called Eve After Dark, which was owned by Alonzo Williams, around 1981{*}82. While working at the club, Dre met DJ Yella, who had learned some of his DJ skills from Kurtis Blow's DJ, Davy D. Dre and Yella became friends and started using the 4-track studio the club had in one of its back rooms to make demos. Dre later hosted a mix show on Los Angeles radio station KDAY around 1983{*}84, along with other DJs from the club. Due to the positive response from listeners, Alonzo Williams decided to form a group with Dre and others, calling it the Wreckin' Cru', later to be known as the World Class Wreckin' Cru'. The group became recognized for songs like "Slice," "Surgery," and "Turn Off the Lights" before disbanding.

Around 1985 Dre met Ice Cube, who was in a group called CIA. Cube had done parties and appeared in skating rinks, and once made the finals at a radio station rap battle at the Hollywood Palladium. Dre had heard one of Cube's tapes and invited him to appear with him at one of his club shows. Dre had advised Cube that the best way to get a crowd was to perform a parody of an existing hip-hop record. Cube did a parody on stage of UTFO's "Roxanne, Roxanne" called "Diane, Diane," which impressed Dre's club crowd.

Around 1986 Cube met one of Dre's friends, Eazy-E, a former drug dealer who had become seriously interested in making records. Eazy used to hang out in Dre's bedroom in the early 1980s when Dre was making tapes. Eazy had just started a label called Ruthless Records, and had just signed a group from New York called HBO, who were coming to California to do their first record with the label. The song that E hoped they would record was "Boys in the Hood," which was written by Ice Cube and Dr. Dre. When HBO heard the work, they decided that it was "too West Coast"-oriented for them and declined to do it. Thereafter, Dre suggested that Eazy should record the piece, making the song the first single for the Ruthless label.

Later, Cube, Easy, Yella, and Dre decided to become a group, calling themselves N.W.A for Niggas with Attitude. Cube wrote two more songs for the group, "Dopeman" and "8 Ball." Both songs continued in the same vein as the "Boys in the Hood" piece, that is, songs about street life. They recorded clean versions of the songs, but the explicit versions were what the people wanted.

Cube then left for the Phoenix Institute of Technology in Phoenix, where he took a one-year course in architectural drafting. Eazy-E, Dre, and Yella began working on other projects for the label as producers, calling themselves High Powered Productions, which also included producer Arabian Prince. Eazy-E's friend, MC Ren, was also involved with some of the recording work at Ruthless Records, as well as Laylaw, future manager of a later Ruthless act, Above the Law.

Dre, Yella, Eazy, and Arabian Prince worked with one of the label's acts, a female group called J.J. Fad, in 1988. Their single "Supersonic" was released in April of that year, and their album *Supersonic, The Album* went gold during this same period. Eazy-E released his own album that year, titled *Eazy-Duz-It*, which eventually went platinum.

N.W.A

Toward September of 1988 Ice Cube returned from college, and the group N.W.A (with MC Ren now a member, along with Arabian Prince) began working on new material. They also had a manager—music-industry veteran Jerry Heller, who was involved with groups like Pink Floyd, Journey, the Guess Who, and Elton John during the 1970s. During this period the group released a compilation album, titled *N.W.A & The Posse*. However, their second album, released in that same year, titled *Straight Outta Compton*, and the single from the work, "Fuck Tha Police," put them on the map with hip hoppers. The album achieved its first platinum status in that same year. Around the same time, Priority Records—which was distributing Ruthless Records' product at the time—received a letter from the F.B.I., which questioned N.W.A's lyrical content in their songs. There was also a massive following of the group by the press when they went on their fifty-city tour, with the press anticipating trouble from the group's concerts.

Later in 1989 Ice Cube was beginning to believe that he was not being properly compensated financially by the group's manager, and by December of that year he decided to split from the group.

N.W.A continued to make records as a group without Cube and Arabian Prince, releasing the EP *100 Miles and Runnin'* in 1990. In 1991 the group released their third album, *Niggaz4Life*. This album gained attention because it entered *Billboard*'s Top 200 Albums chart at number 2. The work had no single to drive it to that position, and by the next week the work was at number 1.

Thereafter, other members of the group gradually began to go in other directions, with Dr. Dre starting his own Death Row Records label, and recording successful solo works like 1993's *The Chronic*. MC Ren and Eazy-E would also release successful solo albums. By 1995 group member Eazy-E had died from complications of the AIDS virus.

Selected albums/CDs: *Straight Outta Compton* (1988, Ruthless 57102); *100 Miles and Runnin'* (1990, 7224); *Niggaz4Life* (1991, 57126).

OTHERZ

NEWCLEUS

Formed in early 1980s, Brooklyn, New York
(Cosmo D, born M. Benjamin Cenac, Brooklyn, New York)

Newcleus was a nine-member group of b-boys (breakdancers) and other hip hoppers from Bedford-Stuyvesant, Brooklyn, who were led by Cosmo D, known for his black derby hat. Their 1984 single "Jam on It" made *Billboard*'s Top 10 Black Single's chart for that year. During the same year Newcleus released the single "Automan" b/w "Where's the Beat" before fading from the scene.

 Selected singles: "Jam on It" (1984, Sunnyview).

NO FACE

(Mark Sexx, born Mark Skeete; Shawn Trone: both born in New York)

No Face initially entered the hip-hop scene as a group whose rhymes focused on sexual subject matter. Their first single around 1989–90, titled "Girl I'll F—You," was released on their own No Face label. In 1990 the group released the album *Wake Your Daughter Up*. In 1994, on the Interscope label, they recorded the single "No Brothas Allowed" b/w "Smashin' Fruit."

 Selected albums/CDs: *Wake Your Daughter Up* (1990, Columbia 46837).

NU-SOUNDS

(Rohan Robotham; Phillip Jordan: both born in New York)

Originally signed to Jazzy Jay's Strong City label around 1990, Nu-Sounds had a hit with the single "Body Slam." Their album *Mackin'* was released in the same period. The group was also noted for its remake of the funk group Ohio Players' piece "Skin Tight."

 Selected albums/CDs: *Mackin'* (1990, Strong City/Uni).

New Jack Swing: A musical style pioneered by producer Teddy Riley combining elements of R&B, rap, and go-go.

ONYX
••••••••
Formed c. 1989, New York
(Sticky Fingaz; Suave Sonny Ceasar; Fredro Starr; Big DS: all born in New York)

Onyx first appeared on the scene in 1989, when they were signed to Profile Records, recording one single for the label.

By 1990 the group had an additional member, Sticky Fingaz, and met Run-D.M.C.'s Jam Master Jay, who signed them to his own JMJ Records. When the group's debut album for the label, *Bacdafucup*, was released in 1993, they made an impression, especially with the younger hip-hop audience, and their album went platinum the year of its release. Onyx had a platinum hit in 1993 with the single "Slam" and another hit with "Throw Ya Gunz in the Air."

Onyx's MC style showed that they were the immediate descendants of Leaders of the New School, in that their rhyme deliveries were loud with occasional ensemble shouts on certain lines of lyrics. However, their subject matter revolved around more ghetto-oriented themes, and their presentation centered on the possibility that the group members themselves were threats to society, as well as to inadequate hip-hop artists. Their logo was the opposite of the happy face: a "madface," or happy face with an angry upside down smile with a blood-drenched "x" hanging over it in the group's name, Onyx. They called their style the grimy style.

 Selected albums/CDs: *Bacdafucup* (1993, JMJ/Columbia 472980).

ORANGE KRUSH

Formed in early 1980s, Queens, New York
(Larry Smith, born c. 1954, St. Albans, Queens; Davy D, a.k.a. Davy DMX,
born David Reeves, Queens; Trevor Gale, born in New York)

Orange Krush's band work provided Russell Simmons and group member/producer Larry Smith with ideas that they used in their work with Run-D.M.C. Of note are Run-D.M.C.'s landmark pieces "Sucker MC's (Krush Groove 1)" and "Hollis Crew (Krush Groove 2)." The parenthetical subtitles refer to the band's name from which that particular beat, or "groove," developed. The drum machine beat on Run-D.M.C.'s "Sucker MC's" comes from the drum pattern on Orange Krush's song "Action," which contained vocals by R&B vocalist Alyson Williams. The group's drummer, Trevor Gale, devised the beat. The group was also noted for its other member Davy D (or Davy DMX), who worked as a guitarist in the group. All Orange Krush members were involved in collaborations with Russell Simmons on some of his early acts.

Orange Krush recorded two songs in 1982, "Action" and "The Bubble Bunch," with rhymes by rapper Jimmy Spicer. By the end of that year Smith and Simmons were planning to use promoter Kool Lady Blue as part of the group, deciding to call it the OK (Orange Krush) Crew, but the group ultimately disbanded. Drummer Trevor Gale and Chyna went on to write a piece for Simmons's brother Run (before he became part of Run-D.M.C.), called "Street Kid," which was never released.

ORIGINAL CONCEPT

Formed in 1977, Westbury, Long Island, New York
(Doctor Dre, born Andre Brown, December 5, 1963, Westbury, Long Island;
T-Money, born in Long Island; the Rapper G, born in Long Island;
Easy-G Rockwell, born in Long Island)

The group Original Concept made a considerable impression with hip hoppers when they made the 1987 single "Pump That Bass"—a work that had continued popularity for nearly two years.

Doctor Dre met friends T-Money, Rapper G, and Easy-G Rockwell in Westbury, Long Island. They soon began working together as DJs, playing at house parties, clubs, school centers, and other available venues.

In 1986 the group had signed with Def Jam Recordings and released the single "Can You Feel It," followed by "Pump That Bass" the following year. In 1988 *Straight from the Basement of Kooley High* was released. The group disbanded around 1989–90. Doctor Dre went on to work as a DJ for the Beastie Boys, and by the early 1990s, became part of the duo Doctor Dre & Ed Lover.

Selected albums/CDs: *Straight from the Basement of Kooley High* (1988, Def Jam/Columbia 462978).

OTHERZ

OAKTOWN'S 3,5,7
•••••••••••••••••••••••••••••••

**Formed c. 1989, Oakland, California
(Sweet L.D., born Djuana Johnican, Houston; Terrible T,
born Tabatha King, Oakland)**

Oaktown's 3,5,7—Sweet L.D. and Terrible T—were originally dancers for Hammer's 1989 "Let's Get It Started Tour." Their debut album, *Wild & Loose*, was released around this same period. Some singles off the work included "Juicy Gotcha Crazy," "Yeah Yeah Yeah," and "We Like It." By 1991 the group's second album, *Fully Loaded*, was released, after which the duo's activities subsided.

 Selected albums/CDs: *Fully Loaded* (1991, Bust-It/Capitol 92996).

Oaktown's 3,5,7

A BASIC RAP ALBUM COLLECTION

Here are the essential rap albums that every listener should own, by year of release.

1984

Run-D.M.C. (Profile 1202). Debut album from the first successful rap group to come out of the suburbs, rather than the Bronx.

1986

Licensed to Ill, the Beastie Boys (Def Jam/Columbia 42038). Best-selling rap album to that date, and the first by a white group to receive wide acceptance by the black rap community.

1987

Criminal Minded, Boogie Down Productions (B. Boy 4787). A pioneering work for its use of gangsta-style lyrics; introduced rapper KRS-One to a larger audience.

1988

Critical Beatdown, Ultramagnetic MCs (Next Plateau 1013). Introduced their unusual rap style, with its off-the-beat rhythms and unusually large vocabulary.

Goin' Off, Biz Markie (Cold Chillin' 25675). The album that launched the career of this comic rapper, who was later involved in legal problems over his use of sampling.

The Great Adventures of Slick Rick, Slick Rick (Def Jam/Columbia 40513). British-born rapper's breakthrough album.

Hot, Cool & Vicious, Salt-N-Pepa (Next Plateau 828246). Debut album by influential female rappers.

He's the DJ, I'm the Rapper, DJ Jazzy Jeff and the Fresh Prince (Jive/RCA 10921). First double album in rap that introduced this popular duo.

It Takes a Nation of Millions to Hold Us Back, Public Enemy (Def Jam/Columbia 44303). The group's second album, on which they turned their attention completely to political themes. The production by Hank Shocklee is very complex, featuring multiple layers of sampled sounds.

Long Live the Kane, Big Daddy Kane (Cold Chillin' 25731). Debut album by this rapper, who became a sex symbol.

Paid in Full, Eric B & Rakim (4th & B'way 4005). Influential duo with a unique rapping style, with lyrics based on teachings of the Five Percent Nation of Islam.

Straight Outta Compton, N.W.A (Ruthless 57102). Their first album, which established their reputation as premiere West Coast gangsta-style rappers.

Strictly Business, EPMD (Sleeping Bag/Fresh 1). First album by this duo, featuring strong funk and hardcore lyrics, and also noted for introducing Eric "E-Double" Sermon's lisp-delivered rhymes.

1989

All Hail the Queen, Queen Latifah (Tommy Boy 1022). Her debut album, which introduced her unique blend of rap, reggae, R&B, and house music.

As Nasty as They Wanna Be, 2 Live Crew (Luke 91651; clean version [*As Clean As* . . .], 91652). The album that started the controversy over obscenity and rap.

Life Is . . . Too Short, Too Short (Jive/RCA 1149; clean version, 1218). Second album by this rapper with a hustler/pimp image, which established his reputation with rap fans.

3 Feet High and Rising, De La Soul (Tommy Boy 1019). Producer DJ Prince Paul drew from a wide variety of musical styles for his samples. The record was also one of the first to feature comedy skits interspersed among the tracks.

1990

History of Rap: Volume One, Awesome 2 (Select). Key early recordings by pioneer rap artists.

People's Instinctive Travels and the Paths of Rhythm, A Tribe Called Quest (Jive/RCA 1331). First album from these rappers, who draw heavily on jazz music for their accompaniment.

Please Hammer Don't Hurt 'Em, MC Hammer (Capitol 92857). Megaselling album that introduced rap to a wide audience.

1991

A Wolf in Sheep's Clothing, Black Sheep (Mercury 848368). Introduced lighter-flavored rap with lighter-textured samples that appealed to a younger crowd.

Future Without a Past, Leaders of the New School (Elektra 60976). First album by this third-generation rap group, which presented louder delivered rhymes and a freer brand of MC'ing from group member Busta Rhymes.

1993

Bacdafucup, Onyx (JMJ/Columbia 472980). Debut album by this group, who follow the Leaders of the New School in style, but with lyrical content touching the more criminal influences of life in the 1990s.

PARIS

• • • • • • • •

(Born Oscar Jackson, c. 1968, San Francisco)

Paris is a rapper whose attire, logo, and political beliefs are reminiscent of the Black Panther Party. His rhymes are almost always politically oriented, and he has also developed narrative rhymes that attempt to educate the black community. Paris is the owner of Scarface Records, and he has developed various acts for the label. He contributes political writings and op-ed pieces on occasion to papers like the *Washington Post*.

Paris was a DJ in college, who was inspired by the works of Public Enemy and other sociopolitical rappers. He graduated from the University of California with an economics degree in 1990. During that same period Paris was signed to Tommy Boy Records, where his first album, *The Devil Made Me Do It*, received some critical notice, selling about 250,000 copies at the time.

In 1992 Paris recorded the album *Sleeping with the Enemy*. Because of a song on the album, titled "Bush Killa," which contained lyrics relating to an imaginary assassination of then-President George Bush, Tommy Boy Records refused to stand by the album and dropped its release. Paris decided to release the album on his own Scarface Records in 1993. The work was critically acclaimed by several music journals across the nation.

Toward the end of 1993 Paris supplied his video for the song "Days of Old" to FOX-TV's *America's Most Wanted* crime program, which aided in capturing a murderer. In 1994 he released the album *Guerrilla Funk*, which was distributed by Priority Records, with the single titled "Outta My Life."

Selected albums/CDs: *The Devil Made Me Do It* (1991, Tommy Boy 1030); *Sleeping with the Enemy* (1993, Scarface); *Guerilla Funk* (1994, Priority 108).

PAUL WINLEY RECORDS

Formed in 1956, Harlem, New York City

Paul Winley and his self-named record company is known for being the first record label to record Afrika Bambaataa and his Zulu Nation members. Winley is also noted for his *Super Disco Brakes*, a series of albums he released in the late 1970s, which contained compilations of popular break-beat records.

Winley started in the music business by writing songs in Washington, DC, for his brother's doo-wop group, Atlantic Records's the Clovers. On travels with the group to New York, Winley began to hang out at Atlantic with the artists, and soon moved there. He would later write songs for Ruth Brown and Joe Turner.

Soon after, Winley began working around the legendary Brill Building with other song-writers such as Otis Blackwell, Jesse Stone (a.k.a. Charles Calhoun), and Winfield Scat. Winley later teamed with Dave "Baby" Cortez, and the two began to write songs and record doo-wop acts such as the Duponts (which featured Little Anthony of the Imperials fame), the Collegians, the Jesters, and the Paragons.

By the end of the 1970s Winley entered the rap market by putting out his *Super Disco Brakes* albums for hip hoppers, featuring just the instrumental breaks from popular disco singles. In 1980 he worked with Afrika Bambaataa's Soul Sonic Force group, Cosmic Force, recording their piece "Zulu Nation Throwdown." He also recorded Bambaataa's "Death Mix" during this same period. Since then, he has ceased to be active on the rap scene.

PETE DJ JONES

(Born in Bronx, New York)

Pete DJ Jones was one of the original DJs during the early 1970s, performing in various areas of the Bronx, Brooklyn, and Manhattan before the emergence of hip-hop culture. He is recognized for the influence he had on hip hoppers like Grandmaster Flash and Lovebug Starski. It was Jones's precision deejaying skill in mixing records that gave Grandmaster Flash the idea to apply precision mixing to Kool DJ Herc's break-beat deejaying style, which Flash and many other DJs were beginning to adapt during this period. It was Flash's discovery that Jones actually cued his records through headphones before playing them (which explained Jones's precision timing) that inspired Flash to apply the technique to break records.

A welfare caseworker during the week at the Bergen Avenue Center in the Bronx, Jones initially deejayed on the weekends. His music sets were disco- and R&B-oriented. Around 1974 he played some of the break records that were associated with Kool Herc, like James Brown's "Give It Up or Turnit Loose."

As with DJ Hollywood and other DJs, Jones had a crew of people that worked under him. Becky DJ Jones was a female who deejayed with Jones on occasion. Jones had three main MCs who worked with him: JT Hollywood, JJ the Disco King, and KC the Prince of Soul. These three MCs would individually get on the microphone and motivate Jones's crowd for a few minutes, then Jones would deejay without the MCs for a half hour.

Some of Jones's famous spots were the Stardust Ballroom, Nell Quinn's, Super Star 33, and Leviticus. His peak period of popularity was during 1973–74, after which his popularity and music activities subsided.

PETE ROCK & CL SMOOTH
• •

Formed c. late 1980s, Mount Vernon, New York
(Pete Rock, born Pete Phillips; CL Smooth, born Corey Penn: both born in Mount Vernon, New York)

Pete Rock & CL Smooth

The Mount Vernon, New York, duo of Pete Rock & CL Smooth attained immediate notice when they released their "Mecca and the Soul Brother" on their 1991 *All Souled Out* EP. CL Smooth's distinctive vocal texture stood out, as well as his phonetically funky rhyme writing style, which initially contained many surreal similes and metaphors steeped in social, political, Hollywood, and ghetto images. DJ Pete Rock had already been recognized as one of the top hip-hop DJs, through his work on Marley Marl's *In Control Radio Show* on New York City radio station WBLS-FM from 1988 to 1992.

Pete Rock began working the turntables at the age of seven when he learned how to scratch. In high school he met CL Smooth and the two soon began working together. They eventually hooked up with another Mount Vernonite, DJ Eddie F, who had been working with Heavy D. Eddie established his own production crew, the Untouchables, and Rock became a member of it. Rock's first production work was on Heavy D's *Big Tyme* LP, for which he coproduced "Mood for Love," "Let It Flow," "Big Tyme," and "Better Land."

Smooth and Rock's debut album in 1992, *Mecca and the Soul Brother*, did well and contained several hit singles—"Straighten It Out," "The Creator," and "T.R.O.Y. (They Reminisce Over You)." Pete Rock became one of the hottest producers and remixers in hip hop, known for his predilection for horn samples. Some of the artists he worked with include his cousin Heavy D, EPMD, Brand Nubian, Johnny Gill, and Father MC.

In 1993 Rock and Smooth recorded the piece "What's Next on the Menu?" for the motion picture soundtrack *Who's the Man*. In 1994 they released the album *The Main Ingredient*, with its single "I Got A Love."

 Selected albums/CDs: *All Souled Out* (1991, Elektra 61175); *Mecca and the Soul Brother* (1992, Elektra 60948); *The Main Ingredient* (1994, Elektra 61661).

PHARCYDE
•••••••••••••••
Formed c. early 1990s, Los Angeles
(Booty Brown, born Romye Robinson, November 13, 1969, Pasadena, California; Darky Boy, born Imani Wilcox, Compton, California; Slim Kid, born Tre Hardison, October 5, 1970, California; Fat Lip, born Derrick Stewart, California)

Pharcyde group members Booty Brown, Slim Kid, and Darky Boy originally started out as b-boys, who breakdanced in their own group, Two for Two. They performed in various music videos, and also on Fox-TV's *In Living Color*.

They attended an A&M Records-funded performance school program in South Central Los Angeles, where they met another dancer, Fat Lip. All four combined their talents, rapping with producer J-Swift, who had been working with Fat Lip. The group was then signed to Delicious Vinyl Records after other labels expressed interest. The group's first work, "Soul Flower," appeared on the Brand New Heavies's album *Heavy Rhyme Experience: Vol. 1*. Then Pharcyde released the single "Ya Mama," after which they presented their debut album, *Bizarre Ride II The Pharcyde*, in 1992. The group had another hit, "Passing Me By," from the album.

 Selected albums/CDs: *Bizarre Ride II the Pharcyde* (1992, Delicious Vinyl 92222; clean version, 92271).

PM DAWN
•••••••••••••••
a.k.a. PM Dawn Infinite
Formed c. 1989, Jersey City, New Jersey
(Prince Be/The Nocturnal, born Attrell Cordes; DJ Minutemix/J.C. the Eternal, born Jarrett Cordes)

The Cordes brothers, known as PM Dawn, are a rap duo with a feel for funk artists like early Kool and the Gang and Sly and the Family Stone, plus pop rock groups like Paul Revere, the Beatles, and the Beach Boys. They are also recognized for Prince Be/The Nocturnal's alternate rapping and singing delivery.

The brothers grew up in Jersey City in the 1970s. Both were influenced by their mother's spiritual studies of the works of Edgar Cayce. Prince Be was deejaying at local parties by the

time he was in the ninth grade. He also began to listen to the vast record collection of his step-father (a drummer, who played for Kool and the Gang and Richie Havens) and his uncle, both of whom had an array of early rock and funk albums.

After he left high school Prince Be landed a job at a homeless shelter as a night guard. The $600 he earned there enabled him to make his first demo recording of the duo, which he was already calling PM Dawn (from the theory that from the darkest hour comes the light). Eventually they were signed to Gee Street Records, and their first single—which was recorded in Britain—was titled "Ode to a Forgetful Mind" and released in late 1989. The British music press gave it good reviews.

By 1990 the duo returned to Britain to record their first album, *Of the Heart, Of the Soul, Of the Cross: The Utopian Experience*. It was released in 1991 to impressive reviews, this time in both Britain and the United States. A single, "Set Adrift on Memory Bliss," reached number 1 on the *Billboard* pop, R&B, and dance charts. The album then went gold two months after its release and soon reached platinum.

Their second album, *The Bliss Album . . .? (Vibrations of Love and Anger and the Ponderance of Life and Existence)*, was released in 1993. The single from that album "I'd Die Without You" was featured in the Eddie Murphy movie *Boomerang*.

In 1993–94 they began producing for other artists, including singers Philip Bailey, Shara Nelson, Chynna Phillips, and Jody Watley. During this same period they changed their group name to PM Dawn Infinite.

 Selected singles: "A Watcher's Point of View" (1991, Gee Street/Island).

 Selected albums/CDs: *Of the Heart, Of the Soul, Of the Cross: The Utopian Experience* (1991, Gee Street/Island 510276); *The Bliss Album* (1993, Gee Street/Island 514517).

POOR RIGHTEOUS TEACHERS

Formed c. late 1980s, Trenton, New Jersey
(Wise Intelligent; Culture Freedom; DJ Father Shaheed: all born Trenton, New Jersey)

The Poor Righteous Teachers made an impression with hip hoppers in 1990 when their single "Rock Dis Funky Joint" appeared on the scene. Lead rapper Wise Intelligent added dancehall, reggae, DJ-style inflections, and occasional quickly delivered lines to his MC'ing, combined with lessons from the Five Percent Nation of Islam. The group's rhymes focus on Afrocentric issues and ghetto themes.

Coming from the Donnelly Homes in North Trenton, New Jersey, group members Wise Intelligent, Culture Freedom, and DJ Father Shaheed have worked extensively with producer Tony (Tony D) Depula on most of their early material, and also with Eric "I.Q." Gray. The group's debut album, *Holy Intellect*, appeared in 1990.

In 1992 the group's second work, *Pure Poverty*, appeared, with the single "Easy Star." By 1993 their third album, *Black Business*, was released, with its single "Nobody Move."

Selected albums/CDs: *Holy Intellect* (1990, Profile 1289); *Pure Poverty* (1991, Profile 1415); *Business* (1993, Profile 1443).

Poor Righteous Teachers

POP ART RECORDS

(Based in Philadelphia)

Pop Art Records was one of Philadelphia's pioneer rap labels during the early to mid-1980s. Owned by brothers Dana and producer Lawrence "L.G. the Teacher" Goodman, Pop Art released records by artists like the Galaxy Five and launched the careers of Roxanne Shanté, Steady B, MC Craig G, and many of hip hop's more successful acts, such as Salt-N-Pepa and DJ Jazzy Jeff & the Fresh Prince. The label's notable releases include Roxanne Shanté's 1984 "Roxanne's Revenge" and "Bite This" singles, and Salt-N-Pepa's "The Showstopper," "Shout" by MC Craig G, and Steady B's "Take Your Radio," all released in 1985.

Around 1986 Dana Goodman started Word Up Records, which launched the duo DJ Jazzy Jeff and the Fresh Prince with their single "Girls Ain't Nothing but Trouble." Their first ten-song album, titled *Rock the House*, was released on the Pop Art label before being picked up by Jive Records. By the early 1990s Lawrence Goodman changed the Pop Art name to Hilltop Hustler Records. He began managing acts like Three Times Dope, and expanded his production duties, producing for that group, as well as Steady B and Cool C. By 1991 on into 1995 he became involved with the careers of his sons, Qu'ran and Taji, and their group, Da Youngsta's, producing material on their albums. Dana Goodman entered the video retail business around the early to mid-1990s.

POSITIVE K

a.k.a. Baby Breed, Positive Knowledge Allah
(Born Darryl Gibson, 1968, Bronx, New York)

Positive K is a rapper who has had an underground following since the early 1980s before he became more widely known with his hit "I Got a Man." He is noted for his phonetically precise lyrics and suave delivery on the microphone.

Positive had the great opportunity of seeing rap legends like Afrika Bambaataa, Grandmaster Flash, DJ Hollywood, and Grand Wizard Theodore perform in Echo Park from his grandmother's window in the Bronx when he was 10 years old. He started buying the tapes of those jams that were circulating during that period, and studied them for hours.

In 1980 he formed a crew with his cousin Corey Cor, calling themselves the Disco Cousins. Both were 12 years old at the time, and still learning the craft of MC'ing. By 1981 Positive was calling himself Baby Breed and living in Queens. He continued to keep up with the hip-hop scene, traveling back to the Bronx whenever he got the chance. Positive and his family moved again later that year, to South Carolina. During this time he entered a Schlitz Malt Liquor rap contest, winning the third place prize of $300.

Around 1982 Positive moved back to New York City and became involved with the Nation of Islam. He later formed the Almighty God Crew, which lasted for a short time. Around 1983–84 Positive hooked up with an acquaintance from his Queens neighborhood, Sweetie G.

Positive K

After deciding to record his own material, Positive borrowed $500 from his mother and recorded (with Sweetie G) the song "Gettin' Paid." The piece was eventually signed by Mike and Dave of Mike & Dave Records, who released the work on their compilation album titled *Fast Money*.

Several months later Positive left Mike and Dave and became the client of then-manager Lumumba Carson (who would later form the group, X-Clan). Carson teamed Positive with Grand Puba Maxwell and Daddy-O to work on a song titled "Quarter-Gram Pam." Nat Robinson of First Priority Records took notice of the rapper and signed him. Positive did duets with Robinson's daughter, MC Lyte. He also penned several songs for the label's artists, like "I am the Lyte" and "Rhyme Hangover" for MC Lyte, and "Many Styles," "Peer Pressure," and "Start It Up Y'all" for Lyte's brothers, the Audio Two.

Disappointed with his First Priority deal, Positive left the label and recorded a cut on Brand Nubian's *One for All* album, titled "Grand Puba, Positive & LG," which became an underground favorite with hip hoppers. He then hooked up with Big Daddy Kane around 1991, recording and co-producing the song "Nightshift," which he financed himself (putting it on his own label, called Creative Control) with another loan from his mom, this time for $15,000. The record sold over 20,000 copies. Island Records signed Positive to a deal in 1991–92 and the same record sold approximately 40,000 more copies. With his earnings, Positive developed his own company, called Creative Control Studios.

His single "I Got a Man" was released in 1992, and later the album *The Skills Dat Pay Da Bills* appeared. "I Got a Man" went gold the following year.

 Selected albums/CDs: *The Skills Dat Pay Da Bills* (1992, Island 514057).

PRINCE IKEY C

See COSMIC FORCE

PRINCE MARKIE DEE

See FAT BOYS

PRINCE PAUL

(Born Paul E. Huston, April 2, 1967, Queens, New York)

DJ Prince Paul was originally known for his work with the group Stetsasonic, but became widely recognized as a producer after his work with the group De La Soul on their *3 Feet High and Rising* LP. It was Paul's work on this album that freed hip-hop production from the

Prince Paul

traditional James Brown samples that were used at the time. Paul sampled every type of music and idea he could come up with for the production of this album, and included comedy skits as well, introducing a new era in hip-hop production. The album went gold in 1989.

Paul began to deejay by the age of 11, and by the eighth and ninth grades he was able to successfully battle other DJs. While in the eleventh grade, Paul participated in a DJ battle in Brooklyn, where he was spotted by Daddy-O and other Stetsasonic members. Impressed with his skills on the turntables, they soon asked him to join the group.

After his initial success with De La Soul, Paul continued to work on their subsequent albums, and he produced and/or remixed works for 3rd Bass, Big Daddy Kane, Queen Latifah, and KRS-One. Around 1992 he established his own label, Dew Doo Man Records, which premiered with his group, Resident Alien, and Mic Tee Lux. In 1994 he became part of the group Gravediggaz, with fellow Stetsasonic member Fruitkwan, rapper Too Poetic, and Prince Rakeem (The Rza) from the Wu-Tang Clan. Their album *6 Feet Deep* was released that same year.

 Selected albums/CDs: *3 Feet High and Rising* by De La Soul (1989, Tommy Boy 1019); *6 Feet Deep* by Gravediggaz (1994, Island 524016).

PRISM RECORDS
See COLD CHILLIN'/PRISM RECORDS

PROFESSOR GRIFF
(Born Richard Griffin, New York)

Professor Griff was originally a member of the group Public Enemy, until a May 1989 interview with *Washington Times* reporter David Mills—in which Griff reportedly made anti-Semitic statements—was made public, forcing group member Chuck D ultimately to fire him from the group.

Griff (one of thirteen brothers and sisters) grew up in Long Island, and during his years at Roosevelt Senior High School, was introduced to the teachings of the Nation of Islam by one of his older brothers. He also was friends with Hank Shocklee, Chuck D, and Flavor Flav. He eventually worked with Shocklee's mobile DJ unit, and they did parties throughout Long Island. Griff also formed the Universal Revolutionary Freedom Fighters Society (TURFS), an organization that provided martial arts and political education to underprivileged youths. Griff provided security to his friends' parties and functions as well.

Chuck D invited Griff to participate in the formation of Public Enemy, and he soon became known as the Minister of Information of the group before he was forced to leave.

Thereafter, Griff worked at Luke Skyywalker Campbell's Luke Records before forming his own group, called the Last Asiatic Disciples, and signing with that label around 1990. He released the album *Pawns in the Game*, along with the single of the same name. By 1991 his *Kao's II Wiz*7*Dome* work appeared, and in 1992 his *Disturb 'N Tha Peace* was released. All albums contained rhymes from Griff centering on sociopolitical themes and black history.

Selected albums/CDs: *Pawns in the Game* (1990, Luke 111); *Kao's II Wiz*7*Dome* (1991, Luke 91721) *Disturb 'N Tha Peace* (1992, Luke 124).

PROFILE RECORDS

Formed in May 1981, New York

Profile Records was one of the early labels to market rap in the 1980s, whose major success was established by acts like Run-D.M.C., Rob Base, Dana Dane, and Special Ed.

Cofounder Cory Robbins had experience deejaying in upstate New York, and worked at MCA Records, before hooking up with partner Steven Plotnicki. Plotnicki (a salesman who worked at Win Records, a distribution company) had written and produced a 1979 dance work called "Love Insurance" for the group Front Page, who recorded for one of MCA's labels, Panorama. Robbins was also involved with the Front Page song as a producer, and soon Plotnicki and Robbins decided to buy the Panorama label, changing its name to Profile Records.

The label was originally established to release alternative dance music. A few of the early records they released were by artists like Grace Kennedy and Lonnie Love (who would later go on to become part of the duo Dr. Jeckyll & Mr. Hyde). Dr. Jeckyll & Mr. Hyde gave the label their first hit in 1981. Spending approximately $750, the company released that group's single called "Genius Rap," and sold 150,000 copies of the work.

The label's biggest success was the signing of Run-D.M.C., whose 1983 "It's Like That" and "Sucker MC's" effectively made Profile a major rap label.

A few other important records for Profile include Rob Base's *It Takes Two*, Special Ed's *Youngest in Charge*, *Dana Dane with Fame* by Dana Dane, and *Quik Is the Name* by DJ Quik. By 1994 Robbins sold his interest in the company to Plotnicki, who then renamed it Profile Entertainment. The company continued to release rap music, as well as dancehall reggae.

PUBLIC ENEMY

●●●●●●●●●●●●●●●●●●●●●●

Formed in 1987, Hempstead, Long Island, New York
(Chuck D/Carl Ryder, born Carlton Douglas Ridenhour, August 1, 1960, Roosevelt,
Long Island; Flavor Flav, born William Drayton, March 16, c. 1959, Roosevelt,
Long Island; Terminator X, born Norman Rogers, New York; Professor Griff,
born Richard Griffin, New York)

Public Enemy is known as the group that brought politically conscious lyrics back to music. They are recognized for reporting on situations in the African-American communities, and for reviving black political heroes of the 1960s, like Malcolm X. Their appearance suggested these times as well, with their background group of steppers, the SLWs, attired in Black Panther Party-type military gear, influenced by mid-1980s underground dance artist Strafe. The group's music is also noted for its multilayered, atonal production style, primarily created by Hank Shocklee, his brother Keith, Eric "Vietnam" Sadler, and Chuck D (a.k.a. Carl Ryder), known collectively as the Bomb Squad.

Group member Chuck D was attending Adelphi University in the early 1980s, majoring in graphic design. He was the first black student there to write and draw his own comic series, titled "Tales of the Skind." He was also part of a party promotion crew at the time called Spectrum City, along with DJs Hank and Keith Shocklee. Chuck designed Spectrum's party fliers, and did occasional rapping, at Hank's request, as MC Chuckie D.

In 1982 Adelphi's radio station, WBAU, broadcast several hip-hop shows. Bill Stephney, a musician whom Chuck had met around this time, had his *Mr. Bill Show*, and would eventually become program director at the station. Stephney offered the Spectrum City crew a three-hour slot there, calling it the "Super Spectrum Mix Show," where the Shocklee brothers, Chuck, and others displayed their deejaying and rapping skills and featured local rappers. One of the favorites on the show was a person Chuck brought in called MC DJ Flavor Flav, who did on the air what he called the "claustrophobic attack." Later, Chuck and the Shocklees created several songs for their show. "Check Out the Radio" was one of the first songs they recorded. Another song they did with Flavor Flav, titled "Public Enemy Number One," was very popular in Long Island and Queens, the station's listening areas.

When Bill Stephney dropped his show, eventually graduating from college and working for *College Music Journal* (CMJ), his radio show was taken over by Doctor Dre, the future host of "Yo! MTV Raps" and member of the duo Doctor Dre & Ed Lover.

In 1985 Stephney, Hank Shocklee, and Chuck D created a short-lived video show called "W.O.R.D.: The World of Rock and Dance." Around 1986 Stephney was approached by Def Jam Recordings cofounder Rick Rubin and offered a position at the label. Stephney accepted, and his first assignment from Rubin was to help him sign Chuck D, whose "Public Enemy Number One" song he had heard from Doctor Dre.

Chuck was reluctant at first to consider rapping as a profession, feeling that he should have something to say if he did it. Eventually, Stephney, along with Hank Shocklee and Chuck, developed an idea for a group that could promote political and social messages. Chuck picked the name for the group, which came from their popular "Public Enemy Number One"

piece. Stephney decided that it would be a good way to market them, as public enemies, because they were young black males, and because the Howard Beach incident had just occurred (where a young black male was killed by angry whites). Chuck also did the logo for the group, which was a silhouette of a black man placed inside a shooting target.

Hank Shocklee's mobile DJ unit partner Professor Griff (who also ran a martial arts school) was also brought into the group as the Minister of Information, as well as Flavor Flav and Eric "Vietnam" Sadler, a musician who early on had played against Stephney in competing bands. Sadler handled the production with the Shocklees and Chuck D. An additional local mobile DJ named Mellow D, later named Terminator X, was also brought into the group.

In 1987 the group released their first album, *Yo! Bum Rush the Show*, which was received successfully in underground circles. Immediate attention went to the production style of the album, which contained many noise-oriented loops on top of funk rhythms, especially on the "F" side of the work. Bill Stephney handled the production here, while Hank Shocklee and Chuck did the coproduction.

The year 1988 saw the release of their second album, *It Takes a Nation of Millions to Hold Us Back*. Here, Chuck D's lyrics became more politically oriented, and Hank Shocklee came more into his own on the production end, beginning to layer more sampled tracks for each song, in the manner of 1960s pop producer Phil Spector's "Wall of Sound." The album went gold that year, and platinum the following year.

In 1989 Public Enemy recorded "Fight the Power" for film director Spike Lee's *Do the Right Thing* soundtrack, which was well received and gained the group even more attention. In May 1989 Minister of Information Professor Griff gave an interview to *Washington Times* reporter David Mills, which contained some quotes that were viewed as anti-Semitic. The incident nearly destroyed the group, with the media's increased coverage of the situation forcing the group to leak several reports about their possible disbandment. Finally, all the attention forced Chuck D to fire Griff from the group. Griff later signed his own deal with Luther "Luke Skyywalker" Campbell's label.

Public Enemy's *Fear of a Black Planet* came out in 1990 and went platinum that same year. Singles from this work include "911 Is a Joke" and "Welcome to the Terrordome." In 1991 the group released their next album, *Apocalypse 91 . . . The Enemy Strikes Black*, a two-record set. The work went platinum, and its single "Can't Truss It" went gold that year. During this period rap activist Sister Souljah became a member of the group, after doing cameos in some of their past videos.

For 1992 the group released *Greatest Misses*, an album that contained remixes of some of their songs that appeared on past albums. The album went gold that year. Later that same year Chuck D created his own "hip hop apparel" company called Rapp Style. In 1994 the group released the album *Muse Sick-N-Hour Mess Age*, which went gold by November. In 1995 during a summer tour of Europe, Flavor Flav broke both his arms in a motorcycle mishap in Milan, Italy. The group went on temporary hiatus, with Chuck D announcing a new multimedia company, including plans for a hip-hop talk show.

Selected albums/CDs: *Yo! Bum Rush the Show* (1987, Def Jam/Columbia 40658); *It Takes a Nation of Millions to Hold Us Back* (1988, Def Jam/Columbia 44303); *Fear of a Black Planet* (1990, Def Jam/Columbia 45413); *Apocalypse 91 . . . The Enemy Strikes Black* (1991, Def Jam/Columbia 2-47374); *Greatest Misses* (1992, Def Jam/Columbia 2-53014); *Muse Sick-N-Hour Mess Age* (1994, Def Jam/Columbia 523362).

PUFFY COMBS
a.k.a. Puff Daddy
(Born Sean Combs, 1970, Mount Vernon, New York)

Puffy Combs is a label owner, producer, manager, and former promoter, who is responsible for many gold and platinum acts in hip hop and R&B, including Mary J. Blige, Faith, Notorious B.I.G., Craig Mack, and Jodeci.

Combs grew up in Mount Vernon, New York, and began his career at the age of 19 as a student at Howard University. During his freshman year, Combs began to organize and promote hip-hop parties. He also interned at Andre Harrell's Uptown Records label, eventually bringing the R&B acts Jodeci and Mary J. Blige to Harrell's attention; they were signed to the label and achieved much success, becoming platinum acts in their field. Combs's prestige in the industry began to grow soon after.

He continued to organize and promote parties in the early 1990s, particularly at the Manhattan hip-hop club the Red Zone, where his events were called "Daddy's House." Many club goers and hip-hop celebrities attended the events. Around January 1, 1992, however, tragedy stuck one of his events, a celebrity basketball game held at City College in Harlem. Billed as "The Heavsters [a reference to rapper Heavy D's team] vs. The Puff Daddy All Stars," nine people were crushed to death when a crowd rushed the school's gymnasium where the event was to take place. Combs was subsequently blamed for the tragedy and was forced to explain his side of the story to the press for weeks. His role at Uptown Records was also diminished by Harrell for a few months.

Around 1993, Combs brought rapper Notorious B.I.G. to Harrell's attention. Harrell asked the rapper to record a party song for the motion picture soundtrack of *Who's the Man?*, resulting in the artist's first single, "Party and Bullshit." Soon after, differences arose between Harrell and Combs, with Combs and Notorious B.I.G. leaving the label.

In 1994 Combs established his Bad Boy Entertainment label, signing Notorious B.I.G. and releasing his singles "Juicy" and "Unbelievable." Earlier that year Combs was introduced to rapper Craig Mack outside a club. After hearing Mack perform some freestyle rhymes, Combs offered to sign him immediately, but told him, as a trade, that he had to do a song with Mary J. Blige. By 1995 Combs became involved in several aspects of the music business with his acts, including stage performances (trading rhymes with his artists), co-writing songs, and directing and appearing in music videos. Some of the songs Combs has co-produced are Blige's "Reminisce" and "What's the 411," singer Faith's "You Used to Love Me," and Notorious B.I.G.'s "Juicy," "One More Chance," and "Big Poppa."

PUMPKIN

(Born Erroll Bedward, January 21, 1961, Bronx, New York; died August 24, 1990)

Pumpkin was one of the most important hip-hop producers of the late 1970s and early 1980s. As house producer for Enjoy Records, he was responsible for many of that label's early rap hits. The works that he either produced and/or arranged rank as classics in hip-hop culture. A multi-instrumentalist with a proficiency on drums, guitar, bass, and keyboards, Pumpkin also worked with artists outside the rap genre, including Keith Sweat, Alyson Williams, Johnny Kemp, and Meli'sa Morgan.

Pumpkin began his music career at the age of 6, playing classical piano. He learned the drums as a member of the Junior High Boro-wide Band from jazz drummer Stix Evans. In the mid- to late-1970s, Pumpkin became part of the fusion band Triad, playing drums, as well as bass and synthesizer. By 1979{*}80 he was recommended to Enjoy Records' Bobby Robinson by DJ Breakout, who was acquainted with Pumpkin from seeing him play in his garage. In 1983 Pumpkin also became a recording artist in his own right for Profile Records. He recorded the hit "King of the Beat" for the label that same year, and in 1984 he recorded "Here Comes That Beat!" with the Profile All-Stars.

Some of the important works Pumpkin was involved with include "Rockin' It" and "Problems of the World Today" by the Fearless Four; "Rappin' & Rockin' the House" by the Funky Four Plus One; "Feel the Heart Beat," "Body Rock," and "Put the Boogie in Your Body" by the Treacherous Three; "Money (Dollar Bill Y'All)" by Jimmy Spicer; "Funk Box 2" and "Gonna Get You Hot" by the Masterdon Committee; "Gettin' Money" by Dr. Jeckyll & Mr. Hyde; "Love Rap" by Spoonie Gee; "Move to the Groove," "Country Rock & Rap," and "School Beats" by the Disco Four. The last artist Pumpkin worked with before his death was Busy Bee, on the piece "Jail Bait." He died in 1990 at the age of 29 of pneumonia.

OTHERZ

PAUL C
. . . .
(Born Paul McKastey; died summer 1989)

Paul C was a well-known producer and engineer, recognized for his work with the Large Professor and Main Source, Ultramagnetic MCs, Superlover Cee & Cassanova Rud, and Stezo. Paul was reportedly shot to death in a case of mistaken identity in 1989.

PEBBLEE-POO
. . . .
(Born in New York)

Female MC Pebblee-Poo originally worked with DJ Masterdon. She received some notice when she recorded an answer record to the Boogie Boys's piece "A Fly Girl." Her piece was called "A Fly Guy," and it was released in 1985 on Profile Records.

RAPPIN' ON THE NET

The Internet is bursting with home pages on music, and new sites are developing devoted to rap, hip hop, and R&B music. While many come and go, there are a couple worth a visit.

Jaime's Crackhouse (http://uenics.evansville.edu.80/~jw2/jcrack.gtf) includes music samples, reviews of current rap releases, information on tours and radio shows, room for rap fans to post messages, and, probably most useful, a list of other rap pages on the net.

Individual fans have developed "unofficial" home pages for their favorite groups.

The Unofficial Public Enemy Homepage (http://wwwime.tut.fi:80/2tpaanane/pe.htm) features discographical, biographical, and other information on this notorious group. The site is still "under construction," but there is useful information to be found here.

The Unofficial Wu-Tang Clan Home Page (http://www.voicenet.com:80/1/voicenet/home-pages/ebonie/wu_tang/wutang.htm1) is a more elaborately developed site than the Public Enemy one. It allows fans to sample music and share their thoughts on what the home page calls "the most phat" of all rap groups.

Hitlist (http://www.cldc:howard.edu.80/%7aja/hitlist/htm.ls) is devoted to hip-hop music. It offers a similar array of information to Jaime's Crackhouse, although in a more commercial format.

Streetsound Magazine's home page (http://www.phatom.com80/2 street) is oriented to the professional musician/deejay/music junkie. It provides chart information, mail order sources, radio airplay stats, and other useful information on a wide variety of musical styles.

Most of the major record labels maintain internet sites. Of course, they produce a wide variety of music, but rap is represented in almost all of their catalogs. Additionally, mainstream magazines like *Rolling Stone* have an elaborate presence online, as does the rap magazine *Vibe*.

Wu Tang Clan

P.A.L. (The Police Athletic League): A group in New York City that sponsors amateur sports teams.

Party rocker: An MC (or DJ) who is able to motivate a crowd to dance more, via his or her own distinctive chants and/or phrases.

Props: Proper respect received for something accomplished. The word was originally used as a synonym for girlfriends, "belonging" to a man in the hip-hop community.

QUEEN LATIFAH
• •
(Born Dana Owens, March 18, 1970, East Orange, New Jersey)

Queen Latifah (Arabic for "delicate and sensitive") is one of the first female MCs to successfully combine three careers as a rapper, an actress, and businesswoman. She is also known for the socially conscious lyrics she presents in her songs.

Latifah's career started while attending Irvington High School in East Orange, New Jersey, where her mother worked as a teacher. She became friends with Tangy B and Landy B (rappers, who went by the name Ladies Fresh) during this period, and began performing with them as their human beatbox. She also developed her rhyme skills with this group.

In 1987 Latifah befriended DJ Mark the 45 King and other members of what would later be called the Flavor Unit (a group of friends who did demo recordings with Mark the 45 King, including Apache, Latee, Chill Rob G, and Lakim Shabazz). They took the name Flavor Unit after Latee's record with the 45 King, titled "This Cut's Got Flavor," which was their first production to receive radio airplay.

Queen Latifah

Around 1988 Mark the 45 King recorded a demo of Latifah's material, which he played over the telephone to Tommy Boy Records' then-head of A&R, Dante Ross, who signed her. Her first album for the label in 1989, *All Hail the Queen*, received a Grammy nomination and sold over a million copies worldwide. The songs on the work combined rap with reggae, R&B, and house music. It reached number 6 on the *Billboard* Top R&B Albums chart.

In 1990 she was voted "Best Female Rapper" in a *Rolling Stone* readers' poll. That same year she was named "Best New Rap Artist" at the New Music Seminar.

In 1991 her second album, *Nature of a Sista'*, was released. Shortly after that she began to receive acting roles, appearing in films such as Spike Lee's *Jungle Fever*, Ernest Dickerson's *Juice, House Party 2*, and the television show *The Fresh Prince of Bel-Air*.

Latifah also involved herself with activities outside the music and entertainment industries, speaking at various colleges and raising funds for ecology and AIDS research projects, among other interests.

Responsible for discovering acts like Treach and Naughty by Nature, she launched with her new manager and friend Shakim Compere (Kool DJ Red Alert was her former manager) Flavor Unit Records in 1993. That same year she entered the television market, starring in the successful sitcom *Living Single*, playing an enterprising magazine editor. During this period she left Tommy Boy Records and signed with Motown, releasing the album *Black Reign*. "U.N.I.T.Y." was one of the singles off the work, and the album is noted for Latifah's work as a singer on the track "Weekend Love."

 Selected albums/CDs: *All Hail the Queen* (1989, Tommy Boy 1022); *Nature of a Sista'* (1991, Tommy Boy 1035); *Black Reign* (1993, Motown 6370).

QUEEN MOTHER RAGE
••
(Born S. Dancer, Brooklyn, New York)

Queen Mother Rage was a promising MC from the Blackwatch Movement camp from which the group X-CLAN emerged. She was noted for her lisp-generated MC'ing of rhymes with complex word imagery, delivered in a seductive tone. Around 1990 her single "Slipping into Darkness" was released, and toward 1991 her work *Vanglorious Law* appeared. She soon left the music scene after personal and professional disappointments.

 Selected albums/CDs: *Vanglorious Law* (1991, Cardiac 3-8001-2).

Queen Mother Rage

RALPH McDANIELS

(Born February 26, Brooklyn, New York)

VJ Ralph McDaniels is recognized as being one of the first rap VJs, and is noted for having one of the first black music video shows in the United States. His *Video Music Box* was the only outlet for the emerging rap video market in 1984, and with his partner, Lionel C. Martin (a.k.a. the Vid Kid), he established one of the first black-owned video companies for music video production, Classic Concepts. Airing on WNYC Channel 31 in New York City, *Video Music Box* became one of the highest-rated shows on public television, and one of the most influential music video shows, with significance alongside of cable music television. McDaniels was born in Bedford-Stuyvesant, Brooklyn, but grew up in Queens, where he was originally a DJ from 1977 to 1983. Having a prior background working with bands, McDaniels deejayed in clubs like the Blue Ice where he met and hung out with people from his neighborhood like Davy D and Russell Simmons. McDaniels attended LaGuardia Community College—where he studied communications—and later attended the New York Institute of Technology. McDaniels also did intern work at television stations like then-WNEW-TV's *Midday Live* show.

He eventually wound up at WNYC-TV in the early 1980s, working as a technical director. He later approached that station's programming department with ideas for video shows, one of which was called *Studio 31 Dance Party*, which aired for one year. His next idea was *Video Music Box*.

With Lionel Martin directing the bulk of the music videos Classic Concepts has developed, the company has produced videos for Bell Biv DeVoe, 3rd Bass, Big Daddy Kane, Biz Markie, LL Cool J, and Public Enemy. Some notable videos McDaniels has directed himself include all of X-Clan's early videos and Super Cat's "Ghetto Red Hot," all during the early 1990s.

REAL ROXANNE
(Born Joanne Martinez, Brooklyn, New York)

The Real Roxanne was originally production crew Full Force's response to Roxanne Shanté's "Roxanne's Revenge" answer record, which responded to Full Force's own classic work produced for the group UTFO, "Roxanne, Roxanne." Because of the overwhelming success of Roxanne Shanté's piece, the production crew had come up with an "authentic Roxanne" to repel other Roxanne impostors.

Real Roxanne was reportedly discovered by Full Force's Paul Anthony when she was waitressing tables at a diner. She was initially chosen for her good looks, which UTFO hinted at in their piece, although the Roxanne in the group's record was actually a fictional character. Anthony and Full Force felt that the Real Roxanne looked the way the UTFO character would look, if she existed.

Raised in the Gowanus Housing Projects in Boerum Hill, Brooklyn, Roxanne encountered great difficulty performing, due to the fact that there were several other Roxannes out there already in shows. Hip-hop audiences would become confused (having already seen a Roxanne or two in concert somewhere) and shout out that she was an impostor during her performances.

Throughout, Real Roxanne endured. Working with her DJ, Howie Tee, Roxanne released singles like her self-titled "Real Roxanne" on Select Records, and an album—self-titled—in 1988.

After the "Roxanne phenomenon" subsided, Roxanne released a few singles that got her attention, like "Bang Zoom (Let's Go-Go)" and "Howie's Tee'd Off." In 1992 she began working with Chubb Rock, who produced her album *Go Down (But Don't Bite It)*, with the single "Ya Brother Does."

 Selected singles: "Real Roxanne" (1984, Select).

 Selected CDs/albums: *Roxanne* (1988, Sire 21627).

Real Roxanne

REDHEAD KINGPIN

Redhead Kingpin

(Born David Guppy, 1971, Englewood, New Jersey)

Redhead Kingpin got his name due to his red hair.

Formerly working as a barber, Kingpin began rapping as a solo artist in 1986, and was signed to Sugar Hill Records for a brief period. In 1987 he met GSD, a former camp counselor, who helped Red make a demo of two songs. GSD brought the demo to a former acquaintance, Gene Griffin, who managed the R&B groups Guy, Wrecks 'n' Effect, and Today, and also worked as a producer. Griffin got Red a contract with Virgin Records in 1988.

In 1989 his album *A Shade of Red* was released, with work done by Guy producer Teddy Riley, and featured the F.B.I. (DJ Wildstyle, dancers Bo Roc and Poochie, and GSD). Singles off the work included "Do the Right Thing," "We Rock the Mic," and "Pump It Hottie." He began touring internationally after recording the album.

In 1991 Kingpin released his second work, titled *The Album with No Name*. Around this same period Kingpin was the victim of an impostor who passed himself off as the star, until he was finally caught by police authorities.

 Selected albums/CDs *A Shade of Red* (1989, Virgin 86124); *The Album with No Name* (1991, Virgin 86207).

REDMAN

(Born Reggie Noble, Newark, New Jersey)

Redman's astonishing cameos on the works of EPMD had hip hoppers wondering who he was during the early 1990s. He is known for his powerful, everything-and-the-kitchen-sink delivery, which is rooted completely in the streets, but with underground appeal as well as crossover recognition.

Redman got into the hip-hop scene as a DJ at the age of 10, influenced by his uncle, who used to DJ in a club. His mother bought him a set of turntables, which he eventually learned to use. Redman also did illustrations, a love that would continue. (He served as his first album's art director, as well as creating his own logo.) By the age of 16, Redman began to get into rapping. He soon joined a group called 1 2 + 3 around the mid-1980s, which lasted approximately a year and a half.

In the late 1980s at the Newark, New Jersey, club Sensations, Redman was deejaying for a friend when he met Erick Sermon and Parrish Smith of EPMD. He tried to talk the duo into getting his friend a record deal, when someone mentioned to them that Redman could MC. After the duo asked him a few times to perform some rhymes, they brought him on stage where he was paid to perform the rhyme again. After the show Redman and EPMD exchanged phone numbers.

Months later, Redman was asked to leave his mother's house because of parent-son differences and lifestyle misunderstandings. He wound up living with Erick Sermon for two years, and began learning the ropes of the hip-hop industry. Redman began to do cameos on EPMD songs like "Brothers on My Jock," "Hardcore," and "Headbanger," while at the same time recording his own material.

He was signed to Def Jam Recordings in 1991{*}92. His 1992 debut work, *Whut? Thee Album*, went gold in 1993. In 1994 his *Dare Iz a Darkside* album was released, with its single "Rockafella."

 Selected singles: "A Day of Sooperman Lover" (1992, Def Jam/Chaos); "Tonight's Da Night" (1992).

 Selected albums/CDs: *Whut? Thee Album* (1992 RAL/Chaos/Columbia 52967); *Dare Iz a Darkside* (1994, RAL/Chaos/Columbia 523846).

Redman

RICK RUBIN

* * * * * * * * * * * * * * *

(Born Frederick Jay Rubin, March 10, 1963, Long Island, New York)

Rick Rubin was the cofounder of Def Jam Recordings, and later founder and head of American Recordings (formerly Def American Recordings). With his then-partner, Russell Simmons, Rubin was responsible for shaping the Def Jam label, making it the most influential record label in rap.

During his years at Def Jam, Rubin signed major acts like LL Cool J, the Beastie Boys, and Public Enemy, and gave marketer/producer Bill Stephney his first major entries into the music business. As a producer, Rubin is noted for placing more emphasis on the verse-and-chorus song structure in rap records, and for introducing rock-music elements in its structure.

Rubin grew up in Lido Beach, Long Island, and attended Long Beach High School. His early musical influences were punk and heavy-metal bands like the Dead Kennedys and AC/DC. He took up the guitar and formed a band called Pricks during his sophomore year.

In 1981 Rubin was a film student at New York University (NYU). He formed a band called Hose and released two EPs with the help of record store and label owner Ed Bahlman (99 Records), who was responsible for putting out underground club records by ESG, Liquid Liquid, and Bush Tetras. Bahlman showed Rubin how to get records pressed and where to go to get songs mastered. Rubin also began to work as a deejay. By 1983 Rubin had met Adam (Ad Rock) Horovitz, Adam (MCA) Yauch, and Michael (Mike D) Diamond of the hardcore rock band the Beasties. Rubin deejayed for the band on stage as DJ Double R.

Attending NYU put Rubin closer to the downtown club scene. At the club Negril, he met DJ Jazzy Jay (Afrika Bambaataa's Soul Sonic Force DJ). Jay turned Rubin on to the records that were hot with the hip-hop crowd. He also showed him how to program beats. In 1983 the two decided to make a record. They tried to interest Special K of the Treacherous Three in the project, but he turned them down, so they asked Special K's brother, T La Rock, to cut their song "It's Yours." The song was first brought to Profile Records—which Rubin turned down—then next to producer Arthur Baker, who had worked with Soul Sonic Force on their "Planet Rock" single, and who had his own Partytime label. Baker offered more money than Profile had to distribute the record, and Rubin accepted. In 1984 "It's Yours" was released and became an underground hit, and was soon heard on radio. Rubin officially set up Def Jam Recordings in his dormitory at NYU. That same year Rubin met Russell Simmons at the club Danceteria. They soon became friends and struck up a fifty-fifty partnership as Def Jam Recordings.

Adam Horovitz had heard a demo recording by LL Cool J that was sent to Rubin. When Rubin heard it, he and Simmons decided to release it as their first record together. "I Need a Beat" was the first song Rubin produced for LL, and it officially launched the rapper's career and the Def Jam label, selling 120,000 copies on its initial release.

In 1985 Rubin continued to work with the Beastie Boys (who were doing all rap by this time) on their songs and as their DJ. He did three songs with them, titled "Rock Hard," "The Party's Getting Rough," and "Beastie Groove." He also produced a novelty record with Jazzy Jay and Russell Simmons, who joked around on the record in a quasi-rap format.

Later that year Rubin and Simmons were approached by CBS Records, where a label deal was made with the company, worth $600,000. The agreement included the promotion and marketing of Def Jam product by CBS. Rubin reportedly xeroxed the check and proudly showed it to his parents. Rubin produced LL Cool J's first album, *Radio*, which eventually went platinum, and the Beastie Boys' single "She's on It." The movie *Krush Groove* was also released this year, which was based loosely on the creation of Def Jam. Many of the label's acts appeared in the movie.

In 1986 Rubin worked with the group Big Audio Dynamite on two songs, titled "Bad" and "The Bottom Line." He also worked with the Junkyard Band on their songs "The Word" and "Sardines." But Rubin's most significant work that year was with Run-D.M.C., co-producing with the group and Russell Simmons their *Raising Hell* album. Selling over a million copies within the first five weeks, it is known as one of the first platinum records by a rap group. The album is also noted for the cover of Aerosmith's "Walk This Way," one of Rubin's favorite groups. Released as a single, "Walk This Way" propelled Run-D.M.C.'s popularity.

Equally significant was Rubin's production of the Beastie Boys' *Licensed to Ill* LP, an album that sold five million copies, the largest selling rap album at that time. The album is noted for its extensive use of tape loops under Rubin's production, which helped initiate and widen the art of sampling in rap music. The work took approximately two years to make, with one to two songs taking about a month to record.

In 1986 Rubin also signed and worked with the heavy-metal group Slayer. When Rubin presented Slayer's *Reign in Blood* to CBS for distribution, the company refused it. Rubin made a deal with Geffen Records to act as the distributor for the record after CBS turned him down.

Later, Rubin heard a demo titled "Public Enemy Number One" from a group called Spectrum City, through Original Concept's Doctor Dre (later one of the hosts of "Yo! MTV Raps"). Rubin signed Spectrum City, which became Public Enemy. In 1987 Public Enemy's debut album, *Yo! Bum Rush the Show*, was released. Rubin was later approached by the group the Cult, and he produced their album *Electric*. Rubin also began working on a script for a movie with Run-D.M.C. titled *Tougher than Leather*, and did soundtrack work on the film *Less Than Zero*.

The year 1988 saw the release of the film *Tougher Than Leather*, which Rubin also directed. Around this time the creative relationship between Rubin and Russell Simmons ended, and Rubin took his share of the company to Los Angeles, where he created his own Def American label.

In 1989, on his new label, Rubin released comedian Andrew Dice Clay's self-titled album, which eventually became the label's first gold album the following year. Some of Rubin's other acts included Slayer (the first group on the Def American label), Masters Of Reality, Danzig, Four Horsemen, the Black Crowes (whose *Shake Your Money Maker* album went gold that year), and the Geto Boys.

The Geto Boys' self-titled album gave Rubin trouble when Geffen Records' president, Ed Rosenblatt, decided not to distribute the work, calling it "the worst thing I ever heard." One song on the album, "Mind of a Lunatic," seemed to cause most of the problems because of its extreme violent imagery. Rubin finally released the album with Giant Records as the distributor.

In 1991 Rubin began to produce more acts, like the Red Devils and the Red Hot Chili Peppers, whose *Blood Sugar Sex Magik*, went gold that year, selling over two million copies by the end of the following year. Rubin also signed a distribution agreement with Seattle rapper Sir Mix-A-Lot and his own Rhyme Cartel label. That same year Rubin produced a 12-inch single containing a remix of two songs by the rock group Queen—"We Are the Champions" and "We Will Rock You," featuring Zulu DJ Afrika Islam.

In 1992 Rubin produced Mick Jagger's solo work *Wandering Spirit*. Sir Mix-A-Lot's album *Mack Daddy* was released in February of that year and went platinum by July. Later, Rubin decided to create a new dance- and rap-oriented label, called Ill Records.

In 1993 Rubin decided to take the "Def" off Def American, changing the name of his label to American Recordings. He proceeded to give the dropped word an honorable burial, which featured an actual funeral procession and a public burial of the word, which was placed inside a coffin and buried. In 1994 he produced rocker Tom Petty's *Wildflowers* album.

 Selected singles: "It's Yours," by T La Rock (1984, Def Jam/Partytime).

 Selected produced albums/CDs: *Raising Hell* by Run-D.M.C. (coproduced 1986, Profile 1217); *Licensed to Ill* by Beastie Boys (Def Jam/Columbia 40238); *Blood Sugar Sex Magik* by Red Hot Chili Peppers (1991, Warner Bros. 26681).

ROB BASE AND DJ E-Z ROCK
Formed c. late 1980s, Harlem, New York
(Rob Base, born Robert Ginyard; DJ E-Z Rock, born Rodney Bryce: both born in New York)

Rob Base is responsible for one of the greatest rap records ever made, 1988's "It Takes Two." Built with samples from Strafe's "Set It Off" and Lynn Collins's James Brown-produced single "Think (About It)," "It Takes Two" was a critically acclaimed work, a true dance record that expanded beyond the hip-hop audience (because of its faster tempo) into dance clubs and, later, other party circles. It is for this reason that the work is also recognized as helping to usher in the hip-house genre. The piece eventually went platinum, as did the album of the same name.

A resident of Lincoln Projects in Harlem, Rob Base and DJ E-Z Rock were originally in the group the Sureshot Seven. As group members began to leave, Base and Rock decided to continue to work as a duo.

They met World to World Records label owner William Hamilton during the mid- to late-1980s, and recorded two songs, "DJ Interview" and "Make It Hot." Hamilton signed a distribution deal with Profile Records, who released the *It Takes Two* album and single, with "Joy & Pain" (featuring R&B singer Omar Chandler) being another hit off the work.

For a time, many tragic rumors circulated about Base, including that he had suffered

Rob Base

from drug overdoses and heart attacks, but he was able to endure. In 1989 he released the album *The Incredible Base* without E-Z Rock, and it went gold that year. A single, "Outstanding," was released in 1990.

 Selected albums/CDs: *It Takes Two* (1988, Profile 1267); *The Incredible Base* (1989, Profile 1285).

RODNEY O & JOE COOLEY

Formed c. 1988, Los Angeles

Rodney O and pioneer West Coast DJ Joe Cooley began to receive attention when they made the songs "DJs and MC's" and "Everlastin' Bass"—the latter being on Egyptian Lover's Egyptian Empire Records. Their debut album, *Me & Joe*, was released on the same label.

Thereafter, the duo recorded for several record labels, including Atlantic, where they made their *Three the Hard Way* LP around 1990. They added an additional MC to their act at the time named General Jeff. In 1991 they signed with Nastymix Records and recorded the album *Get Ready to Roll*.

By 1992 Rodney O began his own label, called Psychotic Records. The duo returned to performing again, and released their album *F—k New York*. Critically regarded as a response record to Bronx, New York, rapper Tim Dog's "F-ck Compton," Rodney and Cooley's work continued to please their fan base. Around this same period the two began working on material for rapper Vanilla Ice.

 Selected albums/CDs: *Three the Hard Way* (1990, Atlantic 1082); *F—k New York* (1992, Psychotic 1101).

ROXANNE SHANTÉ

(Born Lolita Shanté Gooden, March 8, 1971, Jamaica, New York)

Although not the first female rapper, Roxanne Shanté was the first to achieve wide recognition in hip hop. Known for her squeaky youthful voice in the beginning of her career, it was her record "Roxanne's Revenge" (an answer record to the group UTFO's "Roxanne, Roxanne") that spawned dozens of unprecedented answer records in hip hop, all dealing with the same topic: a girl named Roxanne. Shanté's rhymes are known for their abundance of caustic diss lines that are usually aimed at other rappers. She paved the way for female MCs to get record deals by themselves.

Shanté was a neighbor of producer Marley Marl in the Queensbridge Housing Projects in Queens when she approached him in 1984 about making a record with her. She wanted to respond to UTFO's "Roxanne, Roxanne" single that was out at the time, a record that she felt dissed women. Although she was only 14 years old at the time, Shanté had already developed a unique rapping style, based on her sharp-voiced attack.

Marl recorded "Roxanne's Revenge" with her, giving a copy to his partner, pioneer hip-hop radio personality Mr. Magic. Magic played the tape on his show, identifying it as the real Roxanne's response to UTFO's record. The audience was impressed with the piece, especially the female segment. Marl, Magic, and Cold Chillin' Records' Tyrone Williams played the song for Lawrence and Dana Goodman of Pop Art Records, after which the Goodman brothers immediately decided to release it.

"Roxanne's Revenge" was a landmark recording, inspiring dozens more answer records dealing with a young lady named Roxanne. There were Roxanne imitators, songs like "Roxanne's Psychiatrist," "Roxanne's a Man," "Roxanne's Doctor," and the like. By 1985 Shanté was performing her work throughout the country.

In 1989 Shanté's debut album, *Bad Sister*, was released. Two singles off the work became hits: "Live on Stage" and "Feelin' Kinda Horny." She also did a cameo on funk artist Rick James's single "Loosy's Rap."

In 1992 Shanté's second album, *The Bitch Is Back*, was released. The single off the work, "Big Mama," garnered a lot of attention, due to Shanté's severe dissing of every top female rapper who was out at the time.

Selected singles: "Roxanne's Revenge" (1984, Pop Art); "Live on Stage" (1989, Cold Chillin'); "Big Mama" (1992).

Selected albums/CDs: *Bad Sister* (1989, Cold Chillin' 25809).

Roxanne Shanté

RUN-D.M.C.

Formerly Rundee-MC
Formed in 1983, Hollis, Queens, New York
(Run, a.k.a. DJ Run, born Joseph Simmons, November 1964; D.M.C., born Darryl McDaniels, May 31, 1964; Jam Master Jay, born Jason Mizell, 1964: all born in Hollis, Queens)

The entry of Run-D.M.C. into the hip-hop arena marked the official ending of the old school of rap group originators out of the Bronx, New York, and the beginning of groups from other areas across the nation, including the suburbs.

From the suburbs of Hollis, Queens, Run-D.M.C. is the third rap group to become commercially successful, after the Sugarhill Gang and Grandmaster Flash and the Furious Five. However, they are the first to become internationally successful, hitting the crossover market while still sounding raw and maintaining their longevity and recording status.

Joseph "Run" Simmons is the younger brother of Russell "Rush" Simmons, later Rush Communications owner and hip-hop entertainment mogul. The elder Simmons brought Run (a nickname Simmons gave him, because of his ability to cut records so fast) to the stage in 1978 to be a DJ for one of the acts he was managing at the time, Kurtis Blow. Billed as "Kurtis Blow's Disco Son—DJ Run," Run successfully traded rhymes on stage with Blow at their first show together at Manhattan's Hotel Diplomat.

In 1982 Run bugged his big brother to record him separately. Originally, Simmons had planned to create a group with Run, producer Larry Smith, Davy D (who later replaced Run as Kurtis Blow's DJ), and Kool Lady Blue (the English-born hip-hop promoter who presented acts at the Roxy) to be called the OK Crew, after Larry Smith's group, Orange Krush. However, this arrangement never materialized. Simmons's next move was to record Run by himself, doing a piece titled "Street Kid," written by Chyna and Trevor Gale, a drummer from Orange Krush. The rhymes for this piece dealt with the misunderstanding of youth by grown-ups. The demo of the song was brought to major labels without success.

Later, Run convinced his brother to record him and his friend Darryl McDaniels (a.k.a. D, and later, D.M.C., for "Darryl Makes Cash" or "Devastating Mic Control"). They wrote rhymes for two songs: "It's Like That" and "Sucker MCs." They recorded both pieces, which were arranged by Larry Smith, the latter song consisting mainly of Trevor Gale's drum pattern for the Orange Krush song "Action." The demo of these two songs was brought to Cory Robbins and Steve Plotnicki of Profile Records, a small independent label at the time. They released both songs on a 12-inch single. The record sold approximately 20,000 copies within a month to five weeks.

Run had already promised neighborhood friend Jay (Jason "Jam Master Jay" Mizell) that whenever he got the chance to make a record that he would choose him as his DJ. Holding true to the promise, all three members began rehearsing together.

The group's first important appearance before the hip-hop crowd was at the Disco Fever in the Bronx in the spring of 1983. However, Jay missed the show, because the group's driver forgot to pick him up. Both Run and D appeared at the venue in checkered sports jackets, provoking laughter before they hit the stage. The crowd also had a problem with the duo being from Queens. But by the time they did "Sucker MCs" for them, they were impressed. The group soon began to do shows outside the city.

Their later trademark attire became more akin, for the most part, to what hip hoppers wore on the streets at the time. Run wanted the group to wear their street clothes on stage, which was the opposite of what the standard Bronx groups would wear on stage: loud-colored leather suits, furs, chains, and white or red boots, with their hair either braided or Jheri curled. The Run-D.M.C. style of dress consisted of their own black velour Stetson hats, black leather suits, and white Adidas sneakers without laces. In the summer the hats were terry-cloth Kangol and the suits were Adidas warm-ups. Their hair was worn in short Afros. The look signified the street and solidified their outlaw image.

The group's second 12-inch release was "Hard Times," backed with "Jam Master Jay," which peaked at number 11 on the *Billboard* Black Singles chart. In 1984 the group released their first album, titled *Run D.M.C.*, produced by Russell Simmons and Larry Smith. Containing nine songs (including the four previously released singles), the album also had the innovative "Rock Box," which combined the rap genre with heavy-metal (ten multitracked blaring guitar parts played by session guitarist Eddie Martinez). "Rock Box" also gave Run-D.M.C. their video, which featured Professor Irwin Corey. It was the first rap video that MTV added to regular rotation.

In the summer of 1984 concert promoter Ricky Walker approached Russell Simmons with an idea for a national rap and breakdancing touring show, later titled the Swatch Watch New York City Fresh Fest. Featuring Run-D.M.C. and most of the top rappers and b-boys at the time, the traveling show helped introduce the group into areas where rap had not been exposed. In twenty-seven performances, the tour grossed $3.5 million.

With the release of the group's second album, *King of Rock*, the creative relationship with Russell Simmons and Larry Smith began to dissolve, due to what Smith felt was the rock influence of Rick Rubin, who had just partnered with Simmons to form their Def Jam Recordings label. Although the album contained several good pieces, it was regarded by Simmons as a much softer work.

Run-D.M.C. performed their first political concert with hip-hop pioneers the Cold Crush Brothers at Columbia University in April 1985, where students were striking against the university's investments in South Africa. Later that year the group began filming their first movie, *Krush Groove*, directed by Michael Schultz, which was a Hollywoodized story about Run-D.M.C., Russell Simmons, Rick Rubin, and Def Jam Recordings. Actor Blair Underwood starred as Simmons and Run-D.M.C. starred as themselves, as did Kurtis Blow, LL Cool J, the Beastie Boys, and Dr. Jeckyll and Mr. Hyde. The movie grossed over $3 million in the first weekend, opening in 515 theaters. A second Fresh Fest tour followed that same year, along with an appearance at Bob Geldof's Live Aid concert event. The group also produced the Hollis Crew, on a song titled "It's the Beat."

Also in 1985, Run-D.M.C. was the first rap group to appear on Dick Clark's *American Bandstand*, and the first rappers considered for Little Steven Van Zandt's antiapartheid all-star single and video "Sun City." They also did the single and video for "King Holiday," an all-star

Run-D.M.C.

birthday tribute to the Rev. Martin Luther King, Jr., put together by King's youngest son, Dexter, and co-produced by Kurtis Blow.

In 1986 they recorded the album *Raising Hell*, which was largely produced by themselves, along with Rick Rubin and Russell Simmons. It sold over a million copies in the first five weeks, making it one of the first platinum records by MCs. This album contained a cover of rock group Aerosmith's "Walk This Way." The single and video with Aerosmith solidified their image as trailblazers. Released as a single, the song went to number 8 on *Billboard*'s Black Singles chart. It also reached their Hot 100 chart, marking the group's first appearance on that chart. The New York Music Awards nominated the group in five categories in 1986. They won four: Best Single, "King of Rock"; Best Song, "King of Rock" (writer's award); Best R&B Act; and Best Rap Act. Their competition included the Talking Heads, the Ramones, and Cameo.

They performed in the Raising Hell Tour in the summer of 1986 with some of Simmons's other rap acts. This tour, promoted by Jeff Sharp's Stageright Productions and Darryll Brooks and Carol Kirkendall's G Street Express, received negative publicity in the press for various minor unrelated fighting incidents at several venues nationally. After taking part in an antidrug concert called Crackdown, organized by concert promoter Bill Graham, the group made many television appearances toward the end of 1986, most notably on *Saturday Night Live*, *The Late Show Starring Joan Rivers*, and David Brenner's *Nightlife*.

They starred in the film *Tougher Than Leather* in 1988. This time Rick Rubin directed from a fictional story by Rush Artist Management's vice president of operations, Lyor Cohen, and publicity director B. Adler. Later they released the soundtrack album of the same name, which sold 1.5 million copies.

It was after this period when things began to go downhill for the group. Run suffered a nervous breakdown, chronically depressed over his feelings that his work was not up to par. He began to smoke six to eight bags of marijuana a day. D.M.C. resorted to consuming sixteen forty-ounce bottles of malt liquor daily, eventually suffering from alcoholic pancreatitis and winding up in the hospital. Jay separated and started his own label, JMJ, which signed the group the Afros, and later Fam-Lee and Onyx.

In 1988 both Run and D.M.C. proclaimed themselves born-again Christians, with Run donating $40,000 to televangelist Robert Tilton. The two then tried to start their own label, JDK/MCA, producing rapper Smooth Ice.

In 1989 the group came back with the single "Pause" from the movie *Ghostbusters II*. The song saved their street credibility, while some of the lyrics dealt with their newfound beliefs. It sold approximately 300,000 copies. *Back from Hell* marked their fifth album, released in 1990.

After a release of a greatest hits album in 1991, the group came back strong in 1993 with the single "Down with the King" (the King being God), backing it up with stellar performances at music-industry conventions and outside venues. The single marked their tenth year together as a group. Their album of the same name was released that year and also garnered rave reviews. Run and D.M.C. continued their work in the Christian community, working with televangelist Dr. E. Bernard Jordan.

 Selected singles: "It's Like That" b/w "Sucker MCs (Krush-Groove 1)" (1983, Profile); "King of Rock" (1986).

 Selected albums/CDs: *Run-D.M.C.* (1984, Profile 1202); *King of Rock* (1985, Profile 1205); *Raising Hell* (1986, Profile 1217); *Tougher Than Leather* (1988, Profile 1265); *Back from Hell* (1990, Profile 1401); *Together Forever: Greatest Hits* (1991, Profile 2-1419); *Down with the King* (1993, Profile 1140).

RUSSELL "RUSH" SIMMONS

(Born Russell Simmons, October c. 1958, New York)

Russell Simmons is hip hop's first millionaire entrepreneur. As the C.E.O. of Rush Communications, he successfully expanded into all areas of entertainment media through his co-founding of Def Jam Recordings and Rush Artist Management. His Rush Communications company was ranked the second-largest black-owned entertainment company on the *Black Enterprise Industrial/Service 100* list of 1992, and he is responsible for signing and marketing most of the important rap acts of the early 1980s. At one time all rap entries on the *Billboard* black music charts were his acts, and he is recognized as one of the most influential figures

Russell 'Rush' Simmons

in rap music and entertainment. Simmons, like his product, is noted for his street image, in public and in business dealings. He is the older brother of Run from Run-D.M.C., the group he successfully marketed that helped to catapult his business empire.

Simmons was raised mostly in the middle-class neighborhood of Hollis, Queens, New York. He served as a warlord for the seventeenth division of the Seven Immortals (one of the many gangs in New York at the time) when he was in the tenth grade, and sold occasional bags of reefer for pocket money.

After graduating from high school, he entered Harlem's City College of New York, majoring in sociology. During this time, in 1977, he saw his first rapper, Eddie Cheeba, at a venue called Charles Gallery on 125th Street in Harlem. Cheeba's rapping over a record by funk group Parliament, called "Flashlight," impressed Simmons immensely—so much so that by the fall of that year he decided to become a party promoter (after seeing how a few of his friends did it and made money from it).

Simmons put together a group to help with his promotions. One of his helpers was good friend Kurtis Blow, who went by the name Kool DJ Kurt at the time, and who had been working with Grandmaster Flash. To get to know all the DJs in the club circuit, Simmons went to all the clubs and checked out all the scenes, from heavy metal to yuppie club venues. It was around this time that he earned his "Rush" nickname, because of his energy and enthusiasm for his newfound love.

With flyers that read "RUSH—THE FORCE IN COLLEGE PARTIES, PRESENTS . . ." Simmons announced his first party, held at a club in Queens called the Renaissance. He rented the club for $500, and spent $300 on printing fliers. With approximately 800 people attending, he had exceeded the club's capacity by 200 people. Kurtis Blow rapped that night as well. Simmons's second party was held a month later at the Hotel Diplomat in Manhattan, and featured Kurtis Blow and Eddie Cheeba. Thereafter, Simmons's bills at other parties began to feature other rap acts that were popular at the time, like Grandmaster Flash and the Furious Five, Lovebug Starski, DJ Hollywood, and Grand Wizard Theodore. By 1978 Kurtis Blow became popular enough for Simmons to bill him with his own DJ. He chose his little brother Joey, nicknamed "Run," and the two continued to work at Simmons's parties.

In 1979 then-*Billboard* black music columnist Robert "Rocky" Ford spotted Simmons's promotional stickers on New York's B.M.T. subway line. Deciding to do a story about him, he gave Simmons advice on how to take rap into the record business. It wasn't long before that Ford and his friend J. B. Moore told Simmons about their interest in making a rap record about Santa Claus in Harlem. Simmons suggested that they use Kurtis Blow (instead of their first choice, Eddie Cheeba), and the three of them—Ford, Moore, and Simmons—wrote "Christmas Rapping" for the artist. The single was eventually picked up by Mercury Records, becoming the first rap record to be distributed by a major label, selling nearly 400,000 copies.

In 1982 Simmons began to work as a producer with Larry Smith—the bass player Robert Ford hired for Kurtis Blow's first two singles ("Christmas Rapping" and "The Breaks"). Simmons worked with Smith's band, Orange Krush (including singer Alyson Williams), on a record called "Action." The two also collaborated on a song called "The Bubble Bunch" with rapper Jimmy Spicer.

Toward the end of that same year Simmons initially started to make a rap record with Orange Krush, combining his brother Run, Davy D—who became Kurtis Blow's DJ—and Kool Lady Blue (a promoter for the roller skating rink turned club, The Roxy). However, due to Run's pestering of his brother, Simmons decided instead to make a record with Run and his partner, D.M.C. (Darryl McDaniels). They recorded two songs, "It's Like That" and "Sucker MCs," and shopped the demo to Cory Robbins and Steve Plotnick of Profile Records. They released both songs as a 12-inch single, and the record sold 20,000 copies within the first few weeks.

By 1994 Simmons was not only managing Run-D.M.C. and Kurtis Blow, but also Whodini and Dr. Jeckyll & Mr. Hyde. He met Rick Rubin at a club called Danceteria. Rubin had earlier recorded and produced a record titled "It's Yours," with rapper T La Rock and DJ Jazzy Jay under his Def Jam Recordings label. Together, Rubin and Simmons struck up a fifty-fifty partnership as Def Jam Recordings. The first artist they put out together in 1984 was LL Cool J. His single "I Need a Beat" initially sold 120,000 copies, and, in essence, launched the label.

Later, Simmons signed additional acts Jimmy Spicer, Alyson Williams, Spyder D, and Sparky D to his management roster. Toward the summer of that year Simmons was approached by concert promoter Ricky Walker, who wanted to put together a national rap and breakdancing tour. When the agreement was made, the tour—called the Swatch Watch New York City Fresh Fest—grossed $3.5 million in twenty-seven performances.

In 1985, based on Def Jam nearly selling 500,000 records, CBS Records made a label deal with the company worth $600,000, which included promotion and marketing of Def Jam product. Simmons placed former financial analyst and club owner Lyor Cohen in charge of operations at his Rush Artist Management. That same year saw the release of LL Cool J's first album, *Radio*, which later went platinum, and Simmons's first venture into feature films. The movie, *Krush Groove*, which he co-produced, starred actor Blair Underwood, and was a Hollywoodized version of the story of Simmons, Run-D.M.C., Rubin, and Def Jam Recordings. Michael Schultz directed the film, which featured many of Simmons's acts.

In 1986 Def Jam released the Beastie Boys' *Licensed to Ill* album, which sold five million copies. Later, Simmons coproduced Run-D.M.C.'s *Raising Hell* album (along with Rick Rubin and the group). This album sold over a million copies in the first five weeks. In 1987 LL Cool J's *Bigger and Deffer* sold two million copies for the label. The group Public Enemy was also signed.

By 1988 Simmons had co-produced another movie, *Tougher Than Leather*, starring Run-D.M.C. and directed by Rick Rubin. Around this time the creative relationship between Rubin and Simmons began to sour, and Rubin moved on, starting his own label, Def American. Simmons branched into television in 1989, developing the medium's first "rap/hip hop show." Titled the *New Music Report*, the half-hour show was co-produced with Apollo Theatre Productions, and aired weekly in syndication.

In 1990 Simmons renegotiated his deal with CBS, which had become part of Sony Inc. Rush Associated Labels (RAL) was formed out of this agreement. It was the biggest music industry subsidiary deal of its kind. The joint deal included splitting profits and an annual stipend of $3 million to Def Jam for operating costs.

RAL itself consisted of seven labels headed mostly by artists discovered by Simmons: JMJ, with Run-D.M.C.'s Jam Master Jay as president; P.R.O. Division, with Public Enemy's Chuck D. as head; No Face, with president Mark Skeete; Andy "Panda" Tripoli and Sal Abbatiello's Fever Records; De La Soul's Prince Paul had Dew Doo Man Records; and Carmen Ashhurst-Watson became president of both Def Jam Recordings and OBR labels. By this time these and Simmons's other operations all fell under his parent Rush Communications.

In 1991 the company had reported earnings of $34 million, and consisted of broadcasting, film and television, publishing, and management units, as well as the RAL labels. Simmons produced "Russell Simmons' Def Comedy Jam" with Hollywood producers Bernie Brillstein and Brad Grey for HBO, with comedian Martin Lawrence hosting. Originally starting out as eight half-hour specials, the street comedy show soon became a regular on the channel. The year 1993 saw Simmons entering the fashion world, creating PHAT Fashions with Soho boutique owner Mark Regev and designers Alyasha Owerka Moore and Eli Morgan Gefner.

 Selected albums/CDs co-produced: *Run-D.M.C.* by Run-D.M.C. (1984, Profile 1202); *King of Rock* (1985, Profile 1205); *Raising Hell* (1986, Profile 1217); *Oran "Juice" Jones*, by Oran "Juice" Jones (1986, Def Jam/Columbia 26934).

R&B (Rhythm and Blues): A term first used in the late 1940s to describe the new, heavier rhythmic music played by the small black combos of the day. Later, a generic term for all African-American popular music.

Reggae: A mixture of R&B, rock 'n' roll, and traditional Jamaican music, originated in Jamaica, noted for its heavy rhythmic emphasis.

Rhymes: Verses of lyrics composed by MCs.

Ice T

RAP AT THE MOVIES

Rap songs have been widely used in film soundtracks with great success; perhaps the most famous example is Public Enemy's "Fight the Power" used in Spike Lee's groundbreaking 1989 film, *Do the Right Thing*. Rappers have also appeared in films themselves, both as musicians and actors. Notable among rap films is 1985's semifictional *Krush Groove*, which tells the story of the founding of Def Jam Recordings, and features many of that label's act at the time. The fact that the film was inexpensive to make while being successful at the box office was not lost on other executives. Soon many other rap films, and films featuring rappers, hit the marketplace.

Ice-T is one of the best-known rappers to establish himself as a film actor, with his riveting performance in 1992's *New Jack City*, for which he also performed the song "New Jack Hustler (Nino's Theme)." In the same year that Ice-Cube made his film debut, Ice Cube appeared in *Boyz N the Hood*, John Singleton's successful film about gang life in Compton. Director/producer Doug McHenry commented to the *New York Times* about the trend toward using rappers in urban dramas: "Many of the projects today say, `Urban drama? O.K., we gotto stick in an Ice Cube, Ice-T, Ice Run, Ice-somebody . . . Put some scratching in the soundtrack and put it out there.' That's the type of exploitative approach that was the demise of many of the black films of the seventies that were made by white people." Seeking to offer a more nostalgic look at life in the 'hood, Cube co-produced, co-wrote, and starred in the movie *Friday* in 1994.

Not all rap movies have been serious; the duo Kid 'n Play starred in all three of the very successful *House Party* movies, representing the more lighthearted side of rap. (George Jackson, another prominent producer/director who worked on their films, calls them "the hip, ultra-cool Hope and Crosby of their day," accurately describing their appeal.) Besides film, rappers have also scored success as TV actors, beginning with *The Fresh Prince of Bel Air*, a typical TV sitcom created by noted musician/producer Quincy Jones, and featuring one half of the duo DJ Jazzy Jeff and the Fresh Prince.

Here are some of the films that feature rappers performing and/or acting:

- *Wild Style* 1983. Busy Bee, Lisa Lee, Fab 5 Freddy, Cold Crush Brothers, Grand Wizard Theodore & the Fantastics, Grandmaster Flash, Double Trouble, Grandmixer D.ST

- *Beat Street* 1984. Kool Herc, Wanda Dee, Mele Mel, Treacherous Three, Afrika Bambaataa & the Soul Sonic Force, Lisa Lee

- *Breakin'* and *Breakin' II* 1984. Ice-T

- *Krush Groove* 1985. Kurtis Blow, Beastie Boys, LL Cool J, Run-D.M.C., Fat Boys

- *Who's the Man* 1993. Doctor Dre & Ed Lover, Guru, Freddie Foxxx, Ice-T, Kris Kross, Naughty by Nature

- *The Show* 1994. Documentary and concert footage of rap artists, mostly shot in Philadelphia, featuring the Wu-Tang Clan, Russell Simmons, and Notorious B.I.G. Documentary and concert footage of classic rap artists, including Kurtis Blow.

SALAAM REMI

(Born Salaam Remi Gibbs, New York City)

Salaam Remi is a producer and remixer of many hip-hop and dancehall reggae acts. His work displays the versatility he applies to each artist.

Salaam was born into the music business: his father, reggae street marketer and promoter Van Gibbs, had been a studio musician since 1972, working as a guitarist for singer Taana Gardner, and a promoter for Sugar Hill Records.

When Salaam was 4 years old, jazz drummer Elvin Jones made him a drum set. By high school, Salaam had gotten more into electronics, playing keyboards and learning about drum machines. From 1985 to 1987 he worked with a 4-track tape recorder and started doing demo recordings with friends, including MC Rell and the House Rockers. Salaam's first remix was recording artist Leotis's "Ooh Child" in 1989. His first full-scale production work was on the rap group Zhigge's first album.

Under his father's (and partner Eddison Electrik's) Palm Tree Enterprises, Salaam started his own production company, Dashiki Productions. In 1994 his production on reggae artist Ini Kamoze's "Here Comes the Hotstepper" went platinum by December of that year. The work was also on the motion picture soundtrack for Robert Altman's film *Ready to Wear*.

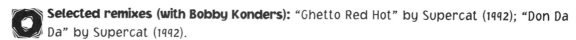 **Selected remixes (with Bobby Konders):** "Ghetto Red Hot" by Supercat (1992); "Don Da Da" by Supercat (1992).

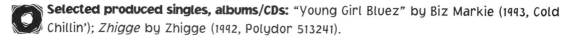 **Selected produced singles, albums/CDs:** "Young Girl Bluez" by Biz Markie (1993, Cold Chillin'); *Zhigge* by Zhigge (1992, Polydor 513241).

SALT-N-PEPA

• • • • • • • • • • • • • • • • • • • •

a.k.a. Super Nature
Formed in 1985, Queens, New York
**(Salt, born Cheryl James, March 28, Bushwick, Brooklyn, New York;
Pepa, born Sandy Denton, November 9, Jamaica, New York; Spinderella,
born Deidre "Dee Dee" Roper, New York; *former member*: Latoya Hanson,
born in Bronx, New York)**

The group Salt-N-Pepa—along with their DJ, Spinderella—are the first female rappers to reach platinum record sales, and to receive a Grammy nomination. They are recognized for their pop-oriented sound and their choreography, both on stage and in videos.

Salt-N-Pepa originally met at Queensborough College. Later they worked in sales at a Sears department store, where they met Hurby Luv Bug Azor, who was a center of media arts student at the time. One of Azor's school projects was to make an actual recording. He used Salt-N-Pepa as rappers to complete his assignment.

Azor took the finished product to his DJ friend Marley Marl, who liked the work and brought it to Lawrence and Dana Goodman's Pop Art Records label. The song, called "The Showstopper," was an answer record to Doug E. Fresh and Slick Rick's "The Show." It was released under the name Super Nature by Pop Art in 1985.

Later, Azor (who was looking for a DJ for the group by this time) was introduced to Latoya Hanson, an acquaintance of Salt's from Lance's Skating Rink in Long Island. She joined the group as their deejay, taking the name Spinderella.

In 1986 Super Nature was now billed as Salt-N-Pepa. Their debut album, *Hot Cool & Vicious*, was released on Next Plateau Records. With most of the material written and produced by Azor, the work was well received in the hip-hop community, and two years later it reached platinum status.

By 1987 creative differences with Latoya Hanson and the other group members arose, resulting in her leaving the group and beginning a solo career as Da Original. Dee Dee Roper was hired to replace her. Around November of that year the group released the single "Push It," which went gold the following year.

In 1988 the group's second album, *A Salt with a Deadly Pepa*, was released and went gold. The group was also becoming internationally known by this time. In 1989 Salt-N-Pepa was nominated for a Grammy, a first for female rappers. However, they decided to boycott the awards ceremony when they learned that the presentation of the award for best rap single would not be televised. That same year their single "Expressions" was released, and went platinum by May 1990.

The group's third album, *Black's Magic*, appeared in 1990, achieving gold status that same year. In 1991 they released two singles, "Do You Want Me" and "Let's Talk about Sex," both of which went gold. The latter song was turned into a successful public service video for AIDS, titled "Let's Talk about AIDS."

After a two-year absence from the charts, the group returned toward the end of 1993 with the singles "Whatta Man" (featuring the R&B group En Vogue) and "Shoop," and their album *Very Necessary*, which went triple platinum by 1995. Also in 1993, they gave a command performance for the children of the Sultan of Brunei.

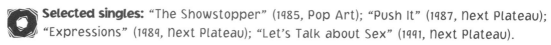 **Selected singles:** "The Showstopper" (1985, Pop Art); "Push It" (1987, Next Plateau); "Expressions" (1989, Next Plateau); "Let's Talk about Sex" (1991, Next Plateau).

Selected albums/CDs: *Hot, Cool & Vicious* (1987, Next Plateau 828296); *A Salt with a Deadly Pepa* (1988, Next Plateau 828102); *Black's Magic* (1990, Next Plateau 828164); *Very Necessary* (1993, Next Plateau 828392).

Salt-N-Pepa

SCHOOLLY D
● ● ● ● ● ● ● ● ● ● ● ● ●
(Born in Philadelphia)

Schoolly D is one of the original MCs who rapped in the so-called gangsta genre. His 1985 single "PSK What Does It Mean?" was a groundbreaking work in hip hop for its rhymes about a Philadelphia gang called the Parkside Killers. Schoolly's lyrics foreshadowed similar imagery from later artists like N.W.A and Ice-T. Schoolly D was also one of the few rap artists to put out his music on his own label—Schoolly D Records—during the early to mid-1980s. With his DJ Code Money, the artist's early work was noted for its production style, which consisted of drums and turntable scratches recorded in heavy reverb. Schoolly is also recognized for his extensive work with film director Abel Ferrara, who has used Schoolly's music in several of his films, including *King of New York* in 1990, *Bad Lieutenant* in 1992, and 1994's *Dangerous Game*.

Schoolly's first single was released in 1984, titled "Gangster Boogie." By 1987, he had released his debut album, *The Adventures of Schoolly D*, and classic pieces like "Gucci Time," "Put Your Filas On," and the album *Saturday Night* on his own Schoolly D Records, which was managed for a time by Chris Schwartz—later co-owner of Ruffhouse Records. (Schoolly was also known for doing his own cover artwork on those records, as well as the distribution.)

Schoolly's other work includes the 1988 album *Smoke Some Kill, Am I Black Enough for You* in 1989 (which was featured in *King of New York*) and another work, called *How a Black Man Feels*. By 1994 he released the album *Welcome to America*, which was recorded with a live band. In 1995 he released *Nigger Entertainment* on his own PSK/Contract Records label, with DJ Code Money.

 Selected singles: "PSK What Does I t Mean?" (1985, Schoolly-D).

 Selected albums/CDs: *Schoolly D* (1986, Jive/RCA 1338); *Saturday Night* (1987, Jive/RCA 1066); *Smoke Some Kill* (1988, Jive/RCA 1101); *Am I Black Enough for You* (1989, Jive/RCA 1237); *How a Black Man Feels* (1991, Capitol 95107); *Welcome to America* (1994, Ruffhouse/Columbia 57632); *Nigger Entertainment* (1995, PSK/Contract).

SEQUENCE

• • • • • • • • • • • • • • •

Formed c. 1978, Columbia, South Carolina
(Cheryl the Pearl, born Cheryl Cook; Angie B; Blondie: all born in Columbia, South Carolina)

Sequence is regarded as the first female group to make a rap record, and are thus credited as female rap pioneers. Originally a singing group from South Carolina, Sequence was discovered backstage at a Sugarhill Gang concert in 1979, when Sugar Hill Records's Sylvia Robinson was introduced to the group by the Sugarhill Gang's road manager. Auditioned on the spot by Robinson, the group was signed to the label. One of the songs they performed was a piece they had written called "Funk You Up," which became their first single for the label. The group made a few other recordings at Sugar Hill Records before business differences with the label and the group forced them to leave Sugar Hill and break up. Cheryl the Pearl went solo and recorded the single "Don't You Sit Back Down" in 1987 with producer Donald Dee.

 Selected albums/CDs: *The Sequence* (1980, Sugar Hill 1003).

SHAZZY

• • • • • • • • • •

a.k.a. Shazzy Quality, Shazzy Q
(Born Sherry Racquel Marsh, Forest Hills, Queens, New York)

Shazzy received critical acclaim for her 1990 album *Attitude: A Hip Hop Rapsody*. On the work, her rhymes showed insight, examining sociopolitical and Afrocentric issues from a female perspective.

Raised in Hollis, Queens, Shazzy began to MC at local parties and school talent shows. Around 1988 she found a producer who helped her construct a demo, which consisted of three songs, "Giggahoe," "Ill Talk," and "The Phantom," which attracted the attention of Elektra Records. Production on her album was handled by the team of A&R man Dante Ross, John Gamble, and John "Geebee" Dajana, known as the Stimulated Dummies. In 1994 she released the album *Ghettosburg Address*, which contained more harder-edged street rhymes, a contrast to her first album.

Selected albums/CDS: *Attitude: A Hip Hop Rapsody* (1990, Elektra 60937). *Ghettosburg Address* (1994, Elektra 61530).

Shazzy

SHOWBIZ & AG
••••••••••••••••••••••••
a.k.a. Show & AG
**Formed in 1990, Bronx, New York
(Showbiz, born Rodney Lemay, 1970, Bronx,
New York; AG, a.k.a. Andre the Giant, born
Andre Barnes, 1971, Bronx, New York)**

The duo Showbiz and AG (Andre the Giant) originally came together in 1990, when the two worked on neighborhood friend Lord Finesse's *Funky Technician* album. Showbiz is also one of hip hop's notable producers, achieving prominence during the early 1990s.

Showbiz started learning production in 1987, laying down music tracks in his home, while Andre practiced his MC'ing skills in the neighborhood and in school. After their work with Lord Finesse in 1990, the duo recorded a five-song demo and pressed it themselves, selling

5,000 copies. They got immediate attention with their 1992 single "Party Groove." Their EP *Party Groove/Soul Clap* was released that same year, as was their album *Runaway Slave*. In 1995 they released the single "Next Level."

 Selected albums/CDs: *Runaway Slave* (1992, London/Payday 828334).

SIR MIX-A-LOT
•••••••••••••••••••••••
(Born Anthony Ray, Seattle)

Computer electronics enthusiast, producer, and rapper Sir Mix-A-Lot put the hip-hop scene in Seattle on the map in 1985, when his number 1 single "Square Dance Rap" got considerable notice across the country. Mix-A-Lot then released other singles, such as "Iron Man" (which was a rap version of the metal group Black Sabbath's piece) and "Posse on Broadway," the latter receiving even more notice.

By 1987 Mix-A-Lot's first album, *Swass*, was released to favorable responses. The work eventually went platinum in 1989 and was on *Billboard*'s Black Music and Top 200 Albums charts for over a year. In 1989 Mix-A-Lot's second album, *Seminar*, was released and also went platinum. By 1991, however, Mix-A-Lot left his Nastymix Records label (which released his previous material) due to financial differences, and began working with Rick Rubin. Mix-A-Lot soon signed a distribution agreement with Rubin, which allowed him to develop his own label, called Rhyme Cartel Records. Under the new agreement Mix-A-Lot released the single "One Time's Got No Case."

In February 1992 Sir Mix-A-Lot's *Mack Daddy* album was released, which went platinum soon after. "Baby Got Back," the single off of that album, remained number 1 on *Billboard*'s Pop Singles chart for five weeks and sold 2.5 million copies. Mix-A-Lot also received a Grammy award for Best Rap Solo Performance for the song, while his video for the piece was banned on MTV, because of the network's feeling that the work displayed women as sexual objects. In 1994 he released the album *Chief Boot Knocka*.

 Selected albums/CDs: *Swass* (1987, Nastymix; reissued Rhyme Cartel 26970); *Seminar* (1989, Nastymix; reissued Rhyme Cartel 26969); *Mack Daddy* (1992, Rhyme Cartel 26765); *Chief Boot Knocka* (1994, American Recordings 45540).

SISTA DEE

See BODY & SOUL

SISTER SOULJAH

(Born Lisa Williamson, c. early 1970s, New Jersey)

Rap activist/public speaker/author Sister Souljah received national attention in 1992, when then-presidential candidate Bill Clinton used her in his campaign speeches as an example of racial hatred, attacking her sociopolitical and historical views on black/white relations. Souljah received wide media attention and rebuked his claims in numerous press interviews and appearances.

Souljah attended Rutgers University and became involved with the Free South Africa Movement toward the end of her sophomore year. During the late 1980s and early 1990s she toured the college lecture circuit, speaking at various campuses throughout the United States, including M.I.T. and Harvard and Howard universities. Souljah had become known in the hip-hop community from her cameo appearances in the group Public Enemy's music videos circa 1988{*}89, and was the manager of rapper MC Lyte for a short time around this same period. She briefly became a member of Public Enemy in 1991, and received her name from that group's member, Chuck D. Also in 1991, she began working with Public Enemy producer Eric "Vietnam" Sadler, recording the single "The Final Solution: Slavery's Back in Effect." Her album *360 Degrees of Power* was released in 1992.

Although this controversy died down, Souljah did not make any further recordings, returning to her role as a speaker/activist. By 1995 she had authored a book, titled *No Disrespect*.

 Selected albums/CDs: *360 Degrees of Power* (1992, Epic 48713).

SLICK RICK
* * * * * * * * * * * * * * * *
a.k.a. MC Ricky D
(Born Ricky Walters, January 14, 1965, South Wimbledon, London)

Slick Rick

Slick Rick is known as a rapper of true originality. With his trademark eyepatch, tons of gold jewelry, suave suits, and authentic English accent, he is recognized for his narrative and sexually explicit rhyme style, centering on ghetto life in the inner city. Rick also portrays different characters in his rhymes, taking on many roles through dialogue.

Rick spent thirteen years of his life growing up in South Wimbledon, London, before coming to the United States and settling in the Bronx with his family in 1976. During his high school years, Rick met and befriended future rapper Dana Dane. They practiced their rhymes in the cafeteria of the Fiorello LaGuardia High School of Music and Art with others, calling themselves the Kangol Crew. Dane encouraged Rick to use his English accent when rapping.

In 1984 Rick met rapper Doug E. Fresh at a rap contest in the Bronx. Impressed with Rick's style, Fresh decided to put Rick on one of his records. He recorded a 12-inch single with Doug E. Fresh, containing two songs, "The Show" and "La-Di-Da-Di." The songs became instant classics in the hip-hop community in 1985, firmly placing both artists on the map. The record went gold in February 1986.

It was three years before Rick returned to the scene with a new recorded work in 1988. His album, with his DJ, Vance Wright, *The Great Adventures of Slick Rick*, is a classic, and fully displays Rick's skills as a storyteller and performer. In April 1989 the album went gold, and by October of that year it went platinum.

In April 1990 Rick was arrested for allegedly shooting at a man (his cousin) who had threatened his mother. After Rick was charged with attempted murder and several counts of possession of a criminal weapon, his bail was set at $800,000, which was paid by Def Jam Recordings's C.E.O. Russell Simmons, who was Rick's label boss.

As he awaited trial, Rick recorded twenty-one songs and five videos in one three-week period for his next album. He later received a jail sentence of three and one-half to ten years for the crime.

In 1991 *The Ruler's Back* was released and was critically viewed as a rushed effort. Toward the end of 1993 Rick was out on a work-release program, recording his third album, which was released in 1994, titled *Behind Bars*. The single off the work, released in 1995, was called "Sittin' in My Car," and featured Doug E. Fresh.

SNOOP DOGGY DOGG

(Born Calvin Broadus, 1972, Long Beach, California)

Snoop Doggy Dog

Snoop Doggy Dogg first burst on the scene with Dr. Dre in 1992, appearing with that artist on the title soundtrack for the movie *Deep Cover*. Dogg's unique drawling MC style and vocal texture, as well as his rhymes and rhyme content (which immediately placed him in the so-called gangsta genre of rap), catapulted him to instant stardom.

Raised by his mother in a house that included two brothers, the 6' 5" Snoop Dogg had the experience of legitimately working four to five hours a day while going to school, before deciding that unlawful measures provided him with more income. He was incarcerated in the county jail several times during the mid- to late-1980s before being convinced by older cellmates that he should consider a more legitimate path in life.

Snoop Dogg began focusing on rap during this same period—something he knew how to do since junior high school—working with rappers like his friend Domino. Dogg began working with another friend, Warren G (a brother of Dr. Dre), who deejayed and produced. The two made tapes during the late 1980s and early 1990s, which Dre eventually heard and liked. Snoop Dogg then worked with Dre on that artist's 1992 multiplatinum album *The Chronic*, on which he appeared and wrote or co-wrote most of the material, including the platinum single "Nuthin' But a 'G' Thang."

Becoming part of Dre's Death Row Records family, Snoop Dogg recorded his first album for the label, *Doggystyle*, which was released toward the end of 1993. By 1994 the work had gone multiplatinum. That same year he gave performances on the "American Music Awards," the "Soul Train Awards," and he also appeared on *Saturday Night Live*. During this period he released the soundtrack album for the movie *Murder Was the Case*, an eighteen-minute film he starred in, based on lyrics from the artist. Dr. Dre directed the film and handled production duties on several songs on the album. By June 1995 the soundtrack album was double-platinum.

 Selected albums/CDs: *Doggystyle* (1993, Interscope/Death Row 06544).

SPARKY D
(Born Doreen Broadnax, New York)

One of the first female MCs who made records, Sparky D made her appearance during the height of the "Roxanne, Roxanne" wars in 1985, recording the piece "Sparky's Turn" for the Aleem's Nia Records, which was co-produced by the Aleems and Spyder D (who would become Sparky's husband).

Recognized for her running battle with Roxanne Shanté, Sparky went on to record for several labels, including Next Plateau, Fly Spy, and B-Boy, recording singles like "The Battle" and "Don't Make Me Laugh." She toured extensively during the late 1980s, especially in the southern states, with Kool DJ Red Alert as her DJ. Her album *This Is Sparky D's World* was released in 1988.

 Selected albums/CDs: *This Is Sparky D's World* (1988, B-Boy 1088).

SPECIAL ED
(Born Ed Archer, 1973, East Flatbush, Brooklyn, New York)

Special Ed immediately appealed to the teenage girls when he appeared on the hip-hop scene. He was noted for his playful teenage battle lyrics, unique vocal texture, and cool delivery.

Ed began working with producer "Hitman" Howie Tee from his East Flatbush neighborhood around the mid- to late-1980s making demos. After being signed by Profile Records, Ed released his debut LP, *Youngest in Charge*. The single off the work, "I Got It Made," brought the rapper immediate notice. After appearances on BET, MTV, and "Showtime at the Apollo," his celebrity status increased. The album reportedly cleared over 500,000 copies in sales.

In 1990 Ed's second work, *Legal*, was released, with the song "Come On, Let's Move It" receiving attention. In 1995 he released the single "Neva Go Back" backed with "Just a Killa," with production work by Ed and Howie Tee.

 Selected singles: "I Got It Made" (1989, Profile); "Come On, Let's Move It" (1990).

 Selected albums/CDs: *Youngest in Charge* (1989, Profile 1280); *Legal* (1990, Profile 1297).

Special Ed

SPICE-1

(Born Robert Lee Green, Jr., 1971, Byron, Texas)

Spice-1 is a rapper who has achieved great success rapping about the crime-ridden street life in California.

Spice was raised in Hayward and Oakland, California, with his grandmother for a year, then lived on the East Bay of Oakland. First getting into the hip-hop scene as a b-boy who performed West Coast dance moves like "popping," Spice soon became so proficient in rapping that, in high school, he ran out of people to battle for a test of lyrical skills.

Spice met rapper Too Short's DJ, Pierre, around 1986{*}87, who introduced him to Too Short. Short liked Spice's skills on the mic, and around 1988, he signed him to his own Dangerous Music label, Triad Records. Spice appeared on the *Dangerous Crew* compilation album that was released during this period.

He was eventually signed to Jive Records, and in 1992 his self-titled album was released and went gold the following year.

Spice-1

In 1993 Spice-1's "Trigga Gots No Heart" from the film soundtrack *Menace II Society* was released. His album *187 He Wrote* was released and went gold during that same year. In 1994 his album *Amerikkka's Nightmare* was released, and went gold by 1995.

 Selected albums/CDs: *Spice-1* (1992, Jive/RCA 41481); *187 He Wrote* (1993, Jive/RCA 41513); *Amerikka's Nightmare* (1994, Jive/RCA).

SPOONIE GEE
(Born Gabe Jackson, New York City)

Spoonie Gee is a pioneer MC, who is remembered for his rhymes that were replete with lyrics boasting about his sexual prowess.

Spoonie attended Townes High School in Manhattan, along with Kool Moe Dee, L.A. Sunshine, and Special K; all four had an interest in the art of MC'ing. They became friends and would occasionally battle each other, and talked about forming a group.

Spoonie was a nephew of the legendary record-store owner and producer from the 1950s Bobby Robinson. Spoonie practiced his MC skills at Robinson's home, using Robinson's records to rhyme over, honing his technique to perfection.

Spoonie was eventually approached to make a record by Peter Brown, owner of the label Sounds of New York USA. Brown recorded Spoonie doing a piece titled "Spoonin' Rap," and Spoonie was soon performing the work at several shows. Later, Bobby Robinson decided to record Spoonie, after seeing the favorable responses he was getting. Kool Moe Dee, Special K, and L.A. Sunshine heard that Spoonie was making another record, and asked if they could record with him, and Spoonie agreed.

In 1980 Robinson recorded Spoonie and the others on his Enjoy Records label. Billed as Spoonie Gee and the Treacherous Three (along with their DJ, Easy Lee), Spoonie recorded his solo piece "Love Rap" on one side of the 12-inch single. On the second side, Spoonie and the Treacherous Three recorded "The New Rap Language." Both works were hits with the hip-hop crowd.

Spoonie was picked up in the early 1980s by Sugar Hill Records, which also put out Spoonie's "Spoonin' Rap" piece. Spoonie was signed to Tuff City Records during the mid-1980s where he did songs such as "The Godfather" and "The Big Beat." Around this same period Spoonie was working outside the music industry as a superviser in a rehabilitation center. During the late 1980s through the early 1990s Spoonie was living in Daytona, Florida. He began associating with Luther "Luke Skyywalker" Campbell, and also began working with producer Teddy Riley.

 Selected singles: "Love Rap" (1980, Enjoy).

STEADY B

a.k.a. the Undertaker
(Born Warren McGlone, 1970, Philadelphia)

Steady B is the nephew of the Goodman brothers, the owners of the influential rap label Pop Art Records.

Steady first entered the scene in 1985 with an answer record to LL Cool J's "I Can't Live Without My Radio," called "Take Your Radio." Two more singles immediately followed, "Fly Shanté" and "Just Call Us Def." He also appeared in the 1985 Fresh Fest Tour with Run-D.M.C. and other hip-hop acts.

Toward 1986 Steady had an underground hit with the song "Do the Fila." Soon, he began performing more extensively, particularly on the East Coast. He was signed in 1987 to Jive Records, which released his debut LP, *Bring the Beat Back*.

His next album was titled *What's My Name?*, and contained the singles "Don't Disturb This Groove" and "Believe Me That's Bad." In 1988 his *Let the Hustlers Play* album was released. By 1989 his *Going Steady* LP appeared, which included popular pieces such as the title track, "New Breed," and "Mac Daddy." In 1991 his album *Steady B V* was released.

 Selected albums/CDs: *Bring the Beat Back* (1987, Jive/RCA 1020); *What's My Name?* (1987, Jive/RCA 1060); *Let the Hustlers Play* (1988, Jive/RCA 1122); *Going Steady* (1989, Jive/RCA 1284); *Steady B V* (1991, Jive/RCA 1428).

STETSASONIC

Formed in 1981, Brooklyn, New York
(Daddy-O, Brooklyn, New York; DJ Prince Paul, born Paul E. Huston, April 2, 1967, Queens, New York; Fruitkwan, born New York; Wise, born New York; DBC, born New York)

The group Stetsasonic was billed as the "first hip-hop band" when they appeared on the scene in the 1980s. They were known for their Afrocentric pieces like 1987's "A.F.R.I.C.A.," as well as lighter works like 1991's "Speaking of a Girl Named Suzy." The six-man group has performed throughout the world, from the Roxy in Manhattan to Senegal, West Africa.

Originally formed by Brooklyn native Daddy-O and his best friend Delite, Stetsasonic was named for the Stetson hats they originally wore. Deciding to combine the talents of MC'ing, beat boxing, deejaying, and keyboard work with DBC, Wise, Fruitkwan, Delite, and DJ Prince Paul, they officially began recording as a group after winning a rap contest held by radio personality Mr. Magic.

The group's first album, *On Fire*, was issued in 1986, and it contained the singles "Just Say Stet" and "Faye." Their second album, released in 1988, *In Full Gear*, scored with several hits such as "Sally," "Talkin' All That Jazz," and "Float On."

In 1991 their third work, *Blood, Sweat & No Tears*, was released. The group then unofficially separated to pursue and/or maintain other projects, with Prince Paul continuing his work with the group De La Soul and Daddy-O developing solo projects. In 1994 Prince Paul and group member Fruitkwan became part of the group Gravediggaz, along with MCs Too Poetic and Wu-Tang Clan's Prince Rakeem, releasing the album *6 Feet Deep* that year.

Selected albums/CDs: *On Fire* (1986, Tommy Boy 1012); *In Full Gear* (1988, Tommy Boy 1017); *Blood, Sweat & No Tears* (1991, Tommy Boy 1024).

SUGARHILL GANG
Formed in 1977, New York City
(Master Gee, born Guy O'Brien, 1963, New York City; Wonder Mike, born Michael Wright, 1958, Montclair, New Jersey; Big Bank Hank, born Henry Jackson, 1958, Bronx, New York)

The Sugarhill Gang is recognized as the first rap group to make a record. Their piece "Rapper's Delight" paved the way for the rap record market, because of its acceptance and airing on primetime radio. "Rapper's Delight" reportedly sold over two million copies in the United States, and eight million copies worldwide.

The idea to form and record the Sugarhill Gang came from Sylvia Vanderpool Robinson— a veteran record-industry label owner, producer, and singer. After hearing the art of MC'ing on a few occasions during the late 1970s, Sylvia decided to record rap. With the help of her son, Joe Jr., she soon began to put together a group.

Big Hank was a worker at the Crispy Crust Pizza Shop in New Jersey, and moonlighted as a manager for the group the Mighty Force MCs, which featured Grandmaster Caz (later a member of the Cold Crush Brothers). Joe Jr. heard Hank rapping over a tape of the Mighty Force MCs in the pizza shop.

Joe Jr. next introduced friend Wonder Mike to his mother. Mike was in a group based in New Jersey at the time, so when he was asked about making a rap record, he accepted the offer. A rapper named Master Gee had also heard about Sylvia's intentions of making a rap record, and soon contacted her for a chance to record with the others.

Around the same period Sylvia and her executive husband, Joe Robinson, acquired a production and distribution deal from Morris Levy of Roulette Records, after which they established Sugar Hill Records. Sylvia rounded up the three rappers she had, calling them the Sugarhill Gang, and recorded the label and group's first record in 1979, "Rapper's Delight." The Sugarhill Gang used R&B/disco group Chic's "Good Times" as the break record to rap over. Some of their rhymes (particularly Big Hank's) were written by Grandmaster Caz. Other rhymes contained certain phrases from DJ Hollywood and other rappers. "Rapper's Delight" hit number 1 in Canada and made the Top Five in South Africa, the United Kingdom, and Israel, while hitting the charts in other countries as well. It ranked number 4 on the R&B charts in the United States.

In 1981 the Sugarhill Gang had another hit with the song "8th Wonder," and later, "Lover in You," before the group disbanded.

 Selected singles: "Rapper's Delight" (1979, Sugar Hill).

SUGAR HILL RECORDS

Formed in 1979, New York City

Sugar Hill Records was known as the first record label fully devoted to rap. Before its demise in 1985, Sugar Hill Records was responsible for signing major pioneer rap acts like Grandmaster Flash and the Furious Five, Sequence, the Funky Four Plus One, the Sugarhill Gang, the Crash Crew, the Treacherous Three, and Spoonie Gee.

The label was founded by Sylvia Vanderpool Robinson and her husband, Joe Robinson. Sylvia once recorded as Little Sylvia for Savoy Records in the early 1950s, and she was also part of the 1956 guitar/singing duo Mickey and Sylvia, responsible for million-selling hits like "Love Is Strange." Sylvia also produced Ike and Tina Turner's 1961 hit "It's Gonna Work Out Fine," the Moments' (later recording as Ray, Goodman, and Brown) "Love on a Two-Way Street," and Shirley and Company's disco hit "Shame, Shame, Shame." Sylvia returned as a single recording artist on her own Vibration label in 1973, with the hit "Pillow Talk," which topped the R&B charts and reached number 3 on the pop charts.

Back in the 1960s Sylvia began doing business in the Bronx with the Blue Morocco Club on Boston Road. Toward the 1970s Sylvia and her husband, Joe, formed several record labels, including All Platinum, Turbo, Stang, and Vibration. All Platinum Records had a total of thirty-five hit records by artists including Chuck Jackson, Linda Jones, and Candi Staton. The Robinsons also later bought the Chess Records catalog of master recordings by blues guitarist Muddy Waters and others.

By the late 1970s the All Platinum label was ailing when Sylvia noticed that her kids were listening to MC and DJ tapes from the Bronx that were circulating around this time. During this same period she also heard people MC'ing over disco records at a party for her sister in Harlem. With her oldest son, Joe Jr., Sylvia began to assemble a group that would provide the same type of entertainment she saw people enjoying around her. At this same time the Robinsons were given a production and distribution deal by Roulette Records' Morris Levy. Sugar Hill Records was established in the Roulette Records offices at 1790 Broadway in Manhattan.

Sylvia first worked with the young men she had gathered, calling them the Sugarhill Gang. They recorded the landmark "Rapper's Delight," which contained rhymes that were written mostly by Grandmaster Caz, who went uncredited. The record reportedly sold over two million copies in the United States alone. She next worked with three female MCs called Sequence, recording the single "Funk You Up." Both of these singles put the label on the map as the premier full-fledged rap label.

After some business differences, Morris Levy asked to be bought out of the deal with the Robinsons for $2 million. The Robinsons moved Sugar Hill Records out of the Roulette Records offices and into offices located in Englewood, New Jersey. At the new location Sylvia set up a studio house band to record her rap records, called Wood, Brass, and Steel. The musicians who made up the house band were guitarist Bernard Alexander, drummer Keith LeBlanc, bassist Doug Wimbish, percussionist Ed "Duke Bootee" Fletcher, guitarist Skip MacDonald, and keyboardists Gary Henry, Duane Mitchell, Reggie Griffen, and Clifton "Jiggs" Chase, who also served as principal arranger on most of the records. There was also a horn section called Chops, and engineering all the records was Steve Jerome.

During the early 1980s Sugar Hill Records turned out a number of hits for its rap roster; however, it was still in serious financial trouble, primarily stemming from the company's desire to distribute its own product. By 1983 Joe Robinson signed a distribution deal with MCA.

Toward 1984 one of Sugar Hill's artists, Grandmaster Flash, saw a conflict of interest in his contract with the label, because Sylvia Robinson managed his group, the Furious Five, and produced their recordings. He sued the company for $5 million in royalties and the right to use his name and the name of his group, the Furious Five. Courts awarded him only the right to use his own name, after which the Furious Five was split down the middle, some members staying at Sugar Hill, others leaving the company with Grandmaster Flash.

By 1985 Sugar Hill Records's financial situation continued to decline, with the added $3.5 million in loans and advances from MCA remaining outstanding. MCA bought the Chess catalog from the Robinsons for $3 million. Sugar Hill Records remained insolvent, and was forced into bankruptcy. In 1995 Rhino Records purchased the label's back catalog and unreleased master recordings.

SUPER DJ CLARK KENT
a.k.a. Superman
(Born in 1968, Panama)

Super DJ Clark Kent became known for his proficiency in all basic forms of trick deejaying during the mid- to late-1980s, and the ease in which he performed these skills. Kent deejayed for rapper Dana Dane (from 1982{*}89), as well as for Hurby Luv Bug Azor and his Idol Makers Management groups. He has hosted the MC and DJ battles that take place at the music industry's New Music Seminars each year, and is remembered for creating Supermen Inc. around 1992, a crew of DJs assembled mostly to battle other DJ crews (like the X-Men), particularly during those New Music Seminar weeks. He is recognized for his versatility; he is able to deejay music from other genres besides hip hop, including dance and reggae, some of which was displayed for a short time on radio station WBLS-FM in New York City during the early 1990s.

Kent grew up in the Bronx and Crown Heights (Brooklyn), and began to practice deejaying at the age of 9, after watching his uncle deejay several times. He began to play in many of the city's parks, and by the mid-1980s he began to explore production, working with artists like Elliot Ness and King Speedy D. After graduating from high school, Kent began working in radio, joining with Pete Nice (of later 3rd Bass fame) on his radio show at Columbia University. He then left and worked at a few stations in Texas before returning to New York.

Toward the late 1980s Kent was deejaying in clubs like Mars, Latin Quarters, the Fever, and the Fun House. Kent began receiving more recognition after being spotted by Kool DJ Red Alert, who was excited about Kent's skills, and decided to look out for him.

Around 1992 Kent was working as an A&R representative for eastwest Records. After about a year and a half Kent left that position and began to focus more on production, working in 1994 on reggae artist Vicious's "Nika" single. In 1995 he produced the single "Player's Anthem" for the group Junior M.A.F.I.A.

SYLVIA ROBINSON
See SUGAR HILL RECORDS; SUGARHILL GANG; GRANDMASTER FLASH AND THE FURIOUS FIVE; SEQUENCE

SERIOUS-LEE-FINE
(Cleveland Delaney; Rodney Bush; Leroy Street)

Serious-Lee-Fine received some attention in 1989 when they released the single "Nothing Can Stop Us Now." During that period they were signed to Arista Records.

7A3
(DJ Mixmaster Muggs, a.k.a. DJ Grandmixer Muggs, born L. Muggerud, Queens, New York; Brett B, born in California; Sean B, born in California)

Los Angeles-based 7A3 released an album in 1988 titled *Coolin' in Cali*. Two singles were released off the work. "Mad Mad World" was a piece that was included on the soundtrack of the movie *Colors*, and the second single was titled "Goes Like Dis." Group member DJ Mixmaster Muggs would later go on to help form the group Cypress Hill.

 Selected albums/CDs: *Coolin' in Cali* (1988, Geffen 24209).

SHANGO

(Afrika Bambaataa, born in Bronx, New York; Amad Henderson, born in Bronx, New York; Hasan Fowler, born in New York; Lovemaster Ace, born in New York)

Shango was essentially a Zulu Nation band under Afrika Bambaataa, which was musically backed up by the Time Zone Band with the Zulu Queens. They released an album in 1984 on Celluloid Records, titled *Shango's Funk Theology*. In 1991 they released their second self-titled album and a single, which was a remake of a Sly Stone-produced piece for Little Sister, titled "You're the One."

 Selected albums/CDs: *Shango's Funk Theology* (1984, Celluloid 207).

SPYDER D

(Born Duane Hughes, New York)

Spyder D was a producer in the early to mid-1980s, who was originally managed by Russell Simmons. He received notice for his production work on DJ Divine's "Get into the Mix," and his own "Smerphies Dance," which was released on Telestar Cassettes. He also became recognized for the work he did with his MC wife, Sparky D. Spyder produced Mr. Magic's 1984 "Magic's Message," and his own "Buckwheat's Beat" in 1985. He also recorded the piece "I Can't Wait (To Rock the Mike)" with DJ Doc.

STEZO

(Born Steve Williams, New York)

Formerly a dancer with the group EPMD, Stezo recorded for the Sleeping Bag/Fresh label c. 1989 and released a 12-inch single titled "To the Max" that received some attention. Around this same period his album *Crazy Noise* was released.

SUPREME TEAM

a.k.a. World's Famous Supreme Team

The Supreme Team was one of the first hip-hop groups to present lessons from the Five Percent Nation of Islam. They were pioneer hip-hop radio personalities on radio station WHBI (along with Mr. Magic, Jerry Bloodrock, and the Awesome 2) during the early 1980s. The duo originally worked with Afrika Islam on WHBI for approximately six weeks before Islam separated from the two and formed his own *Zulu Beats Radio Show*. They also are recognized for their appearance on Malcolm McLaren's classic 1984 album *Duck Rock* and recorded the song "Hey DJ" for Island Records during that year.

SWEET TEE

(Born Toi Jackson, c. 1964, Queens, New York)

Sweet Tee is remembered for the 1986 hit "It's My Beat," which was recorded with DJ Jazzy Joyce, one of the prominent female MCs during this period.

Originally working as a dancer around 1984 for Davy D (during the time of his "One for the Treble" hit), Tee soon began working with producer Hurby Luv Bug Azor, recording for Profile Records. Some of her other hits include "I Got the Feelin'" and "On the Smooth Tip." In the early 1990s Tee put together a group of female rappers known as the Poison Posse. She also appeared in Van Silk's "Sister in the Name of Rap" pay-per-view TV event.

 Selected singles: "It's My Beat" (1986, Profile).

Sample: An audio duplication by a digital recorder of a break beat.

Scratching: The quick back-and-forth spinning of a record under a turntable needle, creating a scratching percussive sound.

Scratch records: Records that were recorded during the early 1980s that contained music combined with the scratching techniques of a hip-hop DJ.

Sound system: DJ equipment, consisting of two turntables, an amplifier, one audio mixer, speakers, and sometimes a microphone.

Speed Rap: Fitting as many as sixteen syllables into a bar of music. This style was pioneered by Kool Moe Dee.

Sweet Tee

RAP RENAISSANCE MAN

Every artistic genre has its Renaissance man (or Renaissance woman, if you will). The hip-hop genre is no exception. Neither are African people. Hip hop's Renaissance man is Fred Brathwaite, a.k.a. Fab 5 Freddy, one-time host of MTV's "Yo! MTV Raps!," formerly a radio show host at Medgar Evers College, a graffiti artist, painter, recording artist, actor, video and television commercial director, associate film producer, and author. Brathwaite's career stretches all the way from the earliest origins of hip hop to the present.

"I was one of the first persons to start taggin' [writing nicknames with black magic markers on walls and trains, the forerunner of graffiti, c. early 1970s]," said Brathwaite, as he reminisced about his Bedford-Stuyvesant beginnings. "Then I got plugged into graffiti. Later, I kinda stopped doin' graffiti [and] I started studying art in Medgar Evers College."

About those early days Freddy said, "The artists weren't in control with what was happening." For him, breakdancing became a "tap dancin' shuffle-along type vibe—not to denigrate tap."

But there are a number of things he misses about those days, when "only tapes were floatin' around, when me and my posse used to walk the street lookin' for jams, the whole thrill of goin' into other boroughs, guys shoutin' 'Dust! Chunky black!,' sheepskins, P.A.L., 183rd Street and Webster Avenue.

"We tried to capture a point in rap, just when people were starting to get money," he said.

Around 1978 Freddy met Chris stein and Debbie Harry (from the group Blondie), along with Glenn O'Brien, who had a show titled *T.V. Party*. Serving as a cameraman for the show for about two years allowed him the opportunity to check out the downtown scene.

"I spent a lot of time studying art, controlling images, understanding the power of the image," Freddy said. Along with his buddy, the late artist Jean-Michel Basquiat, he was the only young African involved in the downtown scene.

With the opening of the Mudd Club (a new-wave hangout), Freddy got a chance to introduce a bit of hip-hop culture by kicking a few rhymes for the audience inside. The intent, he says, was to fuse the two worlds, to show what type of street culture was happening.

Brathwaite appeared in the first, if not only, quintessential hip-hop movie, Charlie Ahearn's 1983 classic *Wild Style*. Realizing that "film making is just another extension of art," Brathwaite effectively portrayed the role of Phade, a promoter who tries to get exposure for hip hop.

Down the road came video direction. "I did the first videos for Queen Latifah, Boogie Down Productions's 'My Philosophy,' Shabba . . . I've directed about twenty videos." Plus, he's produced films, written books, and directed and appeared in TV commercials.

With all these works, one might ask why has Freddy taken so many different directions? "Comin' up the way I came up, I learned how to hustle. I always had to do a li'l bit of this, a li'l bit of that. I only try to do what's in my means."

fab five freddy

TAG TEAM
● ● ● ● ● ● ● ● ● ● ● ● ● ● ● ●
Formed c. 1984, Denver
(Steve Roll'n, born Steve Gibson, c. 1967; DC the Brain Supreme,
born Cecil Glenn, c. 1967; both born in Denver)

Tag Team struck it big in 1993 with the song "Whoomp! (There It Is)," a chant based on a Southeastern slang expression used to cheer on basketball teams. Tag Team took the chant and fused it with the Southern bass sound of hip hop, and their version sold over five million copies by 1994.

Steve Roll'n originally played drums in his high school band before putting together a group with DC the Brain Supreme, a communications major with a knack for words. After working as a barber for a while, while still pursuing a musical career, Roll'n relocated to Atlanta, to attend a music business school and put together a recording studio. DC joined him after graduating from college, originally planning a career in broadcast journalism following up on a job opening at CNN. However, he soon got into deejaying after checking out the local club scene with Roll'n during the late 1980s, particularly after visiting the club Magic City. DC couldn't convince the club's owner to hire him as a DJ, so he worked first as a cook, before he was finally given a chance to work as a relief DJ.

It was while working at Magic City that DC heard the "Whoomp! (There It Is)" expression on one of Roll'n's studio tapes in the early 1990s. DC started using it as well when he deejayed at the club, and the audience there picked up on it. The two decided to record it with a track done in the Miami Bass style (a genre of rap with a faster tempo and high levels of bass). They pressed copies of the song and played it in the club to favorable responses. Within a month's time, other records started to come out with the expression, before the group released their version with the Bellmark label in 1993.

In 1994 they worked with the Walt Disney company, doing a parody of their song with the Disney cartoon characters for a video single called "Whoomp! (There It Went)."

 Selected albums/CDs: *Whoomp! (There It Is)* (1993, Bellmark).

Tag Team

Teddy Riley

TEDDY RILEY

....

(Born c. 1966, Harlem, New York)

Before Teddy Riley was a member of the R&B group Guy, which combined the musical genres of go-go, rap, and R&B to create the so-called "New Jack Swing" style, the producer/writer/performer had been working with rap acts.

Raised in the St. Nicholas Projects in Harlem, Riley was considered a child prodigy at age 5, able to play piano and, later, drums, trumpet, and saxophone by the age of 12.

Around 1978 he joined the R&B band Total Climax as a keyboard player, and the group played local club spots, including the Lickety Split in Harlem and the Blue Note.

Riley's uncle bought the famed hip-hop club the Rooftop around the early 1980s where Riley later set up a recording studio and worked on projects with his then-stepfather, music-industry veteran Gene Griffin. He also took an electronics course at the Manhattan School of Music, to study synthesizers. Around the mid- to late-1980s, Riley worked for the Ya-Maka Records label, which was run by Melquan Shabazz (original manager of Wu-Tang Clan's Prince Rakeem).

Some of Riley's first rap work was done in the mid-1980s with artists like Doug E. Fresh, B-Fats, and Heavy D. He did drum programming (uncredited) on Fresh's "The Show" and Heavy D's "Mr. Big Stuff." He later worked with the Classical Two (whom he also deejayed for occasionally) on "Rap's New Generation," and Kool Moe Dee, on pieces like "Go See the Doctor." Riley also worked with the Wee Papa Girls, Redhead Kingpin, and his brother Markell's group, Wreckx-N-Effect.

Riley formed the group Guy around 1987–88, achieving major success with them. By the early 1990s on into 1995 he was successfully producing other R&B acts, including Michael Jackson, Bobby Brown, and Keith Sweat. Guy broke up around 1992–93, and by 1994 Riley formed another R&B group called Blackstreet, who released a self-titled album that went platinum by 1995.

3RD BASS

....

a.k.a. Three the Hard Way

Formed: c. 1988, New York City

(MC Serch, born Michael Berrin, May 6, 1967, Far Rockaway, Brooklyn, New York; Prime Minister Pete Nice, born Peter J. Nash, February 5, 1967, Brooklyn; DJ Richie Rich, a.k.a. Daddy Rich, born Richard Lawson, New York)

3rd Bass is a group that consisted of two white rappers and one black DJ that gained considerable respect in black hip-hop circles. They were known for their authentic rhymes, MC Serch's dance moves, and Pete Nice's custom-tailored silk suits, walking stick, and big cigar.

3rd Bass

Serch (whose father was a former stockbroker, while his mother was a trained opera singer) grew up in Far Rockaway and hung out in black communities there, like the Hammel and Redfern Houses. It was his African-American friends in those housing projects who gave Serch his name, for what they felt was his "search for knowledge" from them, most of whom were members of the Five Percent Nation of Islam. He attended the High School of Music and Art (rappers Dana Dane and Slick Rick were also attendees) where he learned and perfected his rhymes with others in the school cafeteria.

Pete Nice's father was a basketball coach who taught in Brooklyn's Bishop Ford High School. Pete attended junior high school in all-black South Floral Park, where he started writing rhymes, and eventually attended Bishop Ford, focusing on basketball. He also perfected his rhyming skills in the school cafeteria.

Serch performed in gigs in the early- to mid-1980s with groups like the Gangster 5 and the SZ Connection. Pete enrolled at Columbia University after high school in 1985, becoming a varsity basketball player. He began hosting a rap radio show at the school's WKCR station in the summer of 1986, with Super DJ Clark Kent. Through Kent, Pete later met Daddy Rich.

Serch received his first record deal around 1986, recording one song as a solo rapper for Warlock Records, titled "Melissa." In 1987 Serch recorded for Idlers Records, working with producer Tony D on the single "Hey Boy/Go White Boy," which received some underground recognition.

In 1988 Pete Nice's radio show was taken from him, due to the university's discomfort with the hip hoppers Pete invited to his show. He also left the basketball team and concentrated on rap, making demos with Daddy Rich and working with groups like Sine Qua Non, Servin' Generalz, and doing gigs with others like Divine Sounds and Dana Dane.

Around this time Pete and Serch met each other outside the famed hip-hop club Latin Quarters, and tested each other's rhyme skills. Though they originally hated each other, producer Sam Sever (who had begun working with both Pete and Serch individually) introduced the two, and felt that they would work well together. Serch and Pete eventually got to like each other, later composing rhymes together with ease, working as Three the Hard Way. They were soon signed to Def Jam Recordings and became 3rd Bass.

In 1989 Serch and Pete wrote a song, originally meant for the duo Eric B & Rakim, called "Steppin' to the A.M." 3rd Bass recorded the piece themselves, with Keith and Hank Shocklee producing. It was released during summer of that year to a good response. Their debut album, *Cactus Album*, was released and went gold by April 1990. Other notable singles from the album were "The Gas Face" and "Brooklyn-Queens" (one of the first demos Pete originally made with Daddy Rich).

In 1991 the group's second album was released, *Derelicts of Dialect*. It went gold by September of that year. The single from that work "Pop Goes the Weasel" also went gold that same year. During this period Daddy Rich became the group's permanent DJ. 3rd Bass also began to work with other groups, like KMD, whom they helped get a record deal (with Elektra Records).

By 1992, however, 3rd Bass had broken up "due to creative differences," according to group members. Serch pursued a solo career, releasing his own *Return of the Product* album, starting his own company (Serchlite Productions), and producing songs for female rapper Boss. He also supervised the soundtrack for director Oliver Stone's film *Zebrahead*.

Pete and Daddy Rich continued working together as a twosome, releasing the album *Dust to Dust* in 1993. Pete also started two companies during this period: Suedehead Mezz handled productions, while his label, Hoppoh Records, began working with rapper Kurious.

In early 1994 Serch became vice president of A&R for Wild Pitch Records.

 Selected singles: "Steppin' to the A.M." (1989, Def Jam/Columbia).

 Selected albums/CDs: *The Cactus Album* (1989, Def Jam/Columbia 45415); *Derelicts of Dialect* (1991, Def Jam/Columbia 2-47369).

TOMMY BOY RECORDS
Formed in 1981, New York City

Tommy Boy Records is one of the early rap labels that maintained status and legitimacy throughout the 1980s on into the 1990s. They have been influential in introducing many acts to the hip-hop market, including Afrika Bambaataa and the Soul Sonic Force, De La Soul, Stetsasonic, Digital Underground, Queen Latifah, and a host of others.

The label was started by Tom Silverman, who was, at the time, the writer and owner of a small publication he had started in college called *Dance Music Report*. The publication covered the disco and dance scene during the late 1970s. It was around 1979–80 that Silverman, producer Arthur Baker, and fashion entrepreneur/punk-rock manager Malcolm McLaren began hearing about the type of hip-hop parties Afrika Bambaataa and his Zulu Nation were throwing in the Bronx River section of the Bronx. Silverman eventually visited Bronx River around 1980 and met Bambaataa, after which an article on the Zulu Nation appeared in his publication, and subsequently he became friends with Bambaataa.

The two began working together musically during this same period. They worked out of Silverman's apartment on East 85th Street, trading ideas and working on material. The first result of this collaboration was Silverman's first record (before the Tommy Boy label) called "Let's Vote," which Bambaataa worked on uncredited, with a female group of singers called Cotton Candy, accompanied by Bambaataa's Soul Sonic Force.

The second work Silverman released was "Having Fun," again with Cotton Candy and Bambaataa's Soul Sonic Force. His third release was a piece by another one of Bambaataa's groups, the Jazzy Five, called "Jazzy Sensation." Released on the Tommy Boy label, producer Arthur Baker worked on the song with Silverman and Bambaataa, and it remains a hip-hop classic.

Around 1981–82 Bambaataa met producer John Robie, who had visited him with a record he was trying to release. Bambaataa introduced him to Arthur Baker, and all four individuals collaborated on the now-classic release "Planet Rock." The work went gold in 1982, and with this and the previously issued "Jazzy Sensation," the label was well on its way to success. A few of the many other successful records released on Tommy Boy include De La Soul's *3 Feet High & Rising*, Digital Underground's *Sex Packets*, and Naughty by Nature, Coolio, and House of Pain.

By 1989 Time Warner had purchased Tommy Boy Records from Silverman while Monica Lynch (whom Silverman hired during the "Planet Rock" days) remained as president.

TONE-LÖC
● ● ● ● ● ● ● ● ● ● ● ● ● ● ● ●
a.k.a. Tony Loco
(Born Anthony Terrell Smith, Los Angeles)

Recognized for his trademark deep gravelly voice and appealing personality, rapper/actor Tone-Löc burst on the scene in 1989 with a piece called "Wild Thing." That single and his album *Löc'ed After Dark* were tremendously successful, and both went multiplatinum during that year. Both "Wild Thing" and another hit single from Löc, "Funky Cold Medina," were written by his labelmate at Delicious Vinyl Records, Young MC.

Löc was originally a gang member in Los Angeles before being signed to Matt Dike and Mike Ross's Delicious Vinyl label, where he was offered the "Wild Thing" song by the label owners. (Dike and Ross's reported original choice was Fab 5 Freddy.) Other singles by Löc during this period include "Cheeba, Cheeba" and "Cutting Rhythms."

Löc began to appear in feature films like the 1993 Western *Posse*. He made television appearances also on shows like Fox-TV's *Roc*, and the game show *Wheel of Fortune*. He did animation features like *Bebe's Kids*. In 1991 his second album, *Cool Hand Löc*, was released. After his disappointment with the marketing of that album, Löc concentrated on his acting career, appearing in various films including *Ace Ventura: Pet Detective* in 1994.

Selected albums/CDs: *Löc'ed After Dark* (1989, Delicious Vinyl 92197; clean version, 92198); *Cool Hand Löc* (1991, Delicious Vinyl, 92171; clean version, 92172).

Tone-Löc

Too $hort

TOO $HORT
• • • • • • • • • • • • • • • • • • •
(Born Todd Shaw, April 28, 1966, Los Angeles)

Too $hort is one of hip hop's most successful rappers. His works dealing in the hustler/pimp genre of rap have consistently gone gold and/or platinum with little or no airplay.

$hort was originally a DJ in East Oakland, California, who by 1985 had recorded two albums, *75 Girls Present Too Short* (75 Girls was the name of the record label) and *Players*. Both works sold well locally, but $hort later severed ties with the label toward 1987.

After hooking up with his friend Freddy B around this same period, Short raised enough money to start his own label, Dangerous Music. He recorded a piece titled "Freaky Tales" and an album *Born to Mac*. These works were more explicit in subject matter than his previous recorded work. However, with Short and his partner selling the material from city to city by themselves, starting in the Bay area and winding up in Sacramento, California, sales were modest. Both the single and the album sold 15,000 and 50,000 copies, respectively, enough to draw the interests of music-industry heads at Jive Records, which signed the rapper and re-released his album.

By 1989 Short's next work, *Life Is . . . Too Short*, went platinum, as well as the following album in 1990, titled *Short Dog's in the House*. In 1992 Short released the work *Shorty the Pimp*, which went gold that year. His 1993, album *Get in Where Ya Fit In*, had reached gold by mid-1994. Short's next album, *Cocktails*, went gold by June 1995.

 Selected albums/CDs: *Born to Mack* (1988, Jive/RCA 1100); *Life Is . . . Too Short* (1989, Jive/RCA 1149; clean version, 1218); *Short Dog's in the House* (1990, Jive/RCA, 1348; clean version, 1353); *Shorty the Pimp* (Jive/RCA 41467; clean version, 41505); *Get in Where Ya Fit In* (1993, Jive/RCA 41526); *Cocktails* (1995, Jive/RCA 41553).

TREACHEROUS THREE
●●●●●●●●●●●●●●●●●●●●●●●●●●●●●●●●
Formed c. 1978, New York City
(Kool Moe Dee, born Mohandas Dewese, 1963, New York City:
Special K, born Kevin Keaton, Bronx, New York; L.A. Sunshine, born
LaMar Hill, New York; DJ Easy Lee, born in New York. Former member:
Spoonie Gee, born Gabe Jackson, New York City)

The Treacherous Three was one of the premier rap groups during the late 1970s and early 1980s. They are recognized as being among the first rap groups to make records (along with Grandmaster Flash and the Furious Five, the Funky Four Plus One, and the Sugar Hill Gang). The group—particularly member Kool Moe Dee—is also remembered for introducing speed rapping to the technique of MC'ing.

Group member Special K was formerly a member of the Undefeated Four when he met Spoonie Gee, Kool Moe Dee, and L.A. Sunshine at Manhattan's Townes High School. Because K hailed from the Bronx, he was seen as being a more authentic MC (as opposed to the disco-oriented style of MCs in Manhattan at the time). When Kool Moe Dee met Special K, he was impressed with the quality and quantity of his rhymes. K, Moe Dee, Sunshine, and Spoonie Gee would occasionally battle, and later they talked about forming a group.

After some time, Spoonie's uncle, legendary talent scout, producer, and label owner Bobby Robinson, decided to record his nephew, after Spoonie recorded his first song, "Spoonie's Rap," for Peter Brown's Sound of New York USA Records. Moe Dee (during the summer before Spoonie was to record for his uncle) had been working on a fast MC style that he called speed rapping. When he asked Spoonie if he and Sunshine could record with him, Spoonie agreed. Special K (who had been trying to join the Funky Four) was asked by Moe Dee to join the group to record, and they became known as the Treacherous Three.

Along with their DJ, Easy Lee, the Treacherous Three recorded a 12-inch single for Bobby Robinson's Enjoy Records in 1980. Produced by Robinson, and accompanied by the label's multi-instrumentalist house producer, Pumpkin, the Treacherous Three recorded the piece "The New Rap Language" on one side of the record, while the second side contained Spoonie's solo "Love Rap." Both works were successful with the hip-hop audience. Spoonie Gee left the group soon after and went solo again.

The Treacherous Three recorded other works for Robinson's Enjoy label, including "The Body Rock" and "Put the Boogie in Your Body." By 1982 Robinson sold the group to Sugar Hill Records.

At Sugar Hill the Treacherous Three recorded singles such as "Yes We Can Can," "Action," "Feel the Heartbeat," and "Whip It." Later, due to conflicts of interest and business problems with their label, the group separated toward 1988. Kool Moe Dee had already pursued a successful solo career, beginning with "Go See the Doctor," released by Rooftop Records. DJ Easy Lee toured with Moe Dee during his solo run.

Toward 1992 DJ Easy Lee developed his own Easy Lee Records, and by 1993 the group had reassembled and recorded again for the album *Old School Flava* on Easy Lee's label, cutting the piece "Feel the New Heartbeat."

 Selected singles: "The New Rap Language" (1980, Enjoy).

 Selected albums/CDs: *Old School Flava* (1994, Wrap 8128).

A TRIBE CALLED QUEST
Formed in mid-1980s
(Q-Tip, born Jonathan Davis, April 10, 1971, Harlem, New York; Phife, born Malik Taylor, November 20, 1970, Queens, New York; Ali, born Ali Shaheed Muhammad, c. 1971, Brooklyn, New York; Jarobi, born in Brooklyn)

A Tribe Called Quest was one of the first hip-hop groups to extensively use jazz samples containing electric pianos, acoustic bass, and other instruments. They were also known for the variety of musical genres their samples contained. The group's unique style initially centered on Q-Tip's semigravelly vocal texture and abstract rhyme-writing style.

Group members Q-Tip and Phife were best friends and godbrothers who lived in the same Queens neighborhood. They were known for their MC'ing skills in battles on basketball courts. Q-Tip met the group's future DJ, Ali Muhammad, at Murray Bergtraum Business High School in Manhattan, along with Afrika Baby Bambaataa, Mike G, and Brother J (of later Jungle Brothers fame). During this same period, after Jarobi joined Q-Tip, Phife, and Ali, the group began recording with the help of their future manager, Kool DJ Red Alert.

One of the singles off the group's first 1990 album, *People's Instinctive Travels and the Paths of Rhythm*, was "I Left My Wallet in El Segundo." Most of the hip-hop audience and the

A Tribe Called Quest

DJs, however, took to the other pieces off the work, such as "Bonita Applebum" and "Can I Kick It?" Attention was paid to the group's then-unique choice of samples, such as the intro from rocker Lou Reed's "Walk on the Wild Side" for their piece "Can I Kick It?"

By 1991 the group recorded and released their second album, *The Low End Theory*, which contained the hit single "Check the Rhime." The album was noted for the work of jazz bassist Ron Carter, who appeared on several pieces, and by 1992 it went gold.

By 1993 the group's third album was released, titled *Midnight Marauders*. Two hit singles off the work were "Award Tour" and "Oh My God."

 Selected albums/CDs: *People's Instinctive Travels and the Paths of Rhythm* (1990, Jive/RCA 1331); *The Low End Theory* (1991, Jive/RCA 1418); *Midnight Marauders* (1993, Jive/RCA 41490).

2 LIVE CREW
●●●●●●●●●●●●●●●●●●●●●●
Formed mid-1980's, California
(Luke, a.k.a. Luke Skyywalker, born Luther Campbell, December 22, 1960,
Miami Beach, Florida; Brother Marquis, born Mark Ross, April 2, Florida;
Fresh Kid-Ice, born Christopher Wongwon, May 24, California; Mr. Mixx,
born David Hobbs, September 23, California)

The 2 Live Crew gained international attention in 1990 when their album *As Nasty as They Wanna Be* was declared obscene by a federal judge in Florida. They were the first music group in the United States to have their record declared obscene and, subsequently, have their sales banned to minors, which all raised First Amendment issues. However, because of these actions, record sales for the album continued to climb, even though the album had already reached platinum status and their single "Me So Horny" went gold in 1989.

The 2 Live Crew's sexually explicit subject matter got noticed almost immediately when the group's first single, "Throw the D" (originally "Throw the Dick"), appeared in 1986. They are also known as one of the leading practitioners of the rap genre known as Miami bass, which tends to have a faster tempo (à la Afrika Bambaataa's "Planet Rock" single) and a louder bass sound.

Group leader and label owner Luke Skyywalker had to professionally call himself Luke, after film producer/director George Lucas, who had originally agreed to let the artist use the name (which came from his *Star Wars* film), reversed his decision and threatened to sue around 1990. Luke, who was originally a DJ when he got into the music scene, had got the "Skyywalker" tag from neighborhood friends who said "he had the force" (a recurrent line in the *Star Wars* film) when it came to his deejaying skills.

Working as a cook for a while prior to this, Luke was turned on to the art of deejaying in the late 1970s when he joined the DJ crew known as the Ghetto Style DJs, first as a van driver, carting the group's equipment to parks, then becoming the main DJ with them, adding equipment, attaining more gigs at parks and schools, and, eventually, advertising on radio. When a record producer decided to make a record dealing with a dance done at Luke's parties called the "Ghetto Jump," Luke decided to cut his own record outlining another dance.

There was a group from California called the 2 Live Crew, which consisted of David Hobbs, Chris Wongwon, and another group member who had left. The group had made a record, which was part of Luke's playing repertoire at the time. Luke teamed with the two, along with Mark "Brother Marquis" Ross, and made the record "Throw the D." He sold approximately 250,000 copies of the piece out of his Honda Accord, building up his distribution network store by store. This single officially built his record company, originally known as Luke Skyywalker Records, and later changed to Luke Records. In 1987 Luke and the group recorded the album *2 Live Crew Is What We Are*, which included the single. The album went gold by early 1988.

Also in 1988, the group released the album *Move Somethin'*, which went gold that same year. By 1989 they had recorded their controversial *As Nasty as They Wanna Be*. Florida

2 Live Crew

governor Bob Martinez requested the state prosecutor to investigate the group. Broward County, Florida, sheriff Nick Navarro pressed for obscenity charges after one of the 2 Live Crew's shows was raided by police. A record dealer in Sarasota, Florida, was caught selling the album to an 11-year-old girl; a clerk at another record store was also prosecuted for selling the album to a minor. Former golf pro turned lawyer Jack Thompson faxed copies of the group's lyrics to all sheriffs' offices, police chiefs, prosecutors, and media outlets in Florida, in an effort to bring down the group. This led to some people's claim that the group was unfairly targeted because they were a black group, who recorded for a black-owned record label, which handled its own distribution.

In 1990 the group responded to the brouhaha surrounding their work by recording the single and album titled *Banned in the USA*, both of which went gold that same year. Also during this period the group recorded the first live rap album, titled *Live in Concert*. Toward 1991 Luke released *Sports Weekend (As Nasty [Clean] as They Wanna Be Part II)*, which went gold in 1992. Luke also published the book *As Nasty as They Wanna Be*, which chronicled the controversy that the album inspired.

During the early 1990s Luke was becoming recognized as one of the most important rap moguls next to Russell Simmons, when he branched out and signed other groups to his label. He had set up many scholarship funds and sponsored many kids' programs and charitable organizations.

In 1993 Luke began to tap the R&B market, when his successful R&B act, H-Town, reached platinum sales with their "Knockin' the Boots" single. During this same period Luke and the original 2 Live Crew members split (with the exception of Chris Wongwon) due to creative differences. Thereafter, Luke formed the New 2 Live Crew. In 1994 Luke lost a lawsuit that was filed by one of his former artists, MC Shy-D. A lower-court Miami judge ordered Luke to pay the artist $699,165 in back royalties for two albums, *Gotta Be Tough* and *Comin' Correct In '88*. Luke was also sued by the Acuff-Rose Music company around this same period, because he recorded a parody of Roy Orbison's "Oh, Pretty Woman." In this case, Luke prevailed when his version was ruled a parody by the Supreme Court, protected under the fair use provisions of copyright law.

 Selected albums/CDs: *The 2 Live Crew Is What We Are* (1987, Luke 91648); *Move Somethin'* (1988, Luke 91649; clean version, 91650); *As Nasty As They Wanna Be* (1989, Luke 91651; clean version [*As Clean As . . .*], 91652); *Sports Weekend* (1991, Luke 91720; clean version, 91797).

2PAC
* * * * * *
(Born Tupac Amaru Shakur, June 16, 1971, Bronx, New York)

2Pac (nicknamed "Rebel of the Underground") is an artist who has achieved equal billing as a rapper and a movie star. He is recognized for his powerful film performances, his socially conscious lyrics, and the political circumstances of his birth, as well as his brushes with the law.

2Pac's mother, Afeni Shakur, was a member of the Black Panther Party, and part of the New York 21, a group of Black Panthers who were arrested in 1970 for allegedly conspiring to blow up the New York Botanical Garden and other public areas in that city. A month and three days after her acquittal, 2Pac was born (a name she chose from an Inca chief, meaning "shining serpent").

With famed Panther Geronimo Pratt as a godfather and a stepfather who was on the FBI's 10 Most Wanted List (his real father died a day after being released from jail), 2Pac's early life was filled with poverty and sometimes homelessness. He grew up in Harlem and in 1984 made his acting debut at the Apollo Theater in the play *A Raisin in the Sun*, which was part of a benefit for Reverend Jesse Jackson's presidential campaign.

2Pac, with his mother and sister, then moved to Baltimore, where he attended the High School of Performing Arts. When a high school friend was shot and killed in a gun accident, he was inspired to write his first rap piece. After that, he dropped out of school and decided to pursue music. (He earned his G.E.D. later.)

He moved to northern California, handing out demo recordings of his rhymes. He later found himself homeless and sleeping on park benches in Marin City, California. Finally, around 1989{*}90, he was invited to audition by Shock-G from the group Digital Underground. Shock liked what he heard, but he asked 2Pac to work for him as a roadie, to earn his way on the stage. After months of road work Shock put him on stage to rap. Later he was featured on Digital Underground's "Same Song" single around 1990{*}91.

In 1991 he was signed to Interscope Records, and his first album was released, titled *2Pacalypse Now*. Its two singles "Trapped" and "Brenda's Got a Baby" were hits, and were noted for their ghetto realism.

In 1992 he made his film debut in Ernest Dickerson's *Juice* and won critical acclaim. Later that year then Vice President Dan Quayle blamed 2Pac's *2Pacalypse Now* work for the death of a Texas state trooper, after the man charged with the crime claimed he had been listening to the album.

2Pac's second album, *Strictly 4 My N.I.G.G.A.Z. . . .*, was released in 1993 and went gold. The single from that work "I Get Around" was a major hit. That same year he costarred with singer Janet Jackson in John Singleton's film *Poetic Justice*. During this same period he was arrested for allegedly shooting two off-duty police officers in Atlanta, Georgia, after which the charges were dropped. In November 1993 a 19-year-old woman alleged that 2Pac and three of his friends sodomized her.

In 1994 the artist spent fifteen days in a Los Angeles jail for assaulting film director Allen Hughes (of the Hughes brothers directing team) after he rejected 2Pac for their *Menace II Society* film. That same year he starred in the film *Above the Rim*. He was shot four times in November 1994 while entering a recording studio in New York, and robbed of $40,000 worth of jewelry. He was hospitalized, but checked out after three hours (bandaged from head to torso) in fear of his life. In December 1994 he was found guilty of sexual abuse for the 1993 sodomy charge, and was sentenced to one and one-half to four and one-half years. In 1995 his album *Me Against the World* went platinum.

 Selected albums/CDs: *2Pacalypse Now* (1991, Interscope 91767); *Strictly 4 My N.I.G.G.A.Z. . . .* (1993, Interscope 92209); *Me Against the World* (1995, Interscope 92399).

OTHERZ

THREE TIMES DOPE
. . . .

Formerly 3-D
Formed c. mid- to late-1980s, Philadelphia
(MC E.S.T., born Robert Waller; Chuck Nice, born Walter
Griggs; DJ Woody Wood, born Duerwood Beale)

The Philadelphia group Three Times Dope was originally part of what was known as the Hilltop Posse during the mid-to-late-1980s, which also consisted of Cool C, Steady B, and DJ Tat Money. Formerly managed by Lawrence Goodman of Pop Art Records, the group recorded two notable 12-inch singles for Goodman's Hilltop Hustler label, titled "Crushin' & Bussin'{|}" b/w "On the Dope Side," and "From the Giddyup" b/w "Once More You Hear the Dope Stuff."

The group was later signed to Arista Records around 1989, where their *Original Stylin'* album was released. Hits off that work included "Funky Dividends" and "Greatest Man Alive." In 1990 they released *Live from Acknikulous* . The single off that work was "No Words."

 Selected albums/CDs: *Original Stylin'* (1989, Arista 8571); *Live from Acknikulous Land* (1990, Arista 8615).

T LA ROCK
. . . .

(Born in Bronx, New York)

T La Rock was the first MC to record for the Def Jam Recordings label. His 1984 "It's Yours" single is one of hip hop's classic recordings.

Def Jam's Rick Rubin and Jazzy Jay originally wanted to use La Rock's brother, Special K of the Treacherous Three, for "It's Yours." Due to K's scheduling problems, they decided to work with La Rock. Both La Rock and K shared writing credits on the work.

T La Rock later recorded for Sleeping Bag/Fresh Records during the mid-to-late-1980s, where he worked with Greg Nice of Nice & Smooth and DJ Louie Lou. With those artists he recorded works like *Lyrical King* and *This Beat Kicks*.

Selected singles: "It's Yours" (1984, Partytime/Def Jam).

TUFF CITY RECORDS

Formed c. mid-1980s, Long Island City

Aaron Fuchs's Tuff City Records label officially came into being with the release of Davy D's, a.k.a. Davy DMX's, "One for the Treble" in 1984—one of hip hop's classic recordings.

Fuchs was originally known as a collector of vintage R&B records and an authority on the history of Motown Records. During the late 1980s Fuchs signed DJ Mark the 45 King to his label, where the artist recorded more than fifteen works for the company, one of which was another hip-hop classic, "The 900 Number." Fuchs signed and worked with other artists into the early 1990s, including Lakim Shabazz, Grand Wizard Theodore, YZ, Spoonie Gee, Cold Crush Brothers, Louie Louie Vega, and Lord Ali-baski.

Tag: The street name of a graffiti writer. The tag is then drawn or written on subway trains, walls, overpasses, and other areas where it can be seen by the public.

Tagging: To write graffiti.

Technofunk: See *Electrofunk.*

Toasting: Jamaican style rapping to dancehall music. Also known as DJ style, and chattin'.

3 Times Dope

MR. FREEZE: RAP AND COUNTRY

Mr. Freeze is not only the head of black music at Radical Records, he also released a 12-inch single in 1993 called "Oh Susanna," which features Grand Puba. "It's like a country [and] western hip-hop song," Freeze says.

For those who don't remember, Freeze was once part of the legendary Jazzy Five (which featured Freeze, DJs Jazzy Jay and Kool DJ Red Alert, Master Ice, Master Bee, and the Master Dee), and they had recorded one classic record for Tommy Boy Records called "Jazzy Sensation" (one of the first records on the Tommy Boy label). Freeze says that although the record got them recognized when it was released in 1981, the real recognition came from the tapes they did back then.

"Most of the props we got were from the street tapes," he says, "plus our live performances and things like that. Guys like Run-D.M.C. and them were into our raps."

With Freeze's single and the album titled *Cold Wave* (with production split between Freeze and Jazzy Jay), Freeze reveals, "What I'm trying to get people to see, is that rap is all forms of music. Once you get a flow off a song, then you can go for it.

"You can rap off any kind of music. You have to be able to rap off anything. Back in the days when you were grabbing the mic to get on, you never knew what the DJ was gonna throw on."

ULTRAMAGNETIC MC'S
. . . .

Formed mid-1980s, Bronx, New York
(Ced Gee, born Cedric Miller, August 13, New York; Kool Keith,
born Keith Thornton, October 7, New York; TR Love, born
Trevor Randolph, February 14, New York; Moe Love, born
Maurice Smith, December 13, New York)

When they first appeared on record in 1987, the Ultramagnetic MC's were noted for their heavily sampled sound, constructed in machine-like patterns and textures, but maintaining elements of funk. Their lyrical style utilized deliveries in offbeat musical time, and a larger vocabulary of words than is normally heard in rap. After the appearance of their *Critical Beatdown* album, the group's influence was widely felt, particularly the work of producer Ced Gee, who is also responsible for co-producing Boogie Down Productions' *Criminal Minded*. *Critical Beatdown* has been one of the most frequently sampled records, with users ranging from producers like Teddy Riley, Jimmy Jam, and Terry Lewis, to acts like Soul II Soul and Bell Biv DeVoe.

All members of the group were early hip hoppers, attending the parties of Kool DJ Herc, Afrika Bambaataa, and Grandmaster Flash and venturing to the early clubs like Sparkle, the Audubon Ballroom, and the Black Door.

Ced Gee was in a group called the People's Choice Crew with Moe Love, who was a DJ for the group. Kool Keith originally was a b-boy for the break group the New York City Breakers. TR was working for a while as Afrika Bambaataa's record boy. All four eventually met each other on a basketball court in the South Bronx and decided to form a group.

Ced Gee approached hip-hop radio personality DNA (of the DNA & Hank Love radio show) around September 1986, seeking some help and exposure for the demos he had been recording with his group. DNA gave airtime to Ced Gee's material, and the group was picked up by Next Plateau Records, after which their single "Ego Trippin'" was released in 1987. The piece gained the group immediate attention from the hip-hop crowd. Toward the end of 1988 their album *Critical Beatdown* (which was recorded by engineer/producer Paul C at Studio 1212) was released.

By 1991 the group had switched to Mercury Records, where their second album, *Funk Your Head Up*, was released, with the single "Poppa Large" gaining some attention. During this same period Ced Gee (along with TR and Moe Love) began doing production work on rapper Tim Dog's "Fuck Compton" single and album.

Toward 1993 the group had moved to Wild Pitch Records, where their "Two Brothers with Checks (San Francisco, Harvey)" single was released, after which their album *The Four Horsemen* appeared. In 1995 Tuff City Records released an album titled *The Basement Tapes 1984{'}1990*, which contained previously unreleased material the group had recorded.

 Selected singles: "Ego Trippin'" (1987, Next Plateau).

 Selected albums/CDs: *Critical Beatdown* (1988, Next Plateau 1013); *Funk Your Head Up* (1992, Mercury 510893); *The Four Horsemen* (1993, Wild Pitch 89917); *The Basement Tapes 1984–1990* (1995, Tuff City 618).

UTFO

Formed in the early 1980s, Brooklyn, New York
(Kangol Kid; Mixmaster Ice; Dr. Ice; Educated Rapper, a.k.a. EMD: all born in Brooklyn, New York)

In 1984 the group UTFO recorded a song titled "Roxanne, Roxanne," which started a barrage of response records, Roxanne impostors, and the like. It was a phenomenon, and many careers were built off the success of this one record.

Hailing from East Flatbush, Brooklyn, two of the group's members, Dr. Ice and the Kangol Kid, were b-boys who breakdanced for the group Whodini during their tours. With the Educated Rapper and Mixmaster Ice, UTFO worked with producers Full Force and Howie Tee.

For "Roxanne, Roxanne," Howie Tee laid down the Billy Squire "Big Beat" drum break with Kangol Kid in his basement studio. Due to other commitments, Howie turned the remainder of the project over to Full Force, who completed the recording of the work with the UTFO members. The piece appeared on a 12-inch single with another work, titled "Hanging Out." It was that work that was actually promoted by the group's manager, Steve Salem. However, "Roxanne, Roxanne" is what caught on.

Afterward, they released a self-titled album, and in 1985 they released their second album, titled *Skeezer Pleezers*, which contained the hit single "Split Personality."

By 1987 the group released the work *Lethal*, and in 1989 the album *Doin' It*. Their *Bag It and Bone It* album appeared in 1991. Neither of these albums was as successful as their initial work, and after 1991 the group disbanded. In 1995 the group reunited to appear in a pioneers of rap concert in New York City, performing their famous hit song.

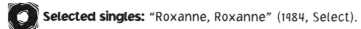 **Selected singles:** "Roxanne, Roxanne" (1984, Select).

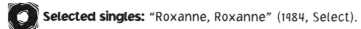 **Selected albums/CDs:** *UTFO* (1984, Sire 21614); *Skeezer Pleasure* (1995, Sire 21616); *Lethal* (1987, Sire 21619); *Doin' It* (1989, Sire); *Bag It & Bone It (1991, Jive/RCA 1326).*

US GIRLS
••••••••••••
Formed in 1984, New York
(Debbie Dee; Sha Rock; Lisa Lee: all born in Bronx, New York)

The Us Girls were a female group of pioneer MCs who combined to perform in the 1984 movie *Beat Street*. The group consisted of Debbie Dee (who had performed with the Mercedes Ladies), former Cosmic Force member Lisa Lee, and the Funky Four Plus One's Sha Rock.

VANDY C
● ● ● ● ● ● ● ● ● ● ● ●
(Born Vandy L. Colter III, September 12, 1962, Brooklyn, New York)

Vandy C is one of hip hop's pioneer radio DJs, whose show ran for nearly eight years (circa 1982 to 1989) in New York City and parts of the tristate area. He was recognized early on for his deejaying abilities, and for being one of the first hip-hop DJs to come out of Brooklyn. He's also known for his work as a record producer. Some of the rap records first heard on Vandy's show were "We're Only Buggin'" by Whistle and "I'll Take Your Man" by Salt-N-Pepa.

Vandy began getting his DJ system together in 1978, and soon formed a group of MCs called the High Powered 3. Booked by then-promoter Cutmaster DC (of later "Brooklyn's in the House" fame), Vandy and the group were involved in many competitions in the Brooklyn area. One of the High Powered 3 MCs, named Freak L, would later be known for underground hits like "Slammin'," "Line for Line," and "When the Pen Hits the Paper."

Around 1979{*}81 Vandy decided to get into radio, and attended a radio broadcast program at New York Tech. Vandy sent out tapes of his radio skills to various stations. Brooklyn's Medgar Evers College's radio station eventually showed interest. In 1982 Vandy was on the air five days a week for the station. Vandy also assembled a crew to help with the show, which consisted of Bill Blast, True Patrick, artist Sammy D, Khadijah, and Irv, who handled the photography.

In 1983 Vandy began to deejay at local clubs like the Latin Quarters and Inferno. He also put on various rap shows. Using his motto on the radio show and at the station, "get busy or get lost," Vandy billed a series of shows, sometimes packing as many as 6,000 people in parks. Some of the popular acts of the day that were featured were the Cold Crush Brothers and the Treacherous Three.

After 1984 Vandy decided to get into the record business, becoming vice president of Wop Records for Charles "Charlie Wop" Sanders. One of the records he recorded for the company was his own, called "V—The Viper," which featured rhymes done by Vandy and Bill

Blast. The b-side of the record contained a session with T-Funk (from the Bad Boys) and Dr. Ice (of UTFO). "V—The Viper" received quite a bit of play from the hip-hop DJs during this period.

A distribution deal for the record was soon worked out between Vandy and Select Records' Fred Munao (who actually got a chance to hear the song before its first release, and suggested the chorus hook for the work). Vandy also did a second song for the label, titled "Let's Feel It."

Vandy continued to do productions and remixes from 1985 on, working with artists and producers such as Kid Flash, Hank Shocklee, Steel Pulse, Tony "Tony D" Depula, and the Jaz. He also did cameos in movies like *Krush Groove* and *Juice* (as one of the judges at the DJ competition).

VANILLA ICE
•••••••••••••••••••
(Born Robert Van Winkle, October 31, 1968, Miami)

Vanilla Ice caused a great deal of controversy in hip-hop circles when he appeared on the scene in 1990 with his single "Ice Ice Baby." Many people in the hip-hop community felt that his rhyme and MC'ing skills left a lot to be desired. That, coupled with the fact that he was a Caucasian, added to the opinion that he was basically taking from the genre, and not adding talent or merit of any kind.

Further controversy revolved around Ice's life before becoming a recording artist. Reports of him living in a rough section of Miami, and attending high school with Luther "Luke Skyywalker" Campbell, turned out to be false. (Ice later denied that he had ever claimed to have known Campbell.) Nevertheless, his "Ice Ice Baby" went platinum in 1990, and his album *To the Extreme* went multiplatinum the same year, first selling six million copies, and by 1994, ten million copies in the United States, and fifteen million worldwide, with one Grammy nomination and two American Music awards. With that (plus a statement from producer Hank Shocklee, claiming he had wanted to sign the artist before he attained his success), Vanilla Ice still remains a questionable figure to those in and outside the hip-hop community.

Ice grew up in Miami, and in Dallas and Carrolton, Texas, moving with his family approximately every year since the age of 11. He began to take up breakdancing when he turned 14, performing in shopping malls for small change. He later won a local rap contest and acquired a manager, who formed a label called Ultrax Records. For that label Ice recorded the single "Play That Funky Music, White Boy" (a remake of the R&B group Wild Cherry's song), with the song "Ice Ice Baby" on the b-side. It was that song that became popular (broken by Darrell J at radio station WAGH in Columbus, Georgia).

Ice performed in two movies: his own *Cool as Ice* and *Teenage Mutant Ninja Turtles: The Secret of the Ooze*. His "Play That Funky Music, White Boy" single went gold in 1991, and his *Extremely Live* album also went gold that same year. In 1994 his album *Mind Blowin'* was released.

Selected albums/CDs: *To the Extreme* (1990, SBK 95325); *Extremely Live* (1991, SBK 96648); *Mind Blowin'* (1994, SBK 28725).

VAN SILK
. . . .
(Born c. 1958, Bronx, new York)

Van Silk is one of the original pioneer rap promoters in hip hop. Beginning in 1978, Silk has promoted over 300 shows in his career, sometimes packing approximately 2,000 kids in one area for six dollars apiece to see a rap artist—before the advent of rap records.

Hailing from the John Adams Houses in the South Bronx, Van Silk originally started working in the peep-show business before embarking on his career in hip hop and joining Afrika Bambaataa's Zulu nation.

Silk is recognized for pay-per-view television events like 1990's "Rapmania" and 1992's "Sisters in the name of Rap." He achieved attention for his work with Furious Five member Mele Mel on the WnBC-TV new York antidrug public service announcement, which won him an Emmy. He has also done community work, visiting schools with former heavyweight boxing champion Mike Tyson, teaching about the dangers of drugs.

Silk has worked as a recording artist as well, writing and producing the 1986 single "Base Pipe." His piece "What's the Matter with Your World?" appeared in the Warner Bros. film *Police Academy 6*, and he has put out various compilation albums dealing with hip hop's pioneer MCs and DJs, like *Posse All-Stars Rap Classics* and *Raiders of the Lost Art*. He wrote "Only the Strong Will Survive" for Kurtis Blow, and worked as a producer for basketball star Earl "The Pearl" Monroe's In Your Face Records.

Van Silk has also managed many of hip hop's pioneer acts such as Doug E. Fresh, Afrika Islam, Rockmaster Scott, and the Force MCs, and as a promoter, he has used most of the classic pioneer venues for hip hop, including the Stardust Ballroom, the P.A.L.'s, and the Roxy.

WHODINI
• • • • • • • • • • • • •

**Formed c. early 1980s, Brooklyn, New York
(Ecstasy, born John Fletcher; Jalil, born Jalil Hutchins; Grandmaster
Dee, born Drew Carter: all born in Brooklyn, New York)**

Whodini was a popular hip-hop act during the mid-to-late-1980s, managed by Russell Simmons. They were one of the first rap groups to have dancers (Kangol Kid and Dr. Ice from UTFO) in their performances, and they also carved out a place for themselves as hip-hop sex symbols. The group first achieved notice in Europe, helping to establish the British Jive Records label, with their recording of the piece "Magic's Wand," which was a tribute to radio personality Mr. Magic.

"Magic's Wand" was recorded around 1982, and was originally an all-music track, recorded by keyboardist Thomas Dolby. The work was brought to executives at Jive Records' publishing company, Zomba, where it was suggested that Dolby record rappers over the track. Brooklyn MCs Ecstasy and Jalil were chosen, and "Magic's Wand" was released. By 1983 their single "Haunted House of Rock" was released, which was included on their debut self-titled album released that same year.

However, it was their 1984 *Escape* (produced by Larry Smith) that put the artists on the map. That work went gold by 1985, and later went platinum, and it contained several major hits that defined hip-hop music for that period, such as "Friends," "Big Mouth," "Freaks Come Out at Night," and the instrumental "Five Minutes of Funk" (which became the theme for Ralph McDaniels's "Video Music Box" music video show in New York City). The group also boosted their popularity by appearing in Russell Simmons's national "Fresh Fest Tour" along with other acts from Simmons's management roster.

Toward 1986 their *Back in Black* album was released and went gold. The work contained the hits "One Love" and "Funky Beat." In 1987 their next album, *Open Sesame*, was released and went gold the following year. They released a *Greatest Hits* album in 1990, and switched labels by 1991, recording the album *Bag-a-Trix* before their popularity began to fade.

Whodini

They made a comeback in 1994. Approached by Public Enemy's Chuck D and Hank Shocklee, Whodini worked with that group's DJ, Terminator X, on his *Godfathers of Threatt* album, contributing the song "It All Comes Down to the Money," which was a hit with the hip-hop audience. The song reteamed the group with producer Larry Smith. That same year they also appeared on the *Raiders of the Lost Art* compilation album, contributing the piece "Do It Again."

Selected albums/CDs: *Escape* (1984, Jive/RCA 1226); *Back in Black* (1986, Jive/RCA 1227); *Open Sesame* (1987, Jive/RCA 1228); *Greatest Hits* (1990, Jive/RCA 1340).

WORLD CLASS WRECKIN' CRU'

Formerly Wreckin' Cru'
Formed c. 1982, Los Angeles

(Dr. Dre, born Andre Young, 1965, Los Angeles; Grandmaster Lonzo, a.k.a. Lonzo, born Alonzo Williams, California; DJ Yella, born Antoine Carraby, California; Cli-N-Tel, born in California; Shakespeare, born Barry Severe, California; Mona Lisa, a.k.a. Mona Lisa Young, born in California)

The World Class Wreckin' Cru' was one of the pioneer rap groups in California in the early 1980s, whose members (Dr. Dre and DJ Yella) later became famous for founding the group N.W.A.

Group member Alonzo "Lonzo" Williams originally opened a club in the South Central area of Los Angeles in 1979, called Eve After Dark. He hired a group of house DJs at the club, among them DJs Dr. Dre and Yella. Dre and the other DJs also did music mix shows on radio station KDAY. Upon hearing the favorable response to the show from listeners, Williams decided to form a group with Dre, Yella, and one of Dre's high school friends, Cli-N-Tel.

First calling themselves the Wreckin' Cru', then later the World Class Wreckin' Cru', the group's first piece was titled "Slice" and released in 1983. Later they began to get more notice with the work "Surgery." Another later single of note was "Turn Off the Lights," which featured vocal work by R&B singer (and Dre's future wife) Michel'le.

The group was eventually signed to Epic Records and released a few albums before separating in the mid-1980s.

 Selected albums/CDs: *Rapped in Romance* (1986, Epic 40324).

WORLD'S FAMOUS SUPREME TEAM

See SUPREME TEAM

WRECKX-N-EFFECT

a.k.a. Wrecks-N-Effect
Formed c. 1987–88, Harlem, New York
(Markell Riley, born Harlem, New York; Aquil Davidson, born in New York; Brandon Mitchell, born in New York, died 1990; *former member:* Keith KC, born c. 1966, New York)

Wreckx-N-Effect gained attention for the work they did with group member Markell Riley's older brother, producer Teddy Riley, particularly on their 1989 second self-titled album, which contained the hit single "New Jack Swing"—a work that paid homage to Teddy Riley's R&B, rap, and go-go combined musical genre.

The group formed around 1987{*}88 by Aquil Davidson, a friend of the Rileys who lived two floors above them in the St. Nicholas Projects in Harlem. Along with DJ Markell Riley, Mitchell, and lead MC, Keith KC, who used to perform with the Masterdon Committee, the four were signed to Atlantic Records and released their first self-titled work in 1988. By 1989 they were with the Motown label where they recorded their second self-titled album, without Keith KC, who had left the group. By 1990 the group lost member Brandon Mitchell, who was fatally shot in the spring of that year. Members Markell Riley and Aquil Davidson continued as a duo.

In 1992 the duo had a multiplatinum hit with their single "Rump Shaker," which appeared on their next album on the MCA label, titled *Hard or Smooth*. The album went platinum that year.

 Selected albums/CDs: *Hard or Smooth* (1992 MCA 10566).

Wu-Tang Clan

WU-TANG CLAN
••••••••••••••••••••••••••
Formed c. early 1990s, Staten Island, New York
(The RZA, a.k.a. the Rzarecta Prince Rakeem, born July 5; the GZA,
a.k.a. Justice, the Genius; Ghostface Killer, a.k.a. Sun God Tony Starks;
Ol' Dirty Bastard, a.k.a. Unique Ason; Method Man, a.k.a. Methical;
Shakwon, Shallah Raekwon, a.k.a. Lou Diamonds, born January 9;
Inspectah Deck, a.k.a. the Rebel INS, born Jason Hunter, July 6;
U-God, a.k.a. Golden Arms: all born in Staten Island, New York)

The Wu-Tang Clan is a huge conglomerate of MCs and groups (the Shaolin Soldiers, the Killer Army, Brothers from the Grain, Shyheim the Rugged Child, and others), reminiscent in quantity and variety to Afrika Bambaataa's Zulu Nation MCs and DJs. Hailing from Staten Island, New York (which group members and Staten Island hip hoppers call Shaolin), the Wu-Tang Clan displays and combines the influence of kung fu movies, Five Percent Nation of Islam teachings, and street knowledge in their rhymes, with production and video concepts handled primarily by group member Prince Rakeem.

Rakeem and his group-member cousin, the GZA (the Genius), were originally signed to Tommy Boy Records and Cold Chillin' Records, respectively, with Rakeem releasing his "Ooh I Love You Rakeem" b/w "Sexcapades" in 1991, and the Genius releasing his "Words from a Genius" (with additional production and remix by Rakeem) that same year. Creative differences with both artists and their labels resulted in the two severing their ties with both companies.

Originally managed by Melquan Shabazz (former manager of Sir Ibu and Divine Force), Rakeem then came under the management of graphic artist/producer and friend Mike McDonald, who formerly worked with Bill Stephney. Rakeem assembled other neighborhood friends and relatives to enhance the Wu-Tang concept and put it into action.

Their debut album, *Enter the Wu-Tang (36 Chambers)*, gained immediate attention when it was released in 1993. Propelled by hits like "C.R.E.A.M.," "Can It Be All So Simple," and "Method Man," the album went gold halfway into 1994.

 Selected albums/CDs: *Enter the Wu-Tang (36 Chambers)* (1993, L.O.U.D./RCA 56363).

WANDA DEE
•••••••••••••••••••
(Born LaWanda McFarland, New York)

Wanda Dee is recognized as one of the first female DJs to appear during the late 1970s and early 1980s. She was also an early member of Afrika Bambaataa's Zulu Nation. Wanda be-

Wee Papa Girls

Wanda Dee

came known for her exotic sexy performances, notably on promoter Van Silk's 1990 "Rapma-nia" pay-per-view event. She also gained wide attention when she performed for famed Pa-terson, New Jersey, school principal Joe Clark, where she put on one of her trademark shows, which reportedly disturbed school officials there. In 1984 DJ Wanda Dee appeared on the turntables in the film *Beat Street*. Around 1989 she released the single "To the Bone."

WEE PAPA GIRLS
a.k.a. Wee Papa Girl Rappers
(Total S., born Sandra Lawrence, and TY-Tym, born Timmy Lawrence: both born in Acton, England)

The Wee Papa Girls were two sisters who were recognized as one of the first group of British female MCs to appear on the hip-hop scene.

One of the duo's first recordings appeared in a compilation album titled *Street Sounds*, where they contributed the work "He's Mine." The piece got the duo some notice, and they toured England with the work and were signed to Jive Records during the late 1980s. They began working with Teddy Riley, who worked with them on their debut album, *The Beat, The Rhyme, The Noise*, in 1989. The following year they released their second album, *Be Aware*.

Selected albums/CDs: *The Beat, The Rhyme, The Noise* (1989, Jive); *Be Aware* (1990, Jive 1377).

Warlord: The person in a street gang who decides whether the gang should go to war with another rival gang. The warlord was usually the third ranking member in the gang, or some-times the leader.

X-CLAN
• • • • • • • • • • •

Formed in 1989, Brooklyn, New York
(Professor X, the Overseer, born Lumumba Carson, 1962,
Brooklyn, New York; Brother J, the Grand Verbalizer,
born Jason Hunter, 1971, New York; Sugar Shaft, the Rhythm
Provider, born Anthony Hardin, New York, died September 1, 1995;
Paradise, the Grand Architect, born in 1965, New York)

X-Clan is a group that performs rhymes of political, historical, and cultural awareness for people of African descent. They are recognized for their tribal/street attire, their adornment of African jewelry (including nose rings), and their 1957 Pink Cadillac, known as "the time machine" and "Pinky." They are also known for Professor X's recurrent slogans, for example, "This is protected, by the Red, the Black, and the Green, with a Key—sissy!" The group is driven by the phonetically funky rhymes of Brother J—formerly a member of the group the Jungle Brothers. They are also a part of the Blackwatch Movement, led by Professor X, known also by his birth name, Lumumba Carson—son of political activist Sonny Carson.

In the early 1980s Carson worked in the music industry as a manager and promoter, handling acts like Positive K, King Sun, and Just Ice, and promoting shows at the hip-hop club the Latin Quarters. Early on in his life, Carson had a chance to experience a full political education from his father, who occasionally had guests over to the house like Malcolm X and other important political leaders of the 1960s.

By 1987, after the shooting death of Boogie Down Productions' Scott La Rock, Carson and others felt the need to put together some kind of organization that would deal with educating the black youth about their rich history in Egypt, and other Afrocentric teachings, to stop the violence that was happening in the communities. Carson called the organization Circle of One, but it soon fell apart. Around 1989 Carson reformulated the concept, this time with two groups in mind: one to handle the overall original concept, and the other to promote the teachings through music via hip hop. Thus, the Blackwatch Movement and X-Clan were born, respectively.

Both came to fruition during the killing of black youth Yusef Hawkins by angry whites in Bensonhurst, Brooklyn. The group helped organize protest marches with Sonny Carson's own organization, and they also worked for a while in the campaign to elect David Dinkins mayor of New York City.

Toward 1990 X-Clan began making appearances between videos on Ralph McDaniels "Video Music Box" show on Channel 31 in New York. Their unique look, and Professor X's catchy slogans, created a buzz. Later that year the group's first album was released on Island Records, *To the East Blackwards*. The work appealed to hip hoppers, fitting right in with similar politically oriented Afrocentric work at the time, like Public Enemy. Hits off the album included the pieces "Raise the Flag" and "Verbal Milk."

By 1992 X-Clan had released their second album, *X-Odus*, this time on a new label, Polydor. On this work, Sugar Shaft had been replaced by DJ Khabir. One of the hits off the work was "Fire & Earth."

In 1993 Professor X put out a solo project titled *Puss 'N Boots (The Struggle Continues)*. In 1995 group member Sugar Shaft died of complications from AIDS.

 Selected albums/CDs: *To the East Blackwards* (1990, Island 4019); *X-Odus* (1992); *Puss 'N Boots* (1993, Polydor 519360).

X-Clan

YOUNG MC
••••••••••••••••
(Born Marvin Young, 1967, England)

Young MC stormed the commercial music scene as a writer of accessible rhymes for rapper/actor Tone-Löc, and as a performer in his own right. His songs "Wild Thing" and "Funky Cold Medina" brought Löc instant stardom. Young MC's own platinum single "Bust a Move" received endless awards in 1990: a Grammy for "Best Rap Performance," the American Music Awards' "Best New Rap Artist," and a *Billboard* award for "Best New Male Pop Artist." The rapper/writer is known for his clean-cut image and clear diction when delivering his rhymes. His 1989 debut album, *Stone Cold Rhymin'*, went platinum the year it was released. When the artist embarked on his first tour, he was on the road for nearly a year and a half.

Young began performing at the age of 11 at various house parties in his Hollis, Queens, neighborhood. He studied classical piano for a few years and worked at night as a DJ where he spinned records by rock acts like New Order and the Pet Shop Boys. By this time he had also discovered the works of Grandmaster Flash, the Fearless Four, and the Treacherous Three.

Young moved to Los Angeles around the mid-1980s to pursue an economics degree at USC, where he later graduated. He was writing rhymes around this same period, and was signed by Delicious Vinyl Records during the late 1980s based on the rhymes the company heard Young deliver over the telephone.

His *Stone Cold Rhymin'* was released by the label in 1989. In 1991 his second work, *Brainstorm*, was released, and went gold the same year, with the single off the work "That's the Way Love Goes." His third album, *What's the Flavor?*, was issued in 1993.

 Selected singles: "Bust a Move" (1989, Delicious Vinyl).

 Selected albums/CDs: *Stone Cold Rhymin'* (1989, Delicious Vinyl); *Brainstorm* (1991, Capitol 96337); *What's the Flavor?* (1993, Capitol 99042).

Yo-Yo

Young MC

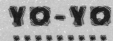

YO-YO
• • • • • • • •
(Born Yolanda Whitaker, August 4, 1971, Los Angeles)

Yo-Yo is a female rapper, who gained a lot of attention when she cameoed on Ice Cube's "It's a Man's World" piece on his *Amerikkka's Most Wanted* album. She is known for her squeaky, high-toned South Central Los Angeles-accented voice, and her strong delivery and lyrical content, which usually expresses a pro-woman stance on issues.

Yo-Yo began to get into the hip-hop scene during the ninth grade, where she performed her rhymes at talent shows and in some of the local clubs. She met Ice Cube in the late 1980s, at a shopping center, and soon began working with him, making demos.

Her demos later made up the songs on her first album, *Make Way for the Motherlode*, in 1991. The remix of the single "You Can't Play with My Yo-Yo" was a hit with the hip-hop crowd. Around this same period Yo-Yo founded the I.B.W.C. (Intelligent Black Women's Coalition) with Ice Cube's manager, Pat Charbonnet, an organization she developed to increase self-esteem in women, as well as their status.

In 1992 her *Black Pearl* album appeared. "So Funky" was one of the popular singles off the work. In 1993 *You Better Ask Somebody* was released. In 1994{*}95 she began to get into acting more (she had a bit part in John Singleton's 1991 film *Boyz N the Hood*), appearing in an episode of the Fox-TV series *New York Undercover*.

 Selected albums/CDs: *Make Way for the Motherlode* (1991, eastwest 91605); *Black Pearl* (1992, eastwest 92164; clean version: 92120); *You Better Ask Somebody* (1993, eastwest 92252).

YZ
• • • •
(Born Anthony Hill, Paterson, New Jersey)

YZ is a rapper who mixes urban street culture and old African griot-flavor rhyming in his work.

YZ started rapping at the age of 9, soon joining the Zodiac Crew in Paterson, New Jersey, where they practiced their work on the streets leaning against mailboxes on the corner. His first single around the mid-to-late-1980s was "I Am Who I Am/Bad" on Rocking Hard Records. His second single, "In Control of Things," was released during this same period on Diversity Records in New Jersey. Next, YZ worked with the BCM label, which was based in Germany. With this label he released the single "P-Funk."

Around 1990 YZ was signed to Tuff City Records, which released the single "Thinking of a Masterplan." The work was co-produced by Tony "Tony D" Depula, and it was a hit in the underground. The piece received extensive radio airplay, along with his album *Sons of the Father*. Tuff City also put out a nonvocal version of the single that appeared on the EP *When the Road Is Covered with Snow*.

In late 1992 to early 1993 YZ signed with Cold Chillin' Records's Livin' Large label, where they released his single "Return of the Holy One," which was popular with the hip-hop underground. The album *The Ghetto's Been Good to Me* was released during this period, as well as the single of the same name.

 Selected albums/CDs: *Sons of the Father* (1990, Tuff City); *YZEP* (1991, Tuff City 8065); *The Ghetto's Been Good to Me* (1993, Livin' Large 3017).

DA YOUNGSTAS

Da Youngstas broke through with their 1993 album *The Aftermath*, and its single "Crewz Pop," which features rhymes by Naughty by Nature's, Treach. I immediately asked them how they felt about somebody like Treach writing rhymes for them on this song, or any other song. People might think, "What's up? They can't write their own stuff?"

Tarik replied, "We knew that some people would be like, 'They sound like Treach,' or this and that. But that's like the only two rhymes where somebody wrote our stuff.

"But it wasn't no problem for us, 'cause we like his style. And the way we tried to kick it was like, his style, plus a mixture of ours—not just all of his. So I think it came out well. It wasn't no ego thing."

There are a lot of young MCs out here these days making records, and I wondered if they felt they were really getting respected as artists instead of little kids.

Tarik responded, "I think young MCs get their respect if they come correct. But the most important thing people don't like is to see little kids with a chance, and not capitalizing on it. You know, comin' out wish-washy.

"I think if you come correct, lettin' brothers know that you're a force to be reckoned with, then you'll get your props."

Blood brothers Qu'ran and Taji, along with their cousin Tarik, hail from Philadelphia. Qu'ran and Taji's pop, Lawrence (L.G. the Teacher) Goodman, was responsible for launching the careers of Salt-N-Pepa and Roxanne Shanté on his own Pop Art label. He's also responsible for Steady B, another well-known Philadelphia rapper, and also his nephew.

Philly hasn't been making too much noise these days. Qu'ran agrees, saying, "Back in the day, there was a lot of rappers comin' out of Philly, like Steady B, Cool C, Three Times Dope, Jazzy Jeff & the Fresh Prince. I think it slowed up now.

"We're the only new group out of Philly. There's a lot of local acts. But they didn't get picked up by major record companies yet. But there's people with flavor here though. People gotta check 'em out. They're sleepin' on Philly."

INDEX

5867